D1523243

How Robert Frost
Made Realism
Matter

How Robert Frost Made Realism Matter

Jonathan N. Barron

University of Missouri Press
Columbia

For Ellen, Liana, and Rafi, without whom no poetry, however real, would matter

Contents

Acknowledgments

I could not have written this book without the aid, support, and inspiration of numerous individuals. I thank the community of Frost scholars from whom I have learned more than I can ever say. In particular I thank Earl Wilcox, who more than twenty years ago got me properly introduced to "the wonderful world of Frost." I also thank Frost's granddaughter, Lesley Lee Francis, a guiding light in Frost scholarship, to whom I owe more than I can repay. Also, I wish to thank Daria D'Arienzo, Robert Faggen, Peter Gilbert, Jack Hagstrom, Robert Hass, Tyler Hoffman, Walter Jost, Karen L. Kilcup, John Lancaster, George Monteiro, Nancy Nahra, Lea Newman, Judith Oster, Tim O'Brien, Jay Parini, Priscilla Paton, William Pritchard, David Sanders, Lisa Seale, Carole Thompson, W. D. Taylor, and J. D. Whitney for many years of fine conversation about all things Frost. More specifically I wish to thank Don Sheehy, Mark Richardson, and Linda Hart for reading portions of this manuscript and offering their commentary on it. Particular thanks go to Pat Alger for permission to use his outstanding Frost collection. I also thank Paige Gray for her design assistance. To Bob Hester I offer my heartfelt thanks for counsel and advice over many years.

To those at the University of Missouri Press, especially Gary Kass, who believed in this project from the very first, I also offer my most heartfelt thanks. I also thank the ever efficient Sara Davis and the sharp eye of Polly Kummel.

I thank the University of Southern Mississippi for a sabbatical leave in the fall of 2011 during which I wrote the bulk of this manuscript. I also thank the University Foundation Fund, established by Dale and Janet Shearer, for aid in producing this volume.

Above all, I thank my first and constant reader, Jennifer Barron, as well as Myra and Jerry Barron, for their advice and reading acumen. To my brother, David, I offer thanks for support and help when needed.

To my wife, Ellen Weinauer, I offer thanks for her hours of conversation about Frost, magazines, and her own beloved world of nineteenth-century American literature. To my children, Liana and Rafi, I extend my thanks for patience, understanding, and even occasional proofreading.

• • •

I gratefully acknowledge Cambridge University Press for permission to publish excerpts of "Robert Frost in the Magazines," by Jonathan N. Barron in *Robert Frost in Context,* edited by Mark Richardson. Copyright © 2014 Cambridge University Press. Reprinted with permission.

All visual reproductions are used with the kind permission of Pat Alger and come from The Robert Frost Collection of Pat Alger.

My thanks to the Estate of Robert Lee Frost for permission to publish manuscript materials.

Grateful acknowledgment as well for permission to cite from the published letters of Robert Frost. Reprinted by permission of Henry Holt and Company, LLC.

How Robert Frost
Made Realism
Matter

Philosophies, whether expressed in sonnets or systems, all must wear this form. The thinker starts from some experience of the practical world, and asks its meaning. He launches himself upon the speculative sea, and makes a voyage long or short. He ascends into the empyrean, and communes with the eternal essences. But whatever his achievements and discoveries be while gone, the utmost result they can issue in is some new practical maxim or resolve, or the denial of some old one, with which inevitably he is sooner or later washed ashore on the terra firma of concrete life again.

—William James, *The Will to Believe*

In a "Meet the Press" interview from the 1950s, Frost was asked by the fearless Lawrence Spivak whether poetry was an escape from life, and without hesitation came back with "No, it's a way of taking life by the throat."

—William Pritchard, *Frost: A Literary Life Reconsidered*

Introduction

IN THE 1890s, when Robert Frost first began publishing in magazines, the art of poetry was already in trouble. By then poetry had become an art of dreams and illusions, of flowers, love, and fantasy. As American culture became ever more materialistic and utilitarian, taking poetry too seriously, either as philosophy or as intellectual critique, seemed little more than absurd. This was, after all, the period that gave rise to the greed associated with the emergence of industrial and financial capitalism, as described in Thorsten Veblen's groundbreaking *Conspicuous Consumption* as well as by other sociologists, economists, and historians.[1]

Even in the magazines that most often published it, poetry's public purpose (and, more generally, the public purpose of literature itself) as a moral, political, and philosophical forum increasingly diminished. Since the time of classical antiquity, it was common to associate literature with the old Roman definition of "instruction and delight"; however, by the late nineteenth century most poetry and fiction published in the leading magazines and newspapers had begun to lose sight of the need to instruct. Instead of raising fundamental questions, such literature primarily offered readers delight, presenting unreal perspectives on the present, through idyllic depictions of contemporary life or stories that recalled the very distant past. The best-selling novel of the era, for instance, was Lew Wallace's *Ben-Hur* (1880), which, after the Civil War, struck the right chord among readers nationwide by offering a Christian alternative to strife and war. In the genre of poetry James Whitcomb Riley—a Hoosier like Wallace—

1

presented picturesque boyhood scenes from a fast-disappearing village culture, poems that offered at least a temporary refuge from the challenges of contemporary American life.

Cultural historians have long recognized the role that realism played as an antidote to the best-selling escapist literature of the period. Although many scholars have drawn attention to American literary realism in fiction, literary specialists have yet to do justice to realism's impact on American poetry.[2] This book attempts to fill this gap. I argue that, if by the 1890s, poetry in the leading magazines appeared to bring as a wide audience of readers into its "stately pleasure-domes" as did Coleridge's "Kubla Khan," poetry was as ripe as the era's fiction for a realist rebellion. Further, I show that it was Robert Frost who gave poetry the realist renewal it required.

Other poets, such as Edwin Arlington Robinson, can certainly be said to share Frost's commitment to realist modes. But I chose to focus on Frost because of his decisive and ongoing impact on American culture. Even today he is arguably America's best-known poet. When, in 2007, the former poet laureate Robert Pinsky began the Favorite Poem Project to see what Americans liked about poetry, he found that a plurality of Americans liked Robert Frost. The project received 17,457 entries, and Frost had a commanding lead, with 970 entries (6 percent of the total).[3]

I argue that, given Frost's popularity and cultural resonance, his poetry, along with his continued legacy, owes as much to the realist period in which he was reared as to anything else. More than that, I believe that Frost's own realism is at once profoundly intellectual and deeply questioning, artistically complex and knowingly humane in its egalitarian desire to appeal. In a recent study of Frost, Tim Kendall writes that Frost made it his goal "to remain a favorite both of a broad reading public and of the university professors."[4] As Frost said, his poetry should reach "all sorts and kinds." Mark Richardson, too, has explored these apparently conflicting goals and the constant struggle they presented for Frost. In Frost's commitment to realism, I say, we can find the key to his ability to maintain both popular and intellectual appeal.

I begin my study by offering a brief history of the cultural conditions that gave rise to American literary realism in the first place. Here I discuss the crucial influence of a particular social cohort, which I call "the genteels"; its members were largely—if not entirely—responsible not only for publishing the era's most influential magazines but also for promoting realism within their pages.[5] This cohort, as I will explain, dominated what sociologists call the public sphere—in large part through the control they exercised over the actively important magazine culture of the time. Furthermore, American magazines, as I also will demonstrate, played a central role in the creation of American literature. In brief, as the United States became an industrialized urban country populated by immigrants from eastern and southern Europe, American poetry in the dominant magazines became ever more idealistic, even escapist. Dedicated to providing antidotes to the perceived dangers of a new America, authors of poems, stories, and serialized novels turned to both idealism and nostalgia while the avant-garde went ever further afield in such new movements as decadence, symbolism, and aestheticism. The realists emerged against that double insistence that the urban, industrial reality of American life had become literature's enemy.

In the same way that realism has been underappreciated for its impact on American poetry, so too have American magazines been sorely neglected as active agents of American literary history. From the eighteenth century onward, American magazines took literature and its ideas seriously, publishing the work of poets and novelists as well as countless essays about them. In the pages of American magazines imaginative literature had been a forum of literary delight as well as of intellectuality, philosophy, and political debate. From Longfellow to Whittier, Stowe to Emerson, William Cullen Bryant to Oliver Wendell Holmes, American writers appeared in the pages of magazines engaging in lively public discussion and appearing as the objects of aesthetic analysis.

After the Civil War, however, rare was the writer, let alone the story or poem, that could engage in controversial discussion. In the magazines, increasingly, the voice of dissent and of so-called objectionable ideas belonged not to poets and fiction writers but rather to essayists, especially (as with the work of the sociologist Herbert Spencer) those writing in the emergent social sciences. This is not to suggest that following the Civil War magazines stopped publishing poetry or fiction—quite the contrary. Rather, such literature attended less to ideas than to pleasure. Literature's classical heritage as a forum for instruction *and* delight had been reduced, it appeared, to delight alone.

This trend is linked to the postwar transformation of American society to an industrial republic of immigrants and cities—what Karl Polanyi has called "the great transformation."[6] The writers emerging in this period considered that literature could best instruct by offering alternatives to the crass new contemporary culture of industrial and financial capitalism. In the poetry of this era, for example, there emerged a genial—what I will call a *genteel*—idealism designed to promote duty, character, and virtue. Such poetry was meant to oppose the perceived greed and amorality of the postbellum American Republic. Riley's wildly popular regional poetry, for example, harkened back to an America of villages, where manufacturers and merchants, not stockbrokers and industrialists, reigned. Other poets of the postwar period, such as Eugene Field, Lizette Woodworth Reese, Louise Chandler Moulton, and Sarah Morgan Bryan Piatt, celebrated ideals that were meant to oppose the increasingly utilitarian and materialistic impulses in American life and culture.[7]

Meanwhile a new group of poets emerged who were even more bold in their dissenting declarations against the new industrial capitalism. Poetic movements such as decadence, aestheticism, and symbolism, which came to the United States from both France and Britain, bespoke a decidedly new artistic sensibility, even a new dissenting idealist philosophy. In the work of such British authors as Algernon Swinburne, Oscar Wilde, W. E. Henley, and Francis Thompson, American readers discovered a hothouse world of fantasy, as well as of ornate rhyme and meter. These authors in turn attracted North American imitators and followers like Clinton Scollard, Bliss Carman, Richard Hovey, George G. D. Roberts, and Louise Guiney, who by the 1890s regularly appeared in the leading magazines.

The realists staged a rebellion against both the idealists and the new avant-garde in the very magazines that published the literature the realists had grown to despise. Notable first in fiction, realism made its mark in new works by Henry James, Hamlin Garland, Kate Chopin, William Dean Howells, Mark Twain, Frank Norris, Sarah Orne Jewett, Mary Wilkins Freeman, and Stephen Crane. By the 1890s they had created a new style of fiction based on new definitions of both *delight* and *instruction*. To them *instruction* meant that fiction must confront rather than avoid the current situation of urbanization, immigration, and industrialism. The modern situation had to be made part and parcel of American fiction. The leading spokesman for realism, William Dean Howells, argued that fiction should neither merely replicate conventional wisdom nor take it for granted. Instead in his own fiction he made drama out of the very problems that such issues as individualism, property, justice, virtue, duty, integrity, and character raised. To do so he took to the pages of such magazines as the *Atlantic Monthly, Scribner's,* and *Harper's Monthly.* Howells and the other writers who embraced the realist creed succeeded to such an extent that today they are the only writers now recalled from this period. Those whom they opposed—Wallace, Aldrich, and Thompson, for example—have fallen far from favor. By the turn into the twentieth century, realist practitioners had proliferated. To Howells and his peers one could now add such writers as Jack London, Theodore Dreiser, Upton Sinclair, Edith Wharton, Charles Chesnutt, and Willa Cather, whose work appeared not only in *Scribner's, Harper's,* and *Atlantic Monthly* but also in the *Nation, Forum, Dial, North American Review,* and *Critic.* In the pages of such magazines works of these novelists often became part of intellectual debates about the very purpose of literature itself, not to mention of the central political, social, economic, and cultural issues of the day. Literature, it appeared, was returning to a sense of public purpose, and this occurred in poetry as well as in fiction. Realist poetry also began to make its presence known in the magazines of the 1890s.

Had Robert Frost been typical of poets born in his generation, he would have written either a genteel idealist poetry or a poetry characteristic of the decadent aestheticism of the avant-garde, with its dependence on lush rhymes, purple diction, and ever more elaborate meter. Instead Frost chose to write poetry in what I call a realist manner. To make that case in a single phrase, I call the period when he first began to publish, 1894 to 1915, his magazine years. In those years Robert Frost published innovative poetry designed to instruct *and* delight. By that he meant to bring to poetry a critique of conventional opinion even as he appeared to endorse it. In his recent study Tim Kendall, citing Frost, calls this "the pleasure of ulteriority," or, said more simply, "saying one thing and meaning another, saying one thing in terms of another."[8]

In the chapters that follow I argue that, in his youth during the 1880s, Robert Frost learned to think of literature—and *especially* of poetry—as a public art with a duty to both delight and instruct, and that he, perhaps inspired by the new realist novelists, decided that *instruction* often meant dissenting from the norm. Beginning in the 1890s, then, whether he consciously intended it or not, Frost began to publish poetry that would ultimately have the effect of restoring to the art an intellectual stature as the voice of critique, even of dissent, a stature that it had begun to lose during the years preceding his decision to publish in 1894.

Chapter One

•

The World That Made Robert Frost
The Genteels, Their Values, and Their Publications

ON A TYPICALLY COLD New Hampshire day, the young Robert Frost, miserable in his first year at Dartmouth, walked to the college library and picked up the *Independent* for November 17, 1892. On the first page he read a poem by Richard Hovey titled "Seaward: An Elegy on the Death of Thomas William Parsons."[1] Did he pick up the magazine because someone told him that Hovey was a near contemporary, a graduate of Dartmouth's class of 1885? Could that someone have been the Dartmouth professor who had once taught Hovey? Or did Frost find that out later? Regardless, the poem had a powerful impact on his future as a poet. As Frost later said, "This experience gave me my very first revelation that a publication existed, anywhere in my native land, that was a vehicle for the publication of poetry."[2]

Finding Hovey's poem on the front page of a national magazine meant that someone like Frost, a boy who had even gone to the same college, could make his thoughts widely known. That *was* the point, was it not? Wasn't literature, especially poetry, supposed to address the fundamental issues at stake at any given moment? For Frost, even in 1894, the answer to these rhetorical questions had to be yes. He was twenty years old and had spent his life immersed in genteel culture—a term that would, about a decade later, be made familiar by George Santayana, but that I mean to associate with a particular cultural elite.[3] Made up of a specific cohort of white Anglo-Saxon Protestant families—a cohort that I will call the genteels—this cultural elite created what I take to be (following but modifying Santayana) a way of life, a system, an ideology that deeply shaped Robert Frost. Born in 1874 to William Prescott Frost and a Scottish immigrant, Belle Moodie Frost, Robert Frost belonged to family steeped in a New England Protestant tradition that went back to 1634, when the first Frost progenitor, Nicholas Frost, arrived in New Hampshire.

Who were the genteels that created the tradition that takes their name? In his study of the American urban social and political establishment, Frederic Cople Jaher writes that "those who exercise authority, accumulate wealth, and command respect may be called elites, upper classes, or aristocracies. Conventional usage designates as elite all groups that wield power or possess fortunes or high status."[4] In the United States the initial Puritans soon gave way, beginning in the 1690s, to merchants and manufacturers from the same demographic group, white Anglo-Saxon Protestants. Between 1690 and Frost's birth, that social cohort, with family roots in New England, dominated the institutions of American power. As Puritan New England gave way to a more bourgeois Anglo-Saxon population, what I am calling the genteel social and cultural code became all the more entrenched.[5] That code depends on the Calvinism that lies at the heart of Puritan heritage, though in many respects it departs from seventeenth-century Puritan theology and ideology. Making this precise point in his famous essay, "The Genteel Tradition," Santayana added with his typical wry cynicism, "Calvinism, essentially, asserts three things: that sin exists, that sin is punished, and that it is beautiful that sin should exist to be punished. . . . To be a Calvinist philosophically is to feel a fierce pleasure in the existence of misery, especially of one's own, in that this misery seems to manifest the fact that the Absolute is irresponsible or infinite or holy."[6] For all his sarcasm Santayana was serious in his claim that the genteel tradition reflected a belief in an unknowable, unfathomable God who will nonetheless ensure that sin will not triumph. To be a human, according to this mind-set, is to do the good work of Jesus in the world. That is, Calvinism begot an ideal of social duty predicated on a specifically Christian understanding of God, sin, grace, and redemption. With the Puritans this theological premise became fundamental to New England life—and after them it became fundamental to a set of genteel ideals. But what, then, is the connection between Calvinism and gentility?

Historians believe that, beginning in the 1690s, what had been an elite consisting of a unique Puritan establishment became, after a century of immigration, a *new* elite first of merchants and later of manufacturers. For all their differences from the initial Puritans, however, these more commercially minded elites nonetheless kept the essential Calvinist moral tenets that Santayana describes. Onto those tenets these new elites grafted gentility, a European aristocratic code associated with refinement.

According to Richard L. Bushman, gentility, a code developed in Renaissance Europe, was first adopted by the English aristocracy in the late seventeenth century and then mimicked by eighteenth-century American elites. Gentility governed "modes of speech, dress, body carriage, and manners" and gave "a new cast to the conduct and appearance of the American gentry," who developed what he calls a "vernacular gentility."[7] Although Bushman finds that gentility came to all of Anglo America in the eighteenth century, in New England gentility developed a decidedly Calvinist habit of mind, or system, and this grafting of the Calvinist to the Renaissance ideal of refinement is what characterizes "the genteel tradition."

The genteel tradition, then, is an odd combination of European refinement on the one hand and Calvinist Puritan moral severity on the other. In 1911 Santayana summed up the tradition with a single image, "the colonial mansion." Comparing that mansion to the newly invented skyscraper, Santayana wrote, "The one is all aggressive enterprise, the other is all genteel tradition." According to Bushman, the colonial mansions were first built in America in the 1720s. The importation of gentility that had begun in the 1690s bore its first tangible fruit, Bushman suggests, in such everyday items as tea services and forks. By the 1720s, however, members of the elite were attempting to distinguish themselves from other groups by constructing what we now recognize as colonial mansions. Today these homes are associated with Georgian style, but Bushman explains that, compared to their predecessors, "no listing of architectural details does justice to the contrasting experience in entering the two houses. Seventeenth-century houses feel low, closed, shadowy; the decoration is invariably simple and severe. The eighteenth-century houses, even those in the middle range, because of their larger windows and higher ceilings, seem open and light." Bushman's larger point—an extension of Santayana's—is that by the 1720s, "the ideal of a cultivated and refined inward life" had become fundamental to the American elite and had begun to shape American cultural institutions, from habitations and household decor to clothing and social interaction.[8]

As Bushman reminds us, "Gentility was worldly not godly, it was hierarchical not egalitarian, and it favored leisure and consumption over work and thrift."[9] In contrast Calvinism was decidedly godly and egalitarian, and it valued above all both work and thrift. But in New England, as it happened, an entire society had found a way to mix the two.

By the 1880s genteel families of Anglo-Saxon Protestants controlled the dominant institutions not only of New England life but also of American *national* life. In the long period from the American Revolution through the Civil War, as the historian Howard Mumford Jones argues, families that could trace their roots to the New England elite "controlled most of the professions [doctors, lawyers, college professors in all disciplines], the world of finance, real estate, education . . . the public school systems, and the arts." And, Jaher notes, the elite exercised profound cultural influence: "When commercial elites evolved into upper classes, the dynastic principle and family loyalty embraced the entire range of group functions. Tribal and kinship ties influenced public office holding, preparatory and college entry, admission to social clubs, militia units, and charity and cultural societies."[10] In this shaping function we find the roots of the genteel tradition, a cultural system that originated among the genteels themselves but subsequently took on a life of its own: it became a way of life, not just for the New England Protestant elite that I have been describing but for mainstream Americans more generally.

That the genteel tradition can be understood as a way of life—or a code, a system—suggests that it has an elusive character. This elusiveness makes it prone to assumptions and misinterpretation. Even Santayana assumed an easy familiarity with the notion of gentility rather than define its parameters for his readers. Much later the historian T. J. Jackson Lears argued that "by the 1880s, whether sanctioned by secular or religious authority, an internalized ethic of self-control had become the unquestioned norm for the middle and upper classes as well as for much of the rest of society." It is here that New England's Calvinist heritage exerted its decisive influence. For while elites who shared similar Anglo-Saxon roots with those in New England dominated Philadelphia, New York, and Chicago (among other cities), they also gave far more license to European ideas of gentility than did their New England cousins. In New England alone the elite insisted on what the literary historian Andrew Lawson refers to as "all that is homely, provincial and modest, as opposed to the sophisticated, pretentious, and superficial."[11] That is, one exhibited one's modesty in order to prove that one had self-control over one's depraved inner nature (the Calvinist element).

In what follows I isolate three particular characteristics of the genteel tradition: virtue, character, and duty. By the 1880s these three ideals had become associated with American success generally and not just with New England. American life and culture increasingly became defined as comprising both refinement *and* modesty, virtue *and* conspicuous consumption. The means by which a particular set of values emerging from one region—indeed one group in that region—became associated with American culture more generally has generated more than a century of historical inquiry. For my purposes it is enough to know that, while there was little reason to predict that American culture—especially as reflected in the public sphere's books, magazines, newspapers, and central institutions—would become associated with New England's distinctive brand of gentility, it nonetheless was.

In the later nineteenth century, changing demographics began to put pressure on the genteel tradition, and the tradition would eventually lose its prominent place. In the 1880s, for example, after forty years of Irish, predominantly Catholic, immigration and newer immigration from Ashkenazi Jews and Italian Catholics to New England, white Anglo-Saxon Protestants no longer constituted the overwhelming majority population. By then they had been joined by nearly a million foreign-born residents, and some demographers estimate that another two million were first-generation Americans. In fact, in the 1880s, when the young Robert Frost came to Massachusetts with his family, Boston was already dominated by Irish Catholics: "The foreign-born and their children comprised three-fifths of the 362,839 populace [of Boston]."[12] In 1885 Boston elected an Irish Catholic mayor, Hugh O'Brien. Nor was Boston unique. Similar demographics applied as well to other New England towns—including the mill town of Lawrence, where the Frost family had settled in 1850.

Nor were demographics the only change to what had long been a predominantly village culture of white Anglo-Saxon Protestants. Even before the Civil War the United States had seen a persistent internal migration from village and farm to newly industrialized cities. In fact, Frost's own grandfather had been part of just such a migration when he left rural Kingston, New Hampshire, for the new mills of Lawrence, Massachusetts, in 1850. Meanwhile, others had decided that New England itself, whether town or city, had little to offer; a steady migration out of the region and to the American West continued the overall depopulation.[13]

Despite all these demographic changes, however, middle-class American life was still broadly associated with the genteel tradition's weird mix of Calvinism and courtier culture–refinement. In fact, just as generations of New Englanders since the late seventeenth century had adopted that genteel tradition as their heritage so, too, by the 1880s did many of the newly arrived immigrants and first-generation Americans. But why and how did this adoption occur? Bushman asserts that "gentility bestowed concrete social power on its practitioners."[14] I agree with that claim, but I press it a bit further in order to understand how the power of gentility came to pass. My answer concerns the publications over which the genteels had long exerted complete control.

Even amid the demographic changes of the 1880s, the genteels still controlled most nationally distributed magazines. Further they still dominated the book trade through such publishers as George Brett (Macmillan), Frank Scott (the *Century*), Charles Scribner, and Henry Holt—who would become Robert Frost's publisher. Editors like Horace Scudder of Houghton, Mifflin and Edward Burlingame at Scribner's also wielded powerful influence on the public sphere. It took little effort to use their power to promote genteel values and to insist that the genteel tradition was the foundation of American civilization itself.[15] As the historian Ronald Zboray puts it, "All the institutions promoting literacy operated under a system of values maintaining that knowledge must be useful first and entertaining second or not at all."[16] Using the publications they controlled, in the 1880s the genteels pushed back against a rampant secularism and materialism to promote in their place virtue, character, and duty.[17] In an era when the traditional bastions of genteel tradition, the church and the economic marketplace, had begun to fall under nongenteel influences, the genteels used their publications to make a case for their way of life as *the* American way of life.

In effect, they argued that the Calvinist element peculiar to New England's genteel tradition was also the American tradition that defined American political, economic, and cultural institutions. They made this claim to counter a rival claim that had appeared by the 1880s. That claim came from the "other America," people who did not belong to the genteel milieu I have been describing. New York and Boston symbolically represent the distinction of this other America from the genteels. New York stood for a mostly European concept of gentility almost bereft of Calvinism, while Boston seemingly had made Calvin an honorary saint. To be less symbolic and more concrete, in the waning years of the nineteenth century a new elite had come to social, economic, and political power within the other America. It did not depend on merchants or manufacturers, as did the genteels, but rather on a new economy of massive corporate industry and finance. This group belonged to a new social cohort of industrial capitalists, barons of finance, department store titans, and other economic industrial magnates. Associated with New York, where their industry was located, and where the most powerful American stock exchange was also located, they had little in common ethnically, religiously, or culturally with the genteels. More to the point, they rejected the genteel tradition. As one historian puts it, "After 1880, money was entering into the American economy and culture in a way it had never done before." Money more than goods produced now held a new "position of eminence in the lives of Americans." As a result "pecuniary values (or market values) would constitute for many people the base measure for all other values."[18] Money, not real property and objects that bespoke genteel values, began to exert a new influence, challenging the Calvinist refinement of the New England genteels.[19] By the 1880s, in short, a ruthless competitive marketplace familiar to all students of the Gilded Age increasingly made a mockery of the genteel tradition: "The older commercial families of the seaboard cities were thrust into the background by new industrial, financial, and utilities magnates, many of them from cities of the interior, who did not share the cultural interests of the older mercantile elite." Howard Mumford Jones renders this conflict well: "The doctrine that the gentleman does not soil his hand with retail trade is old, just as the parvenu is a social type inciting ridicule as far back as Horace and Aristophanes."[20] By the 1880s the difference in American life, however, was that the gentlemen of this equation perceived themselves as morally superior to their parvenu enemies and blasted them with attacks reminiscent of the most severe Puritan jeremiads against depraved heathens. In fact, Oliver Wendell Holmes, recognizing the genteels' sense of themselves as akin to the highest caste in India, went so far as to dub his crowd of white Anglo-Saxon New England Protestants the "Boston Brahmins."[21]

The historian Stowe Persons argues that, by the 1880s, these New England genteels were "caught between a rapidly growing socio-economic elite of wealthy business and financial men on the one hand, and a vulgar mass on the other." That vulgar mass reflected demographic changes that should have put an end to the dominance of the genteels and their tradition. Certainly most of the institutions the genteels dominated had begun to give way to the other America, from local politics to churches and even public schools, whose curricula became ever more secular.

However, in their magazines, newspapers, and books the genteels rode to battle. As Persons puts it, "The gentleman became the apostle of culture in a world of democratic capitalism." In this period the genteels engaged in a new culture war, turning to literature in particular to create bulwarks against what they saw as an encroaching materialist depravity. Against a new literary realism, on the one hand, and sensationalism on the other—modes that I will take up at greater length in what follows—the genteels promoted a literary idealism designed to promote character, virtue, and duty. Their turn to literature was not meant to be simply symbolic or futile. To the genteels literature meant the very stuff of life. There one found the deepest insights and truths concerning human nature. If they turned to literature at the moment their values came under threat, they did so because in literature they saw the full flower of all that the genteel tradition was meant to promote. That tradition, they insisted, was central to nothing less than American civilization itself. In the name of American civilization they took their Calvinist proselytizing urge to their magazines, newspapers, and books and made literature itself not only a forum for the promotion of duty, character, and virtue but a species of work "broadly conceived as the creative exercise of all the faculties and powers." This glorification of work and duty put the genteels at odds with "the older aristocratic ideal of leisure in which labor was despised as menial."[22] It also put them at odds with a new culture of materialism that saw work merely as a means to individual power.

More specifically in the 1880s the genteels promoted in their magazines and newspapers a group of New England authors (eventually known as the Schoolroom Poets) the genteels thought best reflected American civilization. In promoting these authors—William Cullen Bryant, Henry Wadsworth Longfellow, James Russell Lowell, Oliver Wendell Holmes, Ralph Waldo Emerson, James Greenleaf Whittier, to take the most notable—the genteels meant to preach the genteel tradition to those unfamiliar with it. At Houghton Mifflin, for example, Horace Scudder created two series designed specifically for classrooms, the Cambridge Poets and the Riverside Editions, that included not only the Schoolroom Poets but also such novelists and essayists as Henry David Thoreau and Nathaniel Hawthorne.[23] By promoting such writers Scudder meant to remind Americans that one could shun both material excess and spartan asceticism. The genteels also managed to persuade legions of school boards throughout the United States to adopt their books as textbooks for countless children to read. Against the tide of a new financial and industrial capitalism that appeared to put paid to the genteel trinity of duty, virtue, and character, the genteels brought their own cultural evangelism.[24]

Although he had a Scottish immigrant mother and spent his first eleven years in his father's urban political world of Democratic Party politics and Henry George's socialism, Frost nonetheless belonged to the genteels of New England. When, at age eleven, Frost relocated with his mother and sister to Lawrence, Massachusetts, he moved ever closer to the center of a genteel tradition that his own ancestors had a hand in shaping for well more than 150 years.

In this book I argue that Frost's poetry helped to make that tradition more palatable for a modern industrial world. Before turning to Frost, however, I offer a bit more detail about both the tradition Frost managed to revive, if not reconstitute, as well as the magazines and newspapers in which it made its presence known.

THE GENTEEL TRADITION'S CIVILIZING
TRINITY: VIRTUE, CHARACTER, DUTY

Associated with a particularly Americanized Protestantism, the Calvinist valence of virtue, character, and duty underwrote the moral framework of the genteel tradition in which Robert Frost was reared.[25] Of these terms, perhaps *duty* is the most crucial and, for Frost, the most influential. In the genteel tradition duty meant that one put the larger community good over one's selfish individual needs. One historian has called this American phenomenon "collaborative individualism"—an apparent paradox that encouraged in each member of society a reciprocal obligation to that same society's larger goals.[26] The notion of reciprocal obligation derived from the Puritan tradition. Legions of historians have traced its transformation into "a high degree of civic and cultural responsibility."[27] Such responsibility, however, depended on the Calvinist doctrine of work as a communal good. According to the American genteels, labor and work were fundamental and necessary to a good life. For 250 years they had by the 1880s established work as a means whose end was the benefit of the larger community. The historian Daniel Walker Howe adds that this idea of work also incorporated the larger concept of social responsibility. For instance, in the postbellum years the genteels used their tradition's social ideal of duty "to humanize the emergent industrial-capitalist order by infusing it with a measure of social responsibility." This they did through their publications and through their influence on the legislative agenda of the Republican Party during Reconstruction and the Gilded Age.[28]

The emphasis on work also shaped the meaning of the term *character*. Defined as thrift, restraint, and responsibility, character, says Warren Susman, opposes the more modern market-based concept of personality. Personality, Susman says, depends on the logic of consumption, purchasing power, and consumerism. In contrast character had to do with one's inner ability to temper desire rather than act on it.[29] These combined ideals of both duty and character have been traced to the unique culture of Anglo-Saxon New England.[30] As such they also encoded a particular gender theory. Under the rubric of character and duty, a rigorous gender division—historians refer to it as "separate spheres"—defined the particular responsibilities and obligations of men and women.[31]

Virtue, the third cardinal term, parsed the purpose and philosophy behind this strict gender division. To the genteels virtue referred to a philosophical and scientific gender distinction. Taking the family as the fundamental social unit, the genteels made marriage the primary social institution, one that trumped all others. While they endorsed the concept of marriage based on love, an individual affair of choice, they did so because they believed that all men were predatory sexual animals in the state of nature, and all women were potential sexual prey. Virtue invoked a theory of sexuality and gender: Women's virtue was associated with virginity, while men's virtue had to do with control of an otherwise animalistic instinct. The genteel tradition assumed that society, operating through the institution of marriage, had an obligation to ensure the purity of women and the temperance of men. To that end, civil and legal codes were constructed in the name of virtue around such social institutions as marriage and were dependent on a fundamentally patriarchal ideal designed to protect weak women and potentially uncontrollable men. Through their control of legal and political institutions, the genteels throughout the nineteenth century cemented their tradition into American law through a wide array of federal, state, and local legislation. The gender views of the genteel tradition also became part and parcel of both public and private school curricula.[32]

ENFORCING VIRTUE IN PRINT: THE COMSTOCK ACT

Of all the legal mechanisms that brought the genteel tradition into American law, one would have a decisive impact on the culture wars that began in the publications of the 1880s that I have already mentioned. An 1873 act of Congress, the Comstock Act, legally encoded the genteel tradition's idea of virtue in the public sphere. That measure set a sentence of one to ten years in prison at hard labor for anyone convicted of shipping through the mail any "book, pamphlet, picture, paper, print or other publication of an indecent character, or any article or thing designed or intended for the prevention of contraception or procuring of abortion . . . any article or thing intended or adapted for any indecent or immoral use." It also forbade sending information about such "things or articles" through the mail.[33] The Comstock Act codified the genteel idea of virtue for the public sphere; with it the need to publish virtuous literature became law.[34]

In the words of one communications historian, "Congress broke with earlier policy and authorized the Post Office as an instrument of censorship and moral regulation."[35] The power of this instrument was enormous, because the Post Office exercised unprecedented control over the nation's publications after the Civil War. The ability to mail magazines at pennies per pound, a result of the new post–Civil War infrastructure of telegraph and railroads, created a magazine boom. As more magazines relied on the mail, however, the Comstock Act became a powerful weapon. It gave to the Post Office the right to deny its services to anything it deemed obscene. The notion of obscenity was rooted in the genteel tradition's definition of sexuality and gender, as I have discussed. To quote Henry Holt, Robert Frost's longtime publisher, the Comstock Act had one purpose: "The regulation of the sexual instinct."

Officially entitled an "Act for the Suppression of Trade in and Circulation of Obscene Literature and Articles of Immoral Use," the Comstock Act took its nickname from the man who brought it to Congress: Anthony Comstock.[36] Soon after it was signed, Comstock received a commission to be a special agent of the United States Post Office, giving him a remarkable position of unchallenged local and national power. Comstock, from a Vermont village steeped in Protestant values, was a salesman who had become one of the leaders of the new Young Men's Christian Association (YMCA), which in turn sponsored the New York Committee for the Prevention of Vice. Eventually Comstock became the head of that committee and was tasked with enforcing local obscenity laws as they applied to New York's ever expanding publishing industry. When he joined the Post Office, he could, and did, exert influence over every publisher in the nation who relied on the mails to get publications to the hands of readers. Reflecting the fear of the increasing availability of "the wrong sort" of published material, the Comstock Act censored books that might be mailed, and all periodicals that relied on the mail for circulation and profit. The communications historian Paul Starr explains that, "under this extraordinary arrangement, the federal government as well as the state of New York, the leading center of the publishing industry, turned over primary responsibility for the enforcement of moral censorship to a man employed by an elite private society composed of exclusively Christian men."[37] Censorship, in the name of genteel virtue, was soon dubbed "Comstockery" by none other than George Bernard Shaw and would forever alter the publishing landscape of the nation's public sphere.

AMERICAN PUBLICATIONS AFTER 1873

The Comstock Act came about in large part because the genteels saw it as their duty to enforce their ideas of both virtue and character. They saw to it that their views would have the force of law. Susman argues that the idea of character, for instance, defined itself through a distinctly tempered and moderated attitude toward work. To that point Gregory Jackson, in a groundbreaking book, adds that work, labor, or what I have called duty emerge from a fundamentally Calvinist Christian tradition, the very thing Santayana declared to be the case in his 1911 essay. When Santayana made his point, it was already understood as a given. In 1905 Max Weber's landmark *Protestant Ethic and the Spirit of Capitalism* had made the same point with intellectual force and had applied it on a global scale. By the time Robert Frost came of age, then, he inherited a tradition that taught him to expect individuals to do their duty and prove their virtue by restraining desire and enacting in the world only meaningful, necessary labor for the larger communal good. Labor was understood in terms of thrift and responsibility.[38] Labor, in effect, revealed one's character, proved one's virtue, and also became one's duty. Both men and women were understood to have a purpose, which was to labor. This meant that one was active and responsible, hardworking and restrained. It required the tempering influence of character and as such had to be molded and directed. To ensure appropriate labor a community also had to develop appropriate comportment in its people. It had to develop their character. It had to be inculcated—and the genteels used their almost uncontested control of publishing and the force of the Comstock Act to help in the task.

By the end of the Civil War a combination of factors had left the genteels in control of the only publications distributed nationally. As a result the genteels were in a position to promote, even to evangelize, on behalf of their cultural tradition. Nancy Glazener calls their publications "*The Atlantic*-Group," after its most prestigious and influential magazine, the *Atlantic Monthly*.[39] Although Glazener limits her study to monthly magazines, in fact the promotion of virtue, character, and duty could be found in a wide variety of weekly and monthly magazines. Not only did the genteel tradition define such monthlies as the *Atlantic, Scribner's, Harper's,* and the *Century,* it also governed the views expressed in weekly editions of several major big-city newspapers (the *Chicago Evening Post* and *New York Tribune*). By 1880 the magazines, weekly and monthly, as well as the weekly editions of certain city papers mailed to national subscribers, had created national publications dedicated to genteel values. Their editors and publishers deliberately and self-consciously asserted their self-appointed role as custodians of character, virtue, and duty and engaged in a massive campaign of "cultural evangelism" to promote their ideals through poetry, fiction, and drama.[40]

This campaign became but one side in a new culture war that began in the 1880s. But the genteel tradition's three core principles of character, virtue, and duty had always underpinned the genteels' publications. Such principles appeared in the very first American newspaper published in the seventeenth century, and they continued to be heralded. For example, in 1859 George William Curtis, editor at *Harper's Monthly* and *Harper's Weekly,* and "one of the major genteel 'evangelists of culture and civilization,'" used the bully pulpit of *Harper's* to declare that manners—which is to say the associated application of integrity, duty, and character—amounted to little more than the "conviction that we ought to feel kindly and act charitably toward everybody else. Bad manners are merely selfishness expressed in tones and conduct. Good manners are charity in speech and action."[41]

Only when such principles received vociferous opposition from what I have called the "other America" did a singular evangelism on behalf of duty, virtue, and character become, as it were, aggressive.[42] After the Civil War that opposition emerged predominantly in big-city newspapers. By then a combination of inexpensive postage rates and wider distribution made possible by new transportation networks gave alternatives to the genteel tradition an unprecedented voice. The Comstock Act, however, stifled that voice. So, too, did the only nationally distributed publications, which still belonged only to the genteels.

Following the Civil War, it was possible to send published material throughout the continent at low cost, efficiently, and, best of all, rapidly. Given the economics of scale, however, initially the only publications able to afford the capital costs of such massive distribution were those published, edited, and written by the genteels. Given that they had always used their publications to champion character, duty, and virtue, there was no reason to suppose they would not continue to do so in the 1870s and 1880s.[43] Nor were the genteels alone in making such use of the publications they controlled. As Benedict Anderson has argued, "the very idea of 'nation' is now nestled firmly in virtually all print-languages; and nation-ness is virtually inseparable from political consciousness."[44] The "print-languages" are the various institutions of publishing—newspapers and magazines especially. Not only did the genteels put their publications to use but in those publications they also put literature, and in particular poetry, to use in nation building in the name of the genteel tradition. With the rise of industrial urban immigrant America in the 1880s, too, both the publications and the literature they published found a new urgency for cultural evangelism on behalf of character, duty, and virtue.

Faced with perceived threats from urbanization, immigration, and industrialization to what the genteels understood as the core philosophy of nothing less than American civilization itself, they used their periodicals, and literature, to fight these threats. Not only did they convince the nation's public schools to adopt authors said to promote their tradition—"the Schoolroom Poets"—but they also increasingly used their magazines and newspapers as moral instruments.[45] There they made the case for fiction and poetry that not only gave delight but also instructed. Poetry and fiction, they claimed, engaged in intellectual, often philosophical, and political questions. In the antebellum era, for instance, the genteels had put literature to work advocating the abolitionist cause in both the schools and popular periodicals. To the genteels the rise of a "new America" posed a singular moral threat to the nation's health, as had slavery.

Publications such as *Harper's Monthly* (founded in 1850), the *Atlantic* (1857), and the *Century* (founded as *Scribner's* in 1859 and renamed in 1881), as well as several family magazines specifically written with children in mind (*Youth's Companion*), equated the American ideal with the genteel tradition, with the Anglo-Saxon, Calvinist New England village cultural ideals of duty, virtue, and character.

In addition to these national monthlies, the genteels also published daily newspapers such as Samuel Bowles's *Springfield Republican,* the *Boston*

Transcript, and such New York papers as the *New York Tribune* and the *New York Times,* whose first editor, Henry Raymond, was elected to Congress on the Republican ticket in 1865.[46] Using their platform, the genteels published fiction and poetry that treated readers to dramas either opposing or highlighting the dangers of the new materialism that had come in the wake of industrialism and urbanization. Deeply offended by the threats they saw in postbellum America to duty, to work, and to the very idea of character, the genteels promoted and published fiction and poetry that criticized and questioned why consumerism rather than labor, personality rather than character, decadence rather than virtue should be welcomed into American life.

Meanwhile an alternative group of mass-market publications such as *Munsey's* and *McClure's,* became a national phenomenon in the 1890s. These publications advocated consumerism and personality. They drew support from industrialism, the new immigrants, and the very forces of modernity that had panicked the genteel heart.[47]

Although there had long been rival popular publications to the genteel publications, they had not been national. This rich array of newspapers and magazines spoke to and for a far different America of Catholics, Jews, and Orthodox Christians and was resolutely local in the antebellum period. Some of these publications also spoke to and for an African American and ethnic America that rejected the view that Anglo-Saxon ethnicity defined the sum total of civilization. In such "penny-press" newspapers as James Gordon Bennett's *New York Herald,* Benjamin Day's *New York Sun,* and Frank Bonner's *New York Ledger,* as well as in an ever-increasing tide of ethnic, foreign-language, labor, socialist, and other radical publications, the "other America" had a greater voice than ever before.[48] That group did not associate sobriety, rational control, virtue, and social responsibility (duty) only with the example of a small New England village, or with a specifically Calvinist Anglo-Saxon ethnicity.

These rival publications, largely local newspapers, supported the Democratic Party as well as radical third parties and gained national attention in 1882 when Joseph Pulitzer entered the New York newspaper market. Pulitzer, a newspaper publisher from St. Louis, bought the *New York World,* a modest genteel paper with a circulation of twenty thousand, and announced in his own editorial statement of purpose that "there is room in this great and growing city for a journal that is not only cheap but bright, not only bright but large, not only large but truly democratic—dedicated to the cause of the people rather than to that of the potentates—devoted more to the news of the New than the Old world—that will expose all fraud and sham, fight all public evils and abuses—that will fight for the people with earnest sincerity." After just two years the paper's circulation had risen to 153,000, a jump, as Starr notes, that increased by "a factor of ten."[49]

Pulitzer's newspaper not only brought the other America to a national market, it also remade how newspapers looked. Pulitzer's *World* was half the size of a standard broadsheet, in fact the size of a typical genteel magazine. This reduced size also saved on paper costs and became known as the tabloid format. And where most newspapers skimped on visual art, Pulitzer increased it exponentially by using enormous numbers of drawings and photographs and using a wide variety of typefaces. Such became the daily format of the nation's most popular newspapers—the *Daily News, Herald,* and *World,* all published in New York—as well as their imitators throughout the continent.

Like the genteels, Pulitzer brought literature into his newspaper's pages. Rather than reprint the high seriousness of moral uplift associated with the genteels, he instead incorporated its nemesis, melodrama, and its cousin, sensationalism. Ostensibly the literature in Pulitzer's new tabloid endorsed the genteel values of virtue and decorum and followed the letter, if not the spirit, of the Comstock Act. In the stories and poetry he published, more often than not, however, vice received far more column inches than virtue. As he said, "I want to talk to the nation, not to a select committee."[50]

Pulitzer not only brought titillating literature into his daily, he also transformed basic coverage of events—the news stories themselves—into the arc of a melodramatic or adventure tale. As the journalism historian Michael Schudson puts it, the *New York Times* and other genteel dailies gave readers information, while the *World* told stories. In fact, it did more than tell stories; it told realist stories chock full of detail, conflict, and the sort of bad characters genteel literature meant to either condemn or ignore.[51] Thanks to Pulitzer, then, a rival national market had been created for journalism that rejected not only the political ideals promoted by the genteels' publications but also their literary values. The tabloids offered literature of adventure and melodrama, with a sensationalist emphasis on crime and sex that all but made a mockery of the cardinal ideal of virtue.

Meanwhile Pulitzer also gave literature, especially his kind of melodrama, a new forum, the Sunday newspaper magazine. Specifically Pulitzer's *Sunday World* had two to three times as many pages as the daily paper, more illustrations, fiction, poetry, and other feature material than had been published before. The Sunday paper had a dedicated editor, Morrill Goddard, and sold for just a penny more than the regular paper (in 1889 it was raised to five cents). The result of this new concept for the Sunday newspaper was an unprecedented circulation of 250,000 by 1888.[52] Before Pulitzer the newspaper for the working and lower-middle classes had always been the *New York Herald.* By 1890, however, Pulitzer's *World* became the circulation leader for *all* American newspapers. It also had more pages than any other newspaper that sold for two cents, as well as copious illustrations and a singularly liberal editorial bent. Pulitzer's political, social, and literary impact did not go unnoticed. Publishers who sought the mass market soon imitated him, and in so doing they broke the cultural monopoly of the genteels.

With the Post Office Act of 1885 Congress reduced the already inexpensive cost for mailing periodicals to the incredible bargain rate of one cent per pound, the least expensive rate ever (in 2012 dollars, shipping a pound of magazines cost only 25 cents). That rate, as Starr explains, made magazines far less expensive than the already ubiquitous advertising circulars filling mailboxes nationwide. Pulitzer took advantage of the low rates to start a national weekly edition of the *World,* and scores of other publishers decided to start national magazines of their own.

Almost as soon as the Postal Act of 1885 became law, the publishing industry experienced a new boom that affected every element, from daily newspapers to quarterly magazines.[53] To everyone's surprise, however, a plethora of magazines did *not* fill newsstands nationally. Instead only a few managed to achieve what journalism historians refer to as a "super high" circulation (circulations of a half million or more in a country of 72 million people). Nor did these new super high-circulation magazines come from the genteels. Instead they were brand-new publications and often shared Pulitzer's liberal leftist politics. As a group they were distinguished from the genteel publications in four ways: their abundant use of illustration; their copious use of advertising; their unprecedentedly inexpensive cover price; and their inclusion of poetry and fiction.[54]

Above all, these new mass-market publications, which came into their own in the 1890s, depended on advertising in ways that gave the genteels nightmares. The economics became obvious almost as soon as the 1885 Postal Act became law. Whereas selling products once had relied on the direct mailing of expensive circulars, the law now made advertising vastly less expensive because a single ad in a magazine would reach far more people.[55]

As it happened, when the first mass audience magazines began publishing, advertising had just come become a national industry. Advertisers realized that magazines sold nationwide gave them access to huge markets. In an era of overproduction such as the 1890s, producers were willing to pay what might seem like ridiculous prices for advertising their wares. When the publishers began to charge ever higher ad rates and found that advertisers still were willing to pay, a few publishers decided to reduce their cover price and see what happened. One of those new magazines, *McClure's,* was the first to try. McClure decided to sell his magazine for less than what it cost to produce it and to make up the difference through advertising revenue. To the publisher's surprise, a well-produced, thick, heavily illustrated magazine filled with poetry and stories as well as news stories sold in unprecedented numbers at a low cover price.[56]

McClure proved that a magazine publisher who did not share the genteel conception of duty, virtue, and character could triumph in the mass market. He would print huge runs of each issue at a loss in terms of material and labor and still made a profit from advertising revenue. Through his efforts, and those of other publishers like him, American mass-market publishing grew into a formidable industry.[57] Mass-market publishing, unlike the genteel magazines, relied both on abundant advertisements and excessive illustration. These national publications were also huge, often more than a hundred pages an issue, yet they sold for 15 cents compared to the genteel monthlies' 35 cents an issue. The price and visual allure of the mass-market publications appealed to the other America of urban, immigrant, and working-class Americans.

Specifically the 1890s mass-market publishing consisted of such monthly magazines as *McClure's, Munsey's* (founded 1891), and *Cosmopolitan.* For the first time, America had a genuinely diverse national print market.

As Starr says, "The early mass media in America added more to cultural diversity than they subtracted from it." Why? According to Starr, because "the intensely competitive environment of the mainstream English-language urban press was a continual prod to diversification of content and innovation in journalistic practices."[58] Among the new practices were, in addition to advertisements, an abundance of illustration; both resulted from such technological advances as photoengraving that simply made illustrations less expensive to produce.

By the end of the 1890s eighty-five magazines had circulations of more than 100,000. The super high-circulation mass-market monthly magazines, which sold at a cover price of 15 cents (roughly $3.95 in 2012 dollars), became the market leaders. No genteel magazine came close. *McClure's, Munsey's, Cosmopolitan,* and the *Ladies' Home Journal* each had a staggering circulation of nearly or more than 700,000. The genteels could easily have mimicked the methods of these periodicals, but they resolutely refused to do so. Throughout the 1890s, for instance, the Big Three genteel, or "family house," magazines (*Atlantic, Harper's Monthly,* and the *Century*), kept to their expensive 35-cent cover price (roughly $9.20 in 2012 dollars). In sum, they deliberately limited their audience through the mechanism of price. In the words of Frank Luther Mott, they courted only "the moneyed and well-educated classes." In so doing they achieved dramatic subscription and circulation rates of more than 100,000, with the *Century* leading the pack with a circulation of 200,000 by 1892.[59]

• • •

When Robert Frost, as a Dartmouth student in 1892, found Richard Hovey's poem in the New York weekly *Independent*, Frost had unwittingly immersed himself fully in the deep-end of genteel American culture and unknowingly took a decisive stance in an ongoing culture war about poetry. Hovey's poem lamented the death of Thomas William Parsons, who was not only a poet but also the premier translator and scholar of Dante, and one of Longfellow's great friends. In "Seaward," his elegy for Parsons, Hovey also defended a decidedly intellectual, public-spirited ideal of poetry itself. Not content to wrestle only with the angel of beauty and craft, Hovey claimed that poetry was meant to teach, persuade, and change its readers' lives intellectually and emotionally.[60] The weekly's editors heartily agreed. Almost alone among genteel magazines of opinion, news, and culture in 1892, the *Independent* printed a poem on its front page each week.

Hovey's poem lamented the passing of precisely the kind of poetry his own poem represented. As if bidding such poetry good-bye, the poem refers to the Provençal poets of the Middle Ages and the great lyrics of Dante because, Hovey thought, that poetry integrated a social, religious, and aesthetic vision. In 1892 Hovey and his friend Bliss Carman thought such integration as Dante and Parsons represented was no longer possible.

For instance, the poem places Parsons in a long chain of poets that stretched from Virgil to Dante and into the contemporary American present. Imagining Parsons in Paradise, Hovey writes of the poets among whom he now dwells:

> There thy co-laborers and high compeers
> Hailed thee as courtly hosts some noble guest,—
> Poe, disengloomed with the celestial years,
> Calm Bryant, Emerson of the antique zest
> And modern vision, Lowell all a-bloom
> At last, unwintered of his mind's unrest,
> And Whitman, with the old superb aplomb.
> Not far from these Lanier, deplored so oft
> From Georgian live-oaks to Acadian firs,
> Walks with his friend as once at Cedarcroft.
> And many more I see of speech diverse;
> From whom a band aloof and separate,
> Landon and Meleager in converse
> And lonely Collins for thy greeting wait.[61]

These stanzas imply, however, that such poets, and such poetry, can now only exist as something past. Its day is done.

That sadness was as personal as it was theoretical. Both had met Parsons in 1887. Parsons, Longfellow's model for the poet character in *Tales of a Wayside Inn* (1863), had long struck Hovey and Carman as their poetic exemplar.[62] When Parsons died Hovey was primed to write "Seaward: An Elegy on the Death of Thomas William Parsons." Nor was its publication incidental. By then Hovey had become friendly with one of his former English professors at Dartmouth who also regularly wrote for Henry C.

Bowen's *Independent*. Not only was Hovey's poem printed in the first of the front page's three columns on November 17, 1892, but it was given all three front-page columns and thereby filled the entire page, which was unusual even for the *Independent*.[63]

Young Robert Frost likely read the poem as the simple elegy it purported to be. But the only thing that mattered to Frost was that a recent American poet, Parsons, could be so celebrated by another relatively young American poet, Hovey, on the front page of a major magazine.

Chapter Two

•

Realism and Genteel Publishing

IN THE 1890s, when Robert Frost came of age and began to publish his poetry, he was participating in the most diverse, expansive, and eclectic publishing industry in U.S. history. That commercial publishing, both genteel and mass, defined the public sphere and promoted literature as part of a larger social vision. As outlined in chapter 1, by the 1890s genteel publishing promoted a literary standard based on such values as character, duty, and virtue. By then, however, the standard had been challenged on two literary fronts, realism and the aesthetic movement. In chapter 1, I mentioned that the adherents of realism were determined to make literature face the facts of a new materialism and commercialism. That insistence was also an argument against postbellum aestheticism. This new aesthetic movement was meant to counter commercialism and the forces of materialism through literature's creation of a transcendent zone of pure beauty. Beginning in the late 1880s, these new aesthetes, both symbolists and decadents, meant to create not only a new kind of literature but also their own set of commercial publishing institutions, the little magazine and the small press.

Between 1885 and 1900 the American publishing industry underwent a massive boom. According to the 1900 census, there were 15,000 newspapers in the nation (up from 4,500 in 1865). Of them, 2,200 were dailies. More daily papers were printed than at any other time in American history; they included dailies in at least fifteen different languages (the first national daily newspaper with offices in multiple cities was the Yiddish-language *Daily Forward,* which used the telegraph to wire the same story to its branch offices in cities across the nation). Like the older dailies, many of the recent ones had created Sunday editions—four hundred by the end of the 1890s—that regularly printed fiction and poetry. The dailies also began to publish weekly book review supplements. By 1900 the nation also had more weeklies than ever, well more than thirteen thousand, most of which adhered to the local, timely, and, one might say, nongenteel attitudes of the other America. A third of the dailies and weeklies had more than a thousand subscribers.[1]

These papers were divided into two rival and bitter camps. On the one side were the genteels and those who had adopted their tradition of dearly held values, as well as their commitment to the progressive wing of the Republican Party. This camp had long published the only dominant national papers and had seen both its economic slice of the market and its political influence sag significantly. On the other side were the new monthlies, weeklies, and dailies speaking largely for the Democratic Party and for the new immigrant and urban population that comprised the new America of 1900.

This group rocked the publishing world and transformed it into a big industry with industrial-scale profits. These publications combined serious literature, investigative journalism, abundant illustration, and advertising, which took up as much as a third of an issue.[2] Although the publishers, and often the editors and writers, too, detested one another and made no secret about it, the two camps—genteel and mass market—differed only in degree, not kind. While the mass-market publications largely welcomed the new industrialism, and the ethnic and religious variety brought by the tide of immigration that had overwhelmed the country since the end of the Civil War, the genteels opposed all three as somehow un-American. Still, both camps agreed that literature, especially poetry and fiction, ought to serve the public good. And while they fought, often bitterly, about the meaning of duty and virtue, they did not, for all that, deny the centrality of literature to the propagation of their views.

In the mass-market publications that advocacy took on a decidedly aggressive cast both in journalism and in literature, a cast the soon-to-be president Theodore Roosevelt labeled muckraking. In the early centuries of Anglo settlement on the American continent, most homes had only one book other than the Bible, the seventeenth-century allegory of faith, *Pilgrim's Progress,* by John Bunyan. Muckraking was one of Bunyan's most familiar images, and TR applied it to the liberal, leftist brand of investigative journalism practiced by the new mass-market publications. Too often forgotten is the fundamentally literary, and especially Calvinist, context for this epithet. TR used the term in an article he wrote for a genteel publication, which then applied it broadly to its ideological and market rivals; the popularity of the term simply underlines the pervasive influence of the genteel tradition in the 1890s publishing, even as its overall dominance waned.[3]

WILLIAM DEAN HOWELLS AND REALISM

Realism, which could be found in both genteel and mass-market publications, was spearheaded by the writer and editor William Dean Howells. Literary historians continue to debate realism's social role. They ask if it was part of the era's establishment elite or if the elite was generally opposed to realism.[4] In that debate the fundamental values of character, duty, and virtue become either realism's villains or its heroes. Regardless of the social vision, however, scholars agree that as a literary form realism changed the rules for writing fiction. In terms of genre and style the American realists, beginning in the 1870s with Howells as their leading spokesman, championed a new kind of fiction directly opposed to what is now called the romance tradition, the stylistics that had governed what I am calling the genteel literary tradition. Richard Chase's *The American Novel and Its Tradition* (1957) identified the stylistics of the romance tradition. According to Amy Kaplan's summary of Chase, the romance tradition largely avoided topical references and social details. Stylistically it preferred "that American writers characteristically escape from society and history." In place of rigorous attention to the details mimicking everyday reality, and in place of characters that develop "in relation to entrenched institutions and the struggle between classes," American literature prefers "a melodramatic quest through a symbolic universe, unformed by networks of social relations unfettered by the pressures of social restraints," Kaplan writes.[5] As a literary style realism can be traced to the origins of the European novel in the eighteenth century. During World War II Erich Auerbach's *Mimesis,* still the single most influential book on realism in literature, traced the long history of what he termed "the serious treatment of everyday reality."[6] That kind of writing, however, had not taken hold among the genteels who dominated the American public sphere's print publications. They chose instead to champion what Chase identified as the romance tradition. To ensure that readers would adopt their trinity of values—character, duty, and virtue—the genteels promoted the romance literary tradition in their magazines and newspapers.[7] In the 1870s Howells resurrected European realism after reading Zola and Balzac, among others. Howells did not intend to dismiss the core values of duty, character, and virtue associated with that romance or, as I prefer to call it, genteel tradition. Instead he meant to make those values more pertinent, more necessary. Andrew Lawson, in his recent study of American realism, argues that fiction attending to the specific social and particular details of everyday life became the only literary method available "to interpret cohesively."[8] Lawson means that only through strict particulars could writers "give shape to a diffuse, opaque world, to make sense of 'the ephemeral, the fleeting, the contingent,' to fix, or at least to arrest for a moment, the market's chaotic flow of goods, people, information."[9] According to Lawson, Howells's lower-middle-class experiences in his Ohio family and his perspective as an outsider at the center of Boston Brahmin literary culture led him to agree with the Brahmin view that the new industrial financial capitalism lacked character, virtue, and even civic duty. Appalled at the moral turpitude of the United States, Howells saw no benefit from a romance literature that, he felt, had lost all persuasive power to ensure the survival of the genteel tradition. Only if literature took on the aura of fact, empiricism, and science, he argued, would it have a chance of rectifying the nation's moral degeneration.[10] From within the very center of genteel publishing, then, Howells meant to enact a literary reform movement.

More specifically still, realism in this era meant that writers "conceptualized the text as a window or a mirror."[11] In order to make the details and particulars of the social world all the more believable, novelists also began to hide their own role as narrators. In her study of the vanishing narrator of American realist fiction, Barbara Hochman finds that by 1900, "the turn of the century, authorial reserve and impersonality were well established narrative conventions."[12] Howells is the exemplar of American realist fiction because of his leading role in the public sphere as editor of the *Atlantic* and later as a columnist for *Harper's,* essayist for many other magazines and newspapers; his novels were often serialized in leading genteel magazines such as the *Century.*

A rebel in the central genteel institutions that made literature matter, Howells used his public platform to challenge the literary orthodoxy of the romance tradition. His rebellion came not in opposition to the fundamental trinity of character, virtue, and duty but rather as means of preserving their moral necessity. In both his novels and essays Howells argued for a change in literary style, form, and methods. He made this case in his fiction while editor of the *Atlantic* in the 1870s. The magazine, however, and most of its writers, as well as the Boston literary establishment, resolutely opposed the new realism. Charles Eliot Norton, a wealthy merchant who often put his views to paper for the genteel publications and who had been one of the founders of the *Nation* in 1865, drew strict limits around his progressive liberalism when he argued against a democratic literature focused on the lives of the mob. He expected the core civilizing values that defined literature to be written, populated, and promoted only by "the few who have been blessed with the opportunities, and the rare genius to lead." He entered academia in 1873, when he joined Harvard's faculty, and began the first-ever art history classes there. Howard Mumford Jones cites a letter from Charles Eliot Norton declaring his pride in establishing "the first continuous university instruction in the history of the fine arts as related to social progress, general culture and literature."[13] Five years later Josiah Holland, who had worked on the *Springfield (Massachusetts) Republican* and became editor of *Scribner's,* also wrote that literature had to be synonymous with moral goodness to deserve the name and that those who recognized such goodness had to direct readers.[14] At the *Atlantic,* Howells's promotion of realism met with resistance of the staff as well as resistance from readers. Under Howells the *Atlantic* witnessed a steady circulation decline from a peak of fifty thousand subscribers in 1871 to twelve thousand when he left in ten years later. His departure created a scandal in the literary gossip columns.[15] His Brahmin peers were shocked

when, soon after he quit the *Atlantic* he began writing for the less culturally prestigious, though still genteel, *Harper's Monthly*. At the time the
genteels measured someone's commitment to core genteel values through
his attitude toward the new mass culture's commercialism. The placement
and amount of advertising a magazine might use determined its cultural
status, its level of seriousness. The more illustration a magazine carried,
the more commercial, and therefore the less respectable it was said to be.
Harper's Monthly, as an illustrated magazine, was said to have forsaken its
commitment to genteel high seriousness. For Howells to leave the *Atlantic*
and become a columnist for *Harper's,* as he did officially in 1885, when
he moved from Boston to materialist, commercial New York, seemed to
many a signal of the decline and fall of the genteel literary tradition and
the moral standards on which it was based.

What did Howells's departure from the *Atlantic* say about the romance
tradition and the genteel literary idea in the public sphere? It said that the
Atlantic and the Boston literati had no taste for realism. Realizing this,
the *Atlantic's* publisher found a way to remove Howells as editor in 1881.
James R. Osgood by then was paying Howells a commanding $10,000
(equal to $252,000 in 2013 dollars) to edit the magazine, about what the
editors of other large-circulation genteel publications were paid.[16] Evidently Osgood decided to make Howells an offer he could not ignore:
the same annual salary of $10,000 not for editing but rather for exclusive
rights to his future books and in lieu of royalties on initial sales. Howells
took the money. To the literary world, however, it seemed that the writer
had jumped from the most prestigious forum in the land only to wallow
in commercialism and pictures as a writer for *Harper's.* Few people knew
the real reason Howells left.

Meanwhile Osgood replaced Howells with a brash young New England
poet, Thomas Bailey Aldrich, then living and working in New York at a
genteel literary weekly, the *Round Table.* Aldrich had been associated with
the largely bohemian crowd surrounding Walt Whitman at Pfaff's Cellar
Tavern in New York City and had even been assistant editor of that group's
dynamic weekly, the *Saturday Press.*[17] Although Aldrich brought a certain flash to the *Atlantic,* by the time he became its editor, he had left his
bohemian days behind in favor of the genteel tradition. Always opposed

to hard-nosed details and grim depictions made increasingly familiar by realism even when he was at the *Saturday Press*, Aldrich turned the *Atlantic's* attention instead to the lighter side of life and to fiction more laden with symbolism, allegory, and allusive references to history, mythology, and the like. Unlike Howells, Aldrich refused to tempt the stiff boot and sour sneer of Comstockery. His magazine did not criticize duty, character, and virtue as Howells's magazine had so often done. Throughout Aldrich's editorship he maintained a list of topics "not to be touched." As one example, "he enforced a moratorium on religious questions" in any article at all. Under Aldrich the *Atlantic* in the late 1880s returned to a circulation of well more than 100,000 even while avoiding illustrations. In public Aldrich attributed his success to "the hard shrewd sense and the simpler manner" of the New England village.[18]

Howells, still in Boston, wrote for the New York magazines until 1885, when *Harper's* hired him full time to write a new column, "The Editor's Study." He moved to the city with his family, and it became clear to him, as to readers everywhere, that his preferred literary style of realism would thrive only among the New Yorkers. Once there, for instance, Howells not only defended the stylistics of realism with its relentless attention to social detail but he also provided a decidedly liberal moral foundation for it that was at odds with the traditional New England interpretation of both character and duty.[19] Nor was Howells averse to promoting realism in mass-market publications. In 1897 he published, "My Favorite Novelist and His Best Book," an essay about the hard-hitting realist Frank Norris for *Munsey's*.[20]

SYMBOLISM, DECADENCE, AND LITTLE MAGAZINES

Realism was not the only challenge to the genteels' preferred romance standard. In addition to the realists, the 1890s saw writers, predominantly poets, who advocated a new symbolism and decadence within their own social cohort. These new literary forms, often grouped together under the rubric of aestheticism, challenged the chief values of the larger genteel literary idea expressed in the style and technique of the romance tradition. For instance, against duty and its "cult of labor," the new symbolists and decadents became advocates of beauty for its own sake, for leisure, and for play. Like realism, symbolism had come to the United States from Europe.

This movement of poets and painters developed in France in the 1870s and had initially taken such American poets as Edgar Allan Poe and Walt Whitman as its models. The symbolists in France and the United States took a philosophical, intellectual approach to play, beauty, and the delights of words. These writers had as much disdain for the threats posed by immigration, urbanization, and industrialism as did their genteel peers. The symbolists and decadents, too, saw the dangers of a new unfettered capitalist economic engine for publishing. They, too, had little faith in the genteel tradition's ability to combat it. Yet unlike the realists, the symbolists and decadents argued that literature had no business attempting to enforce a social good, nor should literature make cardinal values palatable or even act as a civilizing agent. To the symbolists and decadents any morally instrumental use of literature—be it the genteel romance or the realist alternative—smacked of philistinism. Literature, they argued, should be concerned only with beauty and craft for its own sake. To reduce literature to moral purposes merely cheapened it.[21] Where Howells and the realists in their literature meant to directly confront and face contemporary social problems brought about by modernity and materialism, the symbolists and decadents preferred to transcend (a word they favored) the materialist realm. Typically their fiction and poetry created utopian realms of delight and beauty. In hindsight one can say that the realists succeeded in redefining American fiction, while the symbolists and decadents succeeded in redefining and reconstituting American poetry, although initially their advocates wrote both fiction and poetry.

The American symbolists made less of a dent in commercial publishing than did their decadent cousins, who became hugely influential among the young. According to David Weir, a scholar of decadence's arrival in America, "the weight of materialism seemed so much greater in the United States [in the 1880s]; hence the impetus to aesthetic escapism was greater."[22] Increasingly that escapism took as its heroes poets like Oscar Wilde, Dante Gabriel Rossetti, Edward Burne-Jones, William Morris, and the critic and essayist Walter Pater. Each inspired a rebellious ideal, especially among the young.

In the genteel American publications decadence first came to general attention in November 1893, when *Harper's Monthly* ran Arthur Symons's "The Decadent Movement in Literature." This article made famous a new avant-garde group of English and French writers. According to Symons, the decadent movement had two poles. At one were the Bohemians, generally from the working class and often not from a Christian Anglo-Saxon background.[23] They wrote of their love of the crowd, immigrants, and the new modern America. At the other pole were the decadents, who often came from the aristocracy (what I have termed the genteels) and who shared an elitist contempt and disdain for the mob of immigrants, urbanization, and industrialism. Both the Bohemians and the decadents, for all their differences, shared an equal hatred of the crass materialism of the new industrial capitalist world.[24] Both also shared the view of art's importance outside any need for moral uplift. Symons said the Bohemians-symbolists-decadents expected literature to speak to us "as only religion has hitherto spoken to us." He added that literature "becomes itself a sort of religion, with all the duties and responsibilities of the Sacred Ritual" found in organized faiths.[25] With regard to the symbolist-decadents, Symons said their poetry and fiction largely erased all political and moral advocacy from their works in order to concentrate on beauty. To that end the symbolists and decadents looked to poets like Keats, and to poems like his epic *Endymion,* for their models.[26] Describing their work, he wrote that "it has all the qualities that mark the end of great periods . . . an intense self-consciousness, a restless curiosity in research, an over subtilizing refinement upon refinement, a spiritual and moral perversity." Compared to the high moral idealism of the genteel romance tradition, or even of the new realism, the decadents-symbolists did not aspire to achieve the "perfect simplicity, perfect sanity, perfect proportion, the supreme qualities"; instead "this [decadent] representative literature of to-day, interesting, beautiful, novel as it is, is really [a] new and beautiful and interesting disease."[27] Where the genteel romance tradition had confined writers to the deeper profundities expressed through symbol and allegory, the new symbolists-decadents rejected that tradition's moral urgency. In place of a moral commitment to virtue and duty, they sought instead beauty, pleasure, and leisure for their own sake alone. Nonetheless they typically kept to the genteel romance tradition's dependence on symbol and allegory.

An essay, or even multiple essays, alone do not make a literary event public. A novel, however, did. In 1894 the British writer George Du Maurier met with unprecedented success and put decadence front and center as an American cultural phenomenon when *Harper's* published as a serial *Trilby*, a novel of decadent characters living in Paris. Famous today for its sinister Jewish character, Svengali, and his power over the beautiful Irish model and singer Trilby, the novel made decadence a cause célèbre.[28] Du Maurier put to new, seemingly amoral, use the old symbolist, allegorical technique and incorporated what Barbara Hochman, a recent scholar of realism, refers to as "the friendly narrator."[29] Famously realism had done its best to take the narrator out of the tale, to let the story unfold as if by itself. The earlier genteel romance tradition rarely, if ever, erased the narrator. Instead, as Hochman puts it, the genteel novelists preferred a narrative style that put its arm around the reader and asked him or her to listen to a tale. In *Trilby*, however, the tale was decidedly dark, ending in manipulation and death.

Despite its critics, however, decadence did not have to imply degeneration and death. It did, however, seem suspect (hence its name) because it followed no moral purpose and made no plea for moral uplift. Reveling in beauty, and the making of beautiful poems and stories, Walter Pater was the decadents' singular champion. His novel *Marius the Epicurean* famously ends with its pagan hero converting to Christianity. As if unwilling to avoid the moral element altogether, Pater defended beauty, play, and delight in the name of Christianity, which had a particular resonance in America. As he said, "Art ensures the restoration of the divine within a disfigured world." To prove his case he turned to Shelley, the poet favored by Bohemians and politically radical realists. In Pater's view Shelley ought not be read for his politics but rather as the advocate of beauty. Through Pater Shelley's poetry in particular, and literature in general, became the only human means "to transmute the fugitive moment into enraptured ecstasy." The Horatian idea of poetry as moral intellectual education fell from favor. "The only ideas tolerated are those that help us be ecstatic and allow us forever to be open to new experiences"—such in a nutshell became the new standard for poets in the 1880s and 1890s. Through a new art-for-art's-sake, or aesthetic, movement, poetry had the power to make life not just tolerable but palpably better. Art could transform life by making life itself into art: "Art invents the world and constantly transforms it."[30] By reading Pater a whole host of poets found new possibilities to go against the genteel grain.

Pater provided the deeper intellectual roots for the new turn to what is now called the gospel of beauty but that I will refer to simply as the later nineteenth-century genteel tradition of poetic allegory and symbolism. Like every Jesus, Pater required a Paul to spread the word. Pater's Paul was none other than Oscar Wilde, who in 1882 made an American tour and delivered the epistles of this literary New Testament. When on January 31, 1882, Wilde embarked on his American tour with a sold-out lecture, "The English Renaissance," he popularized Walter Pater's ideas. In Boston, then headquarters of American genteel literature, one recent literary historian writes that, "To say that Wilde received an enthusiastic response that evening in Boston in late January 1882 would be a gross understatement."[31] As a representative of the gospel of beauty, Wilde argued that literature could remove one from the bleakness of everyday life. In literature no one had to abide by duty or virtue, and instead everyone could relax in a utopian space where beauty alone reigned supreme. The irony of this position would come later in the 1890s, after Wilde's conviction for sodomy and the attendant publicity. By then all he represented had become associated with what Max Nordau would call degeneration, the dark side of decadence.[32]

That dark side on the one hand, and the seemingly amoral aestheticism of symbolism on the other, scared most of the commercial publishers in charge of the genteel magazines associated with "*The Atlantic*-group." Happily for the writers, however, the confluence of inexpensive paper, improved printing technology, and lower postal rates made starting a magazine easier and less expensive than ever. In Boston, for instance, members of a decadent circle associated with Harvard contributed to one of the first little magazines of the era, the *Chap-Book* (established in 1894). Members of this circle had gathered around the poet Louise Imogen Guiney (1861–1920). Guiney had gained notoriety for her poetry because it pushed the limits of acceptable decorum concerning sexuality. Like her friend, the young Harvard graduate student and then professor George Santayana (1863–1952), Guiney was a Catholic. Unlike him, though, she did not lose her faith. Also, she made her living as postmistress of Auburndale, Massachusetts. In addition to Santayana, her circle included Bliss Carman (1861–1929), and none other than the poet who influenced the young Robert Frost, Richard Hovey (1864–1900)—and both Carman and Hovey were associated with Harvard. Carman was a recent graduate and Hovey a graduate student. Also in the group were a young Harvard art historian, Bernard Berenson, and another student, Herbert Copeland, as well as Fred Holland Day (1864–1933), an independently wealthy photographer, designer, and artist in whose mansion the group met regularly and even held decadent balls.[33]

These Boston decadents not only admired Keats but also, like the pre-Raphaelites of the 1850s, adored the Middle Ages because of its supposedly organic, holistic culture so unlike, they imagined, the pluralist chaos of the present moment. They also had become ardent admirers of Dante, almost to idolatry.[34] Disdainful of the conventional genteel morality and didacticism associated with the genteel romance tradition, and frank in their literary elitism, they preferred lush, sensual, and sexual poetry.[35] In fact while a member of this circle Hovey had written his 1892 homage to the premier American translator of Dante, Thomas Parsons.

Also associated with this circle were two Harvard seniors, Herbert Stone and Ingalls Kimball, both Robert Frost's age (they, too, were born in the 1870s). In 1894, they decided to start their own publishing firm, Stone and Kimball, and their own monthly magazine, the *Chap-Book*, for which they would solicit contributions from Guiney's circle. The creation of the *Chap-Book* was no immature lark. Its original purpose was to be a platform for advertising Stone and Kimball's list of books. Stone had come by his ability to generate publicity naturally; his father, Melville Stone, was publisher of the eclectic and free-spirited *Chicago Daily News* and head of the country's leading newspaper syndicate, the Associated Press. From the first, then, the Stone fortune bankrolled the firm of Stone and Kimball.[36] In fact it chose as its first book *Sonnets and Other Verses* (1894), by the young philosopher and Guiney's friend George Santayana.

Meanwhile the first edition of their *Chap-Book* sported a portrait by Aubrey Beardsley and carried essays, poetry, and fiction in the symbolist and decadent manner. For instance readers learned in an essay by Bliss Carman about the great renegade Catholic poet Francis Thompson. Carman's cousin, the already well-known poet of symbolism and beauty Charles G. D. Roberts, gave readers a symbolist poem. Altogether this first issue proved an unexpectedly profitable hit.[37] Capitalizing on that success, the two young publishers began a spirited sales and publicity campaign for their new venture.[38] As a result the *Chap-Book* introduced an entire generation to a new kind of poetry and became one of the first American magazines to introduce in translation the French symbolist poets themselves.[39] Above all, the magazine celebrated the carnal pleasures and rejected what Stone and Kimball considered to be the grim moralism of work, duty, and labor. As the two publishers themselves said in one of their first issues, "Is it not enough to be made glad and happy?"[40]

Although a distinctive literary magazine, the *Chap-Book* was never underground nor was it ever meant to be exclusive. Kimball, for instance, always insisted on making a profit. Both he and Stone accepted advertising, kept to a regular publication schedule, and built the magazine as a means of promoting their publishing house's list of books. Given that the family fortune and contacts of Stone's father remained in Chicago, the two men decamped for the great Midwestern city soon after graduating from Harvard even before the end of 1894; the *Chap-Book* would continue its publishing run in Chicago. As Larzer Ziff explained of the magazine in his literary history of the period: "Its habit of free speech produced a curious movement among the young writers of the country. There was scarcely a village or a town which did not have its little individualistic pamphlet frankly imitating the form and tone of *The Chap-Book*."[41]

Meanwhile, also in 1894, a similar magazine was founded in England, the *Yellow Book*. Established by an expatriate American, Henry Harland, it was published by the new English firm of John Lane and became the first successful commercial magazine of the new decadence and other, more exotic, kinds of poetry that Symons had described.[42] In its pages American and English readers were introduced to Oscar Wilde, Ernst Dowson, and Charles Algernon Swinburne, and it too sported art nouveau cover art from Aubrey Beardsley. Issued as a book-length (250 pages) quarterly, "it aimed to be popular and fashionable, if not quite mainstream."[43] Always commercial, the *Yellow Book* did not compromise on its idea of poetry and fiction. In fact it sought to change the direction of the deeply dissatisfying Victorian verse of high moral purpose its editors and writers had come to loathe.

Remarkably no historian believes either the *Chap-Book* or the more well-known *Yellow Book*, though founded almost simultaneously, were aware of each other when they began to publish. Nonetheless, they did affect each other. For instance, the buzz surrounding Stone and Kimball's magazine, writers, and books convinced Lane, the *Yellow Book*'s publisher, to open a New York office in 1896. To run it he sent one of his firm's younger members, Mitchell Kennerley. Trained in this rebellious terrain of symbolism, decadence, and little magazines, Kennerley would soon leave John Lane and found his own eponymous publishing house in New York City. In so doing Kennerley joined a new breed of publishers (Alfred A. Knopf, B. W. Huebsch, the Boni brothers) who were willing to break with the genteel tradition's definitions of literary excellence. After becoming a publisher in his own right, Kennerley would be instrumental in Frost's early career.

In addition to Stone and Kimball and the firm's magazine, the *Chap-Book*, members of Guiney's circle also established another publishing firm dedicated to decadent literature as well as another magazine, the *Mahogany Tree*. Both ventures were started by a young Herbert Copeland, then still in college, and both used the capital of his older, wealthier friend, Fred Holland Day. Although the magazine did not last the year (1894), the publishing company Copeland and Day did produce quality books associated with decadence, especially poetry.[44]

Upon learning that John Lane meant to distribute the *Yellow Book* in the United States, Copeland and Day signed a contract with John Lane to be the *Yellow Book*'s sole distributor in America. As a result, beginning in 1894, decadent literature became increasingly available in the United States, and the concept of a strictly literary, narrowly defined, little magazine began to take hold.[45] Through magazines like the *Yellow Book* and the *Chap-Book,* and such new publishing ventures as Stone and Kimball and Copeland and Day, a new publishing institution, little magazines and the small press had risen to challenge the dominance of genteel publishing. This rival enterprise replaced the genteel value of duty with leisure, pleasure, delight, and beauty. Decadence also signaled ever more clever ways to bring sex directly into literature without risking the sort of explicitness that continued to give realism a bad name. For editors and publishers of any periodical that expected to be mailed, however, the Comstock Act made it all but impossible to reference sexuality openly. The genteel value—virtue—as identified by the Comstock Act, not only limited how far publishers and editors were willing to go in pressing the artistic freedom of their writers but also made it impossible to print most of the new realism, decadence, and symbolism in either magazines or newspapers. The poet, editor, and influential anthologist Edwin Clarence Stedman described such Comstockery as "the *virginibus* maxim," meaning that one should publish only that which might not offend a virgin.[46] "Our Unclean Fiction," the headline for a December 1890 article in Edwin D. Mead's reform-minded *New England Magazine,* typified refined reaction to the new realism. Henry Mills Alden, at *Harper's Monthly,* had been one of the few genteel editors sympathetic to the new realist fiction, but in 1908 even he refused to publish most of it in his pages: "There are doubtless authors who revel in brutalities, who enjoy an infernal habitation not for its purgatorial fires but for its sulphurous airs, and who complain because they may not make their descents before a polite audience; but these things do not come within the scope of the demand of any species of human culture."[47]

Alden had not come to that conclusion lightly. In 1894 he had serialized Thomas Hardy's *Jude the Obscure* in the magazine. Even then, though, Alden feared the censor's wrath and his readers' reactions and so demanded Hardy cut certain passages. Defending the cuts, Alden told Hardy: "Our rule is that the MAGAZINE must contain nothing which could not be read aloud in any family circle."[48] Also that November the *North American Review,* by then a monthly publishing in New York City, ran an essay by the novelist Amelia E. Barr that defended propriety in fiction against a rising tide of indiscretion: "The one thing to be regretted in many of the lighter novels of the day is their kind of heroine. She is not a nice girl.... She is frank, too frank." [49] Despite the decadent-symbolist insurrection, however, the genteels, in both book publishing and the national market, still defined the meaning and contours of American literature through the variety of legal mechanisms collectively known as Comstockery. All this made such upstart publishing ventures as the *Mahogany Tree* and the *Chap-Book* all but impossible to sustain over time. Indeed the former lasted barely a year and the latter just four.

REALISM IS NOT POETRY: THE 1890s

Just as there had been a boom in periodical publishing so too the 1890s saw a boom in book publishing. It had even affected poetry. In a remarkable study of 1890s American poetry, Carlin Kindilien looked at more than twenty-four hundred books of poetry from more than nineteen hundred different authors published during that decade.[50] He found that fewer than 30 percent of the volumes came from genteel publishers in New York or Boston.[51] In other words, just as a new world of little magazines and small presses had emerged, they also resulted in the publication of a plethora of poetry books.

More to the point, of all the books he examined, virtually none incorporated realist themes or techniques. Instead, as he said, they reflected their authors' "worship of the past, their fondness for historical myth and legend, their addiction to the exotic and the picturesque, and especially . . . their peculiar combination of the ideal, the spiritual, and the didactic." When not engaged in utopian dreams, or musical explorations of sonic and imagistic beauty, the work of genteel moral seriousness confined itself to generic ideals rather than topics of the moment.[52] Noting the dearth of realism in the published collections of poetry, one of the first scholars of this poetry, Bruce Weirick, wrote: "The world of cities, of the mills, of railroads, and finance, and technical educations, of Methodism, and invention, and hide-bound custom, the world of drudgery, and immigration, and inartistic day-labor, this world the poets of these two decades [1880s, 1890s] knew little, or considered little, for of it they gave few hints."[53]

That absence was no accident. It was promoted both in mass-market publications and those from the genteel publishers. In 1894 the columnist who regularly wrote "Impressions by the Way" in *Munsey's* declared under the heading "Realism in Poetry" that "these are the days when the romantic in literature—the strong, the shining, the ennobling—flourishes, and holds the ear of the world, while 'realism' and 'veritism' are the languishing cults of the select few."[54]

• • •

In chapter 1, I imagined Robert Frost reading Hovey's poem. For Hovey, though, there was little to celebrate. His elegy for Parsons did more than mark the passing of a great poet; it also marked the passing of the genteel tradition that Parsons had represented. It was decidedly Hovey's farewell to one kind of poetry, a clearing of the brush to prepare for a new Paterian display of decadent fun. Shortly after publishing that poem, Hovey and his friend Bliss Carman set out on a walking tour of the East Coast that resulted in a new poetry of wild freedom and for its day even a bit of lusty joy in beauty and sex, *Songs of Vagabondia* (1894).

Ironically Hovey's successful poem "Seaward" initially made him the epitome of young genteel respectability. After all, following the poem's publication, the *Atlantic Monthly* asked him to write an essay about Parsons. Hovey also received a contract to publish the poem as a small book from the genteel Boston firm of Daniel Lothrop.[55] Hovey, however, was hardly respectable. He had fathered a child with a married woman. By 1894 she had at last divorced her husband, which allowed Hovey to marry her. Soon after the wedding, though, they fled the country to avoid publicity and settled in England and France. There they associated with the circle of decadent and symbolist poets associated with Mallarmé and Verlaine. Hovey, inspired by the new symbolism, began translating the plays of Maurice Maeterlinck.

His reputation as a decadent was enhanced when in 1894 he and Carman published their most popular and successful book of poetry yet, *Songs of Vagabondia*. Published by Copeland and Day, it became that house's first best-seller.[56] The book was released when Hovey was already in Europe and even inspired a new type of "vagabond poet." In *Songs of Vagabondia* Hovey and Carmen recalled their summers tramping around the country. Here, for instance, are excerpts from their title poem:

> What's that you say.
> You highly respectable
> Buyers and sellers?
> We should be decenter?
> Not as we please inter
> Custom, frugality,
> Use and morality
> In the delectable
> Depths of wine-cellars?
> Midnights of revel,
> And noondays of song!
> Is it so wrong?
> Go to the Devil!

> I tell you that we,
> While you are smirking
> And lying and shirking
> Life's duty of duties,
> Honest sincerity,
> We are in verity
> Free!
> Free to rejoice
>
> In blisses and beauties!
> Free as the voice
> Of the wind as it passes!
> Free as the bird
> In the weft of the grasses!
> Free as the word
> Of the sun to the sea—
> Free!

The book's second poem, "The Joys of the Road," made an even stronger case for tramping on the open road in stanzas like this:

> The broad gold wake of the afternoon;
> The silent fleck of the cold new moon;
> The sound of the hollow sea's release
> From stormy tumult to starry peace;
> With only another league to wend;
> And two brown arms at the journey's end!
> These are the joys of the open road—
> For him who travels without a load.

This book made a more vigorous, full-bodied poetry of manliness and realism possible. Not long after it was published, the more vigorous and less polished lyrics of the young Vachel Lindsay (1879–1930) began to attract attention for their realism. Throughout the 1890s he, too, tramped around, mostly in the Midwest. Eventually he sold his "Poems for Bread" in exchange for room and board. In keeping with the genteel commitment to American core values, though, Lindsay's poetry also redefined the male character in such a way that young men, who increasingly had to contend with a public culture that reflected poets and poetry as the arena of children and women, found in this book a new guide. Such machismo was an intentional goal of Copeland and Day's editorial program. The very next year, 1895, the firm even published Stephen Crane's bleak poetic volume, *Black Riders,* another precursor of poetic realism.[57]

Chapter Three

•

An Intellectual Finds His Way
Robert Frost Goes to School

IN 1892, when Robert Frost found both Richard Hovey and the *Indepen-dent,* Frost had long imbibed the traditional genteel concept of poetry as a high-minded, even civilizing, art. He likely also knew about realism, if not yet about symbolism or decadence. Reading Hovey must have confirmed for Frost the genteel tradition's claim that good poetry took on mighty top-ics and made them matter. How had Frost come by that typically genteel view? Biographically he had all the makings of a poet primed for rebellion against everything the genteels stood for, from their Republican politics to their attitude of lèse-majesté. He had been born in 1874 in San Francisco, where he was reared until he was eleven. He had spent his urban child-hood in his father's milieu of Democratic Party politics and among the local newspaper people associated with that party.[1]

A journalist committed to the Jacksonian wing of the Democratic Par-ty, William Prescott Frost had married a literary schoolteacher and Scot-tish immigrant, Belle Moodie, whom he met while he was principal of a school in Pennsylvania. Following their rebellious instincts, the newly-weds set out for the most aggressively wild environment America had to offer in the 1860s and '70s: post–gold rush, post–Civil War San Francisco. Once there Frost's father began what he intended to be a long career in the Democratic Party, beginning with his work in party newspapers and then in the local government itself.

Robert Frost spent his childhood in this urban environment of immi-grants, laboring masses, and newspapers. All the while his father worked on newspapers. First he became an editor of the *San Francisco Bulletin* (established in 1855), one of fourteen San Francisco dailies; the *Bulletin's* intensely radical editorial stance made it stand out from the others.[2] When Robert was just six months old, William Frost left that paper in 1874 to take a position as editor-in-chief of a new, mostly Democratic newspaper, the *Evening Post* (established in 1871). That paper's founding publisher, the soon-to-be-famous single-tax advocate Henry George, put William Prescott Frost Jr. in proximity to those dead set against an entrenched Republican establishment.[3] It also gave the elder Frost access to political life on a national scale. He was a delegate to the Democratic National Convention in 1880. Although the Democratic candidate (Samuel J. Tilden) lost to Rutherford B. Hayes, William Frost's political fortunes continued to rise.

Reared in this world, the young Frost would have taken for granted the coexistence of newspapers and magazines, politics, intellectual life, poetry, and books. Frost's father was not only an editor but a writer and a voracious reader, as was Robert Frost's mother. Her husband regularly ran articles she wrote. Typically she wrote reviews of the latest literature and even contributed her own poems.[4] Frost's relentless biographer, Lawrance Thompson, reprinted one of her poems from the *Evening Post* of 1884, "The Artist's Motive," a poem fully in keeping with the traditional genteel view of poetry as a force for moral uplift. Later Robert Frost himself recalled in a letter that "the first book I remembered the looks of was a book of verse by Robert Herrick that must have come into our house for my mother to review in my father's newspaper when I was seven or eight years old."[5]

In 1884 the local Democratic Party nominated Frost's father to run for the lucrative position of tax collector. However, Frost's father lost that election. He had been so sure of victory that he had resigned as editor-in-chief of the *Post* and now found himself unemployed. Always prone to hard drink and hard living, he soon degenerated, and within the year he was sick with tuberculosis and consistently drunk. By then, too, he had been reduced to working for the rather nondescript, second-tier, Democratic *San Francisco Daily Report*. His diminished role on the *Daily Report* ended with his death in 1885.

He left his wife and two children (Robert had a sister, Jeanie) penniless. Belle Moodie had made no effort to stay in touch with her family back in Scotland. As far as she was concerned, those ties were severed. What of William Prescott Frost's family? As it happened they were icons of New England gentility. With roots in New England going back to the seventeenth century, William Prescott's father belonged to the town elite of Lawrence, Massachusetts, where he managed one of the most powerful and important mills in the state, if not the country. He had seen to it that his son went to Harvard. All through his youth, however, William Prescott Frost Jr. had rejected the New England gentility into which he had been born. Rather than become the lawyer his father expected, the younger William Prescott left New England, first for Pennsylvania. There he married the mystically inclined Belle on impulse and quit his principalship to travel as far from New England as a train could take them. As if to seal the rebellion against his heritage, he named his son after the Confederate general Robert E. Lee, giving the future poet Lee as his middle name. Some biographers claim that the elder Frost had even wanted to join the Confederate Army. With his death, though, Belle Moodie Frost turned to the only family she had, the New England Frosts. They offered their home, and in 1885 she and the children made the long train journey across the country.

WESTERN RASCAL BECOMES GENTEEL NEW ENGLANDER

At the age of eleven, Robert Frost first entered the genteel milieu of his ancestors. This need not have been the case. A city kid reared in urban politics among radicals, Democrats, and free-thinkers the move to the slums of Lawrence could easily have made him an East Coast lefty. As an example, when the Frosts returned to Lawrence in 1885, the Pacific Mill was not only the largest mill in the country but also the second largest in the world, employing five thousand workers, almost all of whom were recent immigrants.[6] And his mother had settled the family in the slums where those mill hands lived. Nonetheless the young Frost became more and more drawn to the ways of New England's peculiar brand of gentility, through the combined influence of his paternal grandfather, William Prescott Frost Sr. and the encouragement of his mother, Belle.

Always strained, the relationship between Frost's mother and her in-laws did provide her with some financial support, if not emotional and psychological warmth. Her own sense of dignity and independence likely led her to settle without their help in Lawrence's tenements and drove her to establish her independence from them as a schoolteacher.[7] Through his mother's literary sensibility, then, Frost learned to value literature. The genteel idea of literature, however, came from high school. This was something he had to learn and learn it he did. To ensure the continuity of genteel American civilization, Lawrence High School (like almost every other public high school) put its students on a college, or classical track, and a regular noncollege English track. From the first Frost was enrolled in the classical curriculum, which emphasized the literary foundation of American civilization through a rigorous course of study. It required, in addition to geometry and algebra, a year of study in ancient Greek and Roman history, as well as British history. Students also had to take three years of classical Greek and four years of Latin. When he entered the classical curriculum, which his sister had also selected, Frost, then fourteen, was introduced to classical Greek and Roman writers, whose work became Frost's lifelong passion.[8]

In high school Frost learned to value literature in the genteel tradition. The emphasis on literature as the source and guide to a fundamentally Calvinist view of character, duty, and virtue belonged as much to an ongoing cultural war as to a dispassionate commitment to ideals. By the 1880s in towns throughout America, not just New England, the genteel establishment saw itself on the front lines of a new civil war between its conception of America—the ideal of the Protestant New England village—and the "other America" of Jewish and Catholic immigrants and the ever-increasing tide of wage-earning mill hands. Through their dominance on school boards, and as schoolteachers and principals, the genteels ensured that their values would be the ones that mattered. As George Livermore, genteel educator and public figure of the day, said, "Let me make the school books and catechisms which the children study, and I care not who makes the laws." Summing up the situation, Howard Mumford Jones explains: "Overwhelmingly of the white, Anglo-Saxon, Protestant tradition, the elite [genteels] wanted to be amiable to agreeable Jews and cultured Catholics. But they had an uneasy sense that their birthright was being threatened by pagan or decadent art, by theories about art imported from

Europe, and by hordes of non-Anglo-Saxon, non-Protestant immigrants from all sorts of places, including Asia."[9]

By all accounts, then, Robert Frost should have been miserable in such a high school milieu as Lawrence High School's classical curriculum and severely abused as little more than a fatherless hick. After all, he had to commute to school because by then his mother, although she was teaching in Methuen, Massachusetts, had moved them out of Lawrence to nearby Salem Depot, New Hampshire, just across the state border.[10] From all accounts Frost became both popular and an academic star. The milieu of this high school encouraged precisely the intellectual curiosity that his mother had encouraged in him all his life. For many poets high school years are marked by trauma and despair. For Frost high school proved nothing less than a revelation. He took with gusto to the combination of literary and intellectual discipline that defined traditional genteel attitudes.

By his sophomore year Frost had become an academic star, even publishing his first poems in the school newspaper, the *Bulletin,* edited and traditionally written only by seniors. In fact the school paper's high school editor, Ernest Jewell, decided to print Frost's first submission, "La Noche Triste," on its front page in 1890. Before the year was over, the sophomore even had two more poems, "The Song of the Wave," and "A Dream of Julius Caesar," accepted by the usually stone-faced seniors. At the outset of his junior year, the upper-crust daily *Lawrence American* published his "Sachem of the Clouds" in honor of Thanksgiving on November 2, 1891.

That acceptance welcomed Frost into the heart of the local genteel society. In his junior year he also became part of the high school's debating society. There it became apparent just how firmly he had latched onto the conventional genteel views of his time. He not only took the side of those arguing against Chinese citizenship and in support of the Chinese Exclusion Act, but in another debate he also took the side of the more refined William Cullen Bryant over his more political and radically egalitarian peer, John Greenleaf Whittier.[11]

Carl Burrell influenced Frost as much as his teachers and their books. Burrell, another student, first introduced Frost to serious poetry as well as to the most modern developments in natural science, including evolutionary biology, botany, and astronomy.[12] Burrell had no interest in separating the humanities from the sciences; literary and scientific pursuits meant the same to him. A genuine intellectual himself, Burrell had become a student of evolution and most likely an atheist, and although a high school senior he was in fact pushing thirty. The teenage Frost became enthralled by astronomy after reading Richard Proctor's influential popular introduction to that science, a general primer on cosmology, *Our Place Among the Infinities* (1876). That primer sought to reconcile empirical evidence from science with belief in God. Frost was so taken by this book that he spent many hours after school selling subscriptions to the *Youth's Companion* to earn a telescope. This family magazine had long been a familiar friend in the Frost household and was responsible for establishing the industry-wide trend of generating enormous subscription sales through such offers as the telescope. Frost won his telescope.[13] By the time Frost had become a regular reader in his teenage years, the magazine had only one page for children. The rest was aimed at what one recent historian of the magazine refers to as "'youths' very broadly conceived."[14]

In high school Frost also found love. Elinor White, two years younger than he, had entered high school so prepared that she easily flew through the required English curriculum in just two years and graduated with Frost in 1892. By the time they met Frost had become a regular reader of the genteel *Century,* from which he learned about Edward Rowland Sill (1842–87), best friend of his future publisher, Henry Holt, and, like Sidney Lanier, whom Sill admired, a poet who died young.

As a seventeen-year-old apprentice poet, Frost so warmly took to the genteel tradition of public poetry invoked by Sill's work that, in courting Elinor, he gave her Sill's collected poems as a present.[15] By then Elinor, as literary as Frost, had not only made her agreement with his views of literature clear but she had also publicly railed against the new realism in an article for the *Bulletin.* By his senior year Frost's academic star was rising ever higher even as his love blossomed. He was elected class president and became chief editor of the *Bulletin,* an echo of his father. Frost also had printed there the poems of his beloved Elinor, also in the pattern of his parents.

By May 1892 the grave illness of his typhoid-stricken sister and his responsibilities on the paper proved so overwhelming that he resigned his position as editor. Soon he and his sister dropped out of school entirely. Still, he did graduate and did attend the ceremony at which he received a prestigious prize from the superintendent of schools. Frost also graduated covaledictorian. The other valedictorian was none other than his sweetheart, Elinor White. Both gave speeches. Frost's speech, "A Monument to Afterthought Unveiled," argued in good genteel fashion for the importance of attending to the past, to the literary heritage of the past on which the present rests. Both speeches received extensive coverage, as did the graduation itself, on the front page of the genteel Lawrence daily *American*.[16]

Frost graduated in 1892 with every expectation that he would go to college and pursue his talents. Determined to attend his father's alma mater, Harvard, and major in classics, he spent the summer taking no less than six of seven entrance exams for admission that fall. Ironically, given his future place in the canon, Frost had to postpone the seventh exam, English literature, the only one for which he actually had to prepare. Ultimately he passed them all.[17] Learning of his Harvard plans, Frost's grandparents thwarted him by refusing to pay, although they had the money. Biographers explain that his grandmother blamed her son's early death on alcoholism, which she ascribed to Harvard's culture of drinking.[18] Told by one of Frost's math teachers about the excellence, sobriety, and piety of Dartmouth, his grandparents insisted Frost enroll there. Perhaps, too, his grandfather, more the Yankee materialist than the genteel intellectual his mother had become, had begun to fear for his grandson's plans to major in classics. The dearth of electives at Dartmouth, the grandfather may well have supposed, would help prepare his grandson to be the lawyer he was expected to become.

DARTMOUTH COLLEGE: DISCOVERING THE GENTEEL PUBLICATIONS AND A GENTEEL POETIC TRADITION

Given that he spent virtually all his free moments with his beloved Elinor, Frost was no single-minded literary intellectual. And already the larger cultural civil war between genteel America and the other America, between the world of his mother and that of his grandfather, had begun to rile him as well. In the summer before his senior year he had, for instance, worked at a local mill. After graduating, he clerked in another local mill. How much sympathy he gained for life in the mills is debatable, but at summer's end, according to Frost, a family blow-out concerning his college plans finally occurred. According to Frost, his grandfather said, "You will go to Dartmouth…. It is a good college, and will prepare you for life as a man of business." Frost had no interest in a life in business or in any genteel professional career. Nonetheless the application to Dartmouth was duly made. He was accepted without having to take any entrance exams (his high school classics curriculum sufficed), and he received a scholarship from Dartmouth amounting to about a third of the total cost. His grandparents were only too happy to pay the rest.[19]

Dartmouth in 1892 proved shocking to young Frost. He did not find the stimulating literary, intellectual, and social world of Lawrence High School. Emotionally, experientially, intellectually the college shook the young Frost. He dropped out before the end of his freshman year. Despite its monastic reputation, Dartmouth was a place of hazing, drinking, and general mayhem; the school's supposed piety and sobriety had created a mostly anti-intellectual culture of class war in which the wealthy and fit bullied the poorer, weaker, and more artistic. Frost may have been physically strong, and so able to fight his own battles and even win respect on that level, but nothing could console him for the loss of the intellectual haven he craved.

Despite the prevailing anti-intellectualism at Dartmouth, Frost did manage to benefit from his three classes that first semester, in Greek, Latin, and math.[20] At the time, Dartmouth had not followed Harvard into the modern education of an elective system (which Harvard's president Eliot had established in 1869). Instead, Dartmouth students followed one of two courses of study for their four-year program: Latin-Science or Classical. Frost had elected to take the Classical program and there can be no doubt about the impact on the future poet of the Greek and Roman poets he read there.[21]

Two other discoveries that Frost made during those first months at Dartmouth also would confirm the importance of literature that his high school years had inculcated in him. The first was his discovery of Francis Turner Palgrave's anthology of English lyric poetry, *The Golden Treasury of English Verse*. The second was his discovery of the *Independent* and of

Richard Hovey's poem "Seaward." That poem proved to Frost that the intellectual life he had experienced in high school had not been a crazy delusion. That poem, its references, and the *Independent* itself proved to him that poetry, politics, and publishers were united in their effort to improve and influence American society for the better. Unfortunately none of it seemed to matter to the other students at Dartmouth College in 1892.

The influence of Palgrave's anthology cannot be overstated. In it he found a personal poetry that went against all that he had learned to associate with the high-toned intellectual seriousness and mighty themes of the genteel tradition. In Palgrave's English lyric tradition, as collected in his *Golden Treasury* (1861), Frost found the power of lyric poetry as if for the first time.[22] After he bought that book, Frost studied its poems as a biologist studies the intricacies of cellular structure. In the 1888 edition, then the latest version and the one he most likely bought, Frost would have read Palgrave's definition of the "lyrical poem" as one that "shall turn on some single thought, feeling, or situation." Taking that definition and the examples found in this anthology as his guide, Frost went to school in this book.[23]

Palgrave's anthology divided nondramatic English lyric poetry into four periods from the Renaissance to 1860. Determined to print only "the best" poems of the culture, Palgrave established the four periods under the names of William Shakespeare, John Milton, John Gray, and William Wordsworth. Palgrave's own sensibility is reflected in the frontispiece, a portrait of Wordsworth. The Wordsworthian egalitarian poetry of the people, which embraced the full range of scientific and philosophical issues of the day, was what Frost would soon adopt as his own poetics. It would also be Wordsworth's insistence that poetry be written according to the way people actually speak that would also prove a lifelong influence on Frost.

BECOMING AN INTELLECTUAL
DECLARING FOR POETRY: 1892–94

Although some biographers believe that Frost decided to drop out of Dartmouth because of the shock of Dartmouth's anti-intellectualism, others attribute his departure to the emotional shock of being away from his mother, with whom he had an extraordinary bond. Most likely it was a combination of the college experience, his connection to his mother, *and* his profound and intense love for Elinor White, who then was attending St. Lawrence University in New York; he had already proposed and missed her to distraction. Still other biographers believe that he used an upsetting letter from his mother as the necessary catalyst to withdraw. Regardless of the cause, before the year was out he had returned home.

After he returned to Methuen, Frost had to face the social cost of giving up a prestigious scholarship. Among the circle of interested adults who had high hopes for the former class president, editor, and valedictorian, the rejection of a prestigious scholarship and of college altogether made Frost a subject of hot gossip. He later recalled, "That I should so treat a grandfather—one who had sincerely offered a college education to a promising valedictorian—put me out of all repute in Lawrence. A cloud of puzzlement hung over me as an obstinate, indecisive young fool." He seemed to have thrown away a fine career, wasting a great opportunity.[24] To make matters worse, his grandmother died shortly after his return home. As his most recent biographer, Jay Parini, puts it, "She had appreciated her grandson's artistic leanings. Her hope was that her grandson would accomplish things her son had not."[25] Her death, and his current failed situation, proved a double blow from which Frost had a hard time recovering.

On his return Frost wasted no time convincing the school superintendent of Methuen to let him take over as a teacher in his mother's classroom.[26] Once in charge he immediately exacted revenge: he beat the obnoxious children with a cane. These Mr. Squeers–like beatings would have, as Jay Parini says, led to Frost's arrest had he done it today.[27] Given that he did it more than a hundred years ago, it led only to the boys' retaliation. The little miscreants waited for him by an alley and mugged him. Perhaps that convinced him to quit teaching. He then began a series of crazy jobs, including impresario to a terrible orator and work in the Arlington woolen mill as a light-trimmer. The latter job was described by his biographer Robert Newdick as "an electrician's helper, tending and trimming the carbons in the arc-lights that hung high over the looms."[28] Frost held this position, which paid ten cents an hour, ten hours a day, for six days a week, for most of a year, a notable descent from the clerk's position he once held in a woolen mill.

Biographers in the past have paid scant attention to this episode in Frost's life. Yet, in the context of dropping out of college and wishing to marry his high-school sweetheart without prospects, its significance stands out. The genteel assumptions he had taken to Dartmouth had already suffered severe shock from his discovery of a general hostility to intellectual and cultural life among the other students. Working a sixty-hour six-day week among the vast tide of Lawrence's immigrants can only have increased a latent sense of Jacksonian democracy and egalitarianism learned at his father's knee. It also seems likely that the liberal sentiments expressed in many of the poems contained in Palgrave's anthology, for instance, may finally have resonated within him.

Meanwhile in these years, 1892–94, American publications, which Frost read assiduously, debated the merits of realism, romance, idealism, and of the new seemingly amoral aestheticism of symbolism and decadence. At this time the young aspiring poet Robert Frost learned about the decadents and symbolists published by Thomas Mosher, Copeland and Day, and Stone and Ingalls. In fact biographers know that one of Mosher's own favorite poets, the mystically inclined, opium-addicted, Catholic priest Francis Thompson had a lasting impact on the poetic light-trimmer. Robert Frost recalled, "I was seventeen, a bobbin-cart pusher in a mill in Lawrence. I rode a train to Boston, stopped at the Old Corner Bookstore, picked up [Francis Thompson's] 'The Hound of Heaven' [1893] and started to read. I kept on reading. I had only money enough for my railroad ticket. I used it all to pay for the book and walked the twenty-five miles to Lawrence reading the poem over and over."[29] The book that contained that poem, Francis Thompson's first collection, *Poems* (1893), pushed Walter Pater's symbolist association of beauty and morality into a theological zone. Rather than aim for easy moral uplift, it charted profound doubt instead. Decidedly not realist, and manifestly allegorical, Thompson's poems offered a psychological drama of religious faith containing as many poems of heretical doubt as of faith as he charted his journey to transcendence. The poem that so impressed the young Frost, "The Hound of Heaven," dramatizes the struggle between faith and science, the chief interest of Frost's debates with his friend Carl Burrell.

In that poem one finds a few stanzas that would certainly have affected a budding young intellectual like the eighteen-year-old Robert Frost. At one point God speaks through an inner voice, a kind of instinct in the poet, saying, as the poet flees from faith and from God, that such flight is impossible: one cannot escape transcendent power:

> But with unhurrying chase,
> And imperturbèd pace,
> Deliberate speed, majestic instancy,
> They beat—and a Voice beat
> More instant than the Feet—
> "All things betray thee, who betrayest Me."

"The Hound of Heaven" convinced Frost that poetry's intellectual work not only mattered but also had immediate consequence. In it Frost saw, as Emerson put it, "his own ideas come back to him with a certain alienated majesty." Frost faced his own struggle with religious conviction as a direct consequence of reading this poem. After all, working as a light-trimmer in a mill with no prospect of college or marriage on the horizon, Frost had never been more adrift than when he came across this poem. If, as he says, that poem reminded him of what matters most, and of what his own talent could do in this world, it was a decisive moment in his artistic life. Far from being a wasted period, 1892–94 saw a humbled Frost reading the genteel literary tradition, even in its newer symbolist phase.

Inspired by Francis Thompson, Frost, even as he worked his many low-wage jobs, renewed his debates about the theological implications of the science of evolution with his good friend Burrell. At the time Frost, a former champion high school debater, took the side of faith, transcendence, and the inexplicable against Burrell's materialism and near atheism.[30] Frost believed that what he eventually called "the God-belief" was at the core of genteel civilization and the literary tradition, from antiquity to the present, and that the God-belief gave rise to that civilization. Given that, one cannot help but wonder what precisely "the God-belief" meant to one so prone to skepticism as was Frost even then. The serious quest for an answer, I believe, became one of the central obsessions of Frost's intellectual life. It began in earnest at about this time when literary and intellectual meteors bombarded him, one after the other in various forms: from a magazine found at random in a college library, from a book found haphazardly in a Hanover, New Hampshire, bookstore, and from a poem read by chance in downtown Boston.

As these meteors—Hovey and the *Independent,* the lyric tradition in Palgrave, the new symbolism of poets like Francis Thompson—struck, one after the other between 1892 and 1894, Frost wrote more and more poetry. Meanwhile his home life became more unstable. Because he had quit teaching for her, his mother returned to the classroom. Without her son's heavy hand of discipline, however, she was soon fired. Meanwhile the financial panic of 1893 was replicated in the Frost household, with his mother out of work, and Frost's meager income in the mill proved insufficient to cover their expenses. In dire straits, the impoverished family left Methuen and moved back to Lawrence, settling in what the Frost biographer Lawrance Thompson recognized as "a four room tenement." Frost's sister, no longer grievously ill with typhoid, and then also a schoolteacher in Salem, already had a severe, though as yet undiagnosed, mental illness. Frost knew he had to do something for the family. Perhaps his increasing commitment to an identity as a poet made him all the more disdainful of a career as a schoolteacher. Regardless, he apparently returned to the classroom quite reluctantly, out of duty to his family to provide a steady income of $34 month, slightly more than he had made in the mill.[31]

All the while he read, he wrote, and, most of all, he talked with Burrell about that era's central intellectual issue, the compatibility of faith and science, Darwin and faith, and poetry's role in that debate. The two young men asked what constituted truth. Did empiricism offer the only access to truth? If this was a materialist universe, did that mean reality was merely a directionless and random set of causes and effects? When these questions were applied to biological, organic life, did they result in the conclusion that life followed only the blind dictates of natural selection? What was poetry's role in this? As a public art composed out of personal interest, ought not poetry reveal what science was saying? If faith no longer mattered or if it did, ought not poetry and poets engage the issue? Or could it be that empiricism had finally proved the positivists correct: that this was a materialist universe and poetry had no place in it beyond its ability to offer entertainment and pleasure? That last was never a conclusion either Frost or Burrell would accept. What Frost did accept was the necessity of poetry to engage such questions and to make them public.[32]

In the year of his first nationally published poem, 1894, did Frost also read Hovey's and Carman's *Vagabondia?* Did he read *Harper's* serialization of the great decadent novel *Trilby?* It is tempting to think he at least read *Vagabondia,* because that fall he embarked on an adventure that, given his personality at the time, seemed thoroughly bizarre and uncharacteristic. Without notice or warning, late that summer he took a vagabond trek sprung from despair but likely inspired by the poets of *Vagabondia,* both of whom had captured Frost's interest two years before. Heartbroken at another rejection from the love of his life, Elinor White, and already a college dropout, he thought about killing himself. He made his way from Lawrence, Massachusetts, where he was living with his mother and sister, to the Great Dismal Swamp of Virginia.[33]

Before undertaking that journey, however, Frost had begun in earnest to find a poetic voice of his own, which I call a poetry of realism. In it he used regular speech and everyday concerns to express the serious intellectual issues he believed poetry ought to tackle. The combination of plainspoken diction and serious genteel intellectual themes came slowly. His poetry from the early 1890s shows that he did begin to let go of archaic diction and of scenes modeled on either classical or American history in favor of more direct episodes based on his own experience. In the style of Wordsworth and of Longfellow he began to write poems that told stories of everyday life in an everyday language.

After she received his poem, "My Butterfly: An Elegy," Susan Hayes Ward, poetry editor of the (New York) *Independent,* had shown it to, among others, the coauthor of *Vagabondia* Bliss Carman. He recommended publishing it. On his return from the trek to the Great Dismal Swamp, Frost found in the mail a copy of the *Independent* with his poem on the first page. Instead of killing himself, he returned from the trek to find himself on the brink of a great career, part of the same literary and intellectual environment as Richard Hovey and Bliss Carman.

Chapter Four

•

Robert Frost, Realism, Poetry, and American Publishing of the 1890s
"My Butterfly: An Elegy," "The Birds Do Thus"

IN EARLY 1894, Frost began submitting his poetry to genteel publishers, striking gold when he placed "My Butterfly: An Elegy" in the *Independent*.[1] That poem also earned him a substantial check of $15, the equivalent of two weeks' wages as a light-trimmer and almost as much as two weeks' wages as a schoolteacher in Salem, New Hampshire.

"MY BUTTERFLY"

This poem incorporates the strange blend of realism and high moral purpose that would define Robert Frost's best poetry. Specifically this poem asks where one can find moral truth: Must it only be through God? In it he questions the source of faith, even the very notion of a transcendent spiritual realm. The poem dramatizes the religion-science conflict he had been debating with Burrell. Is the world just blank and random without direction, as depicted by Darwin, or are Palgrave's hero Wordsworth and the English lyric tradition correct to claim that nature is proof of a spiritually meaningful world of benevolence?

In the manner of American fiction's new turn to realism, this poem dramatizes a typical scene adhering to particular details so as to create what Roland Barthes long ago called "a reality effect."[2] In the poem a young man recalls how a butterfly once brushed against his cheek and in so doing made him feel better. This is a familiar Wordsworthian story about the healing touch of nature and "the spirit that rolls through all things." After a closer reading, however, the poem wryly reverses that idea and wonders whether, in the absence of a connection between God and nature, the universe itself might just be malevolent. That reversal occurs toward the poem's end. There Frost describes the onset of winter. Cold winds blow. Snow lies on the ground.

> Ah, I remember me
> How once conspiracy was rife
> Against my life
> (The languor of it!), and
> Surging, the grasses dizzied me of thought,
> The breeze three odors brought,
> And a gem flower waved in a wand.
>   Then when I was distraught
> And could not speak,
> Sidelong, full on my cheek,
> What should that reckless zephyr fling
> But the wild touch of thy dye-dusty wing![3]

In these two stanzas the zephyr (the west wind) brings life in the form of a butterfly, which so appeases the sad young man that he seems cured. At least one biographer, by the way, believes Frost wrote this poem while at Dartmouth in 1892.[4] If that is the case, then biographically the conspiracy may well refer to his grandparents' insistence that he go to Dartmouth rather than Harvard, that he be a lawyer or a businessman and not a poet. Regardless of the biographical elements, however, the poem tells a simple tale: the poet, in despair and anguish, finds that nature alleviates both.

A poem Frost long admired, "Daffodils," from Palgrave's own favorite poet, Wordsworth, has the same basic idea. There a sad poet sees some wild daffodils, and the very sight of them proves a kind of mental balm. He holds the image in his imagination, in what he calls a "spot of time," and pulls it out for solace when he needs it. The final stanza of that famous lyric reads:

> For oft, when on my couch I lie
> In vacant or in pensive mood,
> They flash upon that inward eye
> Which is the bliss of solitude;
> And then my heart with pleasure fills,
> And dances with the daffodils.

The Independent

Entered at the Post Office at New York, as Second-Class Mail Matter.

"EVEN AS WE HAVE BEEN APPROVED OF GOD TO BE INTRUSTED WITH THE GOSPEL, SO WE SPEAK; NOT AS PLEASING MEN, BUT GOD WHICH PROVETH OUR HEARTS."

VOLUME XLVI.   NEW YORK, THURSDAY, NOVEMBER 8, 1894.   NUMBER 2397.

For Table of Contents see Page 10.

MY BUTTERFLY.

AN ELEGY.

BY ROBERT LEE FROST.

Thine emulous, fond flowers are dead, too,
And the daft sun-assaulter, he
That frighted thee so oft, is fled or dead.
Save only me
(Nor is it sad to thee).
Save only me
There is none left to mourn thee in the fields.

The gray grass is scarce dappled with the snow;
Its two banks have not shut upon the river;
But it is long ago,
It seems forever,
Since first I saw thee glance,
With all thy dazzling other ones,
In airy dalliance,
Precipitate in love,
Tossed, tangled, whirled and whirled above,
Like a limp rose-wreath in a fairy dance.

When that was, the soft mist
Of my two tears hung not on all the fields.
And I was glad for thee,
And glad for me, I wist.

And didst thou think, who tottered wandering on high,
Fate had not made thee for the pleasure of the wind,
With those great, careless wings,
'Twas happier to die
And let the days blow by.

These were the unlearned things.
It seemed God let thee flutter from his gentle clasp.
Then, fearful he had let thee win
Too far beyond him to be gathered in,
Snatched thee, o'er-eager, with ungentle grasp,
Jealous of immortality.

Ah, I remember me
How once conspiracy was rife
Against my life—
(The languor of it) and
Surging, the grasses dizzied me of thought,
The breeze three odors brought,
And a gem flower waved in a wand!
Then, when I was distraught
And could not speak,
Sidelong, full on my cheek,
What should that reckless zephyr fling
But she, mid-touch of our dye-dusty wing!

I found that wing withered to-day;
For you are dead, I said,
And the strange birds say.
I found it with the withered leaves
Under the eaves.

Lawrence, Mass.

AT THE END.

BY DANSKE DANDRIDGE.

Fearlessly into the Unknown
Go forth, thou little soul!
Launch out upon the trackless sea,
Nor wind nor stars to pilot thee,
Alone, alone, alone!

Thine is a helpless plight.
Thou canst not turn thy helm,
Nor reach the harbor any more;
Thou driftest to an unguessed shore.
Dark, dark the night.

Yet launch and take no care;
For what can care avail?
In the dark void, the awful space,
Where wand'rest thou to find thy place,
Thy God is even there.

Shepherdstown, W. Va.

OUTLINES.

BY ELIZABETH C. CARDOZO.

I.—BEFORE THE MERCY-SEAT.

I dreamt that I stood, a naked soul, before the throne of God. And he questioned me, saying: What hast thou with I clothed thee?

I answered in bitter shame: I have trod the paths and breathed the air whereby is innocence crushed. The mire of humanity is upon me.

And God said: What hast thou done with thy courage, that stout shield wherewith I did provide thee?

I answered, bowed unto the ground: Alas, my shield is rent in twain, for it hath indeed been mercilessly battered.

And God said: What hast thou done with thy reason, that keen sword wherewith I did arm thee?

I answered, overwhelmed with shame: The miasmas of the slums breathed upon it, and the sight of misery blinded it, and the voice of unheeded wrong thundered upon it, so that I am clean bereft thereof.

And God said: What hast thou done with thy love, that bright halo wherewith I did crown thee?

I answered, with bowed head: I have so squandered it upon thy creatures that I know not if the remnant be a fitting gift to lay at thy feet. And I stretched out my empty hands.

And God said: What is that in thy hands that shines as fine gold?

And behold, it was human love.

II.—THE CHOICE.

Before my soul had yet endured the pangs of human life, God showed me the earth.

And I beheld a marvelous fair country whereon were lofty mountains and stately edifices, the last being the work of the hands of man.

And I said: The world is very fair, I fear not to be born therein.

God said unto me: Look thou closer.

And behold, when I looked more closely, I saw that there ran hither and thither, over the face of this fair world, a mighty throng of creatures that never rested, but sought perpetually each to destroy the other. Only a few were quiet, and these were speedily overcome.

I asked: What race is this?

And God said unto me: This is man.

I asked: What doth he unto his brothers?

And God said: He preyeth upon him. Behold I have shown thee that thou mayest choose. Wilt thou be born into this world that thou seest. Wilt thou be of them that destroy or wilt thou be the prey?

I answered: I will be the prey.

Pity me not, my brothers, in that I am destitute of the good things of this earth, for I have chosen.

New York City.

REMINISCENCES OF MR. GLADSTONE.

AN INTERVIEW WITH DR. NEWMAN HALL.

It was in the charming house, close by the Heath, that I found Dr. Hall a few days ago, just returned from a busy week of preaching in the country. Dr. Hall travels far and wide, often preaching five and six times a week; but his mind must often wander back to "Vine House," with its pretty garden, and walls covered with climbing vines. Seventy years have passed over his head, and yet he told me that a few days ago he went for a sixteen-mile walk, and climbed a mountain nearly three thousand feet high without fatigue. "And I never feel Mondayish," he exclaimed. Indeed, there was something in his physical vigor akin to that of his great contemporary, Mr. Gladstone, of whom he speaks in terms of great admiration.

"I have known Mr. Gladstone for twenty-five years," said Dr. Newman Hall. "He has spent several evenings at my house, and I honored me with invitations to his own; and, indeed, the chair upon which I am sitting is the very one he occupied on the last occasion. When I first knew him I was coming I used to invite several ministers of the Free Churches and the Anglican Church to meet him. We have had memorable conversations at the universities, Vatican decrees, Disestablishment, Colonial empire, etc. Mr. Gladstone showed himself as good a listener as a talker. I have the greatest admiration for

Mr. Gladstone. I do not agree with his Home Rule policy, because I keep to what he taught six years ago. I have not changed; it is he who has changed his idea of carrying it out. But his kindness has in no degree diminished because of our difference of opinion on that point. He once said to me: 'I am sorry that you and I disagree, Dr. Dale and Dr. Allon do not see as I do.' I replied in substance that perhaps we might all agree better with one another if we all understood better what it is which we individually do really see. It is a mistake to suppose that I object to Home Rule altogether because I object to a particular method. I consider that all matters relating to local interests should be settled in that locality, and not brought to Westminster. There should be Home Administration for Ireland, Wales, Scotland, England alike—neither more nor less; but the Union should remain, in regard to all united and Imperial interests, untouched.

"I am indignant at some of the spiteful things said of him and evil motives attributed, because of difference of political opinion. As the last time he stood before me, when Mr. and Mrs. Gladstone went out during the interval, I saw two ladies, very fashionably dressed, go up behind him, one of whom hissed in his ear. I was some distance off, by reason of the crowd. On returning to hear the second part of the oratorio, I heard a lady say: 'Didn't I hiss in his ear?' I turned round and saw the same two ladies, and not forbear saying, in a loud voice: 'And you ought to be ashamed of yourself. We may not agree with Mr. Gladstone in politics, but we ought to honor him as one of the greatest men of the day, who has spent a long life in the service of his country.' The so-called 'ladies' seemed somewhat crest-fallen.

"By the way," added the doctor, "one day I saw Mr. Gladstone at Dr. Allon's church, listening to Dr. Dale; he also came to Christ Church on a Sunday evening when I was preaching.

"The other day when he was at Dollis Hill, waiting for the operation on his eyes, I sent to ask the doctor's orders whether he could be broken. I had, however, brought his last photograph with me, so I asked whether it would be possible for him to write his autograph on it. The photograph was taken up to him, and came back almost immediately with his autograph appended." It was a pleasant place in the doctor's study.

"About two years ago I also met Mr. Gladstone at Barmouth. Hearing that he was coming there, I went to the station to meet him. I was the first he greeted, and the station a large bouquet of heather, which I gave to Mrs. Gladstone, saying: 'The Welsh hills greet you.' A large crowd followed him to his hotel, where he gave a short speech, while Mrs. Gladstone occasionally waved the bunch of heather.

"Mr. and Mrs. Gladstone once asked me to bring the Negro Jubilee Singers to their house to breakfast, and I took about eight or ten. The Gladstones had also invited some dozen aristocratic people, and the Jubilee Singers were sandwiched between them, and not placed all together; so that you saw in one place a well-known countess, and by her side a full-blown Negress, all waited upon in an equal way. Mr. Gladstone engaged in conversation on matters of interest to them, and showed a wonderful knowledge of Negro character and history. After breakfast the singers sang for about an hour. Mr. Gladstone sat on the sofa for a few days, and his eyes were moist with emotion, while he seemed absorbed in the music. In the next morning's paper I saw that he went by special train at twelve o'clock to see the Queen at Windsor, and in the same afternoon made a great speech in the House of Commons. That was a very important and busy day, yet it commenced in the way I have told you.

"He might well write as he does here," continued Dr. Hall, turning to a letter from Mr. Gladstone—"My daily life is a continual struggle with immediate calls and unfulfilled engagements." That was in 1878."

Resuming his reminiscences, Dr. Hall said: "One morning I met John Bright in the street, looking very downcast. After greeting me, he said: 'I feel very anxious, and should like a long talk with you; but I have not time now.' A few hours later his resignation was announced in the House of Commons. It was the day on which the bombardment of Alexandria took place,

---

"My Butterfly." This is Robert Frost's first significant national publication. From the Robert Frost Collection of Pat Alger.

Frost's poem does not follow the Wordsworthian idealist solution to grief. In Frost's the memory of the wind blowing a butterfly against his face is caught up short by grim reality:

> I found that wing withered to-day;
> For you are dead, I said,
> And the strange birds say.
> I found it with the withered leaves
> Under the eaves.

In Wordsworth the healing touch of nature, even if it occurs just once, becomes a lasting psychological fact that one can reapply in times of distress. In contrast Frost finds the actual wing of the insect, now dead, in the depths of winter. According to the poem, he finds himself once more in similar emotionally dire straits. This time, though, the creature is dead; the wing is detached from the body; the birds are strange; the wind is harsh; the ground frozen.

Just before the lines I quoted, Frost makes the theological dilemma explicit by explaining the butterfly's death not just in terms of naturalist biology, a cold wind, but also in terms of God:

> It seemed God let thee flutter from his gentle clasp,
> Then, fearful he had let thee win
> Too far beyond him to be gathered in,
> Snatched thee, o'er-eager, with ungentle grasp,
> Jealous of immortality.

Biographically, one could read this as Frost explaining his own plight. It is as if he were saying that God let him go to Dartmouth, but in exercising his free will and leaving he found only disaster, which nearly killed him. On that psychobiographical level he perhaps associates the larger forces, whether the wind or God, with his grandfather. Perhaps that is reading too far afield. Sticking to the facts of the poem, the butterfly is killed by a strong, cold wind. This is not because God is cruel, says the speaker, but rather because God loves it and wishes to keep it close, in heaven. Yet this would mean that such love is not gentle. In fact it kills. Is this, then, a testament of faith? By the end of the poem one cannot be sure. Even if there is a God, the Darwinian world He created leaves little room for comfort: the butterfly is dead.

WHAT THE BUTTERFLY PROVIDED

Robert Frost's letters to the editors of the *Independent* survive. In them we can see how important the genteel publishers had become to the young poet. We can also see what publication in one of their periodicals could mean. The *Independent* had been printed continuously each week since 1848, and its current editor, Henry C. Bowen, had ceded most of the duties to William Hayes Ward, who had been on the staff since 1868. When Bowen died in 1898, Ward became the magazine's editor-in-chief. Already in the 1890s, though, Ward had helped transform the weekly into the only genteel general interest political publication that still took poetry seriously. In large part he did this through his appointment of his sister to the editorial staff.[5] In keeping with the antebellum genteel tradition that made poetry central to American culture, the *Independent*, particularly the poetry that Susan Hayes Ward oversaw, had become, as if by default, unique. William Hayes Ward bragged about this in a professional magazine, the *Writer,* which was read mostly by other editors and publishing professionals. "We make a specialty of poems, and pride ourselves on publishing as good verse and as much of it as any journal in the country."[6] In fact in the early 1890s the *Independent* had already been mostly responsible for the new and intense interest in the poetry of Emily Dickinson. The magazine had been championing that poet's work and helped to ensure a market for the ultimate publication of her first posthumous collection in 1892.

As a result of the magazine's moralizing Congregationalist heritage, it had become, for the Protestant elite of the 1890s, the equivalent of what today's *Commentary* or *Tikkun* is for Jewish intellectuals. In the late nineteenth-century culture war between science and faith, the *Independent* committed itself firmly to the side of religious faith and to poetry as the source of ethical, moral truth arising out of such faith. The publication did so, however, always with an eye to the critical, the nuanced, the intellectual. The staff understood empirical science in terms of faith. Its editors rejected a too-easy dichotomy between science and the humanities. In fact each week's issue ran this motto on the masthead: "Even as we have been approved of God to be intrusted [*sic*] with the Gospel, so we speak; not as pleasing men, but God which proveth our hearts." This was also the motto under which the *Independent* would print Frost's poem on its first page.

A magazine whose literary policy opposed much of the brutal attention to the squalid facts of daily life that had come to mark realist fiction also attacked what it called a false and naive belief in beauty that marked so much of the latest symbolist and aesthetically minded poetry. In poetry a new realism of subject matter was joined to a decidedly poetic diction that emphasized the music of meter and rhyme. It was a mixture of realist attention to everyday life and high moral purpose, something that in the realm of fiction has been called "high realism."[7] The magazine's ideal poet of such a blend was Emily Dickinson, who used mundane particulars to explore her complicated views of Christianity and faith.[8] On a more theoretical level the editors regularly adopted and championed Sidney Lanier's treatise on the subject. Ultimately, then, whether intended or not, when Frost published in the *Independent* he also affiliated himself with this more tempered, more realistic, aspect of the genteel tradition.

"My Butterfly" arrived on William Ward's desk sometime early in 1894. It struck exactly the right note at the right time. It insisted that its readers face the actual facts, but it did so using a particularly mellifluous music and diction common to the ongoing genteel poetic tradition associated with allegory, symbol, and what others have called the romance tradition of American literature. After reading the poem and no doubt delighting in its concentration on an everyday butterfly rather than its symbolic representation in some mythic landscape, Ward sent it to his sister, the magazine's poetry editor, Susan Hayes Ward. She took it on trip to Washington D.C., where she met the poets and cousins Bliss Carman and Charles G. D. Roberts. She showed it to both, and they encouraged her to print it. Most likely, they took delight in Frost's unusually dark tale, which he had embedded in what to them may have seemed strikingly beautiful meter and rhyme. My own sense is that they read the poem in light of the era's aestheticism, symbolism, and decadence in particular. At the time Carman (then associated with Stone and Kimball's *Chap-Book*) had also just published *Songs of Vagabondia* with Richard Hovey, the very man whose poem in the magazine had sent Frost to the *Independent* in the first place.[9]

The poem was printed as the first item in the first column of the *Independent*'s three-columned front page. Sometimes that column would have as many poems as would fill it, and the editors often printed poems in the other front-page columns too. "My Butterfly" filled most of the first column, suggesting the Wards were particularly admiring of it. In the second column they printed a deeply religious poem, "Outlines," by Elizabeth C. Cardozo. Her poem, in keeping with the more conventional symbolic, allegorical poetry of that era, had the effect of enhancing Frost's poetic realism. Yet even Cardozo's poem eschews conventional poetic lines for the long Whitmanesque sentence. Her first sentence, also the first stanza, reads: "I dreamt that I stood, a naked soul, before the throne of God. And he questioned me, saying: What hast thou/ done with thy innocence, that fine white garment where-with I clothed thee?" In contrast the quotidian moment captured in Frost's poem stands out all the more clearly.

In keeping with their genteel preference for the romance tradition, the editors often printed the novelist Maurice Thompson. In recent years he had also become a public critic of the new realism. He read Frost's poem and wrote to the Wards about it. Describing the typical rationale for nonrealist poetry, Thompson says that he read Frost's poem after reading the latest saturation coverage of the current election season's political vitriol. While reading the news, he felt as "if a hogshead of salt had rolled over me."[10] In that sour mood he turned to poetry as the place, as the genteels had long argued, where life's serious issues and deepest matters were rendered into beautiful form. Reading Frost's poem he found what he went to poetry to find: "I am not stupid enough yet to fail to see the extreme beauty of that little ode." For all his admiration, however, the thought that young Frost, a man without independent means, was setting out to be a poet in modern America filled Thompson with dread. "It gives me a pang to know that its author is poor. To be a poet and be poor is a terrible lot. What hope is there? . . . If I had a chance to say my say to him I should tell him to forget that he ever read a poem and to never pen another rhyme." To be sure his meaning was clear, he added, "If Frost has good health tell him to learn a trade or profession and carry a sling-shot in his pocket for [the Muse] Aoede."[11] Paying magazines like the *Independent* notwithstanding, Thompson saw no future for poetry in contemporary America. As far as Thompson could see, the genteel idea of making poetry to soothe the cares of those overwhelmed with a world gone mad with materialism was a fool's errand. He meant to warn Frost before it became too late.

Such warnings hit Frost as blanks fired from a pistol. The real bullets—his acceptance for pay into a major magazine—had done no harm and an immense amount of good. Had not an important cultural arbiter, the (New York) *Independent,* singled out one of his poems for publication and praise? As he said, "I am endorsed now by a professional critic."[12] Had they not paid him actual cash worth two weeks' pay from his job in the woolen mill and almost as much as he had been paid for teaching school for two weeks? And, contrary to Maurice Thompson's view of poetry, had not Frost meant to engage the world rather than escape it? Far from following the genteel expectation of creating in poetry the ideals that the world appeared to forsake, Frost meant to use his poetry to engage the world directly.

Eventually Susan Hayes Ward sent the relevant passages from Thompson's letter to Frost. She must have feared for Frost's poetic ambition for she decided to include the more damning passages about being a poet in America. In his reply of January 1895, Frost said he had "undertaken a future" in poetry, come what may: "I cannot believe that poem was merely a chance. I will surpass it. Maurice Thompson will not hope to discourage me by praising me surely? I would tell him that he is not so inscrutable as he might be when he does so inconsistently." In fact, like one made drunk by praise, Frost responded to William Hayes Ward's acceptance and check by writing, "The memory of your note will be a fresh pleasure to me when I waken for a good many mornings to come; which may as well confirm you in the belief that I am still young. I am. The poem you have is the first of mine that any publication has accepted."[13] Meanwhile, struck by the unusual caliber of a poem that combined real detail and idealist, spiritual questioning, William Hayes Ward wanted to know more about the young man. Responding to the editor's questions, Frost wrote, "I am only graduated of a public high-school. Besides this, a while ago I was at Dartmouth College for a few months until recalled by necessity. But the inflexible ambition trains us best, and to love poetry is to study it. Specifically speaking, the few rules I know in this art are my own afterthoughts, or else directly formulated from the masterpieces I reread."[14] As it happened, Ward's sister, Susan Hayes Ward, also found something endearing about Frost and had a profound admiration for his poem. Initiating a correspondence with the young poet, she began a long, caring mentor-apprentice relationship.[15] Susan Hayes Ward also began to mentor him more into the new science of poetics, particularly the poetic theories of Sidney Lanier.

In one of his first letters to Susan Hayes Ward, Frost wrote first of his own training in poetry and then of his thoughts concerning Lanier. Frost acknowledged that hers was "just such a letter as you wrote me that I have been awaiting for two years. Hitherto all the praise I have received has been ill-advised and unintelligent. . . . So that something definite and discriminating is very welcome. My thanks unlimited!" He added: "To betray myself utterly, such an one am I [sic] that even in my failures I find all the promise I require to justify the astonishing magnitude of my ambition."[16] To prove his apprenticeship in the art of poetry, he then describes his literary training, saying he is "fond of the whole collection of Palgrave's" and that his favorite poems, all near-epic poems, were Keats's *Hyperion*, Shelley's *Prometheus*, Tennyson's *Morte d'Arthur*, and Browning's *Saul*, to which he added, "all of them about the giants." He could have offered few better examples of his education in a genteel poetic tradition of public purpose, allegory, and moral idealism.

In response to her question about Lanier, he said simply, "I have never read Lanier's poetry nor the volume of his you mention. I have read no technical works."[17] With her next letter she gave him not only Sidney Lanier's poetry but also, and more important, his treatise, *Science of Poetic Meter.*

SIDNEY LANIER: MAKING GENTEEL POETRY MATTER

When Frost opened Lanier's book, he found a science of poetic music. In a scientific age, when empiricism trumped idealism, Sidney Lanier thought that he could bring rigor to the art of poetry without diminishing its idealist themes or purpose. He did this through the application of a strict science of meter and rhythm in general. He made his scientific case for poetry in a posthumously published treatise, *The Science of English Verse* (1880). There Lanier argued that poetry in English had precise empirically based rules akin to those of musical theory. He further argued that such empirical rules did nothing to detract from, and indeed would only enhance, poetry's deeper thematic purpose.

The book arose out of a series of lectures Lanier gave as part of his effort in 1878 to join the faculty of the newly established Johns Hopkins University in Baltimore.[18] In both lectures and book Lanier argued that American culture, especially in the public sphere of the genteel publications, required empirical scrutiny. As he told an influential editor, "In all directions the poetic art was suffering from the shameful circumstance that criticism was without a scientific basis."[19] He wished to prove that poetry mattered, not based on idealist principle but rather on an intellectually sound set of rules and laws.

In keeping with the latest thinking in the new field of psychology, Lanier argued that poetry and the idealism associated with genteel values referred to a science of the emotions: *"The initial step of every plan and every action is an emotion"* (emphasis in original). Particularly in its linguistic forms and its techniques, poetry followed specific rules for representing emotions.[20] As a science, then, poetry depended more on the methods for creating musicality in words than for what those words might mean. The science of poetry was a science of rhythm, of music made from words. As one critic noted, according to Lanier's view of the science of poetry, any poem rightly understood would "stimulate the reader to feel rightly, think rightly, and finally act rightly." This was inevitable because, as Lanier himself said, "The father of meter is rhythm, and the father of rhythm is God."[21] Because Lanier concentrated on poetry's sound, meter, rhythm, and rhyme, he provided an intellectual, empirically based justification for the use of specialized high poetic diction, rhythm, and meter. It was precisely that distinctive poetic music that the Wards meant to encourage Frost to cultivate.

THANK YOU BUT NO THANK YOU
ROBERT FROST'S REALISM

In his thank-you letter for the gift of Sidney Lanier's treatise and William Ward's article about him, Frost pretended to be enthusiastic and faked an interest, saying, "I have been very much enthused over what I conceive to be Lanier's theory of art." He acknowledged that poetry had technical, empirically arguable, elements, as did any other major artistic medium whether music, sculpture, architecture, or painting. But having already come to believe that poetry's realism had everything to do with the sound of people talking, Frost could not now write according to an arbitrary formula based on Lanier's science. Happily he did not have to because Lanier himself distinguished speech as "a series of tunes."[22]According to Lanier, what we call tone of voice is really just a variation in pitch across a standard rhythm. That variation creates an inflection and tone that can assign meaning to an emotive state, he wrote. There can be no question that this affected Frost deeply. It would eventually undergird his own theory of "sentence sounds." I believe that reading Lanier's discussion of poetic talk as a theoretical justification for Frost's own new ideas concerning poetic speech deeply upset his new mentors, especially William Hayes Ward.

Frost later told his biographer Robert Newdick that he fought with William Hayes Ward over Lanier's book and that their dispute had caused a serious rift. According to Newdick, Frost admitted his dislike of the musical idea of poetry and Ward became disgusted. My own sense is that Ward probably also did not appreciate having Lanier used against him. Said Newdick, "Then why did the *Independent* buy later poems?" Frost attributed that entirely to Susan Hayes Ward. According to Frost, she insisted.[23]

I believe that Frost accepted Lanier's theories about "talk as a series of tunes" only insofar as those "tunes" concerned tone and voice inflection, not music, because Frost's beloved Elinor had by then convinced him to write more according to the way people actually spoke than according to accepted poetic conventions and to write as well about actual particulars, the things and experiences of everyday life. Even in high school they had argued about the new realism, and her defense of talking over artificial literary language was the topic of her valedictory speech, "Conversation as a Force in Life," at graduation. In an 1894 letter to Susan Hayes Ward he declared, "Written poetry is rather ineffectual after all, unless artists are the readers of it." To that he added, "If I were so accomplished as to be able to improvise a few heroic metres for them [my friends] by the camp-fire next summer, be sure they would appreciate me."[24]

Not long after writing this, Frost did spend time by campfires and among the vagabond crowd of hobos populating the other America. In

November, with the commission from "My Butterfly," he printed two copies of a small book, *Twilight*. When he arrived at Elinor's college campus to give it to her and propose, she rebuffed him. Although no biographer mentions it, he must have just read Hovey and Carman's *Vagabondia*. Right after Elinor turned him away in November 1894, Frost left New England on his own "vagabondia." For nearly a month he wandered the Dismal Swamp through Maryland, Virginia, and North Carolina (not, incidentally, in many of the places where *Songs of Vagabondia* took place). Along the way he lost himself among hobos and other refugees of the 1893 panic and subsequent economic depression. Could it be that Carman and Hovey's very first poem, "Vagabondia," inspired Frost not just to dream but also to act? To be "Free as the bird / In the weft of the grasses! / Free as the word / Of the sun to the sea— / Free!" Perhaps the journey south was not a suicide's long dark night of the soul but rather a youthful spur-of-the-moment quest for adventure, for a realism of experience.

His poem had been accepted when he left on this journey. When he returned to Lawrence, he learned that at last it also had been published. In December he wrote to Susan Hayes Ward thanking her. Referring to his trek south, he says it gave him "experiences so desperately absorbing that I am nothing morbid now and I can enjoy the poem as freshly as if it were but lately written and I had not since wasted eight months to ineffectual aspiration." In the hope of keeping him on track to become the poet she imagined him to be, Ward next put one of her friends, a Congregationalist minister in Lawrence, the Reverend William Wolcott, in touch with Frost. William Hayes Ward was himself a minister, and the Wards had contacts with Congregationalist ministers all over the country. Honoring their request, Wolcott reintroduced himself to Frost (he had in fact been enlisted as the judge for the poetry prize in the high school newspaper back when Frost edited it). Soon the two were engaging in the conversations that had once provoked such interest between Burrell and Frost. Later Frost would recall Wolcott as "the great friend of my struggling days."[25]

With Wolcott and Burrell as intellectual companions, Frost in 1894 earned his living teaching in the elementary school classrooms of Methuen, Massachusetts. Meanwhile he renewed his attention to poetry and began to experiment with everyday speech in poetry. To Wolcott he explained the flaw in Lanier's theory. Poetry, Frost said, should not be considered akin to music at all. Instead it should focus on speech, on talk. Years later, in conversation with his friend Louis Mertins, Frost said that his lifelong conviction that poetry concerned speech rather than music stemmed from those conversations: "I'm sure the old gentleman didn't have the slightest idea he was having any effect on a very stubborn youngster who thought he knew what he knew. But something he said actually changed the whole course of my writing."[26]

Despite the Wards' disapproval of a poetry focused on talk rather than traditional rhythms of rhyme and meter, Frost made no secret of his delight to Susan Hayes Ward. He praised the poetry of Kipling for his ability to capture living speech.[27] This was hardly a unique concern of Frost's. In these years "the problem of dialect" beset literary intellectuals, who wrote innumerable essays either approving or denouncing the new phenomenon that had overtaken both poetry and fiction. The genteel *Dial* (published in Chicago) had even devoted a special issue to just that problem.

ROBERT FROST: JOURNALISM AND THE POETRY OF ORDINARY SPEECH

Desperate to leave school teaching, in 1895 Frost found the perfect job for a budding realist. As he said to Susan Hayes Ward, "I am a reporter on a newspaper!"[28] In Lawrence, a town dominated by mill owners, the daily *American,* edited by William F. Gilden, promoted New England's genteel ideas of civilization and Republican Party politics. Its rival, the morning *Lawrence Evening-Tribune,* in contrast, mostly adhered to the Jacksonian Democratic Party line and had the town's mostly immigrant working class for its readership. Hired by the *American,* Frost also wrote for its Sunday edition, the *Sun.* In both Frost mostly wrote the light column, "The American About, and Abroad," which ran on a distinctive editorial page that also carried the local version of the Republican Party establishment line.

Frost's column, purportedly written by the fictive character "The American," was part of a national trend in local newspapers and was based on the success of syndicated columns by the likes of Eugene Field, who had the most popular syndicated column of that era, "Sharps and Flats."[29] A column depicting local hijinks in clear punchy statements had become an expected feature in American newspapers. First developed in the popular penny newspapers in New York, such as Horace Greeley's *Tribune*, James Gordon Bennett's *Herald*, Charles Dana's *Sun*, and Pulitzer's *World*, the concept had spread to almost every newspaper in the nation. The *American*'s column preceded Frost's arrival, and no one who wrote for it, including Frost, received a byline.

Certainly familiar with the concept, Frost had much to learn about the form such writing required. To Susan Hayes Ward he said, "My newspaper work requires a brave effort. They assure me I have much to learn particularly in the way of writing." Most likely he meant this to be a "sarcastic ha-ha-what-can-they-teach-a-genuine-American-poet" quip, but it also contained a harsh truth. Journalism and such man-about-town columns had their own rhythms. Added to that, Frost was still relatively shy and found it difficult to approach people, not to mention find good stories. As a columnist his job was to get around and report on what he saw. By his own account he was awful: "I was young and shy. My editor said I should get around to saloons more. I wasn't a very good reporter."[30] Among the items he did write were short paragraphs on such notable events as "an eagle that alighted on the flagpole of the Post Office. Another was about women and children gathering in the freight yard." Ultimately he decided it would be easier to make up the stories for his column. This gave him effective experience in writing fictive realism. In his prose he tried to detail events with a ring of plausibility. Years later, writing to a friend, he recalled, "I faked in a small way for another paper named the Sun which was published in Lawrence Mass. All I had to do was to claim for my yarns the virtue of fact and I had story writers of twice my art and invention skun [sic] a mile."[31] When he wrote to Susan Hayes Ward in 1895, this was the background for his claims that "my newspaper work requires a brave effort. They assure me I have much to learn particularly in the way of writing: but what care I: I have done the best I can with what I know: and if I know everything I have reached my limit. Let them teach me." He gave the impression that he was far too superior for mere newspaper work and had nothing to learn. But I believe that writing this column in January and February 1895 taught Frost how to look at everyday life, at people and what they do, and render it as exactly and precisely as he could. He attended to the oddities of local speech and learned how to shape what he saw into what he later termed "sort of prose poems." And not just any prose-poem but a form he had become more and more interested in, the eclogue. To his friend Louis Untermeyer, Frost said, "I wrote 'paragraphs' [for the column] some of which though in prose were really eclogues."[32]

After two months Frost suddenly quit. According to Lawrance Thompson, he quit out of high-minded moral disgust at the managing editor. Apparently he proved to be an unscrupulous snake responsible for graft, blackmail, and other shenanigans in the thicket of business, journalism, and politics that defined the Lawrence of the 1890s. There is no way to prove it, but it seems more likely Frost left newspaper work because he had a better job. It so happened that the Jacksonian, populist, working-class evening paper, the *Lawrence Evening-Sun,* had gone bankrupt. Instead of shutting down, however, it was to be revived as a literary weekly, the *Sentinel,* the sort of fashionable publication one found in Boston and other sophisticated cities. I suspect the new editor, a fan of Frost's *American* column, made him a good offer. The facts show that no sooner had Frost left the *American* than he began work on the newly revived and now literary weekly *Sentinel,* where he stayed through the summer. But when he quit that summer, he already had another job waiting, his old fallback, teaching school. By the fall of 1895 he was preparing to renew his teaching job in Methuen. Altogether, Frost worked on newspapers for six months.[33] From his brief career as a reporter and from his reading of the newer realist novels and dramatic and dialect poetry of the era, Frost began to grow ever more interested in bringing realism to his own poetry.

ROBERT FROST 1896: MARRIAGE AND
BOTANY, A NEW DOMESTIC SCIENCE

In June 1895 Robert Frost headed north to attend Elinor's college graduation in Canton, New York, where he again tried to convince her to marry him. This time he succeeded. Meanwhile his mother had founded her own private school. Mrs. Frost's Private School capitalized on the local Anglo-Saxon community's ill will toward the increasingly Irish-dominated public schools. A relatively new phenomenon in Lawrence, the surge in private schools such as Mrs. Frost's met an increasing demand from those who did not want their children to go to school with the children of new working-class immigrants who toiled at the mill. This is not to say

Mrs. Frost's aim was bigoted. A Scot and immigrant herself, she had no animosity toward the newcomers. In fact her landlord was an Irishman with whom she became friendly. But because she still faced economic uncertainty, this became an opportunity almost impossible to ignore. When the new school year began in the fall of 1895, Robert Frost, who had taught briefly in his mother's school, returned to the public elementary school classroom of Salem, New Hampshire. His fiancée, Elinor White, also now in Lawrence, began her first job teaching in Mrs. Frost's school.

It is likely that Frost left journalism and the *Sentinel* and became a schoolteacher to convince Elinor to marry him. He must have figured the steady income of a teacher, unlike the unreliable income from his poetry, or from newspapers, would convince her she had not made a mistake, as her father had declared, when she agreed to marry Robert Frost. No doubt, too, Elinor's father knew the sorry history of Frost's own father's journalistic career and added to the young Frost's desire to prove he was his own person. In 1895, then, both Frost and Elinor worked as teachers and married in December 1895 at the end of the semester.[34] Economic security did not follow. By the time the summer of 1896 rolled around, Mrs. Frost's Private School, despite a noble advertising effort, faced eviction for nonpayment of rent. Elinor was pregnant but morning sickness seemed to derail even that joy.

Meanwhile, even as he experimented in his poetry with ever more precise attention to detail and to the rhythms of speech as set across poetic meter, Frost also began to train himself in another kind of close looking: botany. Frost came to his love of botany as he had found astronomy, through his old high-school friend Carl Burrell. No longer in Lawrence, Burrell was then making his living as a factory worker near Concord, New Hampshire. He gave his friend a peaceful, even bucolic, retreat for his honeymoon, a cottage that he rented for the couple to enjoy that June. While there Frost began to botanize in earnest. Jay Parini, for one, believes that Frost's discovery of botany that June inaugurated his lifelong obsession. Frost relied on the field guide *How to Know the Wild Flowers* (1893), ostensibly by William Starr Dana but in reality by his wife. That guide combined, in the best genteel tradition, botany and literature. Dana peppered the book's descriptive discussions and numerous color illustrations of flowers with quotations from Thoreau, Whittier, Longfellow, Bryant, and Wordsworth and in so doing wove together history, legend, botany, and etymology.[35]

"THE BIRDS DO THUS": A SECOND SUCCESS

In 1896 it had been two years since Frost had published any poems. Newly married and with a baby, Elliot (born in September), the Frosts were living on the second floor of a disheveled house near Lawrence High School. His mother and sister resided on the first floor where his mother struggled to run Mrs. Frost's Private School and where Elinor taught. Frost meanwhile commuted to nearby Salem, New Hampshire, to teach elementary school and wrote his poems in the evening. He also sent them to genteel magazines; he sent two—"Caesar's Lost Transport Ships," which Frost had written in his high school years, and "The Birds Do Thus," of more recent vintage—to the Wards at the *Independent*.

Susan Hayes Ward published both. In a letter to her concerning "The Birds Do Thus," Frost described the poem's psychological theme: "Well I did what I tried to do so that the future is not so uncertain though it is not with success as it is with failure which is final, while success to a coward is only suspense, the most awful of tortures."[36] In keeping with the genteel tradition, the poem was not to be read only as a literal statement of fact. Instead he implied that it should be read as a metaphor, even as an allegory, about success. It is a poignant theme, given that he had immersed himself in a household of women and an infant and spent his days teaching children in what had become a woman's profession. He was perhaps beginning to feel like a failure.

Published in the first column of the first page of the *Independent* on August 20, 1896, "The Birds Do Thus" was also surrounded by women.[37] Because of its short length, it shared the first column with two other poems, one by the decadent poet Louise Imogen Guiney and one by a Canadian poet, Elizabeth Roberts MacDonald. Frost's poem stands out because its diction and its meter contrasts sharply with theirs. This is Frost's poem:

I slept all day.
The birds do thus
That sing a while
At eve for us.
To have you soon

> I gave away—
> Well satisfied
> To give—a day.
> Life's not so short
> I care to keep
> The unhappy days;
> I choose to sleep.[38]

Compare those lines to this opening from Guiney's poem: "Moveless on the marge of a sunny cornfield, / Rapt in sudden reverie while thou standest." Although sexually alluring, Guiney's poem invokes a poetic diction in such archaisms as *marge* instead of *margin*, *thou* instead of *you*, and *standest* instead of *stand*. Her poem in turn was followed by MacDonald's "The Bugle-Call," which begins, "The night loomed black with coming storm / The narrow pass was iron-walled." Although the diction is more realistic, the imagery refers to an entirely allegorical zone where no realistic specificity can be found. In MacDonald's poem, the bugle's sound "in the heavy heart of time" relates in an entirely symbolic register to "Eternity's desire." Compared to those two poems, Frost's three-stanza poem seems stark, even unpoetic.

On the other hand, Frost's poem, too, traffics in poetic cliché insofar as it compares the poet with birds, a figure that goes back to antiquity. Frost, however, turns that cliché around when he uses it as a metaphor for success. On a biographical level the metaphor implies that for a man like Frost in the 1890s, song can be sung only at night. Like a bird that sings only at night, Frost's day job (teacher and before that reporter) allows him to sing only at night too. In this case song is a metaphor for poetry. Associating birds with poets, and their song with poetry through the already conventional association of bird and bard, Frost can be said to connect himself and his poetry to nature in the more empirical biological sense and not in the old romantic sense familiar to lovers of Keats. In actual fact some birds really do sing only at night, and Frost, like them, will write only at night.

On another level the poem can be read as a conventional love poem. Its central metaphor of birds and their song can be read as justifying his current situation as a schoolteacher. He sleeps (a metaphor for being nearly dead) during the day to earn a steady salary. Such sleep, a bad thing, is the price he is willing to pay to have the woman he loves. A third possibility, though, concerns the second stanza, which reads: "To have you soon / I gave away— / Well satisfied / To give—a day." One could read this not as his willingness to give away "the day" of mundane work for a life of night love and poetry but rather as a lament. In this third reading Frost could be saying that he sleeps, a bad thing, because as Maurice Thompson advised, Frost has decided to give up the possibility and bright sun of his dream to be a poet for the security of a job. Sleep could even be literal. During many tedious days he may well have pleaded illness and taken sick leave, if such a thing existed. We know that as a result of his undiagnosed depression and insomnia he often did "choose to sleep." Sleep, in that case, is not natural like that of birds but all too human, a willed reaction in the face of awful reality. Ultimately the final stanza is ambiguous. During the day he sleeps, metaphorically speaking, so that at night he can come alive and sing, like certain birds. That reading also carries a naturalist's pun. For just as the birds who sing at night also mate at night, and come alive sexually, so too does Frost.

We cannot know why Susan Hayes Ward accepted this poem after Frost spent two years attempting to get her to take his work. What we can know is that although it was only the second poem he ever published, Frost refused ever to reprint, collect, or even republish it. Its first and only appearance came in 1896. Still, "The Birds Do Thus," like "My Butterfly," matters because in the context of its day, and of the poems with which it was published, it signals a new poetic turn to realism.

A CODA

Four months after Frost published "The Birds Do Thus," the *Daily American* carried the following headline: "Fisticuffs Followed by a Warrant and Police Court." The headline on December 28 in the new evening paper, the *Lawrence Evening Tribune,* was "Long Police Court Session: Robert L. Frost Fined for Assault on Herbert S. Parker." And that weekend another Lawrence paper, the *Weekly Journal,* also covered the affair, reporting on December 31: "It isn't anybody's privilege to challenge the son of a $20,000 mill agent to mortal combat every day of the week."[39] No. It was only Robert Frost's privilege to beat up a rich man's son, a member of the local gentry. The man, Herbert Parker, had been, like Frost, a worker in the Arlington Mill several years before. Though born well, he was a factory hand and lived in the same tenement as Frost because Parker's parents opposed his marriage and cut him off from family funds. Frost and Parker had a great deal in common and had become friends. But Parker's wife, according to Elinor, had befriended a prostitute and invited her over as a guest. In good New England genteel fashion, Elinor, and likely even Frost, took umbrage and Frost complained to Parker's wife. She called Frost a coward for confronting her and not Parker himself. If he had something to say, say it to her husband. Why wait until he was away? Was he not a man? What was he—schoolteacher, poet—a man living in a house of women? When Parker, who had not been home during the confrontation, returned, Frost met him and dared him to call him a coward. Reading about the fight and the police intervention in at least three local newspapers, Frost's grandfather said Robert had "disgraced the family."[40] Although Parker was the one estranged from his family, and his wife the one consorting with prostitutes, Parker had the upper hand because he had been assaulted. Frost's grandfather made it clear that since his grandson had hit the son of a mill owner, going to court and contesting the charge would be futile. As manager of a mill himself, Frost's grandfather knew that winning a public battle would be impossible. Although Robert Frost wanted to go to court, his grandfather discouraged it. He also helped Frost get out of town.

With his grandfather's financial help Frost returned to college.[41] He decided to go to Harvard as he originally had intended, take a degree in classics, and become a high school classics teacher. He also intended to realize his poetic talent and to make that his real work.[42]

Chapter Five

•

Discovering Realism
Frost, 1897–99

AFTER PUBLISHING "The Birds Do Thus" in 1896, Susan Hayes Ward published two more of Frost's poems: "Caesar's Lost Transport Ships" (January 1897), and "Warning" (September 1897).[1] On April 30, 1897, Charles Hurd, editor of the Brahmin elite's newspaper of choice, the *Boston Evening Transcript*, printed Frost's "Greece."[2] This flurry of publishing occurred at a time when most of the leading national magazines relegated poetry to a single theme, beauty, and dismissed its larger intellectual relevance.[3] Indeed in this same year Charles Dudley Warner, Mark Twain's *Gilded* Age coauthor, defended poetry precisely as the sacred space wherein one could find solace and relief from everyday trials.[4] For the most part the typical poem found in such magazines as *Scribner's*, the *Century*, *Lippincott's*, the *Atlantic*, and *Harper's* corresponded to Warner's views. The poems by Cardozo, MacDonald, and Guiney that I have described, for example, can be taken as parts of the whole of the era's genteel poetic tradition for their use of archaic diction, often fanciful or highly symbolic landscapes, and ever more surprising use of meter and rhyme.

In relation to these works Frost's four poems from 1897 do stand out. Frost's high school effort, "Caesar's Lost Transport Ships," is a poem from the 1880s and had an oddly and surprisingly fresh impact. Its historical specificity struck another realist blow against poetry's idealist turn. In it, for instance, Frost imagines he is one of Caesar's (doomed) sailors. At the poem's conclusion the sailor is below decks, after his compatriots have jumped ship: "And in the hull a tremor of low speech. / And overhead the petrel wafted wide." The poem ends with these last words of resignation to death. Conventional though it was when he wrote it in high school, in 1897 Frost's poem stood out—not only for its plain diction, precise historical moment, and focus on particular details but also for the contrast it presents to the other poems printed alongside it in the *Independent* of January 13, 1897.

That week all of the *Independent*'s poems were published in the first of the three columns on the first page. There readers found Martha McCulloch-Williams's "Alchemy," which begins with a depiction of a sunrise: "A silver streak that rose and fell / As winds blew high, or winds blew low." The figurative language transforms the metaphor into a symbol for spiritual benevolence. After her poem came Frost's and after his, readers found Priscilla Leonard's four-line "Nil Nisi Bonum," a poem with a conventionally uplifting spiritual message:

> Hath thy heart sunshine? shed it wide;
> The wearied world hath need of thee.
> Doth bitterness within abide?
> Shut fast thy door, and hold the key!

In September the *Independent* printed Frost's bleak "Warning" underneath "Ascription" by George G. D. Roberts in the first column on its first page. Roberts was among the most ubiquitous magazine poets of that era. One could hardly pick up either a genteel or mass-market publication and not find one of his poems. The first stanza of Roberts's poem is:

> O Thou who hast beneath Thy hand
> The dark foundations of the land,—
> The motion of whose ordered thought
> An instant universe hath wrought,—

The poem describes a butterfly that (unlike Frost's butterfly from the 1894 poem, "My Butterfly") is decidedly symbolic, a living icon of beauty, "More sweet to Thee than all acclaim." The poem assumes and declares the symbolic connection between God and the natural world in order to encourage and promote an affirmative reading of a life-promoting deity.

In contrast to Roberts's poem in both diction and theme, Frost's "Warning" begins:

> The days will come when you will cease to know,
> The heart will cease to tell you; sadder yet,
> Tho you say o'er and o'er what once you knew,
> You will forget, you will forget.[5]

Frost's diction, one notes, is matter of fact. Even the elision in *o'er*, which maintains the rigorous tetrameter lines of the poem, sounds, when read aloud, more like speech than beautiful song. And rather than make a case for the necessity of beauty in a tawdry world, Frost's poem concerns an intensely modern psychological theme, a lover's inability to maintain constancy in love. As the last stanza has it:

> Blame no one but yourself for this, lost soul!
> I feared it would be so that day we met
> Long since, and you were changed. And I said then,
> He will forget, he will forget.

Neither "Caesar's Last Transport Ships" nor "Warning" suggests realism today. In their immediate context, however, both stand out. They belong to Frost's already-developed belief that poetry had to leave the clouds and attend to the "things of this world," as one of his latter-day followers, Richard Wilbur, would say in his third book.[6]

In 1897 Frost also published "Greece" in Boston's *Evening Transcript*, in keeping with his attention to the things of this world.[7] In keeping with genteel poetry's antebellum ideal of public purpose, this poem referred directly to that year's outbreak of war between Greece and the Ottoman Empire.[8] Frost most likely could not resist the temptation, given his interest in classics and his love of the ancient Greek poets, to write a poem in reaction to these events. The poem concludes with the lines, "Long ago / It was you proved to men, / A few may countless hosts o'erthrow: / Now prove it once again." The poem's publication in this newspaper, too, was no chance event. Frost had earlier introduced himself to Charles Hurd, the newspaper's literary editor. When Frost said he wanted to be a poet and make his living in journalism, Hurd told him to make another plan. Hurd said that he, too, had wanted to make his mark as a poet and had learned only that no poet worthy of the art could write well if he made a living in newspaper work.[9] I suspect that Hurd took a shine to Frost even though the editor popped Frost's dream bubble. Hurd also most likely appreciated the topical theme as particularly well suited to a daily newspaper.

DISCOVERING THE LIFE OF A PUBLIC
INTELLECTUAL: THE HARVARD YEARS

In 1897, when these three poems appeared, Frost again went to college, enrolling at Harvard in anticipation of taking a degree in classics, teaching, and writing poetry in his spare time. But the Harvard years took Frost on a different course, for there he received encouragement not only to see poetry and intellectualism as synonymous but also to recognize the value of public dissent. Among his professors it was common to call "into question the social and political conventions hitherto held sacred." In fact his professors were themselves public intellectuals, regularly writing for the genteel and even the mass-market press. Significantly William James, a professor of psychology at Harvard, brought the term *intellectual* to the United States.[10] During the Dreyfus Affair (1898) he singled out the French adjective *intellectuel* for its reference to "the men in France who still retained some critical sense and judgment." He said such a term ought to be used in America.[11] By the late 1890s it was already a familiar epithet for those who "retained some critical sense and judgment" and who made their views known in plain language without obfuscation.[12] Frost matriculated in the fall of 1897, arriving at Harvard just as it was becoming the seat of American intellectual culture per se.

Nearly twenty years earlier Harvard's president, Charles William Eliot, a chemistry professor and the first noncleric to be named president, had divorced the Calvinist theology of New England from the curriculum. In 1869 he instituted a new curriculum dedicated to creating what would later be understood as intellectuals. Eliot wanted to bring science to the fore and to train students for a modern world that required specific skills.[13] As a result the new curriculum prescribed course requirements only for the freshman year. An elective system allowed students to select their own courses for the following three years.[14] As part of that reform Eliot also secularized the science faculty. Before 1869 Harvard, like most other American colleges, allowed for "the dominance of theology in the curriculum . . . [which] obliged scholars in every field to align their work with Christian orthodoxy." Eliot's elective system effectively brought this alignment to an end—and also ushered in an era of professorial intellectual freedom. That freedom eventually expressed itself as a new philosophy, pragmatism—a concept and term that William James made popular. In the words of Louis Menand, pragmatism embraces the view "that ideas are not 'out there' waiting to be discovered but are tools—like forks and knives and microchips—that people devise to cope with the world in which they find themselves."[15] In his own book on the topic William James referred to it as a method. Said James, "To attain perfect clearness in our thoughts of an object, then, we need only consider what conceivable effects of a practical kind the object may involve—what sensations we are to expect from it, and what reactions we must prepare." As a way of thinking, the pragmatic method asks, "What difference would it practically make to anyone if this notion rather than that notion were true? If no practical difference whatever can be traced, then the alternatives mean practically the same thing, and all dispute is idle. Whenever a dispute is serious, we ought to be able to show some practical difference that must follow from one side or the other's being right," James said. Pragmatism, then, offered a method of thought based not on idealism per se but rather on the testing of what James referred to as "a concrete consequence" that might follow from any belief, supposition, idea, or ideal. The pragmatist, said James, "turns towards concreteness and adequacy, towards facts, towards action, and towards power."[16] Philip Weiner wrote one of the first, and still most comprehensive, books on the Harvard pragmatists and their connection to the era's scientific ideas, especially the theory of evolution. There he says that the pragmatic method defines "the meaning of an idea by reference to its effects or predictable consequences." He then cites Peirce to call attention to "the *raison d'être* of Peirce's pragmatism." Says Weiner, the pragmatic method's purpose, according to Peirce, "is that 'it will serve to show that almost every proposition of ontological metaphysics is either meaningless gibberish . . . or else is downright absurd.'"[17] As a method pragmatism was designed to be part and parcel of scientific inquiry rather than of airy and idealist philosophy. It belonged to a larger struggle about the meaning of *science* and of *objectivity*.

Without going into too much detail concerning that struggle, suffice to say that by the mid–nineteenth century philosophers and psychologists like James and Peirce saw increased threats to what had been a stable concept of individuality established during the Enlightenment. Subsequent philosophical inquiry and scientific discovery following the Enlightenment had revealed what two scholars of this topic, Lorraine Daston and Peter Galison, describe as "the continuity of consciousness and memory." That continuity came to replace, they argue, the Enlightenment's more stable, atomized self. They write: "As the continuity of consciousness and memory came to replace the soul as the definition and expression of the self, introspection seemed to reveal fluid, tattered, and even contradictory identities." Resolving that chaos of metaphor, and convinced that they could resolve the intellectual contradictions such chaos revealed, became the life goal of such pragmatic philosophers and psychologists as William James and Charles Sanders Peirce.[18]

Robert Frost arrived at Harvard and this heady milieu of intellectual exploration, and new methods of thought that concerned the very meaning of individuality, science, and philosophy, as an older student, who was married and had a child. He left his wife and son in Lawrence and took lodging in a rooming house in Cambridge where he earned extra money at a night school.[19] His classes at Harvard included German, English composition, Greek, and Latin. In these classes he first studied Virgil's *Eclogues* and Theocritus's poetry in depth.[20] He did so well that at year's end he received an impressive scholarship that would cover most of his sophomore year's tuition. He also continued to write poetry. Charles Hurd published Frost's "God's Garden," in the *Boston Evening Transcript* of June 28, 1898. The poem adheres to the era's conventional allegorical high poetic style. In a straightforward Christian allegory it tells readers to "Tend flowers that God has given / And keep the pathway open / That leads you on to heaven." This defense of Christian doctrine is odd. None of his other poems had taken either so obvious an allegorical turn nor made its religious sensibility so unambiguous. Some have speculated that the poem is not Frost's. In later years Frost refused to say he wrote the poem, and he never reprinted or republished it.[21] But perhaps the poem's defense of Christianity emerged from the poet's intellectual shock. After all, unlike his high school teachers or his Dartmouth professors, his professors at Harvard resisted the conventional Christian piety to which he had grown accustomed. One can imagine both professors and students mocking such piety, perhaps driving Frost to write this poem not as an act of conformity but rather of dissent. Certainly he left Harvard that summer too full of ideas and poetry to contain himself. He read widely and, always a great talker, engaged his friends in conversations about the implications of the new science on matters of faith.

When Frost returned that fall for his second year, the choices he made for his elected course of study paved the way for what would be nothing short of an intellectual revolution. In particular, such professors as Thomas Shaler, William James, George Santayana, and Hugo Munsterberg would have a long-lasting effect. I turn first to Thomas Shaler, whose course in geology Frost took that year. In 1869, when Eliot instituted the elective system and divorced theology from every aspect of the curriculum, Louis Agassiz (1807–1873), the head of the natural science department, had been especially unhappy. Agassiz, the nation's premier biologist, had spent his career resisting Darwinian ideas for their lack of religious concern. His student, Thomas Shaler, an evolutionary geologist quite comfortable with Darwin, had carved a middle ground between Darwinian atheism and Agassiz's theology. Shaler's effort to prove the compatibility of faith with empirical science had a profound influence on Frost's understanding of the natural world.[22] Charles Sanders Peirce, who had an enormous influence on William James in the informal Metaphysical Club that had formed at Harvard in the 1870s, expressed this middle ground best. In a letter Peirce made the case directly: "The universe of Nature seems much grander and more worthy of its creator, when it is conceived of, not as completed at the outset, but as such that from the merest chaos with nothing rational in it, it grows by an inevitable tendency more and more rational." As Philip Weiner puts it: "If God is the end of being and highest reality, then God is a growing creature of evolution."[23]

Said Piece, this "satisfies my religious instinct."[24] If this were also the sort of thing Frost gleaned from Shaler, from conversations, and from Frost's reading that semester, it likely satisfied Frost's religious instinct too.

That instinct meanwhile found itself put to the test in two yearlong classes in philosophy. George Santayana and Josiah Royce taught the first, a history of philosophy. No longer a decadent poet associated with the circle of Louise Guiney but rather a tenured philosophy professor, Santayana taught the first half of the course, which covered the ancients.[25] Royce, a Christian idealist, taught the second half, bringing the history of phi-losophy into the Christian era. At the time one of the great debates con-cerned the very idea of truth itself. By the late 1890s reason, the traditional province of philosophy, had become less and less important to a new crop of empiricist scientists who associated reason not with scientific inquiry but rather with fuzzy and deluded idealism.[26] In their lectures, then, both Santayana and Royce gave to their lessons something of an edge, insofar as they meant to defend their brand of reason through idealism.

The other side of that debate meanwhile made its argument in the other sequence of classes Frost took. The first of these focused on logic (taught by George Herbert Palmer), and the second, taught by William James, treated psychology—then still understood as a branch of philosophy but presented according to the new pragmatic method.[27]

Santayana's class on the early history of philosophy gave Frost an in-tellectual surprise, even alarm. Santayana opposed Christian idealism, which in 1911 he famously and disparagingly referred to as "the genteel tradition." He particularly disliked its condemnation of the carnal world of sensual pleasure and with it the visceral joys that beauty made palpable. In a recent study Irving Singer summarizes Santayana's views:

> Santayana believed that the dogmas of all supernatural religions can be justified only as imaginative portrayals of human aspiration. For him religion is, and of a right ought to be, nothing more than poetry supervening on life. As a kind of aesthetic metaphysics or myth mak-ing, religion elicits the most highly elevated feelings, and it provides affective reassurance of a sort that science cannot give. But according to Santayana, religion has no authority to contradict science.[28]

Unlike Shaler, and unlike his pragmatic colleagues, Santayana did not have an interest in proving the truth of spirituality. Nor did he feel com-pelled to connect beauty to God, as had such poets as Walter Pater. Many years later Santayana explained why writers in the 1880s (and he included himself in that crowd) favored an intensely allegorical, spiritual literature that connected beauty and God: "You must remember that we were not very much later than Ruskin, Pater, Swinburne, and Matthew Arnold: our atmosphere was that of poets and persons touched with religious enthusi-asm or religious madness. Beauty . . . was then a living presence, or an aching absence, day and night." By the 1890s, though, as a philosopher and atheist the one-time decadent poet could find no justification for a connection between beauty and spirituality. In his philosophy he explained that beauty, especially the beauty of great art, referred only to order, structure, and pattern. Beauty was synonymous with symmetry. At best artists, and especially poets, made metaphors and analogies for beauty in an otherwise meaningless, empty world. As he said, "the human spirit" is not "anything more than a lonely wanderer in a universe devoid of any basic interest in our welfare."[29]

The year before Frost took his class, Santayana had published *The Sense of Beauty* (1896), in which he claimed that, "We no longer mean by work all that is done usefully, but only what is done unwillingly and by the spur of necessity. By play we are designating, no longer what is done fruitlessly, but whatever is done spontaneously and for its own sake, whether it have or not an ulterior utility. Play, in this sense, may be our most useful occupation."[30]

To that, Santayana added, "work is the disparaging term and play the eulogistic one."[31] Having made the case for play, Santayana argued that "we may measure the degree of happiness and civilization which any race has attained by the proportion of its energy which is devoted to free and generous pursuits, to the adornment of life and the culture of the imagination. For it is in the spontaneous play of his faculties that man finds himself and his happiness." To his students Santayana made the case for the divorce of play from work, God from beauty, by teaching the history of play in the pagan Greeks, especially the Epicureans and Lucretius.[32] Lucretius opposed play to work and favored play and pleasure over a grim puritanical work ethic. Santayana wanted his students to have the same view. In class, he often disparaged American culture's work ethic and materialism—not in the name of genteel Christian piety but rather in the name of Lucretian play and beauty.

Frost's poems, and his genteel upbringing, had not prepared him for such a rigorous and unabashed defense of atheism or of pleasure and play for their own sakes. He could not help but reject Santayana's view and find in the psychology and pragmatism of William James a necessary rebuke to Santayana. Where Santayana mocked the genteel tradition's perspective on a good society comprised of good people, Frost continued to maintain his faith in the necessity, and continued existence, of that tradition's views of duty, character, and virtue. Since high school Frost had cast a skeptical eye on that view—yet he was not prepared for Santayana's cynical, often mandarin, dismissal of it.

Just as Shaler did with natural science, William James with psychology meant to find a compromise between spiritual belief on the one hand and materialist atheism on the other. He did this through his own take on what individuality meant. According to the historians of objectivity, Lorraine Daston and Peter Galison, James, following from Kant, argued that there was a "'self of all other selves'" and that it "is part of the stream of consciousness that endures amid the flux, and it is robust, unified, and above all 'active.'" In sum, such a unified self existed and warranted study by psychologists. In James's most recent book, *The Will to Believe* (1897), which Frost read that summer, one sentence might have struck a particular chord: "There is but one unconditional commandment, which is that we should seek incessantly, with fear and trembling, so to vote and to act as to bring about the very largest total universe of good which we can see." To that James added that one has to believe in "[a] power not ourselves... which not only makes for righteousness, but means it, and recognizes us." James accepted the premise that divinity must exist. In so doing, he argued, "I am something radically other than the Divinity with whose effulgence I am filled."[33] In this way he left it to others to find empirical, objective proof for such divinity. According to James, empiricism stopped at the door of physical sensation, of feelings. The quality one assigned to such feelings and sensation had no province in empirical discussion. This, however, did not mean that what philosophers call *qualia* lacked reality, or truth value, to the one experiencing such sensation. According to James, those who assigned spiritual qualities to feelings had as much right to their belief as did the hardened empiricist. Allowing two seemingly contradictory beliefs to coexist was what James called pluralism. In *Will to Believe* James adopts "the pluralist empiricist point of view."[34] He established pluralism to distinguish his felt perception of the divine from conventional genteel Protestant theology. With regard to objectivity he therefore distanced himself from a European philosophical monism that ran from Plato and that asserted "the notion of the Whole, which is the essence of deterministic monism." Against that monism James insisted on the radical subjectivity of the psychological self, the one who experiences. James argued that one can actively suppress one's own self and so create objectivity, which, say Daston and Galison, allows one "to meet experience with outstretched hand," but finally one is still, perforce, always also inside one's subjective self. The name for such suppression of the self, for the attempt to gain access to the not-me, James called pluralism. That radical separation not only opened the door to humanity's free will, but it also made room for chance. It opened the door for that which we cannot know. As James wrote, "Chance means pluralism and nothing more." Ultimately, to make the case for the divine, for God, James had to make the case for belief as something that humanity wills: "Our ordinary attitude of regarding ourselves as subjects to an overarching system of moral relations, true 'in themselves,' is therefore either an out-and-out superstition, or else it must be treated as a merely provisional abstraction from that real Thinker in whose actual demand upon us to think as he does our obligation must be ultimately based. In a theistic-ethical philosophy that thinker in question is, of course, the Deity to whom the existence of the universe is due."[35]

In so doing, he said, one has to "give up the doctrine of objective certitude."[36] James seemed to say that by an exclusively objective measure God was not necessary to justify morality. James wrote, "No bell in us tolls to let us know for certain when the truth is in our grasp." Typically one fully comprehends the ethical consequences of an action only after the fact, after the evidence of its impact can be discerned. Yet where does the notion of moral consequences come from? Given the lack of any empirical proof, either of God or morality, one must simply believe it to be so: "Believe that life is worth living, and your belief will help create the fact."[37] In his later book, *Pragmatism* (1907) James made it plain that if one has a will to believe, then one is also "willing to live on a scheme of uncertified possibilities which he trusts; willing to pay with his own person, if need be for the realization of the ideals which he frames." In sum, "On pragmatistic principles, if the hypothesis of God works satisfactorily in the widest sense of the word, it is true."[38]

Against Santayana's Epicurean defense of play, delight, and beauty, Frost found in James's books a pragmatic means of justifying his own conviction that the divine must exist. It was enough to feel it, to will it to be so. When the fall semester concluded, and Santayana's class ended, one can only imagine how deeply Frost must have looked forward to James's class that spring. To Frost's lifelong regret, however, James did not teach the class: he was suffering from acute depression and had taken a medical leave for the spring semester.[39] When Frost entered what was to have been James's class, he found Professor Hugo Munsterberg at the front of the room. At the time Munsterberg, William James, and G. Stanley Hall comprised Harvard's psychology faculty.[40] Together they brought the German movement of "physiological psychology" to America. That movement sought to understand "mental phenomena through physical laws."[41] In keeping with the religious tenor of the age, they often fought about whether the "soul and consciousness were part and parcel of human physiology. James made a pragmatic case for the soul's existence. Munsterberg belittled the idea that the soul and consciousness existed. As he said to James, "The story of the subconscious mind can be told in three words: there is none."[42]

James was not offended by Munsterberg's dissent. In fact James recruited Munsterberg because of his empirically based materialism. Once at Harvard Munsterberg created, with the encouragement and even the backing of William James, an experimental psychology laboratory.[43] James may have found a way to rescue the soul, and perhaps even God, from the empirical demand to know even as he preserved the necessity of empiricism itself and its association with objectivity. In sum James did not at any point mean to deny the necessity of empirical evidence for psychological matters. Similarly Munsterberg had an abiding respect for James, who was in many respects his mentor. Not surprisingly, then, Munsterberg used James's textbook, *Principles of Psychology,* for the class Frost took. In that textbook James argued that consciousness *was* real, empirically discoverable, and a result of evolution. Munsterberg evidently taught the subject according to that premise, though he may have told the students of his own doubts. In any case the textbook, and the new field of psychology, proved nothing short of a revelation to the poet. Louis Menand summarizes the textbook as arguing that "there is intelligence in the universe:

it is ours. It was our good luck that, somewhere along the way, we acquired minds. They released us from the prison of biology." He taught Frost that through psychology, one could "solve traditional philosophical problems—and validate traditional philosophical conclusions—using laboratory methods."[44] Along with Shaler and Santayana, Munsterberg and James had introduced Frost to views that would shape his future work. By March 1899 he seemed to be well on the way to engaging ever more deeply with these matters. Instead he abruptly withdrew from college altogether.

AFTER HARVARD

In March 1899 Frost had left his family in Lawrence to take up residence for the spring semester in Cambridge. But his wife's last weeks of pregnancy with their second child required that he commute to Lawrence once a week. Between his responsibilities as husband and father and his classes, he became ill: "I got very sick, terribly so, as if something were very wrong with heart or stomach. Trouble in the solar plexus," he later explained. Indeed he spent most of that spring semester ill, perhaps suffering a bout of severe depression. By the end of March he had decided to leave college. He wrote an apologetic letter to the dean officially asking to withdraw without penalty. The dean granted Frost's wish in a wonderfully encouraging and deeply regretful response. One might say that Frost left, to quote the Ancient Mariner from Coleridge's poem, "a sadder and a wiser man."[45]

Sad that he had to leave, wiser for what he learned, Frost was also now the father of two children. Without a job he was more dependent than ever on his grandfather. No one knows precisely why Frost left Harvard when he did or what he expected would follow. Most agree, however, that from 1899 on he was determined to make his way as a poet. The move was as risky in 1899 as it would be today. Richard Poirier best summarizes the stakes: "Its own 'original intent' is to make us assent to a notion which we ordinarily find presumptuous, namely that poetry is an heroic enterprise and that a poem is made equivalent to a number of activities which belong, as it were, to the real world—of politics, of business—which usually acknowledges poetry, if at all, by condescension." In a biography of her family, Frost's granddaughter, the daughter of Frost's second child, Lesley, writes that after Frost left Harvard, "he and Elinor formed a pact with their marriage to protect the integrity of his poetic talents . . . in spite of constant pressures from his grandfather and from Elinor's parents and siblings to make an 'honest' living and to provide for his family."[46]

Gravely ill when he left Harvard in the spring of 1899, Frost would not fully recover until the spring of 1900. About that time a doctor told him to try farming—counsel that one biographer has called "the best piece of advice he ever got."[47] Frost became a poultry farmer with the help of a veterinarian and amateur chicken farmer whom he knew in Methuen. Even as things began to look up, illness struck again, this time affecting Frost's mother and his wife (his mother had to be placed in a sanatorium). Horrified at the filth of their unauthorized chicken farm, the Frosts' landlord threatened eviction. But the worst was yet to come. In July 1900 the Frosts' first-born child, Elliot, died of cholera.

Elinor fell into a profound depression. Somehow she mustered enough energy, unbeknown to her husband, to ask Frost's grandfather to buy them a farm. Earlier she had admired a farm in Derry, New Hampshire, just twelve miles across the border from Methuen, Massachusetts. When she saw it was for sale she appealed to Frost's grandfather, and he agreed to assist.[48] Often a villain in Frost's memory and in biographies, Frost's grandfather likely knew he had to take desperate measures. He had, after all, lost a son and a great-grandson. He now saw the near mental collapse of his grandson and his wife. He had financed Frost's two attempts at college, and he now decided to do something about the Frost family's situation. Agreeing to Elinor's proposal, Frost's grandfather, with his brother's help, purchased the Derry farm.[49] But there were strings attached, for the grandfather was certainly not thrilled that his grandson intended to pursue the two least profitable jobs in America, poet and farmer. Frost's friend Louis Mertins recalled Frost's saying, "That his grandson should desire to be *both* was almost enough to bring on a stroke."[50]

The terms for the purchase of the Derry farm made Frost a tenant rather than an owner. His grandfather had set up a trust fund such that Frost would have to rent the place for ten years. The trust fund would also pay an annual income of $500. Calculated in 2013 dollars, that $500 would have amounted to only about $13,500. After those ten years Frost would own the deed outright, and the trust would continue to pay an annual income increased to $800. It also required that Frost's high school friend Carl Burrell and Burrell's father, both experienced farmers, live there, too, in order to maintain the daily operations. Although the offer was generous, even with these terms attached, Frost saw it as insulting. Later he recalled his grandfather's saying, "You've made a failure out of everything else you've tried. Now go up to the farm and die there. That's about all you're fit for anyway." Rather than die there, however, he thrived. According to Jay Parini, Frost was a successful poultry farmer, making money from his eggs and from his apple orchard, despite a rotten economy.

Frost's reputation in Derry allowed him to maintain a genteel status despite his downwardly mobile slide from scion of the Lawrence gentry to college dropout and hardscrabble farmer. To his neighbors he was just another dandy playing at farming while relying on a trust fund. As Frost recalled, "They would see me starting to work at all hours of the morning—approaching noon, to be more explicit. . . . When they saw me sleeping away the better part of the day—well, it was quite too much for them. They laid it to a lack of energy on my part. I was a failure in their eyes from the start—very start." The key words here are "in their eyes." If he slept late it was because he wrestled with his poems and read deep into the night, long after his children, whom he and Elinor homeschooled, had been put to bed.[51]

As he had presaged in "The Birds Do Thus," Frost in these Derry years sang at night. The real work of those years would be the poetry he composed after his children were asleep. "The Quest for the Orchis" was the first of these poems to see print. In it one can trace the impact of the intellectual breakthrough of his Harvard years and of his newfound commitment to a career in poetry.

"THE QUEST OF THE ORCHIS" (1901)

On June 27, 1901, the *Independent* published "The Quest of the Orchis." It was Frost's first publication since 1897. Four years later, however, poetry's role in most publications had fallen ever further into decline. Beginning in 1900 the *Independent,* already a holdout with regard to poetry, stopped printing poetry on its first page. Also with the new century the weekly removed the Christian epigraph from its masthead. After 1900 each week's issue began with a series of editorials on the state of world affairs. In the typical twenty-five-page issue, readers often found three poems. For instance in the issue that carried Frost's poem, his was printed last following a Negro dialect poem by the popular white poet Frank Stanton and a conventionally genteel poem, "Bel Canto," by Bessie Miller. Each poem was interspersed among articles by Samuel Gompers and Senator Orville H. Platt. Frost's poem, like the others, was printed by itself at the bottom of a page.

Frost initially composed this poem in 1896, before he went to Harvard. As with almost all his poems, the gestation period from original composition to final publication covered a lengthy period. Scholars have no way of knowing what the poem looked like when he first wrote it or even if he made any changes to it.[52] In general Frost went out of his way to destroy most of his drafts. Regardless, when he first composed it, he and Elinor were on their honeymoon in Allenstown, deep in the White Mountains of northern New Hampshire, and Frost delighted in hunting for wildflowers.

In Frost's New England two flowers would have piqued his interest: the fringed orchid and the fringed gentian. Dana's field guide, *How to Know the Wild Flowers,* which Frost used, describes them both. In the entry for "Purple Fringed Orchises," Dana opens with a quotation from Thoreau's journal:

> June 9th—Find the great fringed-orchis out apparently two or three days, two almost fully out, two or three only budded; a large spike of peculiarly delicate, pale-purple flowers growing in the luxuriant and shady swamp, amid hellebores, ferns, golden senecio, etc. . . . *The village belle never sees this more delicate belle of the swamp. . . . A beauty reared in the shade of a convent, who has never strayed beyond the convent-bell.* Only the skunk or owl, or other inhabitant of the swamp, beholds it.[53]

In this entry Thoreau brings his keen naturalist eye to this flower. Thoreau attends to the sexual derivation of the name in the italicized lines. He implies that the orchid-testicle should not be seen by a demure village belle. Meanwhile the orchid is itself compared to a virgin, insofar as it hides, staying close to the shade of alder trees, its convent. In this brief excerpt Dana draws attention to Thoreau's association of flowers and sex.

Dana's entry on purple-fringed gentians begins with her own commentary, "In late September, when we have almost ceased to hope for new flowers, we are in luck if we chance upon this." She says, "The fringed gentian

The Independent

JUNE 27, 1901

Ten Cents a Copy - Two Dollars a Year

130 FULTON STREET, NEW YORK

"The Quest of the Orchis" was published while Frost lived in Derry, New Hampshire. Note that by this time poetry is no longer published on the front page of the *Independent*. From the Robert Frost Collection of Pat Alger.

1494   THE INDEPENDENT

nesses were so lusty and strong, not to act hastily. He earnestly beseeched them to give all the various industries a proper hearing, and it was through his influence and that of other members who are identified with the textile interests in Philadelphia that the resolutions finally passed by the body were more conservative than the declarations of the various speakers might lead one to expect. It was decided that the whole matter of reciprocity should be referred to a national reciprocity convention to be specially assembled by the National Association of Manufacturers in Philadelphia. To this meeting the representatives of all the industries will be invited to send delegates, and after they are given a fair hearing recommendations will be framed for the guidance of the next Congress.

The convention reflects a change in the sentiment of the business men of this country which has been coming on for several years, in fact ever since they first began to turn their thought and attention to the foreign trade. President McKinley, whose observation no shifting in the current of public opinion escapes, has for some time foreseen this movement in popular sentiment. His strong and tactful speeches assure us that the welfare of the great American industries is un-der his careful scrutiny and that he is ready to second the efforts of the manufacturers to hold their foreign markets by a liberal system of reciprocity.

It is an opportunity, of course, for free traders to declaim very gleefully about a change of faith. One of the humorists in this convention, who is at the same time one of its most useful members, comically declared that so far as his own industry was concerned, cement manufacturing, he thought it would require protection " for a few months yet." He wanted to know whether a man could not change his opinion in the course of ten years if the conditions and circumstances which originally induced him to those opinions had undergone modification. The representatives of many of the greatest industries in this country admitted in Detroit that they had changed their views regarding an important economic question. They had been ardent protectionists, and they still believed in the protective principle. They honored the tariff for what it had done to develop the resources and increase the prosperity of the country. They now wished the policy modified, in order that this development and prosperity should continue without diminution or loss.

PHILADELPHIA, PA.

The Quest of the Orchis.

By R L. Frost.

I FELT the chill of the meadow underfoot,
    But the sun o'erhead;
And snatches of verse and song of scenes like this
    I sung or said.

I skirted the margin alders for miles and miles
    In a sweeping line;
The day was the day by every flower that blooms,
    But I saw no sign.

Yet further I went before the scythes should come,
    For the grass was high;
Till I saw the path where the slender fox had come
    And gone panting by.

Then at last and following that I found—
    In the very hour
When the color flushed to the petals, it must have been—
    The far-sought flower.

There stood the purple spires, with no breath of air
    Or headlong bee
To disturb their perfect poise the livelong day
    'Neath the aldertree!

I only knelt and, putting the boughs aside,
    Looked, or at most
Counted them all to the buds in the copse's depth,
    Pale as a ghost.

Then I arose and silent wandered home,
    And I for one
Said that the fall might come and whirl of leaves,
    For summer was done.

WEST DERRY, N. H.

is fickle in its habits, and the fact that we have located it one season does not mean that we shall find it in the same place the following year. . . . Our search for this plant is always attended with the charm of uncertainty." She then cites Emily Dickinson's poem, "Fringed Gentian," in which Dickinson refers to the gentian as a symbol of beauty's spiritual power and its association with the life force itself. The part of the poem Dana quotes also refers to frost, which would not have been lost on Robert Frost: "The frosts were her condition: / The Tyrian would not come / Until the North evoked it, / 'Creator! Shall I bloom!/'"[54] In Dana's field guide the fringed gentian, unlike the fringed orchid described by Thoreau, is a distinctively literary flower, associated with beauty, femininity, spirituality, and the romance tradition. In contrast the fringed orchid is male and refers to the Darwinian cycle of sexual selection and reproduction.

Dana also cited William Cullen Bryant's famous "To the Fringed Gentian." It is likely Frost would have known and even memorized that poem by 1896. First published in 1809, Bryant's poem had long been a standard in the American schoolroom. One of the founding works of what I have called the genteel tradition, the poem took the lowly New England flower and rendered it a symbol for immortality and the soul. Bryant remarks that the flower blooms just as winter's onset begins. That, says Bryant, makes it an emblem for eternity, for hope, for the soul's immortality.

When Frost wrote his own poem during his honeymoon in June 1896, he would have seen the fringed gentian, the June flower that both Bryant and Dickinson had immortalized. In June there would have been no fringed orchid; they bloom only in September. Yet the poem he submitted to the *Independent* (the poem printed in June) is about the orchid, not the gentian. I submit that the intellectual revolution he experienced at Harvard, coupled with his troubled feelings about being a man doing the woman's work of teaching school, writing poetry, even botanizing explain why he wrote not about the feminine flower made famous by Bryant and again by Emily Dickinson but rather the masculine flower.

Frost's poem tells the story of an active botanist who, almost in desperation, hopes to sight the rare purple-fringed orchid before the local farmers cut it in their next mowing or before the cold weather kills it. As a botanist, the speaker of the poem knows the flower is hard to find. He also knows that alder trees are its natural habitat. He decides to find the flower by first finding the trees. To that end he follows the tree line, all the while keeping his eye to the ground, hoping to spot the flower. He spots a fox trail and follows it to the orchid, which he finds hidden under an alder tree's boughs. He then examines the flower with scientific precision and true botanical detachment. The poem's concluding lines say:

> And I for one
> Said that the fall might come and whirl of leaves,
> For summer was done.

Read metaphorically these lines echo the Old Testament. The mere mention of "the fall"—along with a "whirl of leaves"—alludes to the biblical Fall and biblical whirlwinds. Combined, they paint a bleak future of chaos, as if to say that when "summer was done" the easy optimism and easy faith that so long read flowers as symbols of beauty, and therefore of God, have also come to an end.[55] In Frost's poem, as in Bryant's and Dickinson's, the flower becomes a symbol of a larger spiritual truth, albeit a deeply pessimistic one. Unlike their poems, however, Frost buries that metaphorical connection to such a degree that readers may be forgiven if they miss it altogether. The poem can easily be read as purely descriptive tale of one man's search for a beautiful flower.

Frost's knowledge of botany would suggest that he knew what he was doing when he anachronistically depicted an orchid, rather than a gentian, as blooming in June. Frost's botanical inaccuracy allows him to make a point about male sexuality and its association with flowers, nature, poetry, spirituality, work, and play. In so doing he invokes the association of orchids with testicles and Orpheus, founder of poetry, according to the Greek tradition. With regard to male sexuality, the Greek word *orkhis* means testicle, supposedly as a result of the root's shape. In the late 1880s decadent poets such as Santayana had found their progenitor in Orpheus. Meanwhile critics of the decadent aesthetic found in orchids a symbol of overcultivation and human intervention. A flower beloved by breeders, who had long brought the techniques of artificial selection to bear in their search for ever more outrageous forms of beauty, the orchid also reflected the drive of art to be better than, and ever surpass, nature itself. More than any other flower, orchids proved that even nature could be corrupted and changed for aesthetic ends. Orchids represented the artificial world of aestheticism, art-for-art's sake poetry, and decadence in general.

In his poem Frost takes what had become the decadents' premier symbol of beauty, an amoral human construction, and returns it to the fields and woods where it originated. Removing the hothouse flower from the manufactured world, Frost also removes it from human intervention. In Frost's poem the orchid is dependent only on the raw facts of its own sexuality. Its beauty is not for people, nor is it a symbol of God or beauty for its own sake alone. It is just a mechanism for survival.

As it happens Frost had at this time been arguing about Darwin with his friend and hired man, Carl Burrell. At least one scholar, Robert Faggen, believes that Frost had even read Darwin's book on orchids as part of their debate. As Faggen explains, Darwin argues in his book that orchids are so adaptive that they actually follow no inherent design. Said another way, "Natural selection as opposed to artificial selection does not design for a single purpose . . . but can modify different parts for different purposes." According to Faggen, Frost and Burrell debated the implications of the orchids' natural selection with regard to Christian theology. Darwin proved that orchids' forms and colors had emerged from their adaptive evolutionary process in the struggle for survival. He had, in other words, disproved the anthropomorphic view that the beauty of flowers, and orchids in particular, existed for the sake of beauty alone. The many poets to the contrary notwithstanding, orchids did not exist to please humanity, nor did their beauty exist to suggest a better, moral life. In "The Quest for the Orchis," Frost removes the orchid not only from its association with the decadents but also from the larger genteel association of flowers with God's moral benevolence.[56]

It would seem that the poem sets Darwin in opposition to both Santayana and James. Rather than find proof of faith, and rather than will himself into belief, Frost finds natural selection. The orchid seeks out the alder trees to keep itself safe. The botanist finds the flower only by following a fox. In folklore the fox represents a crafty pragmatic figure. It could be that Frost, by invoking a fox in this poem, means to associate all of nature's flora and fauna with the trickster figure whose elusive, ever-changing ways ensure its survival.

Previously, I suggested that the poem's final lines are metaphorical:

> And I for one
> Said that the fall might come and whirl of leaves,
> For summer was done.

On the other hand, this same pragmatic, realist, Darwinian perspective can also support a more affirmative conclusion than the dark metaphorical one I offered before. With the onset of winter's whirl of leaves, rather than die, the orchid actually resists. After all, it does bloom year after year. One never knows where, yet bloom it does. Read in that light, even a Darwinian tale can make of a flower an emblem for human life, even for the spirit itself. That reading also gives a new view of the allusion to male sexuality. As an image of masculinity the orchid knows how to survive against all odds. Like a Greek hero the orchid triumphs against the odds. There is no moral lesson derived from God's gift of beauty but rather a lesson drawn from the classical tradition and from Darwinian biology. One can survive against all odds. If there is faith in this poem, and a will to believe, it is the will to believe in courage and heroism rather than in beauty.

Perhaps by coincidence, perhaps not, the same issue of the *Independent* that carried "The Quest of the Orchis" also carried an essay, "The Geology of the Soul," by the pseudonymous Dicast (probably William Hayes Ward himself). The essayist engaged the problem of faith and science in what was ostensibly a review of essays by Lafcadio Hearn—essays in which Hearn attempts to fuse the philosophy of East and West, Darwin and faith: "Evolution is a theory," Dicast writes, "drawn from the observation of outer phenomena, that man is the last product of myriads of generations of life reaching back to the past; but evolution has forborne to make any appeal to the inner consciousness of the human soul."[57] Frost's small poem engages precisely that dilemma.

• • •

In 1942, more than forty years after the publication of "The Quest of the Orchis," Frost published this poem in one of his books, *A Witness Tree*. There he made a significant change, retitling the poem, "The Quest of the Purple-Fringed." What had already been a deeply buried metaphorical connection to masculinity, decadence, Darwin, and faith through the association of orchids, Greek antiquity, and testicles now became even more buried. "Purple-fringed" could refer to the purple-fringed orchid or to the purple-fringed gentian. The poem does not explicitly say. The change did, however, make the connection to Bryant's famous poem all the more explicit. In 1942 it was as if Frost meant to highlight the idealism that had become Bryant's poetic legacy. I cannot help but feel that by publishing this poem in the middle of World War II, Frost meant to call attention to the peril facing what had once been the essence of American exceptionalism, its idealist faith in a benevolent God of nature.[58]

Chapter Six

•

Robert Frost's Poetry of Ideas, 1906–8

"The Trial by Existence," "The Lost Faith,"

"A Line-Storm Song," "Across the Atlantic"

WHILE ROBERT FROST wrote his poetry on his farm in Derry, New Hampshire, the genteels wrestled with the forces of commercialism that continued to overwhelm the publishing industry. In 1906 Frost's future publisher, Henry Holt, declared that book publishers in the United States cared only about market trends and making money. As a publisher of books on science (especially the works of Herbert Spencer), as well as literary works of poetry and fiction, Holt argued that the publishing industry had fallen prey to business interests and commercialism. He made the sorry state of intellectual publishing clear in the *Atlantic Monthly* of 1905. That article drew an intense reaction in England from the *Fortnightly Review*. The editors there did not disagree. Rather they said the situation was even worse and applied as much to magazines as to book publishers.

Holt took umbrage at that claim. He declared that while book publishers had fallen to mammon, magazines had not. In the vast sea of ink, he said, only magazines still carried the torch for intellectual thought, even for poetry. To prove it in 1906 he helped sponsor the revival of *Putnam's* (once the most important of American monthlies) to compete with *Harper's*, the *Century*, *Atlantic*, and others. In a 1907 follow-up to his *Atlantic* essay, Holt recalled in an issue of *Putnam's Monthly* the publishers who made the genteel publishing industry in antebellum years: "I cannot imagine any chaffering going on with (not to mention living men) the first Charles Scribner, or William H. Appleton, or Daniel Macmillan, or the original Harper Brothers." In 1907, though, he only found chaffering (haggling). "It would be an immense gain for the cause of literature, and to the profit of all worthy authors . . . if the 'commercial enterprise' that has come in from the Wall Street and the energetic West, were taken out of the publishing business," he continued. That utopia would not come, he said, because "the literary standards of people are of course, affected by what they read, and what they read is too much determined by the publisher who brays loudest and pounds hardest." Holt knew that his lamentation would have little effect: "I am perfectly aware that in a day when the gods of Heathendom, excepting Mammon, and those of Christendom too, have pretty much disappeared, to many readers this cry in the wilderness will seem unpractical to the extent of foolishness."[1] Still, he made it and sponsored the forum for it, a new monthly *Putnam's* that meant to insist on the genteel tradition's relevance and importance.

Though they did not know each other, and were separated by two generations, Frost was writing poetry that meant to keep the genteel tradition's idea of an intellectual public poetry alive and relevant to the new century. Nor was he alone. In 1906, the *Atlantic Monthly* published a simply titled essay, "Three American Poets of To-Day." In it the British novelist May Sinclair singled out Edwin Arlington Robinson, Ridgely Torrence, and William Vaughn Moody for precisely the elements that I am attributing to poetic realism.[2] Frost met Sinclair seven years later and, from what he wrote to her, seems to have read her article when it first appeared. If he did, it likely made quite an impression, proving that his attention to the living voice and the emotional facts of psychological experience were not misbegotten.

For all his efforts, though, between 1901 and 1906 Robert Frost did not publish a single poem. It was not for lack of trying. In 1903 he went with his family to New York City for a month. There Frost made the rounds of magazines and publishers, while his wife and children enjoyed New York as tourists. Ultimately he failed to secure either a book contract or publication for any of his poems.[3] Then, in 1906, he published poems in a local Derry newspaper, the *Enterprise,* and in two genteel magazines, the *Youth's Companion* and the *Independent.*

The continued development of Frost's poetic realism is evident in these poems. To his interest in a more accurate rendition of speech and local particular detail, he now added his current thinking about the conflict of faith and science. To his slight experiments in poetic diction and description, he now brought a new thinking about psychology, Darwin, and the problem of materialism.

"THE TRIAL BY EXISTENCE"

This poem had a long gestation. Frost first drafted it in 1892, the year he went to Dartmouth. Most likely inspired by the Plato he had to read for class there, it also likely underwent substantial change when in 1906 he submitted it to the Wards.[4] Reading it that February, William Hayes Ward called it "uncommonly good" and accepted it. It was published in the issue of October 11, 1906, and given almost an entire page, a major feat for any poet. Typically even this magazine relegated poetry to filler spaces at the end of articles.[5]

In the poem Frost retells Plato's tale of souls who gather before they are born to ask fundamental questions about the life they will lead once given earthly form.[6] The story asks whether Darwinian science's view, that life is just random chance, is more accurate than the conventional Platonic, and later Christian, view of divine design. Beginning with the title, Frost subtly makes a strong case in favor of a will to believe, of a universe open to faith and the divine. By 1906 the sociology of Herbert Spencer had become an intellectual dogma in many genteel publications. Spencer had been the one to claim that life was a "struggle for existence," where Darwin had never said any such thing. Subsequently an entire school of realist literature, naturalism, had designed stories around Spencer's premise. Struggle, chance, and brute forces inevitably overwhelmed individuals. Happily, said Spencer, evolutionary history among people proved that individualism would always triumph in the end. According to Spencer, the individual, not the collective, and the singular person, not the larger species, class, clan, or tribe, was nature's sole concern.[7] Frost likely had little interest in this idea. His reading in Darwin likely made him doubt Spencer's separation of individual from species and humanity from the rest of nature. At any rate Frost's poem changes the already familiar phrase "struggle for existence" to his own, "Trial by Existence," and in so doing removes Spencer from biology and locates him where he belongs, in moral philosophy. Both *trial* and *by* return individual volition, even free will, to the human story Frost means to address. It also raises the specter of guilt.

876   THE INDEPENDENT

will not lose interest in the little republic that was founded by her citizens. Tho its future history may be a good deal more concerned with the development of the British colony of Sierra Leone and the French colony of the Ivory Coast, the United States may at any rate take to itself the credit of having founded the first civilized independent negro state in West Africa, a land in which, if the negro have but patience to bear with us for a while, and with our help to frame a civilization of his own to suit his own environment, he may come to find himself independent of white tutelage, and an equally endowed collaborator with the Caucasian in a world-wide civilization.

LONDON, ENGLAND.

The Trial by Existence
BY ROBERT FROST

EVEN the bravest that are slain
  Shall not dissemble their surprise
On waking to find valor reign
  Even as on earth in paradise:
And where they sought without the sword
  Wide fields of asphodel fore'er,
To find that the utmost reward
  Of daring should be still to dare.

The light of heaven falls whole and white
  And is not shattered into dyes,
The light forever is morning light;
  The hills are verdured pasturewise;
The angel hosts with freshness go
  And seek with laughter what to brave;
And binding all is the hushed snow
  Of the far-distant breaking wave.

And from a cliff top is proclaimed
  The gathering of the souls for birth,
The Trial by Existence named,
  The obscuration upon earth.
And the slant spirits trooping by
  In streams and cross- and counter-streams
Can but give ear to that sweet cry
  For its suggestion of what dreams.

And the more loitering are turned
  To view once more the sacrifice
Of those who for some good discerned
  Will gladly give up paradise.
And a white shimmering concourse rolls
  Toward the throne to witness there
The speeding of devoted souls
  Which God makes his especial care.

And none are taken but who will
  Having first heard the life read out
That opens earthward, good and ill
  Beyond the shadow of a doubt.

And very beautifully God limns,
  And tenderly, life's little dream,
But naught extenuates or dims,
  Setting the thing that is supreme.

Nor is there wanting in the press
  Some spirit to stand simply forth
Heroic in its nakedness
  Against the uttermost of earth.
The tale of earth's unhonored things
  Sounds nobler there than 'neath the sun;
And the mind whirls and the heart sings
  And a shout greets the daring one.

But always God speaks at the end:
  "One thought in agony of life
The bravest would have by for friend,
  The memory that he chose the life;
But the pure fate to which you go
  Admits no memory of choice,
Or the woe were not earthly woe
  To which you give the assenting voice."

And so the choice must be again,
  But the last choice is still the same,
And the awe passes wonder then
  And a hush falls for all acclaim.
And God has ta'en a flower of gold
  And broken it, and used therefrom
The mystic link to bind and hold
  Spirit to matter till death come.

'Tis of the essence of life here,
  Tho we choose greatly, still to lack
The lasting memory, at all clear,
  That life has for us on the wrack
Nothing but what we somehow chose:
  Thus are we wholly stripped of pride
In the pain that has but one close,
  Bearing it crushed and mystified.

WEST DERRY, N. H.

"The Trial by Existence" as it appeared in the *Independent*. From the Robert Frost Collection of Pat Alger.

The word *trial* implies both a test and a forthcoming judgment. To speak of a trial *by* existence suggests that life itself will determine whether one is guilty or innocent, whether one deserves mercy or damnation. Darwin had put paid to the notion that morality had anything to do with natural selection. In contrast Spencer brought morality back to what he called the struggle of existence.[8] In this poem Frost addresses the moral quandary the two thinkers had raised. In particular the poem, like "The Quest for the Orchis," addresses the meaning of courage. It wonders whether courage has any moral value. In the poem the souls who have already lived one life choose to be born again and once more inhabit a body and live a human life on Earth. If they choose hard lives full of suffering, they prove their courage. Frost says they also prove that "the utmost reward / Of daring should be still to dare."

In paradise the souls are told that they can elect to undergo a "trial by existence"—they can prove their courage if they choose to return to earthly life. Why would they? It must be for some good. As Frost says, only those souls "who for some good discerned / Will gladly give up paradise." In the consummate exercise of free will the souls agree to suffer. "And none are taken but who will." To make sure they know what life they are about to lead, each soul is told the history of the life it will lead on Earth. They choose to endure pain for the sake of proving their own strength of will. Their courage merits their reward, a return to paradise. Each time a soul decides to endure the trial by existence, "a shout greets the daring one." There is a trick to this exercise in free will. Upon birth in human form each soul is made to forget that it had chosen the life it will lead:

> 'Tis of the essence of life here,
> Tho we choose greatly, still to lack
> The lasting memory, at all clear,
> That life has for us on the wrack
> Nothing but what we somehow chose:
> Thus are we wholly stripped of pride
> In the pain that has but one close,
> Bearing it crushed and mystified.[9]

To avoid the sin of pride each soul must live unaware of its choice. Suffering cannot be suffering if it appears less than random. The life of the soul is the life of any modern person in a Darwinian universe; not only is there no foresight, but the pain and hardship that ensue appear most often as chance and random happenstance rather than inevitable and designed. In this poem life is a paradox. Everything is known even as nothing is known. In the absence of foreknowledge one has only two choices: face the bleak fact of random chance or accept, through what William James called "the will to believe," that there must yet be a purpose. Rather than reject belief, the poem through this myth instead offers a compromise between blank meaninglessness and modern Christian faith in salvation.[10]

When the poem was published, Frost wrote to Susan Hayes Ward to complain that the magazine got his town wrong (West Derby instead of West Derry) and for using the word *life* where he had written *strife* in line 50. He also noticed that his poem was relegated to the bottom of an interior page. In a subsequent issue he found it carried only one poem and that a reprint of one it had already run. He could not let that lapse go unremarked:

> These things were not thus in the old days when I read your editorial accompanying Hovey's Elegy on the Death of Parsons, and then and there gave you my allegiance whether you had need of it or not. I call it your editorial—I think likely you wrote it. It was in the fall of 1892 and I was at Dartmouth . . . neglecting my studies for Palgrave, which I had just got hold of (Halcyon days!) I remember your generosity to Hovey very well: you likened the exaltation of his close to Milton's sunken daystar that yet anon repairs his drooping head. . . . And only last spring the Independent took a whole page to declare itself the immemorial friend of poets. But if it expects the slightest poets to believe its protestations, it must not get into the habit of stopping a gap twice with the same poem. Now must it?[11]

He soon regretted sending that letter. After he did not hear from Susan Hayes Ward, he convinced himself that he had offended her. In January 1907 she wrote to say she had been ill and had not been angry. His relief was palpable.[12] He thought of himself as a public poet, a genteel poet, and, as I am arguing, as a realist poet. None of those self-perceived views, however, could be viable if magazines like the *Independent* abandoned the art.

Meanwhile, the Derry farm idyll came to an end by late 1906 after several disasters in quick succession. First, in an effort to supplement his income, Frost determined to be a commercial writer. In 1903 he began to write and publish short stories for the poultry industry's trade press. By 1906 he had published eleven stories. The idea had not been his. His neighbor, John Hall, also a poultry famer, had given him the tip. Hall was a longtime subscriber to *Farm Poultry,* and thought that since Frost was a writer, he might gain some extra money if he sent stories to that trade magazine. Before the electronic entertainment of television and radio, even industry magazines routinely carried fiction and poetry to attract readers. There were, for instance, a number of trade magazines competing for poultry farmers' subscriptions and one, *Farm Poultry,* routinely printed fiction to attract more readers than its rival.[13] Unfortunately in 1906 Frost made a simple error in one of his stories that betrayed a fundamental ignorance of poultry. As a result he lost his contract.

Also that year Dr. Bricault, Frost's main egg buyer, retired from the trade. This was a serious blow, for with Bricault went the majority of the income from Frost's farm. He was suddenly left with only an uncertain apple harvest and his grandfather's annuity of $500. As good as the years had been on the Derry farm, they had also done little to change the general impression locally that he was a dandy living off an inheritance. Biographers report that one year, when he deposited his annual check, the snide bank teller could not help but comment, "More of your hard-earned money, Mr. Frost?"[14]

Faced with financial disaster, and now with several more children to support, Frost returned to teaching. As it happened, the Pinkerton Academy, a prestigious private boarding and day school not two miles from his farm, hired him that year. Through a circuitous route, and a series of contacts that led from Lawrence, Massachusetts, to Derry, New Hampshire, Frost was hired to teach English in 1906.[15] As he did not have a college degree, he landed the job in large part through his poems. His minister friend from Lawrence knew the principal at Pinkerton and apprised him of Frost's intellectual acumen and of his poetic talent. The minister also saw to it that for his job application, as it were, Frost should read his poem "The Tuft of Flowers" to the school board. Frost had written it in 1897 while at Harvard. Like "My Butterfly," it tells a story of accurate botanical and biological fact mixed with existential questioning. The poem so impressed the school board—after he read the poem its members crowded around him—that it secured him the position. As he said, "Again my poetry saved me."[16] Somehow, too, the poem was also published in the *Derry Enterprise* on March 9, 1906. The paper, one of two dailies in town, was marketed to the middle and working classes, and members of the Democratic Party, and was the less prestigious. One would have thought it would be published in the *Derry News*, written for and read by the mostly Republican town elite and business class. Already, though, Frost was living in both worlds, barely straddling the fence between them. At Pinkerton, for instance, he was not hired full time but had to prove himself first.

As he said, he began "at fearfully low pay," teaching the children of the local wealthy gentry, readers of the *Derry News*. Their children made their disdain for Frost apparent. In his first semester a student put on the chalkboard the insulting phrase, "Hen Man," meant to belittle Frost. Never one to take an insult lightly, he fought with the administration to have the student permanently expelled and succeeded.[17] Worse, when "Trial by Existence" was published that October in the *Independent,* even though the poem was given a generous allotment of nearly an entire page, that compliment was undermined by the misidentification of his town of residence. He imagined the worst, believing his ideas had been too provocative. In the end his colleagues were angry because Pinkerton Academy had not been mentioned. The school wanted a share in the glory of publication.[18]

1907: "THE LOST FAITH"

In 1907 Frost placed another poem, "The Lost Faith," in the more elite of Derry's two dailies, the *News,* and another, "A Line-Storm Song," in the *New England Magazine.* Of these two, "The Lost Faith" better reflects his continued commitment to a new realism of diction, as well as to a poetry of ideals in keeping with the genteel tradition's ideal of public poetry. Individual states assumed the task of memorializing the war dead in the era before a federal Memorial Day. In New Hampshire the annual event was called Decoration Day and specifically honored the Civil War dead. The Reverend Charles Merriam, Frost's Lawrence friend and mentor who had helped Frost land the teaching job in the first place, now secured for Frost an invitation to recite the honorary Decoration Day poem for the Derry Men's League Banquet of the town's First Congregational Church.

It was more than just an honor. Merriam knew that Frost had not yet been hired as part of the permanent faculty. He hoped that this recital would persuade the school board to hire Frost permanently. For the February 29, 1907, banquet, Frost wrote "The Lost Faith," one of his few commissioned occasional poems. Too nervous to read it to the assembled high and mighty of the town, in the end, Frost sat in the audience while Merriam himself read the poem. It proved a success. Shortly after Frost delivered this poem, the *Derry News* printed it.[19] Shortly thereafter the school board offered Frost a permanent position.

With seventy-seven lines the poem adheres to the classical ode. It speaks in a collective voice for the Union dead. As do few of Frost's poems, it also wears its genteel moral and cultural evangelism on its sleeve. Perhaps that explains why he chose never to reprint it.[20] The poem's views, however, are not conventional. This poem challenges its era's standard interpretation of the Civil War, the American South, and the so-called Negro problem, in keeping with the model of the intellectual as dissenter that Frost had first witnessed at Harvard.

In 1906 the conventional meaning of the Civil War for both North and South buried the issue of race relations and civic equality, preferring instead to understand the war as a political contest about states' rights. Racial equality had been effectively repressed, if not overtly denied, in most public discussions of the war's meaning. Meanwhile African Americans had been migrating to northern industrial cities, which led to increased racial tensions in those cities, while in the South, the early twentieth century saw the rise of Jim Crow legislation and the rollback of the civil rights African Americans had gained during Reconstruction. As racial integration became more and more of a reality in the North, public discussion of racial equality became more and more of a political liability. By 1907 the Civil War's meaning had changed. No longer a moral cause in the name of abolition and equality, it had become a political contest between state and federal authority.[21]

In his poem Frost resurrects what had been repressed. In place of a struggle about appropriate political authority, Frost read the war as fundamentally concerned with racial equality. The lack of commitment to the ideal of equality became the acerbic, pointed implication of his title, "The

Lost Faith." By making racial equality a central issue, Frost means to re-cover a lost meaning for the Civil War and even to redeem the dead in the name of something moral and good. Adopting the public rhetoric of the Greek Pindaric ode, the poem alludes to abolition without ever naming it directly:

> We shrine our fathers as their wars recede
> With the heroic dead that died of old,
> We shall strew flowers for them year after year;
> They shall have flowers themselves more than they need!
> But for the cause that was to them so dear,
> Where shall it be so much as justly told
> What that cause was?—which, as they lie in mould,
> In our hearts dies as cold.
> Have we for that no flowers, no mournful rhythm,
> The soldiers' dream, that when they died, died with them?

When the poem asks, "Where shall it be so much as justly told / What that cause was?" Frost refers to the cause of abolition. He calls attention to the premise behind freeing the slaves: that all people are equal. The first stanza's pessimism says that such a dream died with the soldiers. To honor the soldiers, says Frost, ought not one to honor their dream? What they fought for?

One of the major political issues of 1907 was the renewal of the 1885 Chinese Exclusion Act then before Congress and a topic of much debate. Alluding to that debate, Frost writes in the second stanza:

> The Californian, by the western sea
> Exults, and by the Gulf they laugh,
> Saying, "How can all men be free,
> How equal, when God made them wheat and chaff?'"

The 1907 audience would have known that the California argument for limiting Chinese immigration and citizenship arose from a racial theory that declared the Chinese "chaff" to the Anglo-Saxon "wheat," although the poem does not mention this directly. At the time, more than forty years after the Civil War, Frost said, the principle of racial equality still had no footing in America.

The poem's fourth stanza makes this lack of principle, or failure of prin-ciple, explicit:

> It was the dream that woke them in the north,
> And led the young men forth,
> And pitched against the embittered foe their tent;
> And fought their fight for them on many a field,
> Their sword, their shield,
> The still small voice that like a clarion pealed;
> Strong as a dream and deathless as a dream,
> As it did seem,
> (Though destined to go down the way they went.)

In this stanza Frost alludes to 1 Kings (19:11–13), where God makes his presence known to Elijah. In so doing, God chooses not a mighty form but rather a small still voice. This same image also had captivated Wordsworth, who famously invoked it in his own meditative ode on the necessity of adhering to moral principle, "Ode on Immortality." Rather than associate that voice with God, however, Wordsworth called it "the still small voice of humanity." In Frost's poem the "still small voice" is the dream of racial equality, a dream he fears "is destined to go down the way they [the soldiers] went."

To emphasize just how little of that dream existed in contemporary America, Frost's sixth stanza laments the failed dream in the current industrial city:

> we saw it fade from sight,
> Not while we slept, but while we strove too much
> For things that were not beautiful and bright.

In the final stanza, rather than make a stirring cry for racial justice, Frost simply asks a question. Is the vanishing dream of racial equality an inevitable consequence of industrial progress and a materialistic age? Imagining racial equality as a Platonic ideal, Frost wonders if those souls who had such a dream have the capacity to bring such an ideal to pass.

> Truer than aught recovered from the vast
> By souls that could not slumber, but must climb
> The starlight in far suns to dwell a time—
> So true in passing, if it must be past.

The last five words—"if it must be past"—offer the poem's only hopeful note.

On the strength of "The Lost Faith," and his publication of "Trial by Existence" in the *Independent,* Frost was hired full time as a permanent teacher at Pinkerton. He took to the job bursting with fresh educational ideas. He expected to, and did, shake up the small school based on his reading, on his previous experience as a schoolteacher, and on his own experience during the previous seven years of homeschooling his own children.

1907: "A LINE-STORM SONG"

In addition to "The Lost Faith," Frost also published "A Line-Storm Song" in the *New England Magazine.* It seems likely that Susan Hayes Ward led him there. The two had finally seen one another when she visited the Lynch farm in northern New Hampshire, where the Frosts summered. In a letter to her that August, he thanked her, saying, "I have sent the inoffensive poem to the unoffending editor and soon, I expect, I shall be enough richer to buy a few more books—[George] Meredith, [Sidney] Dobell, [William Butler] Yeats, and one or two others I shall have to think up. (Have you anything to suggest?)" Most likely the "inoffensive poem" was "A Line-Storm Song," and the "unoffending editor," was Winthrop Packard of *New England Magazine.*[22]

In 1907 *New England Magazine* was a regional monthly that had begun in Boston in 1884 as the *Bay State Monthly,* and it had begun to enjoy the fruits of an editorial change of direction. Sold in 1901 when it became the *New England Magazine* under the patrician editor-publisher James A. Garland, it could hardly be called inoffensive. A genteel magazine of politics and literature, it championed both progressive Republican politics and literary realism, especially in fiction. Today the magazine is recalled for publishing the early stories of Willa Cather. After 1905 its editor, Garland, turned its editing over to another patrician who was something of a dandy, Winthrop Packard. When Frost submitted his poem to them, the magazine was in transition. At the time Garland was looking to sell it. While not intended to be either as intellectually severe or exacting as either the *Independent* or the *Atlantic,* the *New England Magazine* took seriously its role as titular voice of New England gentility's more reformist wing. To that end both Garland and Packard filled each issue with a combination of light and serious poetry and fiction, in addition to the articles focused on what was still considered the birthplace of America.

"A Line-Storm Song" was published on almost an entire page. It followed a comic narrative poem by the then-well-known dialect poet, Holman Day.[23] This mix of lighthearted and serious literature was typical of the magazine. Its articles had the same eclecticism. This issue, for instance, included an article by G. Stanley Hall, the new president of Clark University, the psychologist who invited Freud to America, and a former Harvard professor who had been a colleague of William James's.

Frost's poem was written in rhyming quatrains to emphasize its musical rather than speech qualities as Frost tells a simple story. A lover calls to his beloved and asks her to walk with him in a storm. A closer reading, however, reveals a subtle continuation of Frost's exploration of the meaning of morality in a Darwinian, empirical age. The poem begins romantically enough:

> The line-storm clouds fly tattered and swift,
> The road is forlorn all day,
> Where a myriad snowy quartz-stones lift
> And the hoof-prints vanish away;
> The roadside-flowers, too wet for the bee,
> Expend their bloom in vain.
> Come over the hills and far with me,
> And be my love in the rain. (*lines* 1–8)

From a naturalist's perspective the scene reveals a paradox. The life-giving rain proves so overwhelming that pollination during the storm becomes impossible. The flowers bloom in vain. The bee will not pollinate; the power of the rain proves so overwhelming that sexual reproduction is impossible.

Yet during this overwhelming downpour Frost calls to his love in song. The song itself—poetry, with its obvious meter and rhyme—becomes a metaphor for love. In a world that cares only about natural selection, sexual propagation, and nothing more, the sound of the poet becomes the only sound besides the rain: "All song of the woods is hushed like some / Wild, easily shattered rose" (lines 13–14). His song, as something distinctly human, becomes something different from nature, as if to say that love must reside, as Plato said it did, apart from nature. Human choice confronts nature's indifference. In the final stanza Frost makes an analogy by means of a simile to draw attention to the division between people and nature.

> Oh, never this whelming east wind swells
> But it seems like the sea's return
> To the ancient lands where it left the shells
> Before the age of the fern;
> And it seems like the time when, after doubt,
> Our love came back amain.
> Oh, come forth into the storm and rout,
> And be my love in the rain (*lines* 24–32)

The poem depends on that small verb *seem*. When he says to his beloved, "Be my love in the rain," he implies that their love is somehow eternal, natural, part of the natural cycle. A closer look at the language, however, shows that the declaration of their connection to nature is simply a wishful, imaginative desire. It "seems like," but it is *not*. All that can be certain is that the power of rain will make "the hoof-prints vanish away" and that the flowers in the storm will "Expend their bloom in vain." Despite that bleak view, the poem ends with Frost's declaration of faith in their love. Again Frost returns to a willed belief. A faith that has no ground, no context, no larger system other than itself for its justification.

1908: "ACROSS THE ATLANTIC"

In "Trial by Existence," "The Lost Faith," and "A Line-Storm Song," Frost enacts his will to believe. Each poem testifies to the need to maintain a belief in some larger purpose, some design, even the divine. In the absence of empirical proof Frost makes use of a new kind of realism in his poetry—a straightforward diction that mimics the regular sound of everyday speech, along with a rigorous and often exacting attention to specific detail. His poems from 1900 to 1907 are at once bleak and hopeful as they manifest a pragmatic poetics.

This new poetics can also be found in the only poem from 1908 that he published, "Across the Atlantic." Published on March 26 in the *Independent*, the poem received the unusual, even lavish, merit of almost a full page.[24] It tells the story of someone, perhaps Frost, who is staring off into the ocean. Looking at the sea, the person does not find the conventional genteel allegory and symbol. A frank imitation of similar poems by both William Wordsworth, "The World Is Too Much with Us Late and Soon," and Matthew Arnold, "Dover Beach," Frost updates their disillusionment by bringing the problem of technological advances and scientific amoral detachment to this ocean scene. Where Wordsworth and Arnold play on various symbolic associations of the sea's moral, ethical meaning—Arnold's "sea of faith," Wordsworth's pagan "creed outworn" that had once assigned Neptune to the sea—Frost sees in the sea only another terrain for modern technological advancement.

In his poem the ocean no longer threatens. In the modern world of 1908, the ocean is little more than another highway. The era of giant ocean-going vessels and luxury travel on those vessels, not to mention international trade, has riddled the sea with ships: "Too many have come with sails, to sink them all; / And now they trample flat the waves they run. / Ever the sea is less the sundering sea." The Atlantic had once kept people and continents apart. What had been a mighty metaphor and symbol has now been "trampled flat." The poem's refrain, "Ever the sea is less the sundering sea," laments the fall of this symbol, of symbolism itself.

Chapter Seven

•

Robert Frost's New Poetic Realism, 1909–10

"Into Mine Own," "The Flower Boat"

IN 1909 Robert Frost published two poems, one of which, "Into Mine Own," defends and describes the philosophy behind his realism.[1] That poem, I believe, should be read as his first published *ars poetica*. Published in the *New England Magazine* in large font, on its own page, the poem asserts the need for the will to believe.

> One of my wishes is that those dark trees,
> So old and firm they scarcely show the breeze,
> Were not, as 'twere, the merest mask of gloom,
> But stretched away unto the edge of doom.
> I should not be withheld but that some day
> Into their vastness I should steal away,
> Fearless of ever finding open land,
> Or highway where the slow wheel pours the sand.
> I do not see why I should e'er turn back,
> Or those should not set forth upon my track
> To overtake me, who should miss me here
> And long to know if still I held them dear.
> They would not find me changed from him they knew—
> Only more sure of all I thought was true.[2]

The poem's sonnet form does not follow a conventional Shakespearean or Petrarchan pattern. It is divided into five stanzas and ends in a couplet according to the Shakespearean model. It also neatly divides into an octave of exposition and a sestet of explanation according to the Petrarchan model. It is at once both and neither. The form nicely complements the thematic dilemma.

That dilemma is stated in the poem's first two stanzas. There Frost says that to look for value and meaning in otherwise random events requires heroism and courage. For instance, rather than invoke a symbol that would adopt the conventional association of nature with God and spiritual design, Frost says instead in realist fashion that the woods refer only to themselves. The dark trees from an empirical point of view support no final teleological interpretation. Knowing that stark empirical fact, however, Frost cannot help but bring to those woods the long history of literary symbolism associated with the adjective *dark*. The woods are just trees, even as they are also the place of evil, death, and suffering. Knowing all this, he says, he would go into those woods anyway: "Fearless of ever finding open land, / Or highway where the slow wheel pours the sand." Read literally, which is to say, realistically, these lines declare his goal of plunging into the heart of the dark woods. Like a contemporary scientist, Frost would go to the uncharted area with the goal of finding out more. Never mind that no road, no map, no path exists. Courage, says the poem, comes from an acceptance of random purposelessness and from a willingness, despite that knowledge, to seek answers all the same. In that sense he mirrors the courage of Charles Darwin, whose book, *Voyage of the Beagle,* Frost loved and kept with him wherever he moved. Darwin had to give up the Christian view of design if he wished to undertake his trip around the world in search of origins.

This is also a poem about poetry, or about the poetic tradition of heroes who search for meaning. For instance, I noted that its sonnet form alludes to Petrarch. Its subject also alludes to Dante, who opens his great *Divine Comedy* by saying that he was lost in a "*selva oscura,*" a dark woods, which becomes his metaphor for a lack of faith and certitude. Like Dante, Frost associates the woods of his poem with intellectual, spiritual ignorance, darkness, and the inability to know. Unlike Dante, who conjures Virgil to be his guide, Frost has no guide, unless one reads the poetic tradition in this case, the sonnet form itself, as his guide. Petrarch made the sonnet into what he termed "a little house," where one could construct an argument in eight lines and then elaborate and explain it in the following six. Dante follows Petrarch's example, and Frost follows both.

In his concluding sestet, divided in two stanzas, Frost meditates on the implications of his courage and in so doing also alludes to Dante's progenitor Virgil and his *Aeneid* and even to Homer and the *Odyssey*. To undertake the journey into the woods in the hope of finding some meaning does prove Frost's courage, but it also requires him to be entirely alone. He will have to leave behind all those "who miss me here." The quester as hero returns the poem to the long heritage from Homer to Virgil and to Dante. Recast here the solitary journey means that, like Ulysses, Frost must leave behind family, friends, everyone. He undertakes an individual's solitary, heroic quest for meaning and faith in a world that lacks both. Aware of that implication, the narrator of the sestet imagines how those left behind might react. If they really missed him, they could go into the woods and follow. Finding him, they could then ask if he loved them so little that he abandoned them in quest of some larger sense of meaning. In other words, the quester must have the courage not only to take the journey alone but also the courage to ignore and even abandon those loved ones.

In the final couplet Frost offers a conclusion, an epigram similar to the conventional closing couplet of a Shakespearean sonnet. If those he left behind nonetheless went in search of him, "They would not find me changed from him they knew— / Only more sure of all I thought was true." The implication is ambiguous at best. If they went in search of him, they would find that he was all the more convinced, but of what? Would he be more convinced than ever that he did not really need those he left? That relationships, family, love are not the real source of value in this world? Or, when they found him, would they find a man satisfied that his quest, in yielding nothing, had given him the answer that there is nothing to find? No Platonic or Christian value is located somewhere outside the woods, the natural world we all inhabit. Might this be his subtle way of saying such a quest is needless? Might he be saying that true meaning resides in the relationships people develop where they live? Perhaps. As with "Trial by Existence," this poem not only combines two kinds of sonnet but also the older symbolic, highly allusive poetry of the genteel tradition and a new realism. By combining those two styles, the poem brings the genteel concept of heroism and courage, even of duty, into the contemporary scientific world of strict empiricism.

It is impossible to know what the editor of the *New England Magazine* made of this poem. We know he liked it enough to publish it. Something of the way he read it can be gleaned from its placement a little more than halfway through the issue on a full page. The poem was printed at the top of the page, and below it is a lovely design that filled the rest of the page. Following the poem was "Our Birds," a field guide to local New England birds, illustrated with photographs.[3] Nor was this that issue's only poem. Also included were William Addison Houghton's "Colonial Dames" and Anna Perlsius Chandler's allusive and symbolic hymn to the beauty of birds. That poem again demonstrates through its contrast with Frost just how far he had taken realism into American poetry.

> **To a Brown Thrush**
> Thou voice of spring at floodtide, sing again!
> I feel the season's joy, yet mutely long
> To give it utterance, for words were vain
> To body forth the gladness of thy song.
> Poised on the topmost twig of yonder tree,
> In rapt abandon, thou dost sway and sing,
> Perfect expression of the ecstasy,
> Which cometh with the glad, life-giving spring![4]

Compared to Chandler's poem, Frost's diction in "Into Mine Own" stands out. Unlike Chandler, who addresses "Thou voice of spring at floodtide," Frost's poem uses only sparse everyday language. And while Chandler draws the connection between bird, beauty, and God directly, Frost breaks the all-too-easy symbolic association of nature's fauna with spiritual essence only to ask if one ought to make such breaks at all.

In her study of the era's fiction Nancy Glazener makes the point that readers had to learn how to "read for realism." Similarly one could say that for a hundred years most American readers had been trained not to read realism in poetry but rather to read for symbolism and allegory. Although I believe Frost questions that tradition in this poem, it seems likely that the editors of the *New England Magazine* missed the realism in this poem and read it as they read Chandler's. Even today critics and scholars attentive to Frost's subtleties have largely overlooked this poem. Of those who discuss it, Richard Poirier's comments from 1979 remain the most pertinent.[5] Attending to the poem's grammar, Poirier writes, "it is consciously designed to make [it] more accessible than in fact it is." In other words the grammar tells us that the poem is just a thought experiment, a speculation, a "what-if?" As Poirier reminds us, the poem concerns "a journey that he had never started, a journey which would in any event depend on conditions . . . that do not exist." Rather than read the allusion to Dante's *selva oscura*, Poirier picks up on the Shakespearean sonnet form and reads the poem in light of Shakespeare's sonnet 116. There the final lines before the couplet (lines 10–11) say that "Love alters not with his brief hours and weeks, / But bears it out even to the edge of doom." Love, says Shakespeare, is eternal, and Robert Frost, says Poirier, tests that declaration by wondering what would happen if he left his beloved and ventured far into the woods. Would his beloved follow? And even if she followed him to prove her love, would he still love her for all that? In my view Frost's poem, a meditation on love more than a meditation on meaning and belief, brings the fundamentally genteel interest in serious matters to a time when readers trained in genteel poetry were more interested in "the gladness of thy song" and "life-giving spring," to quote Chandler's poem.

1909: "THE FLOWER BOAT"

In the spring of 1909 Frost published "The Flower Boat," his second poem to appear in the *Youth's Companion,* the favorite magazine of his youth and a household favorite among his own children.[6] Frost's poem told just the kind of story the *Youth's Companion* typically printed. The magazine printed stories and poems for families to read aloud for entertainment and edification on cold nights and boring afternoons. The poem tells the story of a fisherman retired from his dangerous, even heroic, life in the cod fisheries off the George's Bank. Now old, the sea captain cultivates a garden planted in the very boat he had once taken out to sea.

> The fisherman's swapping a yarn for a yarn
> Under the hand of the village barber,
> And here in the angle of house and barn
> His deep-sea dory has found a harbor.
>
> At anchor she rides the sunny sod
> As full to the gunnel with flowers a-growing
> As ever she turned her home with cod
> From George's Bank when winds were blowing.

> And I know from that Elysian freight
> She will brave but once more the Atlantic weather,
> When dory and fisherman sail by fate
> To seek for the Happy Isles together.

In three rhyming quatrains of mostly tetrameter lines, Frost tells a tale suited for a ballad. The next time the fisherman and his dory go out to sea, the poem implies, they will go in a classic fisherman's funeral that sends the old man's corpse to rest in the Atlantic itself. It is just the sort of tale that the editor, Mark Antony Dewolfe Howe, admired and the kind of tale his readers expected him to publish.[7]

If one reads this poem in the earlier context of "Into Mine Own," and "Across the Atlantic," rather than as an adventure tale for the *Youth's Companion,* its realist subtlety stands out. Like those two poems, this poem mourns the loss of meaning. The profundity associated with the sea and even the meaning of heroism become diminished things. The icon of coastal New England, the image of New England self-reliance and indus- try—the lone fisherman—finds himself retired in a village getting his hair cut. His vessel is now little more than a bower for blossoms. The boat be- come a garden becomes an apt metaphor for the transformation of a poetic tradition that had once been vital, pragmatic, full of things. No longer fit for anything but beauty, American poetry, like the boat—and American poets, like the fisherman—should only wait to die. Read in the context of Frost's other published poems, and of realism, this poem's final quatrain implies that the individual courage of either poets or poems (captains or boats) is no longer possible.

Chapter Eight

•

Coming into His Own
Robert Frost, 1910–12

"Reluctance"

IN THE FALL of 1909 the Pinkerton Academy's longtime headmaster, Dr. George Washington Bingham, retired. The new principal, Ernest Silver, a man younger than Frost, was the son of the man who had taken such a shine to Frost a decade earlier, the man from the school board who had procured Frost's teaching job in Salem, New Hampshire. Like his father, Ernest Silver admired Frost, although their relationship initially suffered from no small amount of tension. In fact Silver at first expected to fire Frost and came to admire him only after the state superintendent, Henry C. Morrison, came for a visit and did little but praise the poet's unique teaching style.[1] From that point on Silver treated Frost with respect and eventually even asked him to recast the English curriculum for the school.

Frost probably had as little respect for Silver as he at first had for Frost. While Silver may have marked Frost for termination when he arrived, Frost likely had little admiration for Silver either. As the new principal, Silver represented what Frost most detested in American culture. Against the classical curriculum beloved by genteels like Frost, Silver advocated a modern instrumental, practical education. As principal, Silver wanted to see "new teachers, newer courses.... Domestic science and Agriculture, with more up-to-date emphasis on 'practical learning.'"[2] When Super-intendent Morrison found in Frost the kind of teaching that he thought should occur throughout the state, Silver, to his credit, changed course and asked Frost to redesign the school's English curriculum. Savvy in this as in his poetry, Frost made the new curriculum *seem* practical even as it preserved the genteel tradition's attention to moral and ethical values. As

129

a practical matter Frost did away with traditional textbooks in favor of teaching the actual literature, unexpurgated and unexcerpted. He also had students read the same poetry anthology that had changed his life, Palgrave's *Golden Treasury*.[3] Such innovations appealed to Silver, but when it came to the fundamental ideals of humanities for their own sake, Silver had little interest in Frost's educational theories.

In 1911, after two years as principal of Pinkerton Academy, Silver was offered the presidency of Plymouth Normal School, the New Hampshire state teachers' college in Plymouth. By then Frost, through the superintendent, had gained a reputation on the speaking circuit (lecturing to other teachers) and had gained respect from Silver with his new literature curriculum. Obviously an intellectual, Frost made no secret of his interest in William James, Henri Bergson, and psychology. When Silver accepted the position as head of Plymouth Normal School, he asked Frost to join him. Unfortunately Plymouth's English department had no openings, so Silver asked if Frost would leave Pinkerton to teach psychology and the history of education; Silver wanted Frost to join him regardless.[4]

Several weeks before receiving that offer, horror again entered Frost's life. To be close to Pinkerton Academy, the Frost family moved from their Derry farm to a rented house in Derry Village in 1911. That same year their landlord killed himself. Shortly after that traumatic event, Silver made his offer and Frost, at thirty-seven, almost the age of his own father when he died, immediately agreed. The family moved north to Plymouth, and Frost became a college teacher.

Although he took the job and quit his post at Pinkerton Academy, he did not intend to make his appointment permanent. Over Silver's objections he signed a one-year contract. As it happened, 1911 also marked the end of his grandfather's ten-year trust fund lease on the thirty-acre Derry farm. At last Frost could claim ownership. To write his poetry he expected to sell the farm and intended to live for a year off the windfall and the new bump to $800 a year from his grandfather's trust fund. But first he had committed himself to teach for a year at Plymouth.

After moving there with his family Frost began the fall semester teaching prospective teachers William James's *Psychology: The Briefer Course*, as well as James's more recent collection, *Talks to Teachers on Psychology*. Sidney Cox, whom Frost befriended that year, recalled the intellectual atmosphere of the time. Cox was but a twenty-two-year-old local teacher at Plymouth High School when he met Frost at Plymouth. The two, however, soon became lifelong friends. Said Cox of that era: "We were rid of the old taboos, the fear of the supernatural was weakening, the primacy of reason was more generally acknowledged, art was more and more directed to the solution of the human problem, and when the profit motive had been discredited and war eliminated progress would be swifter."[5]

In this context Frost submitted his poems, among them, another *ars poetica,* "Reluctance." He submitted that poem to the *Atlantic,* where the first reader, a subeditor, rejected it outright and never forwarded it to the editor, Ellery Sedgwick. Much later Frost recalled that "during the years on the farm I had given all the good magazines a chance at my work. The office readers were dead set against me."[6]

Frost was not the only poet to incorporate realist techniques in his work. By 1911 enough such poets had been publishing realist work that more than a few literary cognoscenti discerned a movement. It would eventually be labeled "the New Poetry," signifying poetry that favored regular diction, avoided archaisms, and wrote about the conditions and people of urban and rural America. The first indication that there was such a movement afoot came as a result of a contest. In 1911 the intellectual general-interest magazine the *Forum* sponsored a well-publicized contest for an anthology, the *Lyric Year* to include one hundred poems.[7] Notably it offered a large prize for the best poem. Once published, the *Lyric Year* brought together a host of older and new, otherwise mostly unknown, poets. Reading it, one could hardly fail to notice that reform of the sort Robert Frost had been writing was now in the air.[8]

Although no record exists to prove it, it seems all but certain that following his rejection from the *Atlantic,* Robert Frost submitted "Reluctance" and another poem, "My November Guest," to the *Lyric Year* contest. It seems likely since we know he submitted both poems to the *Forum,* whose editors rejected "Reluctance" and accepted "My November Guest." Why did they reject "Reluctance"? I suspect that, compared to "My November Guest," it seemed too much like a conventional genteel poem. I say this because somehow "Reluctance" ended up with the aestheticist publisher of decadence and symbolism, Thomas B. Mosher. While there is no record to support my supposition, it seems likely that after rejecting it, the

Forum's publisher, Kennerley, who knew Mosher quite well, forwarded "Reluctance" to him. Mosher likely thought it belonged in his magazine or in one of his publishing company's book catalogs, which often included poetry. At any rate, however it happened, Mosher, editor of the beautifully produced magazine of aesthetic poetry the *Bibelot*, and publisher of similarly beautiful editions of poets associated mostly with British aestheticism, received "Reluctance." He admired it so much he decided to publish it and saw to its second publication, sending it along to his friend, the editor of the *Youth's Companion*. Out of the blue, Frost not only learned that Mosher would publish the poem but also received a check for the amazing sum of $25 (nearly $600 in 2013 dollars).[9] Frost wrote to Mosher saying, "What should my poetry bring me but a check for twenty-five dollars, which is more than it ever brought before at one time. Some part of this belongs to you in simple poetic justice. Five dollars, say. . . . But I can and herewith do, send five dollars for books; . . . I copy on the inside of this sheet the poem by which I earned it, glad of the chance to show poem of mine to one whose life is so conspicuously devoted to the cause of poetry." The poem he copied was "Reluctance." In a later letter, again referring to "Reluctance" and "My November Guest," Frost wrote, "I do not say that

The *Youth's Companion* was a decidedly family-oriented magazine. From the Robert Frost Collection of Pat Alger.

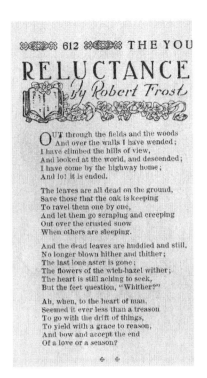

612 THE YOU

RELUCTANCE
by Robert Frost

OUT through the fields and the woods
    And over the walls I have wended;
I have climbed the hills of view,
And looked at the world, and descended;
I have come by the highway home;
And lo! it is ended.

The leaves are all dead on the ground,
Save those that the oak is keeping
To ravel them one by one,
And let them go scraping and creeping
Out over the crusted snow
When others are sleeping.

And the dead leaves are huddled and still,
No longer blown hither and thither;
The last lone aster is gone;
The flowers of the witch-hazel wither;
The heart is still aching to seek,
But the feet question, "Whither?"

Ah, when, to the heart of man,
Seemed it ever less than a treason
To go with the drift of things,
To yield with a grace to reason,
And bow and accept the end
Of a love or a season?

"Reluctance" as it appeared in the *Youth's Companion*. From the Robert Frost Collection of Pat Alger.

either of them heralds a new force in literature. Indeed I think I have others still under cover that more nearly represent what I am going to be. . . . My great difficulty is going to be to get a hearing with the crowd-deafened editors."[10] Perhaps because Frost had lamented his luck in getting his poetry published, Mosher decided to forward "Reluctance" to his friend at the *Youth's Companion*. Whatever the reason, he did send it to Mark Anthony Dewolfe Howe, who did publish "Reluctance" in the November issue. Given that at least four editors at some of the most interesting and influential magazines in the nation had taken a look at the poem, I turn to it.

"RELUCTANCE" (1911)

Unlike "The Ghost House" (1906) and "The Flower Boat" (1909), which the *Youth's Companion* had also published, "Reluctance" told no tale and offered no family entertainment. Instead it charts a philosophical, ethical problem and engages the psychology of the speaker. A relatively old poem by 1911, it had been in Frost's files since at least 1899.[11] As with so many of his poems, it is not clear what, if any, revisions he had made during that time. In its published version, though, is a mix of genteel symbolism and allegory and the particulars of the actual world as in "Quest of the Orchis." That mix also explores a similar theme concerning the validity of faith in a world of scientific empiricism. As published the poem relates an anecdote in four stanzas:

> Out through the fields and the woods
> And over the walls I have wended;
> I have climbed the hills of view
> And looked at the world, and descended;
> I have come by the highway home,
> And lo! it is ended.
> The leaves are all dead on the ground,
> Save those that the oak is keeping
> To ravel them one by one,
> And let them go scraping and creeping
> Out over the crusted snow
> When others are sleeping.
> And the dead leaves are huddled and still,
> No longer blown hither and thither;
> The last lone aster is gone;
> The flowers of the witch-hazel wither;
> The heart is still aching to seek,
> But the feet question "Whither?"
> Ah, when, to the heart of man,
> Seemed it ever less than a treason
> To go with the drift of things,
> To yield with a grace to reason,
> And bow and accept the end
> Of a love or a season?[12]

The poem tells the story of a man who leaves his beloved in search of something, an "it." Returning in the dead of winter, he says, "And lo, it is ended." What is the "it" that has come to an end? The season he left behind? Or is it belief in something larger, such as a transcendent Platonic realm where value, ethics, morality, ideas of the good can be said to reside? Has his faith, in the religious sense of the term, come to an end?

The poem's rhyme scheme echoes its ambiguous theme. The end rhymes of the first three lines mirror the sound of the second three lines, a pattern continued in each of the four six-line stanzas. The first two stanzas assert the theme. The verb *ravel*, which is unusual in Frost's poetry, suggests that action, when it happens in nature, has no ulterior transcendent meaning.[13]

No figure, human or god, plays with the leaves, as if to say that nature, in and of itself, offers no metaphors of hope or transcendence. In itself nature exists as an amoral scientifically objective set of facts. As such life and death have no other meaning than chance survival permits.

In the fourth stanza Frost becomes dissatisfied with that perspective. He asks, "But the feet question 'Whither?'" *Feet* in this line do not refer just to his walking in the woods. They also refer to a unit of metrical measurement, the poetic line's anapests. The metrical feet, in other words, ask Whither? as if to ask, "What *is* the purpose even of poetry?" What might poetry have to say about the era's fundamental question: In the absence of traditional faith is any moral meaning certain or valid? The final stanza gives an answer very much in keeping with Frost's intellectual guide, William James's argument in *Pragmatism* (1907). Rather than commit to some proof one way or the other, Frost instead says he is simply "going with the drift of things":

> Ah, when to the heart of man
> Seemed it ever less than a treason
> To go with the drift of things,
> To yield with a grace to reason,
> And bow and accept the end
> Of a love or a season.

Pragmatically these lines say that he must rationally accept that death is the only certainty, not just for him but also for all organic life. In these woods no flowers bloom, leaves are dead, and none of that has moral purpose or significance. It is just decay and death. The drift of the then-current intellectual climate also would have seen Frost reach such a conclusion. His feet, poetic and corporeal, however, resist that drift. They will not take that trip.[14] As a matter of pragmatic necessity he again wills himself into belief, into faith. The very words, meter, and rhymes of the poem, I submit, stand metaphorically for the genteel tradition of belief. Poetry in and of itself, as words set into rhythmic patterns, becomes a means by which Frost can reject the materialist drift of empiricism. In this poem, and in poetry as such, empiricism also refers to what one feels, the facts of one's emotional, psychological state. This is what Frost had learned from James and even from Munsterberg. To allow empiricism to apply only to reason and not one's emotions, he says in this poem, is nothing less than becoming a traitor to one's own heart.

FROST, REALISM, AND HENRI BERGSON

"Reluctance" gave voice to Robert Frost's dissatisfaction with the current intellectual and artistic "drift of things." It expressed his reluctance to follow the empirical path of reason into the dead end of belief's absence. The will to believe expressed in this poem, as I have argued, depended mostly on the theories of William James. As James had said in *Pragmatism,* "The essential contrast [with pragmatism] is that for rationalism reality is ready-made and complete from all eternity, while for pragmatism it is still in the making, and awaits part of its complexion from the future." By this he meant to make room for belief, such as one finds in this poem. As James said, "Let us apply this notion to the salvation of the world. What does it pragmatically mean to say that this is possible? It means that some of the conditions of the world's deliverance do actually exist. The more of them there are existent, the fewer preventing conditions you can find, the better-grounded is the salvation's possibility, the more PROBABLE does the fact of the deliverance become." James made a point of insisting, too, that the French philosopher Henri Bergson had made these points already. By 1911 Frost, too, had found Bergson. Frost's discovery was not unusual. Given his intellectual preoccupations at the time, it would have been more strange for Frost not to read Bergson's *Creative Evolution* when it was published than to read it. At the time Bergson had become an international figure. In a recent reconsideration of his impact, for instance, the editors explain, "In the early years of the twentieth century, it appeared, then, that Bergson, not, say, Sigmund Freud, would lead the revolution in understanding memory, time, and more generally, human consciousness." In 1912 Bergson's chief advocate other than James, Edouard Le Roy, a philosopher, mathematician, and a member of the College de France, published a book on Bergson (translated into English in 1913) in which he declared, "Beyond any doubt, and by common consent, Mr. Henri Bergson's work will appear to future eyes among the most characteristic, fertile, and glorious of our era. It marks a never-to-be-forgotten date in history: it opens up a phase of metaphysical thought." It would have been surprising had Frost not read Bergson, given how often Frost's intellectual hero, William James, referred to Bergson and how often he appeared in the magazines Frost typically read. As the editors of the recent assessment of Bergson's influence on modern writers put it, he was "widely popular during his lifetime, within and without literary circles." Recalling a dinner with Bergson in 1911, Bertrand Russell, the British philosopher, wrote, "All England has gone mad about him for some reason."[15]

What did Frost find in Bergson's *Creative Evolution* (1911)? Most likely he found the empirical proof of faith he craved, a proof that went beyond James's pragmatic test of mere usefulness. Bergson made it possible to claim that faith, belief, and consciousness itself were empirically verifiable and real. According to Bergson, life, "the force that through the green fuse drives the flower," as Dylan Thomas puts it in his poem of that title, is such that contemporary empirical science has no way of isolating and measuring it. Referring to it in French as an *"élan vital,"* this life force is empirically verifiable. It is, says Bergson, apprehended and obvious to each individual through her or his instinct. In their study of the changing idea of objectivity throughout this period, the historians Lorraine Daston and Peter Galison describe Bergson as a "radical empiricist" and associate his brand of empiricism with that of his great admirer, William James. By *empiricism* they mean to point to the importance of experiential firsthand verification of any object of inquiry. Not for Bergson, James, and their admirers the pure speculative logic and other types of idealism. Bergson meant to counter any logical defense of a life force through firsthand verifiable experiential encounter. A recent Bergson scholar, for instance, summarizes the book as follows: "If there is a conclusion that emerges from *Creative Evolution,* it is, on the contrary, that human intelligence and positive science, there where they exercise their own object, are very much in contact with the real and more and more penetrate the absolute."[16]

In *Creative Evolution* Bergson meant to prove the existence of what so many philosophers and scientists had dismissed as "consciousness," "the soul," "the psyche"; he wanted to do so to further prove the existence of a particular life force in all organic matter. To make his case Bergson first describes the present materialist moment as "a certain new scholasticism that has grown up during the latter half of the nineteenth century around the physics of Galileo, as the old scholasticism grew up around Aristotle." Against such materialism Bergson would offer empirical proof of the *élan vital*. In *Creative Evolution* he argues that one must take intuition seriously as empirical data. In the book's last paragraph, for instance, Bergson concentrates on the intuitive and linguistic use of a particular set of metaphors, ascent and descent. According to Bergson, when we refer to biology and organic life, we use metaphors of ascent. Is this not because we assume organic life implies a unique force, an élan vital? To speak of such a force as an ascension, as an upward movement, is a result of our intuitive sense that such a force is associated with a moral good, also reflected in metaphors of ascent. Against such metaphors of ascent, Bergson also explains that language uses metaphors of descent for inorganic matter as well as for the dissolution and decay of the life force. Why, he wonders, do intuition and language associate the third law of thermodynamics, that all things tend toward dissolution and decay, with metaphors of descent? Our language draws attention to their moral failings. These metaphors of upward and downward motion, Bergson says, refer not just to organic and inorganic matter but also to a material and immaterial view of the life force. He writes, "Matter, we have said, is weighted with geometry; and matter, the reality which *descends,* endures only by its connection with that which *ascends*. But life and consciousness are this very ascension. When once we have grasped them in their essence by adopting their movement, we understand how the rest of reality is derived from them."[17] For Bergson the life force (élan vital) that every person recognizes through his or her own intuition has already long been associated with moral belief through the metaphors of ascent and descent.

Is it, however, accurate to make that connection? Not necessarily. According to Bergson, the impulse, the force, the élan vital that we recognize as instinct and that we routinely confirm in daily language can only be apprehended through an understanding of time which he calls *durée*. Rather than understand time as a series of points, a static sequence on a line easily divisible into segments, Bergson understands time as a kind of momentum in which we are implicated. According to him, we cannot put ourselves outside of time. Furthermore, as durée, time does not, he says, necessarily head towards some greater good, as religious people insist. Nor does durée necessarily imply a universe whose life force is subject mostly to random chance as Darwinians and strict empiricists insist. In a recent overview of *Creative Evolution's* argument, David Scott explains that change, development, even Darwinian natural selection itself, "exists according to the *internal* necessity of its own nature. The movement of immanence that compels something to exist determines what compels the production of the new, of change."[18] Scott calls Bergson's concept of time, or *durée,* a "reformed finalism." By that he means that in Bergson the creative element of evolution is precisely the impulse toward design. Bergson's understanding of biology, of life, of natural selection accounts for design. Bergson, in short, makes plain that such design cannot be understood outside its own terms. It can only be understood, he argues, as coming from within the life force itself. Through his concept of *durée,* then, Bergson dismisses blind chance as the only source of causation, finality, of life's ultimate purpose. Given that one *can* find design, a theological purpose for life is made possible. So long as one accounts for durée, for that particular understanding of time, one may very well locate the absolute and call it God. If not, one finds oneself trapped either in linguistic illusions or in a "radical mechanism" that is equally illusory.

Through his study of durée, and of intuition, Bergson meant to prove to science that it needed metaphysics and philosophy. "So understood, philosophy is not only the turning of the mind homeward, the coincidence of human consciousness with the living principle whence it emanates, a contact with the creative effort: it is the study of becoming in general, it is true evolutionism and consequently the true continuation of science." Without philosophy, without the metaphysical understanding of time, evolution as natural selection itself will forever remain incomplete, only half-understood, Bergson says. Evolution, he says, needs to be understood as the philosophical concept of *becoming.*[19] Without going into more detail, suffice to say that Robert Frost found Bergson's arguments deeply compelling.

In one of the few documented instances of his reading, biographers know Frost read *Creative Evolution* on the train after leaving his home in Plymouth that December.[20] The occasion was his visit to his mentors the Wards in their New Jersey home. On the train ride down, he likely read the book in preparation for his visit to the Congregationalist minister and editor, William Hayes Ward. Recall that, even as a high schooler, Frost had annoyed William by defending realist ideas of poetic speech against the musical views of Sidney Lanier. Frost also had far more interest in Darwin and was far more skeptical about faith than the minister. Bergson, he must have thought, would allow him to forge a rapprochement in what he expected to be a fine debate. Shortly after arriving at their Newark home, the debate did occur. The two did not agree. Ward had no interest in finding empirical proof for faith, as he was content to accept God on the terms of that faith, which by definition required no proof at all.

It seems likely, then, that after defending Bergson's philosophy to Ward, Frost returned to New Hampshire where he began to incorporate Bergson's ideas into his poetry. In an odd way, even "Reluctance" made a Bergsonian argument. It became, as every poem could be said to become, a tangible manifestation of the poet's inner intuition and consciousness. In microscopic form does not a poem mimic Bergson's large-scale conception of creative evolution? Many years later, in 1939, in the introduction Frost wrote to accompany his collected poetry, he used a simile to define his poetry that seems to emerge from the pages of Bergson: "Like a piece of ice on a hot stove the poem must ride on its own melting." There he implies that the internal dynamics of the poem itself, the creative evolution of its own inner necessity, compel its forward drive to meaning. Said another way, Frost defined poetry in this same essay as that which "begins in delight and ends in wisdom."[21]

AUGUST 1912: ROBERT FROST GOES TO ENGLAND

Shortly after his discovery of Bergson, Frost finalized the sale of the Derry farm, quit his teaching position at Plymouth Normal School, and with his family embarked on a new life in England.[22] Why England? Frost family legend says that Elinor very much wanted to go to England and "sleep under thatch."[23] In fact the decision was a bit more complicated. When Frost had taught at Pinkerton, he had become friends with one his students, John Bartlett. By 1911 Bartlett had married and moved to Vancouver, British Columbia, to make his living in journalism. Like Frost, Bartlett was a literary and athletic young man and had abandoned college to marry his high school love. In fact, according to Bartlett's daughter, Frost had encouraged her parents' romance when both had been his students at Pinkerton. Frost played the role of mentor to Bartlett, the same role that Susan Hayes Ward played for him. In one of his letters to Bartlett, Frost said he had bought himself a year or more to write. At the time the Frosts had made no decision as to where they would go. Bartlett invited the Frosts to Vancouver. In another family legend Elinor and Frost are supposed to have flipped a coin to see where they should go. When it came up tails for England, they went. No biographer, including me, believes the choice to have been that simple. Much later, to his friend Louis Unter-meyer, Frost said, "I went to England to write and be poor." And to Susan Hayes Ward, he wrote, upon settling in England, "my soul inclines to go apart by itself again and devise poetry."[24] According to one of his British friends, Frost said he "came to England to get his poems published where *The Golden Treasury* had been."[25] Whatever the rationale, in August 1912 the Frost family of six left New England, arriving that September in London.

At thirty-eight Frost had published fewer than twenty poems, barely enough to constitute a collection. He had never lived among literary men and women nor experienced the heady atmosphere that defined cultural centers like New York and Chicago, let alone Paris or London. Even as "the New Poetry" was becoming a fully recognizable movement in American letters, Frost had as yet been only on its outer periphery. During the next two years he would move to the center of that new movement. Through two books, *A Boy's Will* (1913) and *North of Boston* (1914), both published by a well-regarded British literary publisher, David Nutt, Frost would shape and even change the course of American realist poetry.[26]

Chapter Nine

●

Robert Frost in England
A Boy's Will

ROBERT FROST CAME to England with every hope of refining, collecting, and publishing his poetry as a book. Remarkably, six weeks after his arrival, he had the interest of a prestigious publisher, David Nutt, for *A Boy's Will*, which they would publish by the end of 1913.[1] Then, more or less by accident, in late December 1912 he just happened to walk into the very heart of the modernist explosion in New Poetry, the Poetry Bookshop, a small store and publishing house that had just opened. Learning that it would have a grand opening soirée on January 13, 1913, with readings from all the major poets, Frost made sure to be there, and the rest, as they say, is history.

On a cold evening Robert Frost walked into the grand opening celebration of the Poetry Bookshop. One of the older people present, and one of the few foreigners, he arrived with the knowledge that his book of poems would soon be published. At the time he and his family had settled into a rented cottage in Beaconsfield, "officially a town but in reality little more than a large village." It was twenty-three miles northwest of London, but it did not isolate him from literary London.[2] Wondering what he had gotten himself into, he had written in despair that September to his mentor Susan Hayes Ward:

> And now that I have proved myself as a teacher in two departments of learning [English at Pinkerton, psychology at Plymouth] without benefit of college, my soul inclines to go apart again and devise poetry. Heaven send that I go not too late in life for the emotions I expect to work in. But in any case I should not stay [in America], if only

143

for scorn of scorn—scorn of the scorn that leaves me still unnoticed among the least of the versifiers that [fill] a gap in the magazines. [By this he refers to editors' routine use of poetry as a means to fill out a page when articles ran short.] *The Forum* [which had just accepted "My November Guest"] gives me space for one more poem this year; the [*Youth's*] *Companion* [which had just accepted "October," and "Reluctance"] for two. *The Independent* [Ward herself], longest my friend, has held one of my poems unprinted now these three years [neither biographers or scholars know which poem that may have been]. So slight is my consideration. I may be too old to write the song that once I dreamed about.[3]

He had written that letter from his house, called "the Bungalow" after the English fashion. He found it through reading *T. P.'s Weekly*, a relatively new mass-market leftist publication. While still in New Hampshire, Frost had become a regular reader because John Bartlett, then living in Vancouver, regularly mailed the weekly to Frost from Canada. The weekly had been "designed by the Irish Nationalist T. P. O'Connor as a literary paper for the expanding working class and lower middle classes living in the new suburbs and reached a circulation of around 250,000."[4] Modeled on the American mass-market weeklies like *Leslie's* and the new *Saturday Evening Post, T. P.'s Weekly* had also adopted the innovations of Joseph Pulitzer and so became one of the first American-style general readership weeklies in England. In 1907 the magazine passed to the control of Holbrook Jackson, a Fabian Socialist, who, like intellectuals on both sides of the Atlantic involved in publishing, wished to assert literature's role in shaping a more democratic society.[5] Whatever Frost may have thought of Jackson's editorial socialism, he liked to read its literary coverage so much that, upon his arrival in London, he went to the magazine's offices. There he befriended a columnist, a former police officer, one of whose jobs was to write about walks in the countryside around London. Given his knowledge of the area, the columnist had been the one to suggest Beaconsfield in the first place.[6]

According to biographers, this same columnist also told Frost that the Bloomsbury publisher David Nutt would be receptive to an unknown poet with a manuscript. On this advice Frost took the manuscript for *A Boy's Will* to the Nutt firm. As Frost said later, "I showed my manuscript to the one firm. It was as simple as that."[7]

A BOY'S WILL

Robert Frost's first published book had thirty-two poems. Only eight had ever been published, either in American newspapers or general readership magazines: "Ghost House," "My November Guest," "Trial by Existence," "The Tuft of Flowers," "A Line-Storm Song," "October," "My Butterfly," and "Reluctance." He excluded four others he had published elsewhere: "The Flower Boat," "The Quest for the Orchis," "The Lost Faith," and "Across the Atlantic." Also, for some reason (biographers debate why) Frost decided to organize the book's thirty-two poems into three sections depicting the inner life of a single character called "the youth."

Combined, the poems told the inner psychological story of a boy's development into manhood. Jay Parini offers the best single-line description of the book: "The refusal to relinquish control of the self becomes, poem by poem, the unspoken subject of this collection." To that end each poem, even the ten he had previously published, carried an italicized gloss relating it to an instance in the youth's life.[8] To Jay Parini, Frost's most recent biographer, the mask of a youth was a way to protect him from the charge of sentimentality and naïveté. To others it was a way to establish his relation to two poets he most admired, A. E. Housman and W. B. Yeats. After all, Yeats had himself provided a gloss for all the poems in his collection *The Wind Among the Reeds* (1899), and Housman had a stunning success with a collection of poems telling the tale of a single boy in *A Shropshire Lad* (1896). More recent, and younger poets, such as Wilfrid Gibson, had followed in that same vein.

My view is that Frost adopted the character of a youth as a way to distance himself from the poems. In fiction realist authors had all but erased the narrator from the tale being told. In so doing they meant to remove fiction from what they considered the taint of subjectivity. A detached narrator, as Barbara Hochman argues, enabled the story's details to become more convincing, to stand out more clearly. I believe Frost feared that his poetry's psychological, philosophical, and ethical issues would too easily be read as manifestations of his own sensibility. He wished to combat the still-present genteel convention of the nineteenth century that encouraged readers to read poems as autobiographical expressions of the poet's soul. I believe Frost meant to encourage readers in a different direction. He wanted his readers to "read *for* realism," to use Nancy Glazener's choice phrase. To do so they had to be given signs and guides that would encourage them to read for the ideas and emotions contained in his poems and not just to join with him in fellowship and fine feeling.[9] To be the public poet he meant to be in the genteel tradition he had for so long imbibed, Frost found, through this narrative framing device of the youth, a way to be subjective in the poems and objective in the book. The device let him become "a transparent eyeball," as Emerson had said in his great essay "Nature," when speaking of perception itself. Frost, like Emerson walking across Boston Common, had to allow his poems to see everything while he, their author, became nothing. The mask of a youth and his biography, I submit, is Frost's attempt at such invisibility and transparency. He was so committed to that frame that, I believe, he decided not to include such already published poems as "The Flower Boat," "The Quest of the Orchis," "The Lost Faith," and "Across the Atlantic" because they did not lend themselves to the narrative arc he established for the book. Regardless, the frame failed from the first and even to Frost seemed clunky almost as soon as he published the book. After the book's first edition Frost removed the epigraphs for the poems. In so doing he removed a rather heavy-handed device for guiding his readers toward objectivity even as they engaged the subjective facts of experience.

The book's title, meanwhile, came from Henry Wadsworth Longfellow's poem "A Lost Youth." In Longfellow's poem, however, those lines are themselves a quoted refrain from an old Lapland song: "A boy's will is the wind's will / And the thoughts of youth are long, long thoughts." Using them as his title, Frost sets his book in the tradition of public poetry attentive to historical detail and social accuracy that Longfellow's poetry had encouraged. Even today Longfellow is remembered for "Hiawatha," "The Midnight Ride of Paul Revere," and "The Jewish Cemetery at Newport," poems still found in textbooks. For Frost to claim Longfellow as his progenitor in 1912 was a bold move because his tradition of genteel realism had fallen almost entirely out of fashion for poetry.

It was not certain that such a book as this should get published at all, let alone by such a prestigious press. According to Frost, M. L. Nutt, the founder's widow and owner of the publishing house, had given up on new poetry books by unknowns; she had also decided that even the knowns no longer had much of a market. As Frost recalled, she initially told him, "No market for poetry! Nobody would read it even if they bought it! After all, the day of poetry was past, and all that."[10] Frost's persistence, her perusal of the manuscript, and the nice little series of modern poetry that remained on her list convinced her to send Frost's manuscript to a poet, probably John Drinkwater, to see if it was worth publishing. Whoever her expert reader was, he recognized originality in Frost's work, finding in it an antidote to the hackneyed Edwardian poetry that filled itself with as much idealism and flowers as did its American counterpart.[11] On that poet's recommendation M. L. Nutt accepted Frost's book for her modern poets series, on October 25, 1912.

A sharp, not to say callous, businesswoman, M. L. Nutt was a French immigrant who had little faith in the economics of poetry. To compensate for what she believed would be a money loser, she had Frost sign what in any era would have been an insane contract: she would publish his book if he would agree to give her the rights to his next four.[12] Given that this first book had been at least fifteen years in the making, for Frost at the time it was a lifetime contract. Frost signed in part because he had no one in England to whom he could turn for advice about the contract. He did not want to lose a chance at publication and knew he was out of his depth when it came to London publishing; he did write of his anxiety to his few friends in America who might at least offer some insight, if only after the fact.

Meanwhile, out of the blue, just after he received the Nutt contract but before he signed it, he got a letter from Thomas B. Mosher asking if Frost had a collection he might include in Mosher's Lyric Garland Series of poetry books.[13] Frost responded that it was too late, adding, "I should like nothing better than to see my first book, *A Boy's Will*, in your Lyric Garland Series." Each book Mosher published in that series received extraordinary attention in the genteel media, often garnering reviews not just in the national but also in local newspapers and magazines. As if speaking without his internal censor, Frost essentially says in his letter to Mosher, "Why couldn't you have spoken two weeks sooner and saved me this perplexity?" Was he lying, playing to his audience, or telling the truth when he added, "It even crossed my mind to submit it to you. But under the circumstances I couldn't, lest you think I was going to come on you as the poor old man comes on the town. I brought it to England in the bottom of my trunk, more afraid of it, probably, than the Macnamara of what he carried in his." The year before, in 1910, James McNamara had bombed the *Los Angeles Times* by smuggling dynamite into the building in his trunk. In this fitting metaphor Frost does more than compare his poetry to dynamite; he also suggests it might have the power to blow up conventional genteel thought so prevalent in newspapers like the *Los Angeles Times;* Frost's manuscript was just such explosive dynamite as Mosher had long been publishing, and no doubt Frost was sorry to lose the chance to publish with him. Not willing to let Mosher's offer go to waste, Frost told him he was working on three other volumes, which he listed as *Melanism, Villagers,* and *The Sense of Wrong.* This may well have been true because of the Nutt contract's requirement. At the very least, Frost would have been thinking about them. He then asks for Mosher's advice: "Won't it seem traitorously un-American to have all my first work come out over here?" He concludes, "Have I made a serious mistake in going to David Nutt?"[14] Whatever Mosher had to say, Frost nonetheless would publish *A Boy's Will* in January 1913 with M. L. Nutt as his publisher. While he waited for publication day, he inhabited the quiet success of a man who had come to England and accomplished his primary goal.

Meanwhile, in those same months huge change occurred in the London literary world, particularly with regard to poetry. No less than three distinct types of poetry had emerged—Georgian poetry, imagist poetry, and futurist poetry. New magazines to trumpet them had also begun publishing. To provide a better sense of the revolution that occurred in London literary culture by 1912, I offer a brief tour.

A NEW REALISM FOR BRITISH POETRY

Just as in America, so too in England: poets increasingly had begun to turn away from genteel allegorical and symbolic poetry, late Victorian verse. Reacting to the Victorian limitations to tone, voice, meter, rhyme, and rhythm, younger poets turned to alternative traditions preferring rough everyday diction, plain detail, and working- and middle-class subjects, people, and scenes to the felicities of rhyme and meter. Modeling their poetry on the early Wordsworth and on the works of Virgil and Horace that had influenced him, they "had grown tired of poetic language, of huge indigestible slabs of blank verse, of [Alfred Lord Tennyson's] *In Memoriam* and [Matthew Arnold's] *Sohrab and Rustum* and all they stood for; and it became fashionable to write poetry in the idiom of everyday speech and to celebrate the little things rather than the great, the world-shaking."[15]

This was particularly true of the recent poetry of Thomas Hardy. But it could also be detected in younger poets such as John Masefield and Wilfrid Gibson, both of whom would soon spark a Georgian school (for George V, who became king in May 1910) of what I am calling realist poetry. Of these younger realists, the first to hit the market, Wilfrid Gibson, had been publishing Victorian-style poetry since 1902. His two 1907 collections, *The Stonefolds* and *On the Threshold,* made the turn to realism. They were published by a small publishing house, the Samurai Press, that had been started by Harold Monro on Fabian socialist principles. Between the press's obscurity and the poetry's unconventional topics and rhythms, they received little attention. Then, in 1910, Gibson published *Daily Bread,* a starkly realistic portrayal of working-class Britain. In 1912 he published *Fires,* a book consisting of depictions of the coal miners of northern England. Those did garner attention and began to make the realist turn in British poetry a noticeable event.

Another poet, John Masefield (1878–1967), meanwhile published a similarly realist long narrative poem, *The Everlasting Mercy* (1911), and far more than Gibson's collections this book did capture the attention of newspapers and magazines. Most likely that attention had to do with Masefield's connections. He was already earning his living on the *Manchester Guardian.* Regardless, he, like Gibson and Thomas Hardy, helped make the turn toward realism not only noticeable but also artistically viable. In *The Everlasting Mercy* (1911) one finds, for example, a poacher and a drunk—"I drunk, I fought, I poached, I whored," says the lead character.[16] This long poem resists the more conventional rhythms and themes associated with Victorian and Edwardian gentility. It instead represented the harsh realities of everyday village life in relatively plainspoken everyday language. As Edward Marsh, one of the major promoters and patrons of this New Poetry, later put it in a letter, "The vague iridescent ethereal kind [of poetry] had a long intermittent inning all through the nineteenth century, especially at the end, and Rossetti, Swinburne, and Dowson could do things which is [sic] no use trying now." Compared to that, Marsh said of *The Everlasting Mercy,* "I read [it] in such a turmoil of excitement that I have never dared read it again, for fear of not recapturing the rapture."[17] Among them, Hardy, Gibson, and Masefield seemed to have established something of a new direction for British poetry by 1912.

FALL 1912: THE MAGAZINES AND LITERATI OF LONDON

England in 1912, like America at the same time, had just experienced its own marketing revolution, much of it based on the American model, whose massive, systematized, efficient assembly lines, mass advertising, and public relations had begun to appear in Europe and especially in England. In the previous thirty years British intellectuals had witnessed an ongoing struggle between an economic system dedicated to profit at any cost and a set of older humanist ideals. The struggle put the humanists on the losing side, as had been the case for intellectuals in the United States. To make their case in the public sphere, British poets had chosen to pierce the Victorian veil of mediocrity just as American poets had begun to do with the American veil of Comstockery.

Unlike the Americans, British writers, especially poets, often belonged to the political and economic elite and were fixtures of that elite's publications. Magazines like the *Athenaeum, Academy, Spectator, Saturday Review,* and *Cornhill*; quarterlies like *Blackwood's* and the *Edinburgh Review*; and other reviews, such as the *Westminster, Fortnightly, Contemporary, Nineteenth Century,* and *National,* included on their staffs no end of poets. At the same time a great many poets were also members of the ruling caste. For instance the senior poet of the era, Robert Bridges (1844–1930), was appointed poet laureate in 1913, sealing his reputation as "the figurehead of English poetry on any fair adjustment of seniority and merit." A doctor and wealthy patrician, graduate of Eton and Oxford, he had made purification of the English language his singular passion. Reminiscent of Sidney Lanier's view, Bridges held that poetry, as a language's purest expression, had to follow precise, even scientifically accurate, metrical and rhythmic patterns.[18]

Another peculiarity of the British publishing scene compared to the American is the relatively late advent of stark commercialism there. Based on the American example, it arrived in British newspapers (leading to the famous "tabloid press") only in 1896, when the *London Daily Mail* brought to England the same kind of journalism, though dedicated to largely different political ends, as that of Pulitzer's and Hearst's newspapers. The *Daily Mail* soon became the leading daily in the nation and forever changed the landscape of mass-market publishing. The paper even went so far as to establish a separate weekly book review supplement with the simple title of *Books*. The *Pall Mall Gazette,* another mass-circulation newspaper, soon added to the surge in British publishing for the general readership of this era. *T. P.'s Weekly,* Frost's favorite British periodical, was founded in this new publishing industry in 1902. These new mass-circulation dailies, weeklies, and monthlies, like their American counterparts, also covered books. In a defensive reaction the distinctly upper-class *Times* of London (a newspaper that traced its lineage to the beginning of the eighteenth century) introduced its *Times Literary Supplement* in 1902. By 1912 the *TLS* had become the leading voice of respectable opinion (*Books* actually went out of business in 1907).

In general, the British genteel publications found themselves drawn increasingly into a competitive relationship with the British mass-market publications. By 1912 intellectual mass-market weeklies included the politically oriented *New Age, Athenaeum, Academy, Spectator, Saturday Review,* and *Cornhill,* and new mass-market weeklies included *T. P.'s Weekly* and the *Strand.* As for the monthlies—some, like *Blackwood's,* were nearly two hundred years old— and others, like the *Westminster Review,* the *Fortnightly Review, Contemporary Review, Nineteenth Century Review, National Review,* and *English Review,* appealed to the same genteel readership as did *Blackwood's.* To these, one could add some intellectual quarterlies, like the venerable *Edinburgh Review* (which had actually defined the very concept of a commercial intellectual quarterly two hundred years earlier). Other magazines devoted to books, such as *Book Monthly* (established in 1903), followed.

Just as in America, too, a distinctively literary group of little magazines associated with small presses also began publishing in these years, including the *English Review, New Age, Poetry Review, Poetry and Dra-*

ma, Rhythm, and the variously named entity *Freewoman/New Freewoman/Egoist.* Because each of these publications would have some impact on Robert Frost's poetic life while he lived in England between 1912 and 1915, I turn to an extended treatment of a few. Again, there is a difference between the British and the American publishing scenes. In England the editors and publishers of these little magazines intended them to be commercial ventures. They were meant to shape and influence the literate population and to shape the direction of British literature. In the United States, in contrast, few "little magazines" had such grand designs.

THE *POETRY REVIEW* AND HAROLD MONRO

Before he opened his Poetry Bookshop, Harold Monro (1879–1932) had spent more than a decade instigating a quiet revolution in British literary circles. By the time he opened his shop, British poets had established a number of professional organizations, including the Poetry Recital Society. By 1912 it had dropped its middle name and become merely the Poetry Society. It published a newsletter, which it transformed that year into a full-fledged literary magazine. Harold Monro, the first editor of the newly named *Poetry Review,* would later be described by Frost as "the gloomy spirit that edits it. No one can laugh when he is looking. His taste in literature is first for the theological and after that for anything that has the bite of sin. He got up a penny sheet of Blake to sell in the slums and you ought to have seen the risky selections he made. But dear me everybody is writing with one foot in the red-light district."[19] Long associated with the more salacious poetry of symbolism and decadence, Monro had a deeper poetic imagination than Frost gave him credit for.

When Monro became editor the *Poetry Review,* he had just returned to London after three years in Italy recovering from a failed marriage and from his first literary venture, the Samurai Press, which had published Wilfrid Gibson and John Drinkwater, among others.[20] Monro financed the venture with his inherited fortune and meant "to make poetry popular." As one literary historian says, "To that end he devoted his energies, his zeal, and a not inconsiderable private purse."[21] Always, though, Monro had an eye on the social purpose of his beloved art. His biographer, Dominic Hibberd, explains that "freedom was to be his most positive theme:

freedom from God, from political oppression, from social, sexual and literary convention."[22]

As a subscribing member to the Poetry Society from the first, Monro once back in London made enough of his experience as a publisher and editor to convince the director of the Poetry Society, Galloway Kyle, to turn the *Poetical Gazette* into a full literary magazine. As he said, "I practically sold myself to the society." Monro's idea was to turn the *Gazette* (essentially a newsletter for subscribers) into a commercial magazine with a new name, the *Poetry Review*. Kyle agreed only after Monro committed part of his fortune to financing it. In January 1912 the *Poetry Review* began publishing (with a separate section reserved for the society's *Poetry Gazette*). Both tied to and independent of the Poetry Society, the *Poetry Review* and its schizophrenic nature made 1912 a tumultuous year for the staff and for Monro. But it gave the art of poetry a much-needed presence in literary publishing. Publicity immediately followed on the announcement of an annual *Poetry Review* prize that would award a substantial 30 pounds (a little more than $3,200 in 2012 U.S. dollars) to the best poem published each year as selected by a prestigious board of judges.[23]

From the start the magazine had, through the society alone, a ready subscription base of a thousand people a month.[24] Expecting to increase that base, along with the profile of the new realist turn in contemporary British poetry, Monro also began a massive advertising campaign on behalf of the new magazine on both sides of the Atlantic.[25] In his second issue Monro reciprocated, selling advertising space to American publishers, including a full-page advertisement for Thomas B. Mosher's magazine, the *Bibelot,* that led to new British subscribers.

Turning to his first issue, then, Monro's essay "The Future of Poetry" decries the mistaken view that poetry offered only "repose from material and nervous anxiety" or merely "tickled the imagination."[26] "Poetry," he said, "is uninteresting to-day in that degree only that it is remote from life." The poet, he said, "must include, apart from the natural adoration of beauty, a clear and sound grasp upon facts, and a stupendous aptitude for assimilation." Rousingly he concluded that poetry "must be fundamental, vital, innate, or nothing at all."[27] To emphasize his realist thrust he followed that editorial with an article celebrating the work of Wilfrid Gibson, calling attention to the "raw chunks of life" that marked his poems. Unusual for a literary magazine, the *Poetry Review* initially carried more prose about contemporary poetry than the poetry itself. In fact the first half of each issue carried essays while poems appeared in the second half. In this first issue readers found three lengthy essays followed by new poetry and then a variety of poetry reviews (including a review of Ezra Pound's troubadour imitations and translations, *Canzoni* [1911]). This did not sit well with the ostensible publisher, the Poetry Society. The director, Kyle, for one, thought it had altogether too much prose and not enough poetry.[28] Holding firm, however, throughout that first year Monro and his former Samurai crowd (he had brought to the new magazine's staff at least three former members of that failed press) continued to publish.

In addition to editing the magazine, Monro throughout the summer and fall of 1912 also made plans for a former leather merchant's shop at 35 Devonshire Street in Bloomsbury (in the same neighborhood as Virginia Woolf's Hogarth Press). In 1912 the Bloomsbury of Devonshire Street was a very inexpensive locale. Although not far from the British Museum, it was "a narrow street . . . rather dark, but given over to screaming children, lusty small boys armed with catapults, and to leaping flights of eighteenth-century cats." [29] The neighborhood provided a fit metaphor for the condition of contemporary British poetry in 1912.

From the first, though, Monro had big plans. Writing to Drinkwater, he described a tremendous new idea: "To read poetry in villages without formality, payment, condescension, propaganda, or parson. You give it to them like Eastern story-tellers, who gather people together at street corners." [30] That idea never went beyond that enthusiastic letter, but its spirit could be felt in the Poetry Bookshop. He also began plans for his own literary magazine, *Poetry and Drama* (its first issue would come out in March 1913).

EDWARD MARSH AND GEORGIAN POETRY

In 1912 British poetic realism soon had its own movement, dubbed Georgian. As a movement or school it made big news in literary circles and made the turn to realism in poetry impossible to ignore. That year, too, another school of innovative realists known as the imagists sprang into print. Of the two groups, literary history now recalls only the free verse insurrection of the imagists. But in 1912 the imagists had little role to play in the larger public arena of British publishing. Compared to the onslaught of Georgian poetry, the new imagism could easily have gone entirely unnoticed. Although today imagism takes history's laurels as the English-speaking world's most important and innovative twentieth-century poetic avant-garde, initially the crown went to the far better-known Georgians. This had as much to do with Edward Marsh (1872–1952), the patron of another literary magazine, *Rhythm*, as with the self-declared Georgian poets, Masefield, Gibson, Drinkwater, and others, like Lascelles Abercrombie, Rupert Brooke, and W. H. Davies (author of the *Autobiography of a Super Tramp*).

In September 1912 Edward Marsh, whom everyone knew as Eddie, in conversation with his good friend Rupert Brooke (1887–1915), remarked on the realist turn in contemporary British poetry, particularly in the work of such poets as Gibson, Masefield, Abercrombie, Davies, and Walter de la Mare (1873–1956), a poet who had been publishing collections since 1902 but had only just begun to receive serious attention. During that conversation "Marsh pointed out that the natural thing was to name eras after reigning sovereigns," and so he came upon what he termed "my proud ambiguous adjective—*Georgian*."[31] *Georgian* was meant to associate poetry less with a technique (realism) than with an era, a zeitgeist, an attitude, "the Georgian age." The Georgians argued that with the end of the Edwardian age came an end to the ineffective, unimportant poetry of insipid idealism. The entire point of realism, as a revival of the social purpose once heralded by genteel poetry, had been lost in the Victorian and Edwardian quest for beauty. By naming the poets he admired as Georgian, then, Marsh wanted to return poetry to its cultural evangelical role.

In 1912 the wealthy Eddie Marsh had established himself as a literary and artistic patron. His inheritance had come from a typically eccentric source, a government trust fund established by the government in compensation for the assassination on the steps of the House of Commons of his maternal great-grandfather, Spencer Perceval, who was prime minister in 1812. The trust fund sent Marsh what he liked to call "murder-money," and he used it to patronize the artists and poets he admired. Officially, however, he was a government official, no less than private secretary to Winston Churchill, first lord of the admiralty.

To literary historians Marsh has the uncanny ability to know every circle of British writers and artists worth knowing. Plump and sporting a monocle, he once invited the poet Lascelles (it rhymes with tassels) Abercrombie to spend a weekend with him in London. Said Abercrombie of that weekend: "I seem to have been in the visions of God, on a Miltonic mount of speculation, viewing the whole of modern life in an amazing succession of dazzling instants, from Henry James to Austin Harrison, from Lovely Ladies to Cubists. Henceforth, you stand for London to me."[32] Marsh not only consorted with cubist painters, fashionable young things of the upper crust, Henry James, Thomas Hardy, and other writers, but he also proved to be a hearty and generous patron to painters and poets alike.

After giving the poetry movement a name, he decided to make his observations public. He worried that "openly shepherding a group of poets might strike the uninitiated as a trifle absurd," so he kept his role discreet even as he gathered the poets together in a single volume to be called *The Georgian Poets.* Altogether he and Rupert Brooke enlisted seventeen poets, including Ezra Pound, who was then living in England.[33] For various reasons Pound refused to be included. In the end the Georgian anthology carried the poems of Brooke, Masefield, D. H. Lawrence, Gibson, Drinkwater, and Abercrombie.[34] Marsh dedicated the anthology to Robert Bridges (1844–1930), who had just been declared poet laureate, calling Bridges "the figurehead of English poetry." Upon learning of the dedication, Bridges suggested that Marsh in a preface make the connection between poetry and the current state of British civilization more plain: "Considering the condition of both home and foreign politics [rebellion in Ireland, Balkan war] I would suggest your introduction should be dated from the admiralty." Marsh refused, preferring to keep his role anonymous.[35] In place of a preface readers found only a small prose "Prefatory Note" that discreetly bore the initials E. M., and the date, October 1912. It read: "This collection, drawn entirely from the publications of the past two years, may if it is fortunate help the lovers of poetry to realize that we are at the beginning of another 'Georgian period' which may rank in due time with the several great poetic ages of the past."

Once published, *Georgian Poetry* made an immediate sensation in the literary pages of genteel and mass-market publishing. As Marsh's biographer Christopher Hassell put it, "Once again men talked about poetry in pubs, instead of only in drawing-rooms and studios." For British publishers the Georgian poets represented the modern era.[36] For the most part the reviews emphasized the poets' rejection of late Victorian musicality in meter, diction, and rhyme. This did not apply to all the poets. For instance, anyone might have found the opening lines of "Hesperus" by Sir Ronald Ross—"Ah whither does thou float, sweet silent star, / In yonder floods of evening's dying light?"—the same tired conventions that had taken poetry out of newspapers and magazines to begin with. Of the poems included, however, Ross proved the exception, not the rule. Mostly the poems in the collection mimicked the techniques of realist drama and fiction in favor of more spare, realistic tales and intellectual critiques of modern life.[37]

The British Georgians believed that poetry did not just reflect the times but also played a fundamental role in society itself.[38] Abercrombie, for instance, summarized their views in a review of the anthology by writing, "The present resembles more the time of the pre-Socratic Greek philosophers . . . than any other time." By that he meant "the present is a time wherein the world, and the destiny of man in the world, are ideas different from anything that has ever been before."[39] Marsh's anthology meant to bring those ideas to the public through poetry.

The most innovative feature of the anthology, however, proved to be its publisher, Harold Monro's own Poetry Bookshop. *Georgian Poetry, 1911–1912,* was published in November 1912, with a first printing of five hundred copies.[40] Although Monro published the anthology, Marsh agreed to cover any losses and so freed Monro from financial panic—he was risking more money than he could afford at the time.[41] Also, Marsh applauded Monro's opening the Poetry Bookshop to make poetry part of the public sphere in far more visible ways than currently existed. Meanwhile Monro had learned from the Italian futurists, who had made a huge splash in the British newspapers and magazines, that innovative poetry could provoke essential questions about literature's relationship to society, not to mention provoke fundamental questions about society itself.[42] Amazed that *I Poeti Futuristi* had sold more than thirty-five thousand copies in its first year in Italy, Monro wanted to give contemporary British poetry the same public exposure the futurists had given to the Continental avant-garde. He hoped that the Georgian anthology might be a way to do this.[43] Monro's goal always had been to give poets an audience, not to make a profit. For instance, in keeping with Marsh's philanthropy, and with Monro's own Fabian principles, 50 percent of the anthology's profits went to finance the *Poetry Review* (which Monro still edited for the Poetry Society), as well as to underwriting the costs of his Poetry Bookshop, while the other 50 percent was evenly divided between each contributing poet.[44]

JANUARY 8, 1913

Harold Monro's bookstore had been open for a few months and had already achieved notice by publishing *Georgian Poetry*. On the night of January 8, 1913, the official opening celebration for the store was held. A substantial crowd, mostly poets, gathered in the small rundown neighborhood, a slum, really, on Devonshire Street.[45] Gathered there were the leading poets of the day as well as the young upstart Georgians and the imagists associated with Ezra Pound. Among those attending was the unknown American poet Robert Frost.

Soon after entering the crowded shop, the English imagist poet F. S. Flint befriended Frost, asking if he was American. Since he had not said anything to betray an accent, he asked how Flint could have known. Shoes, Flint said. Not many years later P. G. Wodehouse wrote a similar scene to comic effect. An Englishwoman discerns an American: "She was thinking how hopelessly American Mr. Pett was; how baggy his clothes looked; what absurdly shaped shoes he wore."[46] Mr. Pett could just as well have been Mr. Frost, arrived with square-toed shoes, so unusual in round-toed England. Far from scorning Frost's absurd and provincial demeanor, however, Flint instead began a conversation that Frost could happily join. Soon Frost had a copy of Flint's *In the Net of the Stars* (1909), while Flint had learned that Frost's own first book would be published by Nutt.[47] Flint then offered to review Frost's book. Given his friendships with T. E. Hulme and Pound, and his regular articles for the *New Age*, and *Poetry Review*, not to mention Chicago's newly founded *Poetry* magazine, Flint's offer was welcome. During their conversation they discussed the

French influence on the new imagism, a school of English free verse poets championed by the American expatriate Ezra Pound. In a letter to Flint shortly after that party, Frost wrote, "I was only too childishly happy in being allowed to make one [a splash] for a moment in a company in which I hadn't to be ashamed of having written verse. Perhaps it will help you understand my state of mind if I tell you that I have lived for the most part in villages where it were better that a millstone were hanged about your neck than that you should own yourself a minor poet."[48] In that same letter he also declared his place in the current scene, saying, "I don't know what theory you may have committed or dedicated to as an affiliated poet of Devonshire St. [home of the Poetry Bookshop] but for my part give me an out-and-out metaphor. If that is old-fashioned, make the most of it." He then went on to praise the metaphors Flint had used in his *Net of Stars* and singled out "brindled for the bees, 'gauze' for the sea-haze, 'little mouths' for the half-opened lilac flowers, 'wafer' for the moon, 'silver streak' for the swan's mirrored neck and 'tarnished copper' for her beak." In addition to the metaphors he praised the rhythm, what he called cadence, and the diction of Flint's poetry. He saw in Flint's work the sort of accurate sound of talk that Frost had been striving to capture too. As he said to Flint, "Something akin to that effect [the cadence] is what I go reading book after book of new poetry for—if you know what I mean."[49] In return Flint, as he had on that opening night, insisted Frost see Ezra Pound. He sent him Pound's calling card, which made that poet's precious, often high-handed, if also deeply funny and sarcastic, personality clear; it simply stated that he was "At Home, Sometimes." That sort of personality never sat well with Frost, and he took his time before meeting Pound.[50]

• • •

Meanwhile *Georgian Poets* and the individual poets in that anthology received a plethora of coverage in British publications. Still an observer, Frost, thanks to Flint and then Pound, would in the next six months become an active member of both the imagist and Georgian scene, earning the respect and attention of Monro, Abercrombie, Gibson, Pound, Flint, and T. E. Hulme.

Chapter Ten

•

Robert Frost: Public Poet at Last
"The Death of the Hired Man"

FROST HAD REACHED a pinnacle when *A Boy's Will* was published. After meeting the Georgians and imagists, he must have realized that the philosophical ideas his private study of natural science, James's psychology, and Bergson's philosophy had given him helped to explain the radical changes then occurring in contemporary poetry. He had found a theoretical justification for his realism, and now he had a group of peers with whom he could share those ideas.

MARCH 1913: ROBERT FROST MEETS EZRA POUND

Although they had a nine-year difference in age, Frost and Pound had both been reared in America's genteel culture. Both men expected not only to see their poetry in the public sphere but also to shape that sphere. Of the two, Pound already had become a public figure, especially as a result of his advocacy for free verse imagism. In a letter to his friend Ernest Silver, Frost best captured Pound's milieu: "The dazzling youth who translates poetry from six languages. . . . He lives in Bohemia from hand to mouth but he goes simply everywhere in great society. A lot of daffy duchesses patronize him and buy tickets to expensive little lecture courses he gets up when he has to raise the wind."[1] (Pound gave a series of lectures that would become the substance of his book on Provençal poetry.)

In late 1912 a new magazine, *Poetry*, located in Chicago, began publication. Very much like England's *Poetry Review*, it even had a Monroe, Harriet, as its editor. The American magazine was dedicated to promoting "the New Poetry." To that end Harriet Monroe had appointed Ezra Pound as foreign editor. He was supposed to give the magazine's readers the news of European, especially English and French, poetry. He also took it upon himself to send Monroe manuscripts from poets he discovered. In England, meanwhile, Pound had been promoting what he termed "the school of images," or imagism, in a variety of venues. For the English socialist magazine *New Age,* he wrote that the new imagist free verse poetry "presents. It does not comment. It is irrefutable because it doesn't present a personal predilection for any particular fraction of the truth. . . . It is not a criticism of life. I mean it does not deal in opinion. It washes its hands of theories."[2] If he read that essay, Frost would have seen in it the same sort of realist attention to detail he had been attempting in his poetry. Pound, like Frost, preferred poetry that did not blindly adhere to the moral idealism of Comstockery or Victorianism but instead depicted the facts of things and situations, emotions and sexuality, as they existed.

In March 1913, just before Robert Frost introduced himself to Ezra Pound, Pound had written to Harriet Monroe to rail against the poetry she had been publishing in recent issues. Referring to the last issue, he said only one poem—by Witter Bynner, an old friend of Pounds'—"is at least aware of life apart from brochures." Even that poem, Pound said, "smacks of the pretty optimism of McClure and E[dna].W[heeler]. Wilcox. If America should bring forth a real pessimist—not a literary pessimist—I should almost believe."[3] He did not have long to wait. Shortly after Pound wrote that letter, Frost came to visit.

During their conversation Frost said his first book, *A Boy's Will,* was about to be published. In fact, Frost said, as far as he knew, the book was printed and simply waiting for its April publication date. Hearing this, "the stormy petrel," as Frost called Pound, insisted they march over to Nutt's offices on Bloomsbury Street and demand a copy. Once there Pound weaseled a copy for review. Frost watched as Pound began reading. He is said to have turned to Frost, saying, "You don't mind our liking this, do you?" In his typically wry voice Frost replied, "Go ahead and like it." Not only did Pound like it, he also saw in Frost's poetry the sort of thing he wished Monroe would publish more often. Excited not only to have proof that such poetry existed but also to have "discovered" it for *Poetry,*

Pound wrote to the associate editor, Alice Corbin Henderson: "Have just discovered another Amur'kn. VURRY Amur'k'n, with I think, the seeds of grace. Have reviewed an advance copy of his book." This was not just Pound's bluster. In a letter to his father he also praised Frost's book and added, "I'll try to get you a copy of Frost. I'm using mine at present to boom him and get his name stuck about."[4]

Pound, true to his word, used his contacts at British and American publications to get Frost's book known, beginning with Pound's review for *Poetry*. Meanwhile *A Boy's Will*, officially published in April, began to attract reviews almost immediately, including Pound's, which *Poetry* published in May. Pound not only boomed Frost, he also introduced him to Pound's wide circle of writer friends, including Yeats and May Sinclair, both of whom Frost had long admired, particularly Yeats. At Pinkerton, Frost had his students perform Yeats's recent plays and had likely followed Yeats's example in *A Wind Among the Reeds* for the explanatory epigraphs in *A Boy's Will*. Pound had become Yeats's friend, and not long after this meeting with Frost, Pound also became Yeats's secretary.[5] Few introductions could more have ingratiated him to Frost. "I spent the evening with Yeats in his dark-curtained candlelit room last week. We talked about [Yeats's] *The Land of Heart's Desire* [which Frost's students had performed]." Better still, at that meeting, as Frost wrote to Thomas B. Mosher, "Yeats has said in private that the book is the best thing American for some time. May Sinclair has been showing it to people."[6]

Pound also introduced Frost to May Sinclair, who made her reputation in 1904 with a philosophical novel, *Divine Fire* (1904), a best-seller on both sides of the Atlantic.[7] By 1913 she also was known for realist novels that depicted the spiritual essence of things from an empirical perspective in the manner of William James and Henri Bergson. Pound and Sinclair had long been friends, and she had introduced him to the London literati when he first came to England. Frost, meanwhile, knew her as the author of "Three American Poets of To-Day," which apparently had impressed him when it was published in the *Atlantic Monthly* in 1906. As he told Bartlett, he thought of her as having "made the reputation of [William] Vaughn Moody, [Ridgely] Torrence and Edwin Arnold [*sic*] Robinson by naming them as the principal poets in the States." When Frost met her, he returned to that essay. "I was asking May Sinclair, if she shouldn't have put him [Robinson] ahead of Moody and Torrence in her article of a few years back in the *Atlantic*. She said that Robinson was the only one of the three she still cared for."[8]

Frost looked back with affection on those first meetings with Pound and his friends, recalling that, "among the things that Pound did was show me Bohemia . . . he'd take me to the restaurants and things. Don't forget that our first moment together—Pound's and mine—was happy, even romantic. Pound showed me London's bohemia—he was boyish about it. He presented me with two little books of his verse, *Personae* [1909] and *Riposres* [1912]."[9] These and other introductions overwhelmed Frost—"Gosh" was about all he could say in summarizing the whirlwind of introductions Pound made possible.[10]

IMAGISM AND THE NEW POETRY IN MARCH 1913

In the same month that Frost met Ezra Pound, the new imagism had begun to create a stir in the literary world. Provoked by the Italian futurists, Pound had convinced Harriet Monroe to publish in her March issue a set of essays on his new "school of images." Those essays, one by Pound and one by F. S. Flint, explained the school. In his essay Flint writes that the imagists should not be confused with the new postimpressionist artists then gaining so much attention, nor with the futurists.[11] Compared to such postimpressionists as cubists, fauvists, or futurists, Flint said, the imagists "had nothing in common with these schools." Quoting an anonymous imagist poet (actually Ezra Pound), Flint reported that the imagist poets sought to return poetry to its roots, to its core purpose as a literary art derived from the poets of classical antiquity. Specifically imagism demanded that poetry adhere to three principles: "1. Direct treatment of the 'thing,' whether subjective or objective. 2. To use absolutely no word that did not contribute to the presentation. 3. As regarding rhythm: to compose in sequence of the musical phrase, not in sequence of a metronome." In his essay "A Few Don'ts by an *Imagiste*," Pound summarized Flint by writing "don't retell in mediocre verse what has already been done in good prose."[12]

Those essays were the culmination of what had been a slow introduction of the free verse school in *Poetry*'s pages. Pound had convinced Harriet

Monroe to include in the first three issues of her new magazine the imagist poetry of his friends, the American expatriate Hilda Doolittle (H. D.), and the English poet Richard Aldington. When published, the poems were always identified as belonging to the new imagism.

One should not underestimate the effect the futurists had on any poet who wished to see poetry make a difference in the meaning of art and of art's relationship to the public sphere. Pound's imagism had been provoked by the futurists, just as had Harold Monro's publicity on behalf of his Georgian poets. When Frost met Pound in March 1913, the futurists had returned for a second year in London. They followed from the Ballet Russe, which had broken all the rules of classical ballet. The Russians had brought to London bizarre costumes, sets, and even more strange music by the likes of Eric Satie and Igor Stravinsky. The futurists meanwhile brought their "art of noise" and their poetry in both 1912 and again in 1913 as a series of spectacles incorporating composers, choreographers, sculptors, painters, and poets under the leadership of the great impresario of the avant-garde, Mario Marinetti.

Turning the idea of cultural evangelism on its head, Marinetti had created a touring road show that performed in a popular music hall rather than in a more traditional elite venue for the high arts.[13] Thanks to the music hall environment and the general weirdness of the acts, the futurists attracted massive attention from reporters. Mass-circulation publications like the *Pall Mall Gazette, Illustrated London News,* and *Daily Mirror* began to run articles on the new futurists, including their poetry, and continued to run them even after the futurists had left. In the April 11, 1913, edition of the *Daily Express*, for instance, one of the leading futurist painters, Gino Severini, explained the futurists' odd method: "A picture will no longer be the faithful reproduction of a scene, enclosed in a window frame, but the realization of a complex view of life or of things that live in space."[14] Even he appealed to a new realism as his guide and purpose.

Nor was Frost himself immune. His new English friend, the poet Mary Gardner, recalled a debate she had with a futurist painter. "I ran up hard against another Futurist, and told him my opinions, hard and good, about a picture he invited me to admire. Items: the drawing was bad, the colouring dirty, the pattern—save the mark—ill-conditioned and unnatural; and so on. Strange to say, we parted on quite good terms. Suppose now we of the non-existent art of literature threw over the alphabet. It is just possible to start too far back, & yet hold on to too much."[15]

Pound, like Harold Monro, had also been impressed by the sales and attention *I Poeti Futuristi* had received. Like Monro, who published *Georgian Poetry*, Pound was determined to bring his views of English poetic realism into the public sphere. In 1913, about when Frost met him, Pound had begun compiling an anthology of imagism, which he would call *Des Imagistes*. When Monro heard about it that June, he raised a skeptical eyebrow: "Wilfrid [Gibson] tells me there's a movement for a 'Post-Georgian' anthology, of the Pound-Hulme-Flint school, who don't like being out of G.P. [*Georgian Poetry*]." He added, "But I don't think it will come off."[16] In fact, it did come off, and he would be its English publisher.

In March 1913, only two avant-garde movements could be said to have garnered serious attention in the English press, futurism and the new Georgian poets. For all Pound's efforts, imagism was still mostly unknown. And of the options for making poetry seem more accurate, relevant, and meaningful, Frost had from his earliest writing days been sympathetic to the Georgian idea. That idea emphasized individual psychological exploration, character study, even narrative drama with a focus on middle-, lower middle-, and working-class people.

Pound, however, saw in Frost another poet who could prove the power and necessity for the imagism Pound meant to promote. Following their March meeting Pound began pressuring Frost to write in the new imagist style. Specifically Pound urged Frost to abandon meter in favor of free verse.[17] As Frost said to Mosher later that summer, "You will be amused to hear that Pound has taken to bullying me on the strength of what he did for me by his review in *Poetry*. . . . He says I must write something more like *vers libre* or he will let me perish of neglect. He really threatens." Years later, recollecting Pound's bullying, Frost declared his overall sympathy with the larger realist intentions: "The poets were interesting. Flint, especially, became a friend I have kept to this day. But I had to work alone. Pound[,] to illustrate what it [imagism] should be, took a poem of mine [and] said: 'You've done it in fifty words. I've shortened it to forty-eight.' I answered, 'And spoiled my metre, my idiom and idea.'"[18]

Frost resisted Pound's arguments on behalf of free verse. In that resistance he had powerful company among the Georgians. That same March,

Harold Monro had become editor of a new magazine, *Poetry and Drama* (really just the successor to the *Poetry Review*). In its first issue Henry Newbolt had outlined the principles of Georgian realism. He referred to the "poetic imagination" as the psychological penetration of character. He also dismissed the need for free verse, arguing instead that a combination of meter, rhyme, and everyday diction, what he called the "truth of diction," kept poetry true to its own artistic, literary heritage.

When Frost met Pound in 1913, and when Pound began to bully him into imagism, Frost inevitably found it necessary to defend his own poetic principles. It may well be that for the first time in his life, Frost found it necessary to defend the need for meter in poetry. I imagine meter had not been much of an issue for Frost until Pound made it one. When he did, Frost found himself faced with a troubling philosophical, artistic problem. To create a more accurate psychological penetration of character, why did he need meter?

The Georgians insisted on the importance of British poetic heritage. This no doubt played a singular role in Frost's decision not to abandon meter. Still, he could not help but agree with Pound and the imagists that poetry ought not to sing when it could be more honest in talk. Only after his meeting with Pound (and Flint and their imagist friends) did Frost begin to attend to the importance of his rhythm and of meter to the creation of character, drama, situation, and imagery.

Beginning in 1913, then, Frost decided that he, too, would become an experimenter. Confronted with the challenge of free verse yet refusing to reject meter, he began a metrical experiment on his own terms. He asked himself how far he could take a metrical line toward the sound of everyday speech *without* lapsing into free verse. He began to compose poems that asked how natural in sound and diction one could make a metrical line before it lost all metrical integrity. To that metrical question he also added a question concerning the lyric itself. How much drama, how many narrative elements, could a lyric incorporate before it ceased to be a lyric at all? He found the answer in the classics he had long studied, most particularly in Virgil's *Eclogues*.

Frost now began writing psychologically penetrating narratives in blank verse. These new narrative poems depict relationships among neighbors, husbands and wives, workers and employers, boys and girls, men and other men, women and other women, and men and women. In so doing, he raised fundamental artistic questions not only about the nature of meter and the lyric but also about such core genteel concepts as home, neighbor, worker, friend, and marriage. Although he had begun such poems as "The Black Cottage," "The Housekeeper," and "The Death of the Hired Man" as long ago as seven years previously, he now revised them with a new experimental eye. With Newbolt's, Pound's, and Flint's precepts in mind, Frost wrote many of the poems that would ensure his legacy as a necessary public poet.[19]

"THE DEATH OF THE HIRED MAN": EZRA POUND AND ROBERT FROST

Refusing to forgo meter, Frost began to write in the language that was even more colloquial. He now set a character's speech rhythm across the insistent metrical foot. Secretly fuming at Pound's abrasive tactics, Frost likely came to his new method as a result of their arguments. "The Death of the Hired Man" is one of the first poems to result from those arguments. First begun in 1905, he used it, I believe, as proof that his commitment to meter could still yield the results Pound believed possible only in free verse.[20] To that end Frost showed it to "that great intellect abloom in hair," who, after reading it, likely shouted with joy and agreed with Frost, again endearing himself to the older poet.[21] In fact, without telling Frost, Pound sent the poem to a new American magazine, also committed to "the New Poetry," *Smart Set*, hoping to get it published there.

On the strength of his position at *Poetry,* and his work at the *New Age,* the editors of *Smart Set* had hired Pound as their English agent, a talent scout.[22] At the magazine, edited by Willard Huntington Wright, both George Jean Nathan and H. L. Mencken had been declaring war on the forces of Comstockery, which Mencken called the American "booboisie." Wright had only just recently been appointed editor in chief, after the magazine's recent sale to a new owner. Wright enlisted his friend Pound and promoted Nathan and Mencken, who had been there since 1910, into making more editorial and literary decisions. Under their control each issue of *Smart Set* carried the slogan "A Magazine for Minds that are not Primitive." They also committed the magazine to the New Poetry, saying, "Men and women have grown tired of effeminacy and the falsities of current fiction, essay, and poetry. . . . The demand for pious uplift, for stultification, and fictional avoidance of the facts of life has diminished. The reader today demands the truth."[23] As he read Frost's newest poem, Pound thought *Smart Set* was the perfect venue. He even said as much to his father: "He has done a 'Death of the Farm Hand' [*sic*] since the book [*A Boy's Will*] that is to my mind better than anything in it. I shall have that in the *Smart Set* or in *Poetry* before long."[24]

Part of Pound's joy certainly came from the fact that "The Death of the Hired Man" reads like a short story in free verse. In fact, well into the 1950s readers often misread this and other similar poems *as* free verse, so well did Frost incorporate the rhythms of speech to the requirements of meter for his blank verse.[25] The poem's drama derives from the dialog of a husband and wife. There is almost no narrative intrusion. Thematically the poem relates the ethical dilemma faced by an older couple, Warren and Mary, when their very old, and now decrepit, hired hand, Silas, returns, out of the blue, to work on their farm. Every year he has come during haying time to help with the fall haying. This year Silas has not come to do the haying. He has come to Warren and Mary's home to die there. He has elected them as his family although he has a brother in the next town. When he chooses Warren and Mary, he imposes on them an ethical obligation that by rights should belong to Silas's brother. Ought they to obey it? Warren says no. "Home," he famously tells his wife in one of the great cynical lines of American, or any, literature, "is the place where, when you have to go there, / They have to take you in."[26] And she says in reply, "I should have called it / Something you somehow haven't to deserve." Is it something one does not deserve? The poem does not so much answer as provoke multiple answers from readers. Through its multilayered, multivalenced tale it at once dissects the meaning of marriage, home, family, and work itself.

In the first ten-line stanza Frost economically establishes the scene with realist precision:

> Mary sat musing on the lamp-flame at the table,
> Waiting for Warren. When she heard his step,
> She ran on tiptoe down the darkened passage
> To meet him in the doorway with the news,
> And put him on his guard. "Silas is back."

> She pushed him outward with her through the door
> And shut it after her. "Be kind," she said.
> She took the market things from Warren's arms
> And set them on the porch, then drew him down
> To sit beside her on the wooden steps.

In keeping with metrical law each line adheres to pentameter and ends after the regulation five feet.[27] In keeping with the imagist attention to what readers see, each line ends after establishing a single image. Pick any line in the stanza: it will contain an isolated, single image, rendered either dramatically by implication—"And put him on his guard"—or explicitly through simple description—"To sit beside her on the wooden steps." The lines also read as everyday talk. In keeping with the more egalitarian spirit of the Georgians, the poem manifests sympathy for the population of rural New England. When Frost sent this poem to F. S. Flint that July, he wrote, "I am no propagandist of equality. But I enjoy above all things the contemplation of equality where it happily exists." By that he meant to say that the rural people he dramatized were not to be read as some strange species unlike the urban sophisticates of London. Instead Frost meant to show that understood first as individuals, all people face the same ethical issues in the same way. This implied equality also raised the obvious counterproblem. Who, after all, would really believe that rural people are so much less human and less prone to psychological insight and ethical dilemma that they do not deserve to be subjects of poetry? Only, such poetry implied, a bigot or a fool. Later, when interviewed about the poem, Frost said of Silas, "It's interesting to see how country folks are sometimes wise without books."[28] Later, when Frost saw a dramatization of this poem, and the actors played Warren and Mary as clod-hopping rubes, Frost could hardly contain his disgust. That they lived in the middle of nowhere, New Hampshire, did not mean that Warren and Mary had not been to college.

The egalitarian impulse behind the poem also speaks to the egalitarian impulse behind the realism Frost recuperated from Longfellow's example. Such realism, when applied to such genteel concepts as integrity, duty, and character, gained, so Longfellow's poetry proved, both a striking affirmation and a necessary critique. In the tradition of Longfellow and Emerson, Frost's poem is not an easy song of moral uplift, nor is it an allegorical study chock full of symbols. Instead it is a serious meditation on the meaning of duty.[29] Karen Kilcup puts the issue Frost raises in a single sentence: "'The Death of the Hired Man,' at least, epitomizes the ethic of connection and nurturing that undergirds mainstream nineteenth-century poetry and fiction."[30] The old idea of genteel poetry assigned a public purpose to art. In this poem Frost resurrects that old idea through his application of fundamental ethical principles in a contemporary situation. In so doing he removes public poetry from the symbolic idealism and allegory into which it had fallen.

Turning to this poem's view of duty, even before the poem begins, Mary has decided that she and Warren have a duty to their hired man. She tells Warren that Silas thinks he will help with the haying because she knows it to be a fiction that saves Silas's dignity. She reports his conversation about a season long ago when he worked with a young poet, a student of Latin, who earned extra money helping on the farm. Says Mary:

> "Well, those days trouble Silas like a dream.
> You wouldn't think they would. How some things linger!
> Harold's young college boy's assurance piqued him.
> After so many years he still keeps finding
> Good arguments he sees he might have used.
> I sympathize. I know just how it feels
> To think of the right thing to say too late.
> Harold's associated in his mind with Latin.
> He asked me what I thought of Harold's saying
> He studied Latin like the violin
> Because he liked it—that an argument!
> He said he couldn't make the boy believe
> He could find water with a hazel prong—
> Which showed how much good school had ever done him.
> He wanted to go over that. But most of all
> He thinks if he could have another chance
> To teach him how to build a load of hay—"

In 1913 these lines resonated even more sharply. Harold the college boy speaks the language of the decadent/symbolists, and all those whose love of a pure aestheticism that exalts beauty for its own sake relentlessly mocked the pragmatic materialists of their time. Mary says of Silas, "He asked me what I thought of Harold's saying / He studied Latin like the violin / Because he liked it—that an argument!" Silas counters that absurdity with what he thinks is good old-fashioned pragmatic utility and fact: Harold would be better off if he knew how to use a divining rod to find water. Rather than set aestheticism in opposition to some kind of pragmatic utility, as genteel poetry had so often done, Frost undercuts the pragmatism of people like both Silas, whose own facts are but superstition by another name, and the young student aesthete.

Pragmatism, though, does get its moment in this poem. Regardless of his crazy belief in magic sticks, Silas *can* stack hay like no other farmhand. Mary says of Silas, "But most of all / He thinks if he could have another chance / To teach him how to build a load of hay—" To that point, concerning that particular talent, Warren, who initially resisted any obligation to Silas, finds himself admitting:

> "I know, that's Silas' one accomplishment.
> He bundles every forkful in its place,
> And tags and numbers it for future reference,
> So he can find and easily dislodge it
> In the unloading. Silas does that well.
> He takes it out in bunches like big birds' nests.
> You never see him standing on the hay
> He's trying to lift, straining to lift himself."

Practical utility becomes in this poem its own beauty, its own aesthetic, "like big birds' nests," organized and neat. Just as one can read Harold as a stand-in for aestheticism in the arts, so one might read Silas's haystacks as an imagist analog. Those haystacks, like the new realism, the new poetry of facts and regular talk, is also in its own right a type of beauty.

Warren appreciates Silas's unique talent and says so. Mary, hearing her husband's rare praise for Silas, then adds to it, saying that Silas himself had a proper pride in that skill and wished he could have taught it to Harold Wilson, the aesthete:

> "He thinks if he could teach him that, he'd be
> Some good perhaps to someone in the world.
> He hates to see a boy the fool of books.
> Poor Silas, so concerned for other folk,
> And nothing to look backward to with pride,

> And nothing to look forward to with hope,
> So now and never any different."

Silas, come to this farm to die, too easily compares to the plight of the real-ist poetry that Frost and his Georgian friends had begun to write. Proud of a skill that no one wants to learn, disgusted at a world that made a fool of him through the wrong books (the idealist books of a "Gospel of Beauty"), perhaps the new realists, too, will have no choice but to surrender and die.

The next stanza reads very much like an imagist poem:

> Part of a moon was falling down the west,
> Dragging the whole sky with it to the hills.
> Its light poured softly in her lap. She saw
> And spread her apron to it. She put out her hand
> Among the harp-like morning-glory strings,
> Taut with the dew from garden bed to eaves,
> As if she played unheard some tenderness
> That wrought on him beside her in the night.
> "Warren," she said, "he has come home to die:
> You needn't be afraid he'll leave you this time."[31]

Only through her gestures can one glean Mary's thoughts in these lines. In the moonlight she plays with the nearby morning glories. She spreads out her apron to catch the reflected moonlight. The gestures evoked by the imagery, coupled with the dialog, insist on the ethical story of the poem. They ask to what degree do these two people, Mary and Warren, who have no formal bonds with Silas, owe him so high a debt as to welcome him home to die? To what degree is their house his home too?

At the very end of the poem Mary convinces Warren to soften his stance and to accept their ethical obligation to Silas. Willing at last to go see him, Warren rises and Mary issues one last bit of advice:

> "But, Warren, please remember how it is:
> He's come to help you ditch the meadow.
> He has a plan. You mustn't laugh at him.
> He may not speak of it, and then he may."

In these lines Mary reminds Warren of the necessary fiction that will save Silas's dignity Then she comments about what she will do, and Frost, as poet-narrator, intrudes with a description that also reads like an imagist poem:

"I'll sit and see if that small sailing cloud
Will hit or miss the moon."
It hit the moon.
Then there were three there, making a dim row,
The moon, the little silver cloud, and she.

The narrator's three lines follow the imagist rules. They even break with the poem's dominant metrical pattern, moving from dimeter to pentameter, and the lines also use direct language with plain adjectives—*dim, little,* and *silver*—in order to render a scene of despair, even if peaceful and quiet.

"The Death of the Hired Man" combines techniques from both the imagists and Georgians. From the imagists Frost took the attention to each word and to the nuances and implications a well-chosen image could convey.[32] In the dialog between Mary and Warren, Frost not only experiments, as did his Georgian friends, with the ability of a metrical line to replicate the mundane rhythms of everyday talk, he also experiments, as did they, with dramatic technique. The poem asks to what degree can talk alone convey emotion, depth, and tone without having to resort to narrative explanation? Through such talk, as Frost told Sidney Cox, he could create a little drama that shows the gradual change in Warren. Like a good drama, meanwhile, it brings a poetic tour of psychological depth to "four distinctly drawn characters. It has climax and surprise; and it perfectly observes all the old unities."[33]

The poem is as much a drama of poetic possibilities as it is a drama among people. The poetic drama concerns the problem of meter. Rather than make the metrical line obvious to the ear that hears the poem, Frost instead buried the meter to emphasize the speech. When this poem is recited, the audience does not realize it is metrical, let alone poetry.

Pound, as I have said, sent this poem to the *Smart Set,* for which he acted as English agent. When he sent the editors "The Death of the Hired Man," Pound expected them to welcome it into their pages, no questions asked.[34] They did not. Wright rejected the poem. On top of that, Frost was deeply annoyed that Pound had sent it to the *Smart Set* precisely because it was *not* a genteel magazine but, to his mind, a poseur's magazine for annoying bohemians. In a letter to F. S. Flint, Frost says of Pound, "I wrote him—I may as well confess—a rather wild letter demanding my manuscript back for no assigned reason. He told me I was having a fit of nerves and refused to comply."[35] According to Frost's most thorough biographer, Lawrance Thompson, the poet detested the magazine to which Pound had sent the poem even more than Frost hated Pound's presumptive patronizing. The *Smart Set* stood for everything in American society Frost opposed, what he termed in his letters to Flint "the arriviste." Later, writing to his friend Sidney Cox about the incident, Frost said, "He [Pound] *asked* for the poem he speaks of and then failed to sell it. It was even worse than that. I had demanded the poem back when I learned the name of the magazine he was offering it to but he went ahead in spite of me. And then began our quarrel."[36]

When Wright rejected Frost's poem, Pound asked for an explanation. Wright said the poem was not innovative, that he had been printing too many poems just like it. To prove the point he mentioned the vagabond poet Harry Kemp, whose poem, "A Harvest Hand," he had just accepted. Kemp's poem appeared in the July 1913 issue, and had been heavily promoted by the editors. In June they had announced, "There will be other striking features in the July *Smart Set*. The best poetry available will be printed including a long narrative poem called 'The Harvest Hand,' by Harry Kemp. This is one of the first poems of its kind that any magazine in American [*sic*] has thought it 'policy' to print."[37]

Is that poem as innovative as Frost's? In a word: no. An extraordinarily long narrative about a group of men come to do hired work on the wheat harvest in Kansas, it features one young man, John Anson, from the East, a college man who nearly succumbs to the back-breaking work. Inevitably, though, he meets the farmer's daughter and, as Kemp says, "John only did what any man would do." His partner, however, also loves the girl, but she chooses John. The partner leaves in disgust. The formerly effete East Coast snob not only gets the girl but also has his sexual awakening in the Kansas harvest: "Dreams of the future filled his breast with joy— / For all the Man has wakened in the boy; / And in his heart there was a man's desire."[38] So concludes the poem. Rather than ask questions about the meaning of relationships and the implications of friendship, sex, and love, the poem offers the lusty world of the west Kansas plains, where serious hard work and erotic love can flourish away from misbegotten ideas of decorum. Insofar as Kemp did write a poem opposing both moral uplift and all that was effete in the current genteel tradition, and insofar as Kemp's poem championed everyday working people in everyday plain diction, it *was* a fine example of the New Poetry. Wright was not wrong when he told Pound he had been reading a great many poems in the new style.

• • •

By the end of 1913's summer, even though Frost had become angry with the man he called his "quasi-friend," he had a great deal for which to thank him. Pound had published the first serious poetry review of Frost's work in America, and, the *Smart Set* notwithstanding, Pound and F. S. Flint had convinced Harriet Monroe to publish another of Frost's new narrative poems, "The Code." Nor would Pound return Frost's anger. Rather, he kept promoting him. Late in 1914, when Pound gained control of a magazine, the *Egoist,* he solicited Frost's narrative "The Housekeeper" for publication. And when Frost published his second book, *North of Boston* (1914), Pound asked Frost for several review copies and succeeded in booming that book too.

Chapter Eleven

•

Inventing a New Poetry
"A Hundred Collars," "The Fear"

EZRA POUND HAD written for the May 1913 edition of *Poetry* the first substantive review of Robert Frost's *A Boy's Will*. By the fall of 1913 Frost's book had at least been mentioned in *T. P.'s Weekly, Bookman, Athenaeum, English Review,* and *Times Literary Supplement,* as well as in Harold Monro's new quarterly, *Poetry and Drama*. In the United States the *Academy* and Chicago's genteel *Dial* had also reviewed it. Unlike so many new poetry books, Frost's did not sink unnoticed like a stone.[1] Biographies of Frost remark on the minimal attention this book received. Too often overlooked is that it had received any attention at all. Because Frost's publisher was the reputable house of David Nutt, it gained attention where other poetry books by equally unknown writers received none.

In the glossy wide-circulation *Bookman,* edited by Arthur St. John Adcock, who generally wrote most of the unsigned copy, the review of *A Boy's Will* not only carried Frost's picture but also an interview that made much of the American's decision to come to England. The overall impression of the interview was that Frost had become a poet because "he disliked city life and did not number the profitable business instincts among his gifts."[2] That irritated him, but he *had* been interviewed and his picture duly printed (*Bookman*'s policy was to run pictures of every writer discussed). More impressively the twin standard-bearers for genteel literary opinion, the *Times Literary Supplement,* and the *Athenaeum,* both noticed *A Boy's Will*. The *Athenaeum* deemed the book worthy of only two long sentences under a general headline, "Notices of New Books," yet few poetry books received that dignity. Generations of critics have remarked on the dismissive nature of those sentences, especially the second, which said Frost's attempt to tell the tale of one young man was "only half successful." The reviewer speculated, "Possibly because many of his verses do not rise above the ordinary." But of course a reviewer for this weekly *would* say such a thing. After all, this was the standard-bearer of the late Victorian-Edwardian literary tradition. Compared to the flowery diction still so common in both English and American poetry in 1913, Frost's poems *did* seem ordinary.[3]

In *The Times Literary Supplement,* a full paragraph was given to the book. The reviewer noted a distinctive intellectual and philosophical depth to the poems, and though dismissing that depth as "feebly or obscurely expressed" went so far as to call attention to "The Trial by Existence," one of the few poems Frost had already published.[4] Perhaps that attention caused the *Bookman* to revisit Frost. In June the publication gave *A Boy's Will* a full review by Katherine Tynan. She dismissed the book; even so the unknown first-time poet had the rare good fortune to receive two mentions there.

Also that June the *English Review,* one of the first magazines to promote realist literature, carried a paragraph about *A Boy's Will* in an omnibus review written by one of its editors, Norman Douglas. Given that the *English Review* had been established in 1908 to challenge the genteel idea of literature, this review, when read against those of the *TLS* and *Athenaeum,* proved that at least a few among the literati recognized Frost's distinction. The review called attention to Frost's Americanness saying that, "Nowhere on earth, we fancy, is there more outrageous nonsense printed under the name of poetry than in America; and our author, we are told, is an American. All the more credit to him for breaking away from this tradition."[5] Unlike so many other editors, he recognized the new kind of poetry and meant to be its champion.

The most substantive review came from Frost's friend, F. S. Flint. Published in the second issue of Monro's *Poetry and Drama,* it drew on private conversations with Frost. In his review, Flint asserted the need for a new poetic realism saying that good poets engage in "a constant struggle against circumambient stupidity for the right of expression." Echoing what Pound had said in his *Poetry* review, Flint says that, "Mr. Frost has escaped from America," by which he meant Frost had escaped from the undue symbolism, idealism, and archaic diction that still defined so much of American poetry. He praises Frost's "simplicity of utterance," adding that "most characteristic" of Frost's poetry are "direct observation of the object and immediate correlation with the emotion." He singled out "Reluctance" for his highest praise.

ROBERT FROST AND T. E. HULME

At the end of 1913's summer, as these reviews began to emerge, Frost was busy with his new eclogues; his dramatic narrative dialogues and monologues. As he finished these new poems, he sent them to his new poet friends, soliciting their reactions.[6] At the time he had no idea whether abandoning the lyric in favor of long blank-verse narratives made any artistic sense. In July 1913 he wrote to Flint, "I am suffering from uncertainty with regard to the poems and to myself. Sometimes I despair of myself for several kinds of fool."[7] He asked Flint who could help him negotiate the philosophical issues that lay behind his artistic experiments. Flint answered that T. E. Hulme, the man who gave Pound the theory for imagism, would be the best candidate for such a talk. Even more to Frost's interest, Hulme had just finished translating Bergson's *Introduction to Metaphysics* into English (published in 1913).

In the summer of 1913 Hulme had published and delivered a series of essays that had been the talk of the literati. Hulme had associated the new realism with something he called classicism, based on the Greek poetry of antiquity. He set that kind of realism in opposition to what he sneeringly labeled romanticism. Piquing Frost's interest was Hulme's firsthand knowledge of Bergson and contemporary philosophy. Between Hulme's familiarity with the classical tradition and contemporary philosophy, he was quite possibly the best man in London for Frost to meet. Hulme also had established a salon, begun after he had founded what was termed his Secessionist Club. His first club had lasted off and on from 1909 until he left England in 1910 and had given birth to what Pound called "the school of images." After he returned in 1911, Hulme continued his studies in philosophy for a doctoral degree at Cambridge. That was not so simple. He had already been expelled. To be readmitted he had Bergson himself write a letter of recommendation. But something in Hulme's nature did not love a school. In 1911 he was again expelled. He went back to London, where he became interested in the visual arts of the postimpressionists. His latest salon was held at an artist's hangout, the Café Royal, and included painters and sculptors associated with futurism, such as the visual artists Henry Wadsworth, Henri Gaudier-Breska, and Jacob Epstein, as well as the writer and painter Wyndham Lewis.[8] When Frost met Hulme, he had just returned from Germany where he had attended the Aesthetics Conference.[9]

It seems likely that the two poets talked about that conference. There Hulme had found an answer to his skepticism that the intangible soul, or "life force," what Bergson called the *élan vital,* could be empirically discoverable and even represented artistically. The answer came from both the German aesthetic philosophy of Wilhelm Worringer, and Action Française, the right-wing aristocratic, monarchist, and French Catholic intellectual and political movement. Both convinced Hulme that language could not represent the life force, or élan vital. By definition chaotic and irrational, it was also unrepresentable. All one could hope to do was control it and find a way to isolate and oppose it with something else. The generally optimistic view of human nature associated with this life force in Bergson and William James no longer seemed valid to Hulme. The best one could hope with regard to its existence was to enlist an external authority and temper and control it. For Hulme the inner life revealed by intuition was chaotic and irrational. Institutions, be they from government or from art, offered the external severity of authority. The rules of art, as an external agent, offered one a solution to the implicit dangers of the life force. This is where Hulme found Worringer's theories useful. Worringer had argued that the elements of visual design established just such a mechanism in form. According to Worringer, form governed and made possible the approximation of a representation of the unrepresentable chaos of the inner spiritual realm. Worringer, unlike the Action Française, did not advocate fascist or monarchist authority. Through the Action Française, however, Hulme connected Worringer to politics.

The Action Française, thought Hulme, made the same argument on behalf of authority as did Worringer, only the French movement applied it to politics. Action Française claimed that the life of a nation, its abstract vitality, its people's soul, could be contained only through the politics of monarchy and elite rule. Without the necessary frame of the elite and the monarch, the mob would erupt. To effect a return to Catholicism and monarchy in France, Action Française organized a youth group, Camelots du Roi. The movement's magazine, the anti-Semitic *Action Française*, dedicated itself to these goals in the names of monarchy and Catholicism.[10] Summarizing the way these two conceptions of authority blended in Hulme, Michael Levenson writes, "On the one side, the key concepts are order, discipline and restraint; on the other, they are freedom, expression, and individualism."[11] When Frost met him, Hulme was awash in these ideas. He wanted to reconcile Bergson's empirical claims on behalf of consciousness and an inner life with the authority deemed essential by the Action Française. This is because he could no longer be an unquestioning advocate of progressive views of unlimited freedom that led only to chaos. He now preferred to focus on the limitations and boundaries of experience.

Frost had been wrestling with a justification for his commitment to meter, given the strong arguments made by Pound, Flint, and others against its necessity. Frost hoped that Flint and Hulme would help him better formulate his ideas. He said as much to Flint: "Do you suppose you could get Hulme to listen with you some night to my theory of what would be pure form in poetry? I don't want to talk to a salon, but to a couple of clear-heads who will listen and give my idea its due."[12]

In Hulme's appeal to authority and to tradition, Frost recognized a cultural justification for meter that, for him, trumped any need for empirical objective justification. Not only was meter a metaphor for the ongoing genteel tradition, it was itself also a metaphor for any public poetry concerned with morality, justice, virtue, duty, and character. On the other hand, it may well be that Frost thought of meter as a metaphor for natural laws, even the laws of physics. Probably to Hulme's disapproval, Frost argued that the human compulsion to go beyond natural limitations, even the laws of physics, could be reflected in poetry by contrasting the wild excess of human speech with the controlled metrical feet of poetry, a control meant to mirror biological and other physical limitations. By playing the freedom of the sentence against the control of the metrical line, one could metaphorically represent the contest between what Bergson recognized as the inherent linguistic compulsion to distinguish good from bad as well as a contest between the obvious scientific facts of nature's physical laws and the human will to believe that something lies beyond them. If Frost did make such a case for meter, I can imagine Flint making a case for grammar as the equivalent metaphor without the need for meter. To that, though, Frost most likely would have appealed to the metaphorical weight of cultural tradition that meter also represented. Ultimately one can only imagine what the conversation must have been. No record exists, but shortly afterward Frost told Flint, "My ideas got just the rub they needed."[13] As if to underline just how powerful those ideas had become for him, after this meeting Frost wrote his most famous letter, a poetic declaration of independence.

FROST'S DECLARATION OF POETIC INDEPENDENCE

Shortly after talking with Hulme, Frost wrote a now-famous letter to John Bartlett in which Frost asserted his newfound poetic principles.[14] Too often biographies and literary histories overlook the context for this letter. Written on July 4, 1913, it not only followed his meeting with Hulme, it also came in the midst of his doubts concerning meter and a narrative poetry of talk. The famous letter begins in medias res. In the first line Frost responds to a question Bartlett had asked about *T. P.'s Weekly's* omnibus review of new poetry books. That review had included *A Boy's Will,* and Bartlett thought it unusually nasty. Given that its signature was only initials, Bartlett wondered if Frost knew who wrote it. Frost begins his letter with the answer. "Those initials you quote from *T. P.'s* belong to a fellow named Buckley [Reginald R. Buckley] and the explanation of Buckley is this that he has recently issued a book with David Nutt, but at his own expense [the book was *St. Francis: A Troubadour of the Spirit,* 1912], whereas in my case David Nutt assumed the risks. *And* those other people Buckley reviewed are his personal friends or friends of friends or not that simply examples of the kind of wrong horse most fools put their money on. You will be sorry to hear me say they are not even craftsmen." Frost then launches into his own poetic theory of craft, of speech, sound, and meter.

He begins by saying, "To be perfectly frank with you I am one of the most notable craftsmen of my time. . . . I am possibly the only person going who works on any but a worn out theory (Principle I had better say) of versification."[15] This may not have been just braggadocio. It may well have come from his realization, after talking with Hulme and Flint, that unlike his compatriots, he had a principle behind his insistence that meter ought to be put in counterpoint with talk. That principle had to do with the lyric heritage of classical Greek and Latin antiquity.

To prove to Bartlett what he meant, Frost next explained his theory of talk set in opposition to meter as a theory of "sentence sounds," or "the sound of sense." Based on the tones of speech, that is, spoken conversation replicated in writing, Frost's theory assumed that, properly done, a written record of spoken language would also incorporate the spoken tones of voice that accompanied any conversation. Those tones, he said, reveal the psychological and ethical essence of both character and situation. The consciousness that Bergson and William James championed could be revealed by poetry through mimicking voice tones. As Frost said in this letter, "The sound of sense, then. You get that. It is the abstract vitality of our speech. It is pure sound—pure form. One who concerns himself with it more than the subject is an artist." The Frost scholar Tom Vander Ven offers still the single best pithy sentence explaining the theory, "A poem is not a sound of sense itself but the context for one."[16] The poetry replicates the conditions that give rise to the various speaking tones that reveal each character's inner psychological state. As such it does not need to describe them secondhand and implicitly proves the existence of such inner states in the first place.

In his discussion of realist theory Dario Villanueva makes the case as much for realism's dependence on readers as on writers. Nancy Glazener makes the same case with regard to American realist fiction. According to Villaneuva, the context a reader brings to any given work is as responsible for its recognition as something real as are the various techniques a writer may employ. Frost, according to this theory, assumes that readers will hear the contemporary tones of voice the poet mimicked. In so doing, they would inevitably associate his poetry with living psychological experiences that they recognized.

In the notebooks Frost kept from this period, he scans lines according to conventional metrical patterns and then scans them again as they would be pronounced when read aloud according to their implied tones. One can see him ask, How much can one make metrical poetry *sound* like talk before it ceases to sound metrical, which is to say, ceases to have the cadence of poetry at all? It was similar to Picasso's asking how much one can reduce the pictorial elements necessary to produce a face before no one can recognize the face at all. Is one large circle with two dots and a half circle in the middle all it takes? If so, what does that imply about both perception and art? In his letter to Bartlett, Frost answers with his own principle. Meter sets a rationale, a limit, a boundary. Within the bounds of meter Frost explores the nebulous, strange, inner psychology, ethics, and morals of the genteel tradition. Newly enthusiastic about these ideas, Frost went so far as to propose to Flint that they collaborate on a book, *On Meter, Cadence, and Rhythm*.[17]

Even as he entertained these experimental ideas, Frost expected his poetry to be accessible and make few artistic demands of his readers. Writing to his Plymouth, New Hampshire, friend Sidney Cox (then a first-year professor in Illinois and fresh from a hard break-up), Frost made the case for hiding his artistic experimentation from the casual reader: "You must not disillusion your admirers with the tale of your sources and processes. This is gospel according to me." Later, after he became well known, he told the critic William Stanley Braithwaite, that above all else, he expected his poetry to appeal to any reader as much for its insights as for its artistry: "A story must always release a meaning more readily to those who read than life itself as it goes ever releases meaning. Meaning is a great consideration. But a story must never seem to be told primarily for meaning. Anything, an inspired irrelevance even to make it sound as if told the way it is chiefly because it happened that way."[18]

Frost, full of these new ideas, also wrote to the publisher Thomas Mosher.

> If I write more lyrics it must be with no thought of publication. What I *can* do next is bring out a volume of blank verse that I have already well in hand and won't have to feel I am writing to order. I had some character strokes I had to get in somewhere and I chose a sort of eclogue form for them. Rather I dropped into that form. And I dropped to an everyday level of diction that even Wordsworth kept above. I

trust I don't terrify you. I think I have made poetry. The language is appropriate to the virtues I celebrate. At least I am sure I can count on you to give me credit for knowing what I am about. You are not going to make the mistake that Pound makes of assuming that my simplicity is that of the untutored child. I am not undesigning.[19]

Frost did not exaggerate when he said he had dropped his diction, nor did he exaggerate Mosher's terror. A longtime publisher of aestheticism, of symbolists and decadents, Mosher had long resisted publishing the everyday diction and narratives that defined Frost's new realism. When Frost says that his new poetry contains "the language [that] is appropriate to the virtues I celebrate," he meant to reassure Mosher that they still shared the same aesthetic values. He was saying that he understood poetry to be, above all, an art form. He had now come to a new principle for his art but it was art nonetheless. When he said, "I am not undesigning," he may well have meant to let Mosher know that he still carried the flame for beauty and idealism. He was just now more committed to the gemlike quality of that flame than to the amorphous smoke it so often gave off.

"A HUNDRED COLLARS"

"The Death of the Hired Man" had been the first of his new-style poetry to find its way to the magazine market, and it had failed. In contrast two other new poems, "A Hundred Collars" and "The Fear," both were published in Harold Monro's *Poetry and Drama* (1913).[20] The first of these poems, "A Hundred Collars," reproduces a dispute not just between two men but also between two attitudes toward speech and language. The men, and the way they approach language, come from two different social and ethnic worlds. One, Lafe (short for Lafayette) is a working-class French Canadian, and the other, Dr. Magoon, a genteel professor of old New England stock (most likely Protestant Irish, as were those who founded Derry, New Hampshire, and environs). Briefly the poem describes Magoon's plight after missing his train in tiny Woodsville Junction, New Hampshire. The poem tells Magoon's story. Forced to spend the night after missing his train, he discovers to his chagrin that the town's one hotel is full. He is told he might share a room or sleep in the lobby in a chair. Electing to share, he finds that his roommate, Lafayette, could not be more unlikely. Unintellectual, huge, working-class, gregarious, a collector for the Democratic local newspaper, he has nothing in common with the reserved, skinny, upper-middle-class Republican Magoon. The poem asks in its drama, How would such men, if thrown together, get along? Frost answers by allowing their speech to reveal their character, their views, and their feelings.

As with "The Death of the Hired Man," this poem consists almost entirely of dialog. The characters' words reveal the implications of the situation and the issues. Their speech also reveals larger themes concerning the ethics of obligation, family, and home, the same issues that defined "The Death of the Hired Man." Of all the issues circulating in "A Hundred Collars," however, the value of courage and its relationship to the ideal of equality become central. To connect courage to equality, Frost first raises the issue of equality.

As the poem begins, the night clerk tells Magoon that if he wants a room, he'll have to share. The occupant, he says, is a man, and to that he adds, "a man's a man." In nature all are equal. In social philosophy, in contrast, New England progressive liberal Republicans like Magoon, members of the Party of Lincoln still basking in the Civil War's afterglow, may talk a lot about equality, but they are not likely to want to spend the evening with a burly French Canadian representative of the Democratic Party. Reporting Magoon's own private thoughts, the poem satirizes his hypocrisy; "Though a great scholar, he's a democrat, / If not at heart, at least on principle." Small *d*. He rejects bigotry and prejudice on principle, endorsing the spirit of democracy as the spirit of the new progressive age, and of the Republican Party to which he most likely adheres. Confronted with an actual Democrat, perhaps even a populist, certainly a hearty working-class "rough-neck" from New England's marginalized ethnic group of French Canadians, Magoon balks. His ideal of equality meets the stark reality of another man for whom he has nothing but contempt and also fear. Their meeting becomes the poem's drama.

The night clerk's egalitarian philosophy of "a man's a man" makes no allowance for a hierarchy of class, ethnicity, or character. Magoon is tested again by the night clerk and by his philosophy. For in the clerk's tone the poem's drama emerges. Implicitly he challenges Magoon's courage and manliness. He has all but asked if Magoon is man enough to face a total stranger. Has he the courage? The poem adds, "The night-clerk blinked his eyes and dared him on." Magoon looks around the forlorn lobby. Another man sleeps in a chair. "Has he had the refusal of my chance?" asks Magoon. The night clerk says, "He was afraid of being robbed or murdered. / What do you say?" Directly challenged as a man by another man, Magoon feels compelled by his own principles to meet the challenge. He says, "I'll have to have a bed."

Meanwhile in the room Lafayette, aware that someone will likely share the room, anticipates a knock. When it arrives, he yells through the door before he has set eyes on Magoon, "Show him this way. I'm not afraid of him. / I'm not so drunk I can't take care of myself." The humor here is subtle. The poem has given readers only Magoon's perspective. Switching to Lafayette, readers find he has just as much to fear from a stranger as Magoon does. Unlike Magoon, however, Lafayette rises to the challenge immediately. The two men must give the principle of equality a reality test. Just like Magoon, Lafayette is committed to the principle of equality. The first words indicate where they stand on the issue. Says Magoon,

> "Lafe was the name, I think?"
> "Yes, *Laf*ayette—
> "You got it the first time. And yours?"
> "Magoon.
> Doctor Magoon."
> "A doctor?"
> "Well, a teacher."[21]

Caught in his own elitism—"Well, a teacher"—Magoon next assesses Lafe. In so doing he reveals his prejudice and bigotry. "The Doctor looked at Lafe, then looked away. / A man? A brute! Unclad above the waist / He sat there creased and shining in the lamp-light." That is what he thinks. Does Magoon's revulsion also show on his face? I think it does. I think that Lafe sees that revulsion and realizes Magoon is a snob, even a bigot. For a French Canadian in New Hampshire in 1913, though, bigotry would have been all too familiar. Realizing what Magoon thinks of him, he returns the compliment with a clever witticism about Magoon's little skinny self.

Fiddling with his shirts, Lafe launches into a tale about growing out of his collars. In an era when collars were sold separately from shirts, the very idea of a collar itself signified a certain gentility of demeanor. That such decorum stifles the burly, not to say, uncontainable democratic Lafe, adds a humorous symbolism to the poem. Lafe declares that he now wears a size 18. His sudden, seemingly random, disquisition on collars is in no way random. It is Lafe's conscious decision to belittle and mock Magoon as a bigot and a way to confine him to the gentility that he so clearly reflects, a gentility signified by collars. When Lafe says his neck size is 18, he evidently looks significantly at Magoon and asks, "What size do you wear?" Magoon's response is priceless. He understands the implication of the question and the look. In so many words Lafe has just said, *You think I am a brute. OK—I could strangle you in ten seconds.* "The Doctor caught his throat convulsively. / 'Oh—ah—fifteen—fifteen.'"[22] Whether he meant to or not (I think he did), Lafe puts Magoon in his place. It as if he had also said, *You think my body is repulsive? Whose body is less manly?* Magoon walked into the room thinking himself the social and intellectual superior (perhaps also ethnically superior). Within a minute Lafe has asserted his physical dominance and proved the night clerk's point: in nature a man is a man, and the stronger one can rule the weaker, if he so chooses.

But does Lafe so choose? As it happens, having called Magoon out on his bigotry, Lafe then talks about collars in increasingly genial tones. It is as if he means to call attention to what a recent historian of gentility, Richard L. Bushman, recognized as its central paradox: "Rather than liberating people from aristocratic cultural power, the spread of gentility left Americans more in its thrall than ever."[23] Magoon's gentility, and the genteel tradition in general, signified by the collars, become for Lafe not icons of refinement and culture but rather tokens of physical fact, the size and strength of real bodies in real space. No doubt enjoying his little joke, Lafe tells Magoon that if he will give him his address, he will send him "a hundred collars," size 15, that no longer fit. Getting no response, Lafe concludes, "You act as if you wished you hadn't come. / Sit down or lie down, friend—you make me nervous." When Magoon speaks, his fear, coupled with superiority, continues to dominate: "I'll not be put to bed by you, my man." Lafe replies, "'My man, my man.' You talk like a professor." Lafe then adds,

> "Speaking of who's afraid of who, however,
> I'm thinking I have more to lose than you
> If anything should happen to be wrong.
> Who wants to cut your number fifteen throat?"

At this point the poem engages the problem of tone and language. Magoon talks like a book, while Lafayette talks "like a man." Insofar as this is a poem about equality's relationship to courage, one might say that Lafe embraces the spirit of his namesake, the great Marquis de Lafayette of the eighteenth century. Like that Lafayette, who went against his aristocratic heritage in the name of equality, Lafe goes against the brute strength of his physical body and prefers to be generous, gentle, kind, even genteel. In contrast Magoon, the physical weakling, makes up for what he lacks in strength by the social power of his speech and of the genteel tradition.

Biographically Frost had more in common with Magoon than Lafayette. In fact Frost could write the satire of Magoon so well, I believe, because he was more Magoon than Lafe. In fact the farm that Frost owned in Derry from 1900 to 1912 was known, from its first owners, as the Magoon place. Like Lafayette, that name, too, was not chosen simply at random for this character.

As a metaphor of equality, Lafayette in this poem suggests that equality is at once necessary and deeply unnatural. Said another way, a commitment to such a moral principle might well require one to go against the grain of one's own nature. Huge Lafayette, who has every reason to be angry and bitter, instead stands—far more than Magoon—for equality and even lives it every day. During his long monologue he explains that he is a Vermont Democrat who works as a travelling bill collector for the local Republican daily newspaper. His job has led him to know all the people and farms that subscribe to the paper, people whose politics he does not even accept, and who are likely as bigoted as Magoon toward French Canadians. "You see I'm in with everybody, know 'em all. / I almost know their farms as well as they do." The ultimate democrat, he has earned the respect not only of the local farmers but also of the Republican newspaper editor, who asks him to use his influence to garner enough votes to elect the Republican running in the next election.

What began as a put-down with regard to the collars becomes, by the end, an example of Lafe's generosity. He insists on giving Magoon his old collars. In so doing he puts the ostensibly egalitarian Magoon to shame. At the end of the poem Lafe leaves the room for a while. He tells Magoon that he'll be back and asks that Magoon not go crazy when he hears noise later and think that he is being robbed or assaulted: "There's nothing I'm afraid of like a scared man."[24] The poem's final two lines, a separate stanza unto themselves, mark the effect on Magoon. "He [Lafe] shut the door. / The doctor slid a little down the pillow." I read that as a slide of shame. Called to account for his bigotry, snobbery, and general ugliness of character, Magoon has met his own reflection and found it sorely wanting.[25]

As an example of his new poetic theory of sentence sounds, the iambic pentameter of "A Hundred Collars," when set against the two characters' living speech, complemented the theme of equality. Meter produced regular inexorable lines, but the peculiar individuality of these two men produced their unique cadence and tones. Both their cadence and tone are embedded in the particulars of place and time, which are then governed and controlled by the meter to which both must conform. Meter, like equality, is both unnatural and essential. Both men claim to believe in equality, and one even does, yet nothing really encourages its existence. Current social and political institutions actively encourage Magoon's bigotry and Lafe's potentially violent reaction to it. Yet both men restrain themselves, just as meter restrains each poetic line.

"THE FEAR"

In addition to "A Hundred Collars," *Poetry and Drama* published "The Fear." In that poem Frost explores the psychology of a woman, the poem's central character.[26] Like "A Hundred Collars," this poem charts an incipient threat from what should be a simple encounter. It, too, asks fundamental questions about equality and trust among strangers. Briefly the poem takes place at night, far from any town in a rustic home deep in the New Hampshire wilderness. A woman in her house hears noise in the woods and immediately panics. She calls on her husband to check the situation. By the end of the poem, it has become clear that she fears she is being stalked by a former lover. Before checking the woods, the husband and wife debate the noise. The woman is convinced it is a man, perhaps that same former lover. The husband doubts it is any person at all. In their debate the couple reveals tensions and problems in their marriage.

As it turns out, someone *is* in the woods, a man, a stranger. He claims to be a father taking his young son for a night walk to show the boy the stars. Is it true? The son does not speak, and the man remains forever out of the woman's sight, hidden in the woods. Because the poem is told entirely through dialog, readers confront the same fear as the woman, and by the end readers can be forgiven if they wonder whether the man did murder or assault the husband and the wife. By describing a situation that leads to the woman's paranoia, the poem also makes it our paranoia as readers. In so doing the poem questions that familiar genteel belief in the kindness of strangers and in egalitarianism.[27]

Compared to both "A Hundred Collars" and "The Death of the Hired Man," "The Fear" is Frost's most experimental poem yet. It contains almost no narration. In 103 lines readers find only a dialog between husband and wife and brief comments from a stranger. A poetic narrator appears only in the last three lines, which leave out as much as they describe.

> "But if that's all—Joel—you realize—
> You won't think anything. You understand?
> You understand that we have to be careful.
> This is a very, very lonely place.
> Joel!" She spoke as if she couldn't turn.
> The swinging lantern lengthened to the ground,
> It touched, it struck it, clattered and went out.[28]

Hearing the stranger's explanation, the wife appeals to her husband to forgive her paranoia. On the other hand, given the narrative intrusion of the last lines, readers cannot help but wonder whether the stranger has just assaulted her at the very moment when she feels ridiculous and foolish for fearing that a former lover had come to rape her. The poem's drama can be read either as deeply brutal and unrelieved, speaking to the worst in people, or as a case study in fear's destructive power. As the latter it tells readers that fear, the mental inability to know limits and to have a clear boundary between the real and the possible, can ruin an otherwise healthy marriage. It becomes, oddly, a poem in defense of limits. This poem, more than any other poem he had published to date, pits speech against meter. In so doing it proves that speech can be as important an artistic lens through which to view the human condition as any particularly well-wrought descriptive image.

Frost thought he had found something heretofore untried in American poetry. He said as much to Bartlett that August: "I am one of the few who have a theory of their own upon which all their work down to the least accent is done. I expect to do something to the present state of literature in America."[29]

A SUMMER AND FALL OF POETRY IN ENGLAND
FROST IN 1913

Early in August 1913 the Frost family had taken a trip to Scotland with the Gardners, a couple Frost had met at the January soiree at the Poetry Bookshop. There he had befriended Mary Gardner, a poet, and learned that she and her husband, an archeologist, had as many children as did the Frosts. By August the two families had become friendly and had decided to vacation together in Scotland. On that Scottish trip Frost met J. C. Smith, a literary intellectual who also had a profound impact on Frost's new poetry.[30] Smith made his living as the inspector of teacher training schools in Scotland. His literary reputation, however, came from his scholarly critical editions of Shakespeare and Spenser and, more recently, an anthology of English verse designed to compete with Palgrave's. Smith knew as much of the British poetic tradition as anyone Frost had ever met. In their talks Smith tested Frost's new theories against his own extensive background in British literary history.

As he did with so many of his new poems, Frost sent "A Hundred Collars" to friends to see what they thought of his new theory or principle. After reading it, Smith replied, "I know, because you told me, what the central idea is—the dilemma of the theoretical democrat when he's brought up against the real thing." Smith assumes that he and Frost share more with intellectuals like Magoon—"people like us"—than with Lafe. People like us, says Smith, have a rather hard time with equality in practice. And that hard time, that dilemma, makes the poem of interest. Smith read the poem as a parable of the conflict between two types of poetry, the genteel poetic tradition—the aesthetic triumph of beauty over brutality—and the new realism, which sought to undermine many of the foundational principles of that same genteel tradition. And when it came to realism, Smith could not help but add that Lafe, "as a token of his brotherhood and equality," wants to "present you . . . with a hundred old collars. The idea's all right, and quite important—it *is* a real dilemma for the likes of us, but is it a *poetic* idea? Wouldn't you make a better thing of it in prose?" Smith tells Frost that "the only reason for verse is that one has something to say that can't be said in prose."[31]

Frost came up against the same view that poetry ought to sing when he had the good fortune to meet the poet laureate of England, Robert Bridges, that August. Smith had also been responsible for that meeting. He had given a copy of *A Boy's Will* to the poet Laurence Binyon, who admired the poems and asked to meet with Frost upon his return to London in August. Accepting the invitation, Frost went to Binyon's place, only to be told to follow him to a restaurant. To Frost's surprise none other than Bridges himself was sitting at the table. There followed a lunch in which Frost, Binyon, and Bridges debated Frost's new theory of the "sound of sense" and the need to reproduce genuine talk across the fixity of meter.

Reporting the event later, Frost recalled that "Bridges wants to fix the vocables here and now because he sees signs of their deteriorating. He thinks they exist in print for people." Bridges did not agree at all with Frost. He did not trust the fluidity of speech and the variable tones arising from regular conversation. He wanted poetry to insist on the relationship between the line and the sentence, between meter and each syllable. For Bridges each syllable had a fixed stress, a fixed pronunciation; mimicking talk would merely replicate error, which he opposed. Poetry, Bridges said, served society insofar as it ensured proper pronunciation of words for the future. Bridges opposed any natural evolution of language. Frost violently disagreed, saying later, "The living part of a poem is the intonation entangled somehow in the syntax idiom and meaning of a sentence." Bridges, far from being impressed, dismissed Frost as a naive, even unlearned, American. To that Frost had his answer ready: "Foolish old man is all I say."[32]

Happily he had also, thanks to J. C. Smith, at last been introduced to Harold Monro and his circle of Georgians, a group of poets who shared Frost's newfound poetic theory. Of them, Wilfrid Gibson was the first to whom Frost became close. At the time Gibson lived upstairs in the Poetry Bookshop's artist apartments. Frost that summer and fall became a frequent visitor.[33] One afternoon Gibson took Frost to the Mont Blanc restaurant to join a literary salon organized by one of England's leading magazine critics, Edward Garnett (Garnett's wife, Constance, is still known today for her translations into English of the great Russian realists, especially Tolstoy). Garnett's salon included most of the writers associated with Monro's *Poetry and Drama* as well as such luminaries as Joseph Conrad, John Masefield, and W. H. Hudson.[34]

In the fall Frost also met Edward Thomas (1878–1917), the man who would become "the best friend I ever had," Frost said. One of the most influential critics of the day, Thomas had made his living from his pen since graduating from college and suffered profoundly as a result of the compromises required by editors. Though he would eventually become one of England's most important poets, when Frost met him, Thomas had not yet published any poetry.[35] The two realized they led parallel lives. Both were older than most of their peers; Thomas was thirty-six and Frost almost forty. Both were fathers of a substantial brood. Thomas had three children to Frost's four. Most important for both was that they shared the same views about poetry.[36]

By October Frost had become a fixture in the London world of poetry. By then, I believe, Frost thought he might well be able to make a living as a poet. Gibson, Thomas, and so many others made their living from selling their poetry, reviews, and essays, and Frost no doubt expected to do the same. As one biographer says, by the fall of 1913 "a dream of earning much the greater part of his living from poetry had taken possession of him."[37] To view this dream merely as a good way to earn some money, however, forgets why he wrote in the first place.

Writing to Bartlett that November, Frost gave voice to some of these ideas:

> You mustn't take me too seriously if I now proceed to brag a bit about my exploits as a poet. There is one qualifying fact always to bear in mind: there is a kind of success called 'of esteem' and it butters no parsnips. It means a success with the critical few who are supposed to know. But really to arrive where I can stand on my legs as a poet and nothing else means I must get outside that circle to the general reader who buys books in their thousands. I may not be able to do that. I believe in doing it—dont [*sic*] you doubt me there. I want to be a poet for all sorts and kinds. I could never make a merit of being caviare [*sic*] for the crowd the way my quasi-friend Pound does. I want to reach out, and would if it were a thing I could do by taking thought.[38]

Frost implies that poetry has a public role because it has a moral imperative, what Pound would call "news that stays news." Frost understood that news to be necessary for readers of "all sorts and kinds," and such readers could be found only in the so-called crass commercial marketplace of publishing. On the one hand, to be the voice of dissent and experimentation would "butter no parsnips" for his family's dinner table. To find money for butter, as it were, Frost determined to be crafty and secretly bring his ideas and experiments to the public. His new method, burying in subtlety his artistic experimentation with meter and sound and in seemingly straightforward dramas his tricky intellectual views, was, as he said to Bartlett, "a rather desperate game with our little wealth. The poets here are of three kinds the poor rats in one room and a suit of clothes with no family to take care of and much too cunning to be caught in that trap, the gentlemanly minors with a graceful weakness for verse and by common consent quite rich enough to indulge it and the few like Masefield who arrive at one jump. I am like none of these. I must make my way very slowly: such is my doom I am afraid."[39] The "desperate game" was at once economic and artistic. As a matter of artistic principle he refused to compromise with conventional taste, yet also as a matter of principle he expected to have his poetry be a part of the public sphere, and the genteel publications that defined it.

To that end, he and Elinor had begun making plans to move and settle in the Dymock area of Gloucestershire, the region of little towns where the poets he had become closest with, Gibson, Abercrombie, Edward Thomas, and John Drinkwater (who had given the go-ahead for Frost's first book) lived. Sometime that fall Frost heard from a woman, Gertrude McQuestern, whom he had first met while teaching at Pinkerton. A well-known orator in an age that allowed one to make a living giving recitals of famous poems and dramatic monologs, she had come to Pinkerton to recite. The two had become friends. Later, when the Frost family moved to Plymouth, they met again. McQuestern, ten years older than Frost, was then a professor of oratory at Emerson College and came to Plymouth to be with her mother each summer. She wrote to Frost in the fall of 1913, after reading reviews and hearing about A Boy's Will.

In his reply Frost described his ideas about speech, meter, and music in poetry. In the free-verse imagist crowd, he tells her, the all important thing to know nothing about is metre. There are two ways out of it for the candidate: either he must never have known or he must have forgotten. Then there is a whole line of great poets he must profess not to have read or not to have read with attention. He must say he knows they are bad without having read them. [To which, he adds] Their worst fault is their devotion to method. They are like so many teachers freshly graduated from a normal school. I should have thought to escape such nonsense in the capital of the world. It is not a question with them of how much native poetry there is in you or how much you get down on paper, but of what method you have declared for. Your method must be their method or they won't accept you as a poet.[40]

Frost was not arguing against having a method, a poetic theory, or principle. Rather he wished to emphasize that for him a poet's talent lay not in an arbitrary method but only in "how much native poetry there is in you or how much you get down on paper." Said another way, Frost's commitment to talk, to speech, to the "everyday diction" that even Wordsworth would not drop below, was also a commitment to a method that already existed. This genteel tradition, as I have called it, is a tradition he found in the everyday talk of people. The impact of William James and pragmatism can be found in this letter's explanation of method. Following what he had learned from James and even from Bergson, Frost turns to talk as a way to reflect the flux of events from the perspective of an insider who is experiencing those same events. When Frost's poetry mimics a character's everyday talk, the poet, as it were, enters into that same character's lived experience in real time. In so doing the poem inductively explains its own occasion. Talk understood in this way creates the event. To prevent the poem from becoming so subjective as to be meaningless to readers, however, it also carries in its meter the extrapersonal, extrasubjective external agent of the genteel tradition.

For Frost meter had become essential to his poetry precisely for its check on subjectivity, the motley decadence that he associated with the current free-verse school of poets. Rather than adopt their method, Frost prefers meter and the poets who experiment with talk set against meter, as he was doing. He tells McQuestern that compared to the free-verse poets, "my real intimates," "are of another kind. Gibson is my best friend.... He's just one of the plain folks with none of the marks of the literary poseur about him. . . . He will be of the Gloucester colony. Abercrombie is already living in Gloucester."[41] Soon so too would the Frost family.

Chapter Twelve

•

Robert Frost, a Realist in the Magazines of Modernism
"The Housekeeper" and "The Code"

BY THE TIME *Poetry and Drama* published "A Hundred Collars" and "The Fear" in December 1913, Frost had given himself over to the Georgian poets, who had become a literary sensation. After nearly a year their anthology had sparked such interest that many of its contributors, such as John Masefield and Rupert Brooke, would become among the best-read poets in England. In 1923, for instance, John Masefield's *Collected Poems* would sell more than 100,000 copies, while into the 1930s, Rupert Brooke's poetry would sell nearly 100,000 copies.[1] Of the two, Brooke was a rising star in 1913. His killer good looks graced many pictures subsequently ripped from magazines to grace, it is said, more than a few undergraduates' dorm room walls.

An imaginary application for admission to a fictive guild of Georgian poets by the poet Roy Campbell asked a series of questions to determine worthiness for membership. Through the satire one gleans an idea of Georgian poetry's attributes: "Have you ever been on a walking tour? Do you suffer from Elephantiasis of the Soul? Do you make friends easily with dogs, poultry, etc? Are you easily exalted by natural objects? Do you live in one place and yearn to be in another place? Can you write in rhyme and metre?"[2]

The satire could easily have been based on Harold Monro's *Poetry and Drama*. In its fourth issue, which carried Frost's two poems, it also carried the largest selection of poetry Monro had published to date. Because readers had decried Monro's preference for essays instead of the thing itself, Monro had finally capitulated and published poetry by fifteen poets,

199

most of them well known, including Thomas Hardy and the poet laureate Robert Bridges.[3] In addition to Frost, Monro included such younger poets as Walter de la Mare, Brooke, and W. H. Davies. Monro even included his own poems.

In the context of that issue Frost's narrative and dramatic poetry does not look unusual. It looks, all satire from the application aside, Georgian. In every issue, too, Monro published an opening series of editorials. In this issue he defends the need to bring a living voice to poetry.[4] In contrast to the imagists' emphasis on "the thing seen," Monro in his editorial made a case for "the supreme form of verbal expression" that belongs to "the active ways of life"—namely, poetry.

The poet and reviewer Louis Untermeyer read that issue in New York. At the time he wrote a literary column for the *Friday Literary Supplement* of the *Chicago Evening Post*. He right away recognized Frost's unique artistry. Given that Monro included no descriptions of his poets, Untermeyer recalled asking himself, "What Englishman . . . could have written those two poems?" It was not just their nominal references to New Hampshire locales but, as Untermeyer said, their poetics, which he described as "a blank verse so different from the traditional English medium that it had acquired a whole new tone and direction." It took a few months but he eventually learned from Harold Monro that the poet was an American named Robert Frost.[5]

UNTERMEYER, FROST, AND THE STATE
OF AMERICAN POETRY, 1913

Eventually Untermeyer and Frost became best of friends. They first learned of each other from the pages of *Poetry and Drama*. While Untermeyer learned of Frost from the December issue, Frost would learn of Untermeyer from later issues. In addition to Frost's poems, which had impressed him, Untermeyer had also read a column on the state of American poetry by the English poet John Alford. In his "American Chronicle," Alford claimed that American poetry had little to offer but the pale imitations of the worst of English Victorian verse. Robert Frost, too, could not believe how wrong-headed Alford had been. In a letter to Ernest Silver, one-time principal of the Pinkerton Academy, that accompanied this issue with Frost's poems, he referred to Alford's article as a "stupid roast on American literature."[6] To Bartlett Frost added, "This cub doesn't know how to find his way around among American writers. No one he mentions is thought anything of on the other side [i.e., in America itself]—no one of recent date. [Ralph Waldo] Emerson is so American, so original, especially in form." And while Frost complained about the good poets Alford missed, he added of those Alford disparaged, "Not that I weep for these."[7]

Unlike Frost, Untermeyer did not confine his anger to private letters. He wrote directly to Monro, telling him what Alford had gotten wrong. Monro, to his credit, decided to print Untermeyer's response in the next issue (March 1914).[8] There Untermeyer said, "If I were to take . . . one unrepresentative anthology, one mediocre poetic drama, and a dozen volumes" by poets upholding the Victorian tradition and name the result English poetry, no one would take it seriously. To prove that Alford had overlooked the best American poets, indeed the whole of the realist movement then called the New Poetry, Untermeyer offered a countercanon. He singled out Edwin Arlington Robinson, John Hall Wheelock, Joyce Kilmer, Edna St. Vincent Millay, Arthur Davison Ficke, Sara Teasdale, and Bliss Carman (a Canadian), "whose lusty *Songs of Vagabondia* and whose habit make it safe to classify him among the Americans." In his conclusion Untermeyer also made a spirited defense of Richard Hovey. "Which brings us to the curious fact that a critic has written an article on American Poetry (beginning with the New England group [the Schoolroom poets] and ending with Ezra Pound) and not once was the name of Richard Hovey mentioned. Mr. Alford should pay us another visit."[9] Reading that essay may well have been Frost's first encounter with Untermeyer.

In his published response Alford acidly held his ground, claiming that "the present period in perspective with the past . . . will be found to be as diminutive as any." Alford also dismissed the two most famous American poems of the previous twenty years, which Untermeyer had mentioned, Edward Markham's "The Man with the Hoe," and Joyce Kilmer's "Trees," although Alford did admit to the strength of Vachel Lindsay's and Edwin Arlington Robinson's poetry. Yet even they, Alford wrote, did not compare to the nineteenth-century Americans. Alford's two attacks on American poetry provoked an international literary feud. Edward J. Wheeler, editor of the genteel *Current Opinion,* struck a blow for American literary independence against John Bull in his magazine. To that Alford wrote a third attack, published in the September 1914 issue of *Poetry and Drama*. With it he meant to end the debate once and for all. Of current American poems, he wrote, "they are bad, not because they are American, but simply because they are bad, 'and there's an end on't.'"[10]

The spat over American poetry begun by Untermeyer and Alford had come to an end. But there was a surprising denouement. By the time Alford published his final curse, Robert Frost's second book, *North of Boston*, had been published in England. Between the time of Alford's first essay and his final one, he had read Frost's book. Although Alford had put paid to the argument of American poetry's overall merit, at the end of his concluding essay he did single out Robert Frost's *North of Boston*, saying that, of all the American poets, only in Frost's poetry did there appear the democratic "indigenous type of art for which Mr. Untermeyer and I have been searching in these pages."[11]

Nor did readers of that issue have to take Alford's word for it. In the back of each issue Monro routinely published poems from recently published books. In the September's issue he reprinted Frost's "Home Burial." It appeared just four pages after Alford's essay and gave better testimony to Alford's claim than anything Frost had yet published.[12]

FROST AND POUND, "THE HOUSEKEEPER," AND THE *EGOIST*

Well before either the publication of *North of Boston* in May or Alford's praise of the book in September, Ezra Pound had again decided to boom Frost, a man he would not let stay angry at him. In the January 15, 1914, issue Pound published another of Frost's new poems, "The Housekeeper," in the *Egoist,* Pound's magazine. Even today the *Egoist* is remembered as one of the most influential of "little magazines" for modernist poetry, in large part because it published, in addition to the imagists, T. S. Eliot's "The Love Song of J. Alfred Prufrock." For readers who do not think of Frost and modernism together, it often comes as a shock to find one of his poems in this magazine. Despite its reputation as a little magazine, the *Egoist* of 1914 was not meant to be a strictly niche publication preaching to a small literary audience of like-minded believers. The *Egoist*'s publisher, Dora Marsden, expected and desired to reach a general audience more like that affiliated with the *New Age,* a readership far wider even than Monro's venture, which itself was meant to be broadly accessible with large market appeal. To that end the *Egoist* did not confine its interest to literature but also published essays on a wide variety of topics relating to its editorial philosophy, which had begun in radical feminism. The magazine had been founded as the *Freewoman*. That incarnation died in 1912. Revived in 1913 as the *New Freewoman,* it soon fell under the editorial control of Ezra Pound, Richard Aldington, and H. D. In January 1914 Pound convinced Marsden to change the name to the *Egoist.* The feminist origins of that magazine were absorbed by its new orientation as a platform for the individualist philosophy of Max Stirner (author of a popular book of philosophy, *The Ego and His Own*).

When Robert Frost published in the *Egoist,* he was not suddenly deciding himself exclusive or avant-garde, nor was he narrowing his interests. He understood that magazine to have in intent, if not in reality, a goal of reaching a wide array of readers. In their day the *Egoist, Poetry and Drama,* and *Poetry* (Chicago), as well as the American magazines that had published him so far, like the *Independent, New England Magazine, Youth's Companion,* and *Forum,* belonged to the same world of literary and intellectual journalism, aiming their words at working-, middle-, and upper-middle-class readers, not to mention those in the elites of both countries.

Pound probably solicited Frost's poem while the *Egoist* was in its second incarnation as the *New Freewoman.* Even though it had become an outpost for free-verse imagism under Pound's literary reign, Pound still took an interest in any poetry that did unusual and interesting things artistically and thematically. The poem Pound published, "The Housekeeper," not only exhibited Frost's new theory but also took it even further than had "The Fear." Like "The Fear," it contains only two small lines of narrative intervention from the poet (after more than one hundred lines). Aside from those two lines at the end, the poem consists entirely of dialog. Every metrical line also mimics the living speech of the characters, which Frost sets across the rigid formal requirements of iambic pentameter. It could easily have led many readers to think it was in free verse (as it does even today, more than a hundred years later).[13]

Simply summarized, the poem takes place among New Hampshire's remote farms.[14] A farmer has come over to see one of his neighbors, John, who lives with his housekeeper, Estelle, and her mother. Estelle's mother tells the neighbor that John had just left to see him. During their conversation readers learn that John loves Estelle. Two weeks earlier, evidently tired of being unmarried, Estelle left John and married someone else. That implies she had been having an affair, despite essentially being John's common-law wife for fifteen years. Abandoned, John has fallen into depressive ruin, and Estelle's mother tells the neighbor the details. John returns by the end of the poem. He calls his neighbor to come outside, and the poem ends.

Might it be that the neighbor is the very man with whom Estelle is having an affair and even secretly married?[15] The poem never conclusively answers that question, though it offers a great deal of information about John, Estelle, and her mother. Combined, the poem's facts raise such questions as, What constitutes a marriage? What is love? What do lovers owe to one another? Is love synonymous with possession?[16]

Two recent scholars of the poem, Karen Kilcup and Timothy O'Brien, concentrate on Frost's use of speech, his experiment of setting talk against meter. Kilcup, for instance, reminds us that such talk as Frost records already has a long familiar heritage as gossip. Asserting one's power over

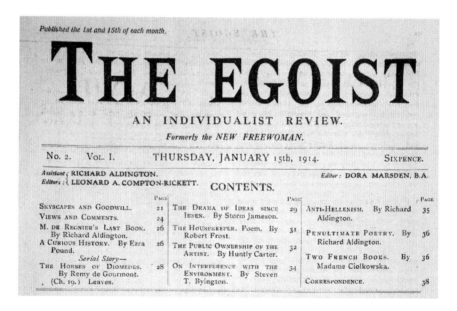

The first page of the *Egoist* of January 15, 1914, with Robert Frost's "The Housekeeper." From the Robert Frost Collection of Pat Alger.

another through the possession of secret knowledge separates gossip from regular conversation. This poem, even more than "A Hundred Collars," which also records the speech of two people who suddenly meet one another, thrives on the meaning and implication of gossip. In effect Frost, having absorbed William James and Henri Bergson, recast conversation from its common perception as a mere throwaway means to pass the time and made it instead a source of genuine poetry.[17] This poem begins when the neighbor learns that John has left. During the neighbor's conversation with the housekeeper's mother, readers quickly realize that, as in all good drama, there is a subtext. The mother wants to know what the neighbor knows, and John wants to find out what the mother knows. That the mother is morbidly obese and cannot move, and that she has a shotgun next to her armchair, hardly goes unnoticed in this little story of brinksmanship.

As she tells her version of events to the neighbor, Estelle's mother often quotes John. Until Timothy O'Brien drew attention to it, though, few had noticed the significance of John's speech. Like so many of the farmers that populate Frost's poems, John speaks in familiar country sayings and parables. His words, in short, are not necessarily his. He is the sort of man who finds it easier to quote conventional wisdom, such as when he offers his excuse for not marrying Estelle, than to invent new tropes. As he says, "Better than married ought to be as good / As married." O'Brien makes the point that John's own speech reveals his failure as a partner to Estelle and as a farmer. He does nothing on his own initiative. He does not even speak his own words or think his own thoughts. He merely parrots conventional wisdom. His talk makes tangible just how "out of touch with reality" and ineffective he really is (and how powerful the genteel tradition's conventions can become for an individual psyche).[18] John's speech also makes a nice analog for all that Frost saw as wrong with the conventional poetry of the genteel tradition.

"THE CODE"

A month after Pound published "The Housekeeper" in the *Egoist*, Harriet Monroe's *Poetry* published "The Code."[19] It was one of only three poems in that issue announced on the front cover. Pound had a role in its publication there too, as he had recommended it to Monroe. Like "The Housekeeper," "The Code" tells a straightforward story in the voices of various characters. Thematically this poem emphasizes the way talk reveals hierarchies of class and culture. It describes how simple speech can limit one's perspective. In particular the poem attends to conversational anecdotes the same way that "The Housekeeper" attends to conversational gossip. The bulk of the poem concerns an anecdote, which becomes the occasion for Frost's deeper meditation on social and psychological issues.

The poem re-creates a seemingly innocent and banal conversation. Consisting almost entirely of talk, its first nine lines rely on the narrator to establish the scene and situation. After that the poem's only voice is that of either the town-bred farmer or of his fellow laborer. Specifically the poem concerns a town-bred farmer who is earning some extra money during haying season; he joins two laborers, local hired men who likely come from nearby farms. Imagining he is just being polite—just, as the saying has it, "making conversation"—the town-bred farmer says something about an approaching rainstorm. This unwittingly provokes one of the two hired men to march off in anger. The remaining man, a local, then tells the farmer what he said wrong. Rather than say what angered his friend, though, the hired man launches into a long anecdote. He describes a time when he tried to murder his foreman for being a bully. The poem ends with the incredulous town-bred farmer's asking if he had been fired for attempted murder. With disbelief he says, "Discharge me? No! He knew I did just right." And so the poem ends. The implication is as sinister as that of "The Housekeeper." At the end of the day the town-bred farmer just wants to fit in. Yet the hired man's murderous anecdote tells the farmer that he will never belong. His tone of voice, his very mannerisms, will prohibit it. If he wants to fit in, he would do well to keep his mouth shut.

"The Code" can also be read as a parable charting the dilemma of being a man trying to make a living in poetry. Where gossip, like the feminine and genteel tradition, drew an intimate circle around both reader and writer, creating the warmth of privately shared information, the new realist methods of the "sound of sense" that Frost had invented dramatize the distance between people that talk often creates. At the same time he expected his poetry not only to reveal that distance but also to bridge it. Frost challenged the genteel tradition, which expected an intimate connection to exist between reader and writer even as he wanted to establish

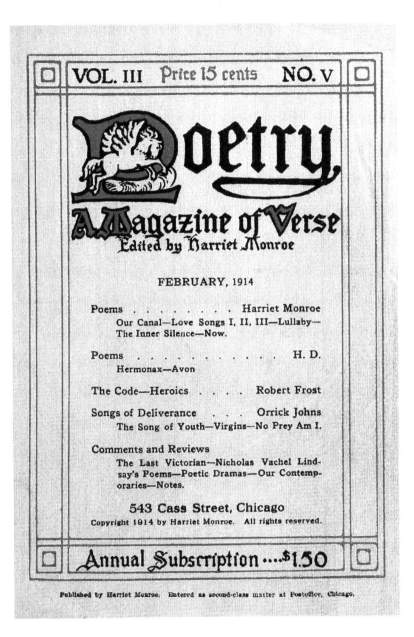

VOL. III   Price 15 cents   NO. V

Poetry

A Magazine of Verse

Edited by Harriet Monroe

FEBRUARY, 1914

Poems . . . . Harriet Monroe
Our Canal—Love Songs I, II, III—Lullaby—
The Inner Silence—Now.

Poems . . . . H. D.
Hermonax—Avon

The Code—Heroics . . . . Robert Frost

Songs of Deliverance . . . Orrick Johns
The Song of Youth—Virgins—No Prey Am I.

Comments and Reviews
The Last Victorian—Nicholas Vachel Lindsay's Poems—Poetic Dramas—Our Contemporaries—Notes.

543 Cass Street, Chicago
Copyright 1914 by Harriet Monroe. All rights reserved.

Annual Subscription ····$1.50

Published by Harriet Monroe. Entered as second-class matter at Postoffice, Chicago.

Of the poems published in this issue of Poetry, Frost's "The Code" is one of the few listed on the cover. From *Poetry, A Magazine of Verse,* February 1914.

it. In this poem, for instance, the town-bred farmer means well and simply says what is on his mind. However, the hired hands hear something entirely different than he intended.

I cannot help but wonder whether Frost wrote this poem out of his own anxiety as both poet and man. To be a man, as dramatized in "The Death of the Hired Man," "A Hundred Collars," and "The Housekeeper," he had to adhere to particularly strict conventions, the genteel tradition in which he had been reared. In these poems a man's relationship to that code, and those distinctions, which is to say, the way he talked, became the very essence of the masculine self.[20] While accent or intonation did not have the same meaning in America as in England, Frost's life in England no doubt drew his attention to the equally rigid speech codes of his own country.

Given that the poem is as much a study in masculine ways of talk as it is of the dynamics of social class in America, is Frost, through this poem's parable, charting the risks he took when he mimicked the voices of New Hampshire's country folk? Like the town-bred farmer, Frost must have wondered whether his poems got the voices right. He must have wondered whether his poetry was accurate to the people he meant to represent. After all, accuracy, precision, le mot juste had become watchwords of the new realism, and Frost meant his poetry to excel in its craft and be accurate in its depictions.[21]

Beyond that personal dimension, this poem can also be read as a parable for contemporary poetry. Poetry as a code could follow either the older genteel model or the newer imagist and Georgian models. And just as blissful ignorance of a code could lead to violence among New Hampshire farmers, as it does in this poem, so ignorance of poetic codes could just as easily cause seemingly poetic friends to throw down their pens and pencils and storm off. Frost did not wish to forgo the fundamentals of the genteel tradition, and I believe he reflected such fundamentals through meter as a synecdoche for the genteel tradition. Yet to adhere to that poetic tradition's metrical heritage meant that he might appear to be a Victorian too. Did he really want to speak in the same voice as the mustachioed Victorian censors or wear the same blue uniform of Comstock patrols?

By the time "The Code" appeared in the February 1914 issue of *Poetry*, Robert Frost had sent the completed manuscript of his second book,

North of Boston, to his publisher, who would publish it in May. It included "Death of the Hired Man," "A Hundred Collars," "The Housekeeper," and "The Code," which, combined with its other poems, appeared to have come from an entirely different poet than the one who had written *A Boy's Will.* Unlike that book, this second book's seventeen poems had only five lyrics: "The Pasture," "Mending Wall," "After Apple-Picking," "The Wood-Pile," and "Good Hours." The rest consisted of blank-verse narratives in the new "sound of sense."

Chapter Thirteen

●

Poet of the New American Poetry
North of Boston, "Putting in the Seed"

ON MAY 15, 1914, David Nutt published Robert Frost's second book, *North of Boston*.¹ In seventeen poems, most written while he lived in England, Frost brought his inherited genteel tradition into the modern world. He made it new. Breaking with that tradition's preference for fluid metrical rhythms based on song, such poems as "Death of the Hired Man," "The Fear," "The Housekeeper," "A Hundred Collars," and "The Code," not to mention "Home Burial," and "Mending Wall," returned poetry to living speech. In this collection Frost tested the metrical tradition on which genteel poetry depended. It was as if he wanted to see just what meter *did* for poetry—what did meter *add* to a poetic line? It was as if he asked, Why should *meter* make a poem? Each poem in this collection uses the language and situations familiar to prose in order to seek answers about the need for meter in poetry. In addition to its narratives, the volume contained five lyrics, including the now famous "After Apple Picking." That poem, too, raises serious questions about the importance and purpose of meter in lyric poetry.

Aside from the artistic questions concerning meter, the poems also raise questions about genteel values, particularly duty. The poems depict, after the example of Virgil's *Georgics,* the everyday work of life on a farm. In so doing they also explore such ethical principles as the purpose of work and the relation of work to play and courage. As Frost well knew, Virgil had inaugurated this type of pastoral poetry, the georgic. In this collection Frost, long a student of Virgil's technique, adapted it to his own poetic principle. Out of Virgil he forged his new realism.

"DEALING WITH REALITY": ROBERT FROST
AND THE NEW POETRY OF 1914

North of Boston came to a literary environment well prepared to receive it. In both England and America, the New Poetry had at last established realism as appropriate to poetry. Editors, reviewers, and others increasingly applauded poetry depicting everyday working-class, low-income, and middle-class lives in the colloquial diction of the day.

In the United States, for instance, Jessie Rittenhouse had edited a widely reviewed and top-selling anthology of such poetry, humbly titled *The Little Book of Modern Verse: A Selection of the Work of Contemporaneous American Poets* (1913). It followed from the success of the *Lyric Year's* one hundred new poems. Riding the wave of interest in such poetry, William Stanley Braithwaite, poetry editor of the genteel *Boston Evening Transcript,* also decided to publish in 1913 what would be the first of an annual anthology of magazine verse. In 1914 the New York publishers the Boni Brothers published Ezra Pound's anthology, *Des Imagistes*; Putnam's published the American edition of *Georgian Poetry, 1911–12*; and Braithwaite published his second *Anthology of Magazine Verse.* Combined, these anthologies proved that there was a new poetry in the United States, a poetry that even went so far as to eschew meter altogether.

Braithwaite's introduction to his second edition reveals an editor grown tired of those who would say, "That poetry has no relation to life." He, like so many other poets and readers, had grown weary of the idealist escapism and beauty that poetry had come to reflect. It seemed as if a law had formed for contemporary poets, which Braithwaite expressed as this: "With reality it must have nothing to do." This Braithwaite meant to oppose and in the poems he selected he meant to prove that "if poetry deals with anything, it deals with reality."[2]

In England, meanwhile, the Georgian poets were standard-bearers of such new poetry, and it was in their context that the English reviews of *North of Boston* emerged. For the most part Frost's book was presented to the public as part of that Georgian turn to the things of this world. Reviewed in the *Times Literary Supplement, Outlook, Nation, Bookman,* and the *Pall Mall Gazette,* Frost's second book received an unusual scrutiny and attention because his poetry was related to the larger realist shift in contemporary poetry.[3] That attention was no accident. Frost's newfound friends among the Georgians wrote the majority of the reviews. It would be a mistake, however, to see these reviews merely as puffery, as one friend's good turn for another. Instead they were manifestos making a case for the new realism. Each review used Frost's book, and often conversations with the poet, to make a larger case for the turn away from the themes and techniques associated with Victorian and Edwardian lyric poetry.

Edward Thomas, for example, was Robert Frost's best friend by the spring of 1914 when his book was published. That spring Thomas wrote three reviews, each for a different audience, and in each he made the case for the new realism and not just for Frost. In the *London Daily News* he wrote, "This is one of the most revolutionary books of modern times, but one of the quietist and least aggressive." He summarized its innovations: "These poems are revolutionary because they lack the exaggeration of rhetoric. . . . Their language is free from the poetical words and forms that are the chief material of secondary poets. . . . In fact, the medium is common speech and common decasyllables. . . . They depend not at all on objects commonly admitted to be beautiful." That Thomas made this case in a daily newspaper rather than in a more genteel publication had the effect of giving Frost the very audience he sought. Thomas's review made the complexities of Frost's themes accessible to the public in one of England's largest circulation newspapers. Nor did Thomas stop there. He also reviewed Frost's book for the August 8 issue of the more literary *New Weekly*. There he said that it "will raise the thrilling question, What is poetry?" In his third review, for the most literary venue yet, the *English Review* (August issue), Thomas went into Frost's poetics, saying that Frost had "got free from the habit of personal lyric" of his first book. He explained that Frost's poems "refused the 'glory of words,' which is the modern poet's embarrassing heritage." According to Thomas, *North of Boston* created "a unique type of eclogue, homely, racy, and touched by a spirit that might, under other circumstances, be pure lyric on the one hand or pure drama on the other."[4]

The reviews did not come only from Frost's poet friends. The founding editor of the *English Review*, Ford Maddox Hueffer (Ford), who had been among the first to champion realist poetry when he had published Thomas

Hardy back in 1908, also praised Frost's book in the popular monthly *Outlook*. There Hueffer said that Frost had written precisely the kind of poetry he had long championed but had so rarely found. At the time, though, Hueffer (Ford) was persona non grata in genteel circles. He had been convicted of adultery, yet he was still quite public about living with his lover. To those who knew his reputation, his praise would have added another dimension of edginess to Frost's poetry.

Less edgy and experimental in their inclinations, Frost's Georgian friends like Thomas were content to make the case for the kind of poetry Frost wrote as much as for his own unique version of it. Another of his friends, Lascelles Abercrombie, for instance, wrote for the large circulation intellectual weekly *Nation*. As Frost's wife, Elinor, said, the *Nation* "is about the best of the English weeklies."[5] To find praise there meant that he had become a public poet at last.

Abercrombie began his review with "poetry per se is one of the most troublesome things in the world to discuss exactly. Like Goodness and Personal Identity, it is a thing which everyone is aware of, but a thing which, when you try to lay hold of it, proves ghost." Using what he calls Frost's idiosyncratic poetry, he then makes a case for realist poetry's relevance more generally. Seeming to agree with Alford's assessment of the general blandness of American poetry, Abercrombie says that Frost is "an American poet who noticeably stands out against tradition." Says Abercrombie, "The first and most obvious novelty in Mr. Frost's poems is their determination to deal unequivocally with everyday life in New England." Describing Frost's poetry as related almost entirely to farming (georgics) as opposed to life in the new American cities, he adds, "The life seems harder and lonelier, and it also seems, oddly enough, more reflexive and philosophical." Ultimately, Abercrombie says, Frost's poetics return not to Latin antiquity but rather to the Greeks: "Poetry, in this book, seems determined, once more just as it was in Alexandria, to invigorate itself by utilizing the traits and necessities of common speech, the minds and hearts of common folk."[6] Of all the reviews, Frost particularly appreciated this one.

September 1914's *Poetry and Drama*, the very heart of Georgian poetry and the publishing center of the new poetic realism, also contained the last round of the debate between John Alford and Louis Untermeyer that

I described in chapter 12. As I mentioned, Alford in his final riposte to Untermeyer had singled out Frost's *North of Boston* as among the best examples of American poetry he had read. Harold Monro also had printed in *Poetry and Drama* "Home Burial" from that collection.[7] In this same issue Monro also reviewed Frost's book, writing that it was "remarkable for its originality and emotional qualities." He added, "Mr. Frost seems to have studied the subtle cadences of colloquial speech with some peculiar and unusual apprehension. . . . Through some acute process of psychological analysis he casts up all the hidden details of a superficially simple tale into stark prominence. . . . All the poems in this book are good reading."[8]

Monro meant what he had written. Between that issue and his next of December 1914, he purchased no fewer than four of Frost's newest poems. Those poems would eventually be published in Frost's third book, *Mountain Interval* (1916). Initially, however, they were published in the December 1914 issue of *Poetry and Drama,* along with a slightly more fulsome treatment of *North of Boston* by none other than John Alford, who wrote, "If Mr. Monro had spoken in any but eulogistic terms of him I should have been in difficulties. As it is, I need only exclaim, 'Hear, Hear!' and refer the unacquainted to his review in Number 7 and the book itself."[9]

ROBERT FROST: LYRIC POET AMONG THE GEORGIANS

In these four new poems Frost left narrative poetry and returned once more to the lyric. These lyrics had been written while Frost himself lived in rural Gloucestershire among his new Georgian friends. When *North of Boston* was published that May, the Frost family had moved there specifically to be near their new Georgian poet friends. They had settled in the Dymock area town of Ledington near the tiny village of Ryton in a small home named, after the English fashion, "Little Iddens."[10] Frost's neighbors included Wilfred Gibson and his new wife (former secretary at the Poetry Bookshop), who lived in "The Old Nailshop" at the Greenway, a hamlet not far away. Lascelles Abercrombie with his wife and children were also nearby in a home they dubbed "The Gallows." Frequent visitors included Rupert Brooke and John Drinkwater.

Also by the spring of 1914 Gibson, Abercrombie, and Rupert Brooke had started a poetry magazine, *New Numbers,* a monthly forum for their brand of rural realism set in meter.[11] In many ways a genuine idyll, Frost's life in the Dymock area nonetheless suffered from plenty of harsh realities. For one thing, after only a few months the Frost family had to move from "Little Iddens" to the now vacated and ironically named home of the Abercrombies, "The Gallows."

In the Dymock area Frost lived a life he may well have thought a dream come true, insofar as he spent his days writing poetry and his evenings talking with his close poet friends. All the while he found himself writing lyrics rather than narratives. Like the longer narratives of *North of Boston*, his new lyrics exposed the hypocrisies of class, sexuality, and gender, and like those earlier poems, they investigated such genteel values as courage and duty.

In a letter to the Russian Jewish emigrant to Britain John Cournos, another one of Pound's young poet friends and part of Pound's English circle, Frost revealed his latest views about "the sound of sense." He had come to know Cournos, and the younger poet had offered to write a review of *North of Boston*. In reply to that offer Frost wrote:

> My versification seems to bother people more than I should have expected—I suppose because I have been so long accustomed to thinking of it in my own private way. It is as simple as this: there are the very regular preestablished accent and measure of blank verse; and there are the very irregular accent and measure of speaking intonation. I am never more pleased than when I can get these into strained relation. I like to drag and break the speaking intonation across the metre as waves first comb and then break stumbling on the shingle. That's all. But it's no mere figure of speech, though one can make figures enough about it.[12]

The letter explains the theory behind both his lyric and narrative poetry. In the new lyrics he applied the same principle he had applied to his longer narrative poems. They, too, should be written as talk. In his new lyrics he tested his theory's artistic integrity. It was one thing to have characters in narrative poems speak to one another or to mimic speech in dramatic monologs. A better test of his principle would be to apply it to the lyric speaker. In his new lyrics he meant to rescue poetry from the mauve glow of antiquated rhythms.

The results of his new lyric experiments were published in the December 1914 issue of *Poetry and Drama*. That issue included "The Sound of

Trees," "The Cow in Apple Time," "Putting in the Seed," and "The Smile," the largest selection of Frost poems yet published in a magazine. Together the poems engage contemporary poetry's singular obsession with sex and eroticism. Having come to know Monro rather well, and know a great deal about him from others' gossip, Frost thought of him as somewhat sex crazed. He said as much to Bartlett. As a Christmas present Frost sent Bartlett this same December 1914 issue. In the margins he included abundant annotations. After Monro's name, for instance, he writes that Monro always kept one foot in "the red-light district." Frost likely thought it humorous, a private joke, to submit these four poems to Monro precisely because of what they had to say about sexuality. Because space prohibits a full treatment of all four, I turn only to the most obviously sexual of the group, "Putting in the Seed."

"Putting in the Seed" is the third of the four poems.[13] It follows from "The Sound of Trees" and "Cow in Apple Time." Those poems made only the most careful and veiled allusions to sex. "Putting in the Seed," in contrast, is one of the most erotic of Frost's published poems. It turns the central metaphor of planting into an explicit metaphor for sex. The poem is also a triumph of his "sound of sense" because it places talk in opposition to the rigors of the iambic pentameter sonnet. Not only is the sonnet a form for love and sex, it is also among the most rigorous of lyric forms. The wildness of passion is set into the rigid requirements of meter and rhyme. The sonnet had been invented to express, and then impose restraint on, the otherwise rapacious passions of sexual courtship in thirteenth-century Italy. As a little song of love it was designed for courtiers as a little argument for having sex. Through the imposed restraint of the sonnet form, men would prove their intellectual wit by trying to convince women to sleep with them. Knowing the history of that form, Frost in this third poem of the sequence offers a sonnet about sex.

Specifically "Putting in the Seed" is both an Italian and an English sonnet. As an Italian sonnet it states its argument in the first eight lines, the octave. It then extends that initial argument with a convincing conclusion in the final six lines, the sestet. It is also an English sonnet that makes its argument in three quatrains and then seals the case in a powerful concluding couplet. In the poem's first printing it was broken into four distinct stanzas to emphasize the English pattern of three quatrains and a couplet. The poem's logic, however, follows the Italian two-part sonnet. By combining both traditions Frost invokes the heritage and history of one of the most influential and significant poetic forms for love and sex.

The poem's first eight lines, the octave, equate sex with farming. From the classical era to the modern era farming was a metaphor for sex. Unrestrained, unchecked sexual desire, a thematic convention of the sonnet, is tied to the domestic enterprise of farming and so made wholesome. In classical georgics, nature propagates itself where and howsoever it will, while humans who farm tame and control such propagation according to fixed boundaries and rules. By tying the sonnet's erotic heritage to the georgic's tradition of farming as sexual restraint and decorum, Frost links both classical and modern metaphors for bounded, controlled sexuality.

> You come to fetch me from my work to-night
> When supper's on the table, and we'll see
> If I can leave off burying the white
> Soft petals fallen from the apple tree
> (The petals, yes, but not so barren quite,
> Mingled with these, smooth bean and wrinkled pea),
> And go along with you ere you lose sight
> Of what you came for and become like me,
> Slave to a spring-time passion for the earth.

These lines trade on double entendre. They also contain Frost's own secret language of love (his wife's maiden name was White). The lines literally declare Frost's intention to go to his wife rather than stay in the garden. As a metaphor of sex, the lines assert his sexual desire through the metaphor of planting. They say that, far from uncontrolled desire, such sexual urges make both husband and wife slaves to a "springtime passion for the earth." Their sexual urges are part and parcel of the animal kingdom and organic world of nature.

In the poem's concluding lines that sexual metaphor becomes even more pronounced:

> How love burns from the putting in the seed
> On through the watching for that early birth,
> When just as the ground tarnishes with weed,

> The sturdy seedling with arched body comes
> Shouldering its way and shedding the earth crumbs.

Depicting the sexual act as "putting in the seed," Frost celebrates both its pleasure, the joy of "the arched body" that "comes," as well as its product, the new life that "comes / Shouldering its way." Plant and baby, Frost says, are as fundamental as pleasure.

By combining classical and modern metaphors in his combination of georgic and sonnet, Frost makes a strong case for sexual pleasure and passion. At the same time he also makes a strong case for control, temperance, and order in keeping with the classical georgic tradition. This poem associates the pleasure and passion of sex with the temperate domains of both farming and marriage. The most wild, excessive, passionate act—putting in the seed—when associated with farming, cooking, home, and marriage becomes its own controlled ritual. The Italian two-part form of the sonnet even draws attention to that contrast. The poem also contrasts Frost's new concept of poetic diction, his "sound of sense," with the older conventions of poetic cadence. The first eight lines mimic the language of everyday talk, while the final six lines return to the old-fashioned heightened abstract language still all too common in the majority of lyric poetry of the 1910s.

Despite the return of such exalted diction in the final six lines, the poem divides neatly into the English sonnet's four-stanza division. In that structure the logic of the sentence as regular talk, like desire itself, often overrides the stanza divisions. In the first three quatrains the poem establishes the connection between sexuality and domestic labor. Then in the final couplet it emphasizes the new life that results from planting and sex, as if to suggest that ultimately the new life produced will trump the singular pleasure both husband and wife feel. As examples of talk the poem's sentence structure runs riot over its metrical lines. The poem's sentences do not follow the stanza divisions of either an English or an Italian sonnet. Metaphorically the sentences as talk stand for precisely the wild uncontrollable passion that poetry, the metrical lines, means to control and tame. In keeping with the New Poets' insistence that erotic passion be made acceptable once more, this poem, through its subtle metaphor of sentences and talk, makes a case for a pleasure that breaks barriers down rather than succumbs to them. In his wily way Frost's at once adheres to a convention as old as classical antiquity and breaks free of it in his sonnet. In both life and poetry wild untamed passion is as much an essential feature of poetry and of life as are the checks that limit such passion.[14]

In the selection's final poem, "The Smile," Frost reveals the obvious danger of unchecked passion. In twelve lines Frost records the dramatic monolog of a young newlywed woman who answers the door to a stranger who asks for bread and makes odd comments with an even stranger smile and leaves the reader in the grip of doubt.[15] After beginning with a simple country meeting, and a portrait of newlywed domestic bliss, the poem concludes with fear of sexual violence, even rape. Combined with the other poems of the sequence, and read as the concluding poem *to* those others, this poem is a sinister commentary on unchecked sexual desire. It is as if this poem were mocking the belief that one might temper hunger with simple bread.

Together these four poems depict sexuality's excess, appetite, and extravagance. Each poem highlights unbridled passion, yet each also makes an argument in favor of some sort of control. Combined they argue for the necessity of brakes to the onslaught of sexual excess that filled so many pages of contemporary magazines. At the same time these four poems also indicate just how useless such brakes often become.

LEAVING ENGLAND, FINDING AN AMERICAN PUBLISHER

The idyll in the English countryside was not without hardship. For one thing the Great War began that August, and Frost's English friends were necessarily in much turmoil. On a far more personal level Frost suffered from severe financial hardship. He had never been as publicly known or as impoverished. His publisher, Mrs. Nutt, was of no help. In fact she refused to pay royalties despite what were clearly large sales of his second book. Biographers speculate she refused to pay his royalties to punish him for selling four of its poems without first asking her permission. Whatever the cause of her penury, it meant that after two years in England, Frost, his savings diminished, had only the annual legacy from his grandfather's estate on which to live.

The pressure of finances convinced him to act on his own. In the fall of 1914, without telling Mrs. Nutt, to whom he was still contracted for future books, Frost began negotiating with Mosher for an American edition of *A Boy's Will.* Calling himself one of Mrs. Nutt's "indentured poets," he said, "All I have in mind is to reach through you an American public. So long as you get me read I shall ask no questions about royalties."[16]

Coincidentally, even as Frost negotiated with Mosher, Mrs. Nutt herself, without telling Frost, also had begun negotiating with an American publisher. The negotiations had not been her idea. She had not intended to market Frost in the United States. As a rule she did not market or advertise her authors much, least of all her poets, and least of all Frost. To Mrs. Nutt's surprise, though, the American publisher Henry Holt wrote to her, asking permission to publish an American edition of Robert Frost's books. Never one to lose a financial opportunity, she began negotiations immediately.

Eventually, in December 1914, when his four new poems were published in *Poetry and Drama,* Frost learned about the negotiations and discovered to his delight that he would have an American publisher. He wrote to Mosher to say, "It turns out that my American publisher is Henry Holt. I have just learned the fact lately, and I don't know how it came about unless it was through someone of the name Holt who wrote me an appreciative letter from Stowe Vermont in the summer."[17]

Indeed it was that "someone named Holt." Florence Holt had discovered Frost, thanks to her good friend the American poet Amy Lowell. By 1914 Lowell, sister of Harvard's president and a relative of none other than the great schoolroom poet James Russell Lowell, had become a force in the American New Poetry movement. While Robert Frost enjoyed his idyll in rural England, Amy Lowell had come for her second visit to London in the summer of 1914. On this visit she meant to gather the poems and meet the poets for her own imagist anthology, which she intended to publish that same year. The story of her fight with Ezra Pound during the summer and fall of 1914 for control of imagism is now a regular part of literary history. Less well known is how that battle changed the course of Robert Frost's American career.

Lowell browsed one day in Harold Monro's Poetry Bookshop. Frost's *North of Boston* was still new, and Monro had given it a prominent display. Lowell bought it and became a great admirer. She liked it so much that she sent a copy to Henry Holt's wife, Florence; the Holts were part of Lowell's social circle. She knew that Florence Holt would like it and duly sent it to her vacation home in Vermont. After reading Frost's book, Florence Holt not only wrote to Frost to express her admiration, but she also gave it to her husband and most likely encouraged him to acquire the rights for its publication in America.[18] On the other hand, Henry Holt likely did not need persuading. He had long taken an interest in serious poetry. At Yale his best friend had been William Henry Sill, one of Frost's favorite poets. In 1911 Holt had been instrumental in editing his firm's *Household Book of Verse*. All through the declining fortunes of poetry in the public sphere that marked the early twentieth century, Holt had been one of the few commercial publishers to insist on poetry's cultural importance. In fact that anthology was still a best-seller in 1914.

He certainly admired Frost's poetry. At the same time Frost was an unknown, and his poetry did not quite achieve the musicality Holt, as a genteel man of the old school, still expected to read. He feared Frost's book was not poetic enough. Holt decided to hedge his bets and wrote in September 1914 to Mrs. Nutt. "The two readers we had look at these poems found them uncommonly interesting, and while we cannot see a paying market here for this particular volume, still we are so interested in this author's work that if you have some later books of his for which you would care to offer us the American rights, we would be most happy to consider it."[19] Mrs. Nutt, despite her famous crotchetiness, wrote back, saying, reasonably enough, if Holt did not want *North of Boston* enough to pay for it, why should she offer any others? She then reminded Holt that England had just begun a war with Germany. She wondered why her American friends might choose not to help their English counterparts. If nothing else, the emotional blackmail worked. Holt agreed to print 150 copies of *North of Boston,* and in December Mrs. Nutt wrote to tell the news to Frost.[20]

Also that December, Edward Marsh visited the Dymock area, having decided to produce a second edition of the Georgian anthology. Marsh was there to solicit new poems from the contributors, and both Gibson and Abercrombie insisted he include Frost in the new edition. Marsh, however, said it was a British anthology (had he forgotten that he had invited Pound to participate in the first edition?), and that Frost, as an American, could not properly be called a Georgian. My suspicion is that Marsh's newly engaged nationalism in a time of war —he was after all working for Winston Churchill at the navy—caused Marsh to champion the British in all things.[21] Had Frost been included, it would certainly have increased his public reputation, given that the Georgians in 1914 and 1915 had become the most important poets of that era. Alas, it was not to be.

More troubling news, meanwhile, came as a result of the war. With each passing week the Atlantic Ocean became less safe. Frost worried that the Germans would soon make any return home to the United States impossible. He and Elinor had never intended to stay abroad more than two years. By the turn of the year, though, it seemed only wise to ensure his family's safe passage back to America while he could. Early in 1915 the Frosts began to make arrangements to return home.[22]

Chapter Fourteen

•

The American Magazines of 1915
and the Making of Robert Frost

RETURNED to the United States, Robert Frost, in the course of six months, would become a major poet celebrated in the genteel publications. The negotiations between Holt and Nutt had moved rather quickly, and by the time Frost secured passage back to the United States, Henry Holt had published an American edition of *North of Boston*. A few months later Holt also published an American edition of *A Boy's Will*.

When various publications received review copies of the American edition of *North of Boston*, it struck just the right chord. By early 1915 the American literary interests continued to mark public poetry's turn to experimental free verse. Such anthologies as *Des Imagistes* (1914) and *Georgian Poets* (1914), just published in new American editions, had become literary causes célèbres. Frost's narratives, which many thought to be in free verse, gained the attention of some of the country's most influential reviewers.

Meanwhile the New Poetry movement had itself spawned an ever-growing market of new literary magazines, many of which published only poetry. By 1915, for instance, Alfred Kreymborg, editor of *Glebe* and first publisher of *Des Imagistes*, had created another poetry magazine aimed at a far more commercial market and called simply *Others*. Describing his new magazine in the *New York Morning Telegraph*'s literary magazine section of August 8, 1915, he wrote, "Vers libre, or free verse, as we have come to call it, has taken the place of cubism and futurism in public popularity. The painter has had his inning. The poet is our hero now, to mock and jeer." While in Chicago, Margaret Anderson rivaled *Poetry* with her *Little Review*. In its pages Arthur Davison Ficke defended free verse, writing, "All outdoors is just what vers libre affords the poet of today. He is no longer under the necessity of moulding his thought into an artificial pattern, expressing it to a predetermined form; it can remain fluent, unsubjugated, formless, like a spontaneous emotional cry."[1] That same year also saw the publication of *Rogue,* which announced itself as "the Cigarette of Literature." Even in the genteel bastion of Boston, the poetry editor of the staid *Boston Evening Transcript,* William Stanley Braithwaite, in 1915 launched a competitor to Harriet Monroe's *Poetry,* which he called simply the *Poetry Journal.*

AMY LOWELL AND THE *NEW REPUBLIC* OF 1915

Among the many new magazines advocating on behalf of the New Poetry, one of the most influential, not just in literary contexts but also in cultural and political matters, the *New Republic,* elected early in 1915 to review the American edition of *North of Boston.* None other than Amy Lowell, then putting the finishing touches on her own anthology, *Some Imagist Poets,* wrote the review. In 1915 Lowell had become the voice of imagism and of free-verse poetry. In American genteel publications her influence exceeded that of Pound. That Lowell had elected to review an unknown poet in the *New Republic* all but guaranteed Frost's success.

Nor was her review there a coincidence. As she later put it, "I asked—nay demanded—to review the volume." Fate or accident, however, saw to it that her review appeared in the February issue, sold on newsstands just as Robert Frost and his family disembarked from their ship. In another one of those odd chance events that punctuate Frost's early career, he became one of the random readers of the first major American review of his work. Legend has it that "he had barely left the docks when he found at a newsstand that the current issue of a magazine he had never seen before . . . carried a long, favorable review of *North of Boston* by Amy Lowell" in the issue of February 20.[2] That review, really an article, sparked such enormous interest in the book that it caught Holt by surprise and led to the need for more printings of that first edition. Within the month Holt had reset the book and printed it again, with a new binding and in new paper.

While the power of Frost's poetry cannot be denied, the prominence Lowell had given Frost in the *New Republic* had as much to do with his startling initial success as did his own intrinsic artistic merit. The magazine itself was a fledgling, having begun publishing only on November 7, 1914. After less than three months, the weekly had become deeply influential in American circles of power, as part of what historians would later dub the Progressive movement. A must-read among policy makers and power brokers, this new magazine devoted itself to a distinctive brand of liberal thought that inspired the creation of the Progressive Party. It meant to unite both Republicans and Democrats in a new political spirit of liberal reform within capitalist economic structures. The magazine was edited by two young men, Herbert Croly and Walter Lippmann, and ideas first floated as articles in their pages often became federal law. Shortly after its initial issue, it had achieved an impressive weekly circulation of fifteen thousand copies, a subscription base that included most of the power elite of the nation at that time. Soon its editors would join that elite. Lippmann, for instance, was appointed an assistant to Newton Baker, Woodrow Wilson's secretary of war.

Both editors came from a younger generation than Frost yet; from the first they insisted and required that their magazine take literature seriously. To that end each issue's back section included review essays about new fiction and poetry. Whether intended or not, then, Lowell's review of Robert Frost's *North of Boston* aligned his poetry, and the New Poetry generally, with that magazine's brand of liberalism.[3]

Lowell's review builds on a fundamentally liberal premise. For instance, when she calls attention to the stark realities of Frost's poems, and singles out his talent for rendering the speaking voice in verse, she does so out of a fundamentally liberal conviction that individualism ought to trump elitism, both in theme and form. While the subject matter of regular farm folk made that point only too obvious, Frost's style, Lowell says, makes the same case: "No hint of European forms has crept into it. It is certainly the most American volume of poetry which has appeared for some time." To this she adds that the book "is American in the sense that Whittier is American, and not at all in the subtler sense in which Poe ranks as the greatest American poet." By invoking the name of Whittier, Lowell means to associate the lack of fantasy, exoticism, historical landscape, rich imagination, and abundant lush language, rhyme, and diction with a far more genuine American quality. She meant to associate realism itself with American society's current state. In this review she associates decadence, symbolism, and aestheticism generally with Europe and fantasy. Bold, brash, and honest, Robert Frost's poetry, she says, contains "an irony, sardonic and grim. Mr. Frost's book reveals a disease which is eating into the vitals of our New England life, at least in its rural communities." Realism, now equated with a distinctive American tradition, makes Frost's poetry matter, she says. But in making that case, she also betrayed her own inability to get behind the assumptions so common to the wealthy Brahmins from whom she came. For what she admired in Frost's so-called honest portrayal of rural New England was that it conformed to her stereotype of that abandoned and distressed place.

Historians report that in fact the impact of industrialism and urbanization on New England farm towns had been devastating. Reading Frost's poems about the people of such towns, Lowell tells the *New Republic*'s audience that at last they can see what most of rural New England has become. She asks rhetorically: "Have the sane, full-blooded men all been drafted away to the cities, or the West, leaving behind only feeble remainders of a once fine stock?" She answers simply enough, saying, "It is a question for the psychiatrist to answer, and it would be interesting to ask it with 'North of Boston' as a text-book to go by."[4]

In her eyes Frost's book told the grim facts of New England's farm folk. To her mind they were just short of the "ape-like" Sweeney that T. S. Eliot would soon mock. They were half-degenerate semihumans living bestial lives without humor. To make her point more evident, she offers extended treatments of "The Housekeeper" and "The Fear." These poems, she says, prove that "the book is the epitome of a decaying New England." Frost, she said, had written an extended elegy lamenting the end of a once noble Anglo-Saxon Protestant community. As she read the book, Frost proved that white Anglo-Saxon Protestant ascendancy had had its day and its place and had now come to an end. "He tells you what he has seen *exactly* as he has seen it. And in the word *exactly* lies the half of his talent. The other half is a great and beautiful simplicity of phrase. . . . Mr. Frost is as New England as Burns is Scotch, Synge Irish, of Mistral Provencal." And like them he tells the truth about his place and his people, no matter how uncomfortable that truth may be. As she says, "Mr. Frost has done that remarkable thing, caught a fleeting epoch and stamped it into print."[5] One might as well have given her essay review the title "Degenerate Land and Forgotten People," given the sociological implications she made of Frost's poetry.

Needless to say, Frost had not written that book. Proud to be reviewed by so important a literary figure, he was nonetheless deeply unhappy with the review's larger point. He had not written a collection of grotesques, nor had he charted a degenerate fall from some glorious cultural height. To see that theme extracted from his book annoyed him. Yet, as he had with Pound, Frost kept his view hidden from Lowell. Writing to his friend Sidney Cox, Frost said only that Lowell "will pervert me a little to her theory." He knew, even then, that the real point of the review had not been a supposed theme of degenerate failure as a result of unchecked industrial exploitation and urbanization but rather the welcoming of a new poet who had found a new language for depicting the life actually lived by men and women. As Frost said not much later to another influential admirer, William Stanley Braithwaite, "Say what you will[,] effects of actuality and intimacy are the greatest aim an artist can have."[6]

FROST IN NEW YORK: MEETING LOUIS UNTERMEYER

Frost chanced upon Amy Lowell's review shortly after disembarking from the ship in New York. While in New York City he secured for his family a place to stay with their old friends the Lynches, who lived in the northern White Mountains of New Hampshire, near Franconia. Staying behind in New York City after his family made the journey north, Frost made his initial visit to the Holt offices. There the editor in charge of trade books, Alfred Harcourt, told him that the initial 150 copies of the Nutt edition of *North of Boston* had sold out after less than a month. The publisher had since ordered two hundred more and had decided to print an American edition of his first book, *A Boy's Will*, as well.[7] Harcourt also told Frost how much he respected his poetry, a respect Frost would have appreciated because it had been hard earned. At first Harcourt wanted nothing to do with Frost's work. When Henry Holt decided to go ahead with a small edition of *North of Boston* based on his wife's recommendation, he had given the project to Harcourt. Harcourt had thrown the manuscript in the trash in disgust, annoyed that the boss's wife was now making editorial decisions. Eventually he retrieved the manuscript from the trash, his initial and most likely sexist reaction erased by the sheer power of Frost's poetry. As Florence Holt had realized, Frost's poetry was honest and carried a psychological and ethical depth like nothing in contemporary poetry.[8] A literary intellectual, Alfred Harcourt had genuine respect for the innovations, thematic and artistic, of the New Poetry, and he understood at once that Frost belonged to that circle of poets.

To facilitate Frost's career, then, Harcourt introduced the poet to the relatively new Poetry Society of America, a rallying forum for the New Poetry's realism. A result of that meeting would be an influential review of *North of Boston* in the *New York Times Book Review* by the poet and anthologist Jessie Rittenhouse, the society's president. Harcourt also knew Lippmann and Croly's *New Republic* circle of friends, and, given the review they had just published, he arranged for the poet to meet the young editors at lunch. There Frost likely met Louis Untermeyer, who, though of their circle, wrote for their far more radical rival, the *Masses.*

Untermeyer, already keen on Frost after first reading him in the December 1914 issue of *Poetry and Drama,* determined that he, too, would champion the poet. He wrote a review of *North of Boston* for the *Chicago Evening Post*'s weekly *Literary Supplement,* a separate weekly akin to today's *New York Times Book Review,* and with the same amount of influence. An unlikely pair, Louis Untermeyer, the Jewish New Yorker ten years younger than the Yankee farmer, and Robert Frost remained fast friends for the rest of their lives.[9] When Untermeyer published his first review of Frost in 1915, he was as powerful a reviewer as Amy Lowell and William Stanley Braithwaite. For him to assess Frost's work as and where he did carried an inordinate amount of weight among literary men and women.

Like Lowell, Untermeyer also was a poet. He had become well known in addition to his reviews for his poetry of heterosexual love and for his radical politics of egalitarianism. In 1919 he would publish one of the first primers on the New Poetry movement, *The New Era in American Poetry,* through Holt. That book explained the poetic turn to realism as a swing back "to actuality, to heartiness and lustihood." To those three adjectives he added that, "most of all, it [contemporary American poetry] has returned to democracy. . . . The most exclusive and aristocratic of the arts, appreciated and fostered only by little salons and erudite groups, poetry has suddenly swung away from its self-imposed strictures and is expressing itself once more in terms of democracy." In 1915 he made the case for democracy, heartiness, and actuality through the poetry of Robert Frost's *North of Boston*. In his review Untermeyer defines poetry as "removed from prose not only because it tells a thing more nobly but more quickly."[10] That word, *nobly,* refers to Untermeyer's view that whatever else poetry may do, it also has a decidedly public civilizing purpose. In keeping with an older genteel model of poetry, Untermeyer championed poetry of "actuality" against what he believed to be the falsehoods offered by the poetry of escape and beauty that still dominated. Nobility in poetry meant to Untermeyer that poetry expressed moral principles no matter how unconventional such principles may appear to be. In his case, for instance, he praised the principles of a radical leftist vision in keeping with the editorial policy of the *Masses* the other magazine on which he worked.

Untermeyer expected the best American literature to manifest a fundamentally egalitarian premise. Turning to Frost's poems, he argues that his poems matter precisely because Frost's poetic style rejects the language of idealism and beauty: "There is, for instance, a lack of 'poetic' figures and phrases in this volume: a lack of regard for the outlines and fragility of the medium, a lack of finesse, of nicely rounded rhetoric and raptures. . . . Robert Frost neglects them—and still writes poetry." Referring to Frost's theory of "sentence sounds," Untermeyer adds that "these poems should be read in batches and out loud. Most poems should, for that matter, but these, particularly, because of their colloquial give-and-take, call for the tongue."[11]

With a hardly disguised patrician tone Lowell had read the characters in *North of Boston* as proof that only the least fit had been left behind in rural New England. She felt sorry for these American peasants who, through no fault of their own, had been left behind as a result of the American race to industrialism and urbanization. In contrast Untermeyer read these same characters as proof that whether one lived in a city or on a farm, the problems of virtue, duty, and character were just as acute, just as real. People have the same ethical soul and must confront the same issues wherever they may be.

In his review Untermeyer also compares Frost to already established New Poets such as James Oppenheim. According to Untermeyer, Oppenheim had condensed "the force of psycho-analysis in less than a quarto volume," through his "prophetically synthesize[d]" poem "The Unborn." So, too, says Untermeyer, does Frost's poetry capture the force of the interior life. Frost not only incorporates his own unique artistry but also, like Oppenheim and the other New Poets, follows in the tradition of Walt Whitman, offering "the same clear sight [as Whitman], honesty of expression, freedom from pose and old patterns (patterns either of speech or thought) and fidelity to his times."[12]

Frost wrote to Untermeyer praising his understanding: "You make the point that there must be many poetical moods that haven't been reduced to poetry. Thanks most of all for seeing that, and saying it in a review of a book by me."[13] Frost believed that poetry incorporated the language people used, the speech rhythms of talk, so that it could bring readers out of a false view that poetry, like an ostrich, should avoid the things that matter most. He particularly admired Untermeyer's review for making that point.

ROBERT FROST AMONG THE BRAHMINS:
WILLIAM STANLEY BRAITHWAITE

After a whirlwind week among the literati and political young intellectuals of New York, Frost next met the most prominent members of the Boston publishing establishment.[14] Frost arrived in Boston after attending to personal business (seeing his sister in Pennsylvania and catching up with family friends in Lawrence, Massachusetts); he met the *Atlantic Monthly*'s editor in chief, Ellery Sedgwick; the literary editor of the *Boston Evening Transcript*, William Stanley Braithwaite; Sylvester Baxter, a journalist for the *Boston Herald*; and the *Herald*'s editor, Walter Prichard Eaton. Like January 8, 1913, when Frost entered Harold Monro's bookshop in London, March 5, 1915, is among the most important days of Frost's early career. What the earlier meeting did for Frost in England, this next round of introductions on Friday, March 5, did for his American reputation.

Initially Frost came to Boston from Lawrence only to see Sedgwick. While he was visiting the editor, the Boston Authors' Club chose to discuss *North of Boston*. Less than a week later Baxter, a member of that club, wrote about the sequence of events in the *Boston Herald*'s "Talk of the

Town" column. He began, "Boston's literary sensation of the day has been the home-coming of Robert Frost." Baxter aligned Frost's poetry with the new work of American realism, writing that "last Friday they were discussing Frost as the monthly 'shop talk' of the Boston Authors' Club, [when] one of the members[,] reading from his work, said that Frost was doing for New England in verse what Alice Brown, Mary Wilkins, and Sarah Orne Jewett had been doing in prose."[15]

Given Frost's reputation, then, it was hardly surprising that, when he announced himself to Sedgwick's secretary, he was invited to meet the editor. Charming the man easily, Frost unexpectedly won an invitation to Sedgwick's home for dinner. At that dinner, with other literary men and women, too, Frost explained his theory of the sound of sense, detailing his understanding of poetic realism. Describing both that dinner and the impression Frost made, Sedgwick found himself converted to Frost's views:

> I took him [Frost] home with me to dine and we had much talk about his theories of poetry which seem to me intelligent and genuinely distinctive. They concern themselves especially with his attempts to reproduce in his lines the very tones of the voice. The magnificent rotundities which have created our English tradition of poetry have, he thinks, served their great purpose. He does not, like the futurists, with whom he is in little sympathy, attack the parent stock of poetry, but holds with justice that the piping modern voices we have so long heard about us are simply thin echoes of sounds once great. In place of all this copying, he would substitute a new attempt to interpret human nature by the slight inflections of the voice which in our common speech means so much. The word, oh, for instance, interprets a whole series of moods according to its inflection.[16]

He was impressed enough to have Frost call up Sylvester Baxter of the *Boston Herald* to set up a meeting, as well as to have Frost call one of Boston's most prominent literati, the poet Nathan Haskell Dole, who, born in 1852, had become an elder statesman of the Brahmin crowd. Dole proved so excited to receive Frost's phone call that on the spot he invited the poet to his home following the dinner. Arriving late, Frost ultimately spent the night there.

The next morning Dole introduced Frost to his friend William Stanley Braithwaite of the *Boston Evening Transcript*. At the time Braithwaite, one of the only black intellectuals to have a platform in genteel publishing,

edited an influential annual anthology of magazine poetry and had begun his own *Poetry Journal.* For Frost to meet Braithwaite, as Dole knew,
would be to give the poet a striking new public presence. And so it trans-
pired. The editor devoted not one but two major essays to Frost for his
newspaper and also included no fewer than three of Frost's new poems in
the third *Anthology of Magazine Verse* (1915).

Braithwaite, like Untermeyer and Lowell, had read Frost's poetry even
before he met the poet and even before Frost's book had been published
in an American edition. Most likely Braithwaite was thrilled when Dole
called. A champion of just the sort of poetry Frost wrote, Braithwaite
rushed over to Jamaica Plain, Dole's home, to meet a poet whom he had
already come to admire. Even while Frost was still in England, Braithwaite
had reprinted almost the whole of the (English) *Nation's* review of the first
British edition of *North of Boston* for his "Listener" column in the *Boston
Evening Transcript* of July 8, 1914. He wanted to give his readers the news
of a book that, at the time, was still not available in the United States. After
meeting Frost, Braithwaite, like Pound before him, determined to make
Frost's poetry better known.

In the first of his two newspaper articles about Frost, "A Poet of New
England: Robert Frost a New Exponent of Life," Braithwaite used Frost's
poetry to make a larger case for realism in poetry generally. Braithwaite
said that, until Frost, American poetry had not given attention to the precise details of everyday life. As Braithwaite said, "Half a century of the
famous New England poets never did more than scratch the surface of
this life." Long an advocate of realism in poetry, Braithwaite believed that
Frost had found a way to bring to artistic fruition the ideas Braithwaite
had long championed. Before *North of Boston,* Braithwaite said, only fiction had addressed the "qualities of inner and outer existence, moral and
social, individually and collectively" together in a single literary work. But
fiction, he believed, did not suffice. As he said, "The natural expression of
New England . . . is a poetic expression," and only in Frost's poetry did
it seem possible for poetry to come "back to New England as its natural
voice." In his praise of *North of Boston* Braithwaite lauded its forsaken
regional tradition as well as a larger ideal of public poetry. He explained
that the book's poems worked "against the tradition of blank verse. In the

first place it is not literary. That is, the language of these poems is not the language of literature, but the speech of life and a very particular quality of life." Making use of his long talks and subsequent correspondence with Frost about his poetic theory of "sentence sounds" and "the hearing imagination," Braithwaite summarized Frost's views for his newspaper's readers. Frost's "new form of verse is that the meaning has the same absolute actuality and intimacy with life as the tones of words with the voice. The result of this thoroughly sincere and artistic effort to enhance a more closely knit idiomatic speech into art . . . will at first be a little puzzling to the reader until he has caught the perfect rhythm of its undermeaning."[17]

After Frost met Braithwaite, Dole took Frost to meet Sylvester Baxter, which led to Baxter's article about the poet. In the end Frost's simple intention to visit Sedgwick that Friday had turned into almost a week of literary conversation and introductions. It ended with an invitation to Amy Lowell's for a dinner party at her estate, "Sevenels," in Brookline.

After Frost's excursion among the literary gatekeepers of Boston, he finally traveled, for the first time since disembarking in New York City, to see his family in New Hampshire. Yet after little more than a month there, he was back in Boston to give his first invited public readings as a newly respected poet. Not content with having introduced Frost to Baxter and Braithwaite, Dole had inspired these invitations too. He had convinced both the Boston Authors' Club and Tufts College to invite Frost for paid lectures.

Arrived from New Hampshire on the appointed day, Frost read to the Authors' Club in the morning. That afternoon he read three new unpublished poems at the annual recitation of poetry from a contemporary poet for the Tufts College Phi Beta Kappa Society. Whether coincidence or not, that same afternoon the *Boston Evening Transcript* published another Braithwaite essay on the poet. Then, three days later, the huge Saturday edition published "Robert Frost, New American Poet." That article ran in the sixty-two-page Saturday paper's "Magazine and Editorial Section." Given that the front page reported the sinking of the *Lusitania*, it may well be that the magazine section was a particularly welcome solace for readers that weekend. As it happened, though, the article on Frost made plain his refusal to grant poetry its license to make beautiful and appease alone.

This article, which presented Frost as a realist in no uncertain terms, was the most in-depth account of Frost's poetic ideas yet published.[18]

In this essay Braithwaite discusses Frost's theory of sentence sounds by using an example Frost had often cited himself, Ralph Waldo Emerson's poem "Monadnock." That poem, according to Frost, proved that poets "must convey meaning by sound."[19] Braithwaite quotes Frost saying that "what we do get in life and miss so often in literature is the sentence sounds that underlie the words. Words in themselves do not convey meaning." To get the point across more clearly, Frost told Braithwaite that sentence sounds were "a psychology of sound." Such sounds, he said, are the inflected tones that reveal what a person really feels or thinks, and meter in and of itself cannot mimic them. That, however, did not mean poets should write free verse and overlook meter. Instead, Frost said, the art of poetry revealed itself through a tension between the sentence tones as they worked *with* meter. Quoting Frost, Braithwaite wrote, "The two [tone and meter] are one in creation, but separate in analysis."[20]

To make the case for realism more generally Braithwaite explains the difference between axiomatic principles of poetry that lie beyond argument, and simple disagreements concerning taste. In so doing he means to defy those who would claim Frost's poetry as unpoetic. He uses Frost's theories, as had Untermeyer and Lowell, to defend the poetic realism and the New Poetry. As he says, "Until the public is given the key to the secret by which the fundamental moods of the poet are shaped into expression, the work cannot be appreciatively understood and enjoyed."[21] In this article Braithwaite intended to give that key to his readers.

If that key had two elements, then the first, Braithwaite said, is "the background of his material, his environment and character which belong to a special community." The second "is the background of art in which the fidelity of speech is artistically brought into literature. This latter is a practice that brings up large and important questions of language and meaning in relation to life on the one hand and to literature on the other." According to Braithwaite, other than Frost and Edwin Arlington Robinson, no other American poet successfully combined these two elements. Together those poets, he argued, write "at once both artistic and the literal tone of human talk."[22]

THE *ATLANTIC MONTHLY* AND ROBERT FROST

Shortly after Braithwaite published his articles, Ezra Pound in London learned about them. Enraged that Amy Lowell had, with her imagist anthology, usurped his role as spokesperson for imagism, and increasingly dismayed at the attention given to her, Pound was all the more aggravated to hear that Braithwaite had just discovered a new, exciting poet. Reading Braithwaite's articles on Frost and the New Poetry, Pound could not believe that there had been no mention of him or his role in that effort. In anger he fired a letter off to the *Transcript,* duly printed that August. There Pound claimed credit for "discovering" Frost. He wrote, "I reviewed that book [*A Boy's Will*] in two places and drew it [to] other reviewers' attention by personal letters. I hammered his stuff into *Poetry,* where I have recently reviewed his second book."[23] He also made sure to trumpet his own bigotry by declaring to the paper's editors, "Your (negro?) reviewer might acquaint himself with that touching little scene in Elkin Mathews's shop some years since."[24] Ironically this letter, which meant to bring Pound's role and that of the poets associated with imagism and the publishing house of Elkin Mathews to public attention, did little for Pound. It did, however, have the effect of further bolstering Frost's poetic reputation.

The previous May, the poet and anthologist Jessie Rittenhouse, secretary of the relatively new American Poetry Society, whom Frost had met through Harcourt in New York City back in February, had published her review of *North of Boston* in the *New York Times Book Review.* She praised in particular Frost's realistic portrayal of women. However, she also proved that at least a few people had paid attention to Ezra Pound's insistence that Robert Frost had gone to England because America was too provincial to recognize his talent. In her review, she wonders, with no little sarcasm, "just why a made-in-England reputation is so coveted by the poets of this country." Reading this, Frost winced, as his letters indicate. As was typical of Frost when he was annoyed by an important reviewer, he kept his feelings close, revealing them only to friends such as Sidney Cox, to whom he said, "She has no right to imply of course that I desired or sought a British-made reputation." Alfred Harcourt, Frost's new friend and editor at Holt, however, did more than silently fume. Through his connections he convinced the *New York Times Book Review* to let him publish a correction in the guise of an editorial. He told readers that Frost "happened to be in England when the idea came of collecting his poetry manuscripts into a volume." More to the point, Frost "didn't cross the water seeking a British publisher."[25]

The publicity concerning Frost and his poetry continued apace. Meanwhile his two readings in the Boston area on May 5 bore unexpected fruit, as was becoming only too common on such occasions. At the Tufts reading the head of school, George H. Browne, of a genteel Cambridge prep school, Browne and Nichols, invited Frost to talk there. He offered to pay $200 if Frost would also be willing to speak to four other schools. Frost readily accepted what would have been a fee of roughly $4,500 in 2012 money, and so his trip to Boston grew ever longer. Also, because he had spent an enjoyable evening with the *Atlantic's* Sedgwick the last time he had been in Boston, and given that Sedgwick had made all of Frost's subsequent introductions possible, the poet next went to the *Atlantic's* offices on his second visit to Boston.

In the wake of all the public attention lavished on Frost, Sedgwick now gave Frost renewed attention, even offering to publish his latest poetry, saying, "We are going to hold you up to your best." Frost later claimed that he was asked if he had any new unpublished poems. Pretending to be shocked, he said he was not "the kind of poet who goes around with poems in his pocket." On the other hand, he did happen to have the three poems from the Tufts reading. "Let me have them," Sedgwick said. Ultimately he purchased the poems "Birches," "The Road Not Taken," and "The Sound of Trees" (the last had appeared six months earlier in *Poetry and Drama*) for a substantial $55 (roughly $1,200 in 2012 dollars).[26]

Before he agreed to the purchase, however, Sedgwick decided not to tell Frost that he had already commissioned an article, "A New American Poet," by Edward Garnett, whose literary salons Frost had briefly attended back in 1914.[27] Instead, Sedgwick let Frost assume that Sedgwick could not publish the poems and that he would have Frost's book reviewed only in a general omnibus review. This feigned indifference to his poetry made Frost angry and annoyed and seemed to prove the truth of what Pound had said about poets like Frost among American editors. Eventually, though, Sedgwick let it be known that it was all just a bit of patrician fun.

Eventually he pulled out Garnett's article and read some of it to Frost, a story he delighted in telling Garnett about in a letter: "A few weeks before you wrote, he happened to come into my office. I bade him sit down and then read judicious extracts from your note. His blue eyes opened very wide, and, of course, he is enormously keen to have me print your appreciation—which I shall be glad to do."[28]

As so often happens, though, Frost had the last laugh. Describing when "those blue eyes" opened so wide at the offer to publish his poems, Sedgwick thought he had proved himself an unexpectedly boorish patron unwilling to publish either article or poems. In fact, by then Frost also knew about Garnett's essay because the critic had written Frost to say he had sent it to Sedgwick. Sitting in Sedgwick's office, Frost was not an innocent rube but rather a jaded poet. He likely thought that the editor had rejected not only his poems but Garnett's essay too. Rather than accept the teasing, he felt that what had looked like success was in fact the same old deafness to his brand of realism. According to Frost biographers, Sedgwick waited more than a few days before telling Frost he was publishing the essay. Frost was left to conclude, as he said in a letter, that the *Atlantic* would bury his book in an omnibus review by "some single-bed she professor with a known preference for the beautiful in poetry." That description of the genteel tradition he opposed, rather than the one he meant to revive, expresses as well his familiar feeling of discouragement. Sedgwick, to be fair, claimed he had never lied. From his patrician roost he meant only to tease. When he finally learned the truth, Frost, writing to Garnett, admitted that "Sedgwick was teasing me . . . and I should have known as much, but it has been a long fight with editors, my rage has gathered considerable headway and it's hard to leave off believing the worst of them." He knew enough, though, to credit Garnett more than Sedgwick: "I knew I should never have such another piece of good luck as your help at this moment." And in a characteristically acerbic comment, he added simply, "I have to thank you for these signs of grace in Mr. Ellery Sedgwick."[29]

In any event the September 1915 *Atlantic* carried not only Garnett's essay but also "A Group of Poems by Robert Frost," marking the first publication of two of his most famous poems, "Birches" and "The Road Not Taken." These poems received an unusually lavish treatment. Each was printed in the middle of the page with generous white space for better visual impact.

That September Frost also appeared in *Harper's* in a column by none other than the one man most responsible for making literary realism central to American public culture, William Dean Howells. Howells welcomed Frost to the heights of Parnassus. By the fall of 1915 Robert Frost's public reputation had garnered the two highest honors and seals of approval then possible in American letters.

Recall that in 1915 the *Atlantic Monthly* still retained its status as the pinnacle of American letters. Nearly unique among the commercial monthlies of high circulation, it refused to make concessions to the era's publishing conventions. Instead of adopting smaller articles, and breaking up the relentless two-columned march of closely printed type with a variety of photographs, drawings, color reproductions, and the like, the editors and publishers kept the same look as had first greeted subscribers in the 1850s. Each month readers received well over one hundred pages of a relentless two-column parade of type, broken by an occasional illustration and by advertisements at the back. In the issue containing the Frost essay, for instance, the magazine began with articles about the war in Europe. The essay on Frost, "A New American Poet," was the first cultural item in that month's issue.

Although Garnett had met Frost in England, back then he did not know anything about his poetry and likely paid little attention to the poet. That changed when their mutual friend, Edward Thomas, gave Garnett the English edition of *North of Boston* in March 1915 and urged him to review it. Thomas said Frost "had been at American editors 10 years in vain. But may I suggest it might damage him there if you rubbed the Americans' noses in their own dirt? I know he thought so. Most English reviewers were blinded by theories they had as to what poetry should look like. They did not see how true he was and how pure in his own style."[30] Thomas must have wondered if one of the editors who had rejected Frost's poems had been Sedgwick himself (he had been). Garnett was a well-known essayist not just in his native England but also in the United States. He had made a stir several months earlier in the December 1914 *Atlantic* with an otherwise innocuously titled article, "Some Thoughts on American and

English Fiction." In it he made the case for realism and generated controversy not just in letters to the editor but also in other magazines on both sides of the ocean. The publicity that article attracted convinced Sedgwick to commission another article from Garnett about the precise standards of English criticism.

While working on that commission, Garnett read *North of Boston.* Perhaps the imp of the perverse led him to suggest his essay on Frost in lieu of the essay on critical standards. Perhaps he wanted to tweak Sedgwick's nose about refusal of Frost. If so, Garnett had no idea that, when he wrote to Sedgwick, the editor had admired Frost's work as much as he did. After reading *North of Boston,* Garnett wrote to Sedgwick, "An English friend [Edward Thomas] put in my hands a remarkable volume by a New American poet, whose work I have reason to believe is *quite unknown in America.* The more I studied this writer the more I became penetrated with a sense of the importance to America of his achievement. I have given my reason for my faith, and I have styled my article, 'A New American Poet.'"[31]

He had also sent the completed essay manuscript to Edward Thomas. Thomas wrote Garnett to say, "The article on Frost is absolutely right. I don't think you could have scored more than by insisting on his sublety [*sic*] and truth and quoting the Hired Man, Home Burial and the Hundred Collars. And you have shown his nativeness + his Englishness very delicately and without hurting anyone's feelings." That endorsement was all the confidence he needed. Garnett sent Sedgwick the completed essay. In the cover letter he hinted that it, too, might generate the same attention as had his last essay. It will, he wrote, "not only interest your readers, but may receive attention and comment in the wider circle of the Press." Coming from Garnett, the claim that Sedgwick would be making literary history if he published this first critical assessment of Frost had unusual merit. Nor did Garnett mince words in alleviating Sedgwick's fear that Frost was just another free-verse loud mouth. Garnett added that Frost is "not to be classed with Mr. Undermeyer [*sic*] & his associates, who I see are vociferously advertising the claims of 'The New Poetry,' or with the class of poetic dilettanti who contribute to Miss Harriet Monro's [*sic*] magazine "Poetry."[32] By removing Frost from the New Poets, who belonged to a world of advertisements, graphics, and the like, the ever-steady *Atlantic,* Garnett said, could endorse and promote Frost. After all, "Frost is really representative, carrying on those literary traditions of New England, which are associated with talents as diverse as Hawthorne, Thoreau & Sarah Orne Jewett. If anything I have erred in *understating* Mr. Frost's claims to the attention of American readers; but I prefer that my verdict be cool and unbiased." Again Frost was associated with realism in the older genteel tradition of the writer as gadfly and critic. Sedgwick likely did not need much convincing when he received this letter. By then he had been hearing about Frost from all sides. He told Garnett, "I feel a genuine obligation to print an appreciation of Frost."[33]

EDWARD GARNETT'S ESSAY ON FROST

Edward Garnett's defense of realism in fiction did not initially extend to poetry. Like most of those who read the *Atlantic,* he had all but given up on "the New Poetry [that] was in process of being hatched out by the younger school; and, no doubt, further researches would have yielded a harvest, had not a literary friend chanced to place in my hands a slim green volume, *North of Boston,* by Robert Frost." Relating Frost's book to William Dean Howells's call for a "native touch" in American fiction, Garnett recalls that the phrase "a native touch" itself belongs to Goethe who had written that "a lively feeling of situations and an aptitude to describe them makes the poet." Through that phrase Garnett joins Frost to a realist lineage stretching from Goethe to Howells. Garnett explains that "this definition, though it does not cover the whole ground, is apropos to our purpose." According to Garnett, Frost makes poetry matter once more because his poems are "little canvases painted with quiet, deep understanding of life's incongruous everyday web." That "everyday web" is, as he writes, "the perfection of poetic realism, both in observation and in deep insight into the heart." Goethe, Garnett says, may well have rekindled realism as an artistic method for revealing "deep insight into the heart," but it began in antiquity with Theocritus, "three hundred years before Christ." Referring to Frost's "The Housekeeper," Garnett says that poem is "cast in much the same gossiping style as Theocritus's idyll, 'The Ladies of Syracuse,' with its prattle of provincial ladies over their household affairs and the crush in the Alexandrian streets at the Festival of Adonis. And one may wager that this famous poem shocked the academic taste of the day by its unconventionality, and would not indeed, please modern professors, were it not the work of a Greek poet who lived three hundred years before Christ." According to Garnett, a realist writer, novelist, or poet eschews the large, heroic breadth of topic, diction, and action. To avoid such heroic language and topics carries a risk: "Mr. Frost . . . may disappoint readers who prefer grandeur and breadth of outline or magical depth of coloring to delicate atmospheric imagery." But Garnett writes, to say that aiming for the small everyday life and regular events of small towns somehow diminishes a literary work would be false. Such poetry's commitment to the plausible, he writes, depends on precision, clarity of description, and imagery to allow for both psychological and situational drama. In turn such drama, when incorporated in the compressed medium of a poem, succeeds in "clarifying our obscure instincts and clashing impulses, and in crystallizing them in sharp, precise images."[34]

Garnett asks, "But why put it in poetry and not in prose? the reader may hazard. Well it comes with greater intensity in rhythm and is more heightened and concentrated in effect thereby." Above all else, Garnett says, poetry is the art of intensity, rhythm, and concentration. In poetry great issues, great emotions are condensed to their essentials. Turning to Frost's poetry, he points out that "he is a master of his exacting medium, blank verse, a new master." Insofar as meter is the art of poetry Frost, Garnett says, excels far more than most of his contemporaries. To prove the point about both Frost's artistic merit and the importance of seeming- ly mundane, small dramas as the new realism in poetry, Garnett exam- ines four poems from *North of Boston*: "Mending Wall," "The Death of the Hired Man," "A Hundred Collars," and "The Housekeeper." Through his readings of these poems, Garnett makes the case for a realism. Building on Goethe's comment, Garnett adds the following:

> The dictum is explicit: "A true, real, natural vision of life . . . high descriptive power . . . pictures of lifelike actuality . . . a lively feeling of situation" if a poet possess these qualifications he may treat any the more situation he pleases [sic]. Indeed, the more prosaic appears the vesture of everyday life, the greater is the poet's triumph in seizing and representing features. In the characteristic fact, form, or feature the poet no less than the artist will discover essential lines and aspects of beauty. Nothing is barred to him, if he only have vision. Even the most eccentric divagations in human conduct can be exhibited in their true

spiritual perspective by the psychologist of insight, as Browning repeatedly demonstrates. One sees no reason why Browning's "Fra Lippo Lippi" with all its rough cast philosophic speculation should be "poetry" and Mr. Frost's "A Hundred Collars" should not; and indeed the purist must keep the gate closed on both or on neither. If I desired indeed to know whether a reader could really detect the genuine poet, when he appears amid the crowd of dilettanti, I should ask his judgment on a typical uncompromising passage in "A Hundred Collars."[35]

• • •

After reading the article, Frost wrote to Garnett and explained his poetic principles in more detail. "What you are good enough to call my method they [the critics so far] haven't noticed. I am not supposed to have a method. I am a naïve person." Always suspicious of groups, categories, and movements, Frost disliked the term *realism* insofar as it referred to a particular group of poets. He tells Garnett that a few "get some fun out of calling me a realist, and a realist I may be if by that they mean one who before all else wants the story to sound as if it were told the way it is because it happened that way." Realism for Frost had to be about the art of capturing living human talk into the written word and laying it across the established meters of a long poetic tradition. Frost defined his realism as "the sound of sense." Frost, however, did not want Garnett to think the sound of sense simply meant one's ability to create verisimilitude in the constraints of meter. It was the vessel, the means by which one made visible the larger philosophical, moral, ethical, and psychological ideas his poetry laid bare. "Of course the story must release an idea."[36] Frost's poetry was nothing without ideas.

In this same letter Frost, most likely thinking of Wilfrid Gibson's poetry of the English poor, tells Garnett that he knew an English poet who wrote to the cliché that those in the middle class who read poetry usually have no idea what the poor really think and feel or even *if* they think and feel. If one assumes, as did that poet, that one's readers have no clue about the poor and so takes it upon himself to show his readers that the poor *are* human, too, then one simply proves to the world the truth that one is fundamentally condescending and elitist. Genuine poetry, Frost's idea of realism, had to emerge from an egalitarian and individualist premise that assumes everyone feels and thinks the same if placed in similar circumstances. Given the chance, anyone can behave as well or as badly as anyone else. Above all, Frost detested formulaic thought and thanked Garnett for finding a nonformulaic heritage for his brand of realism.

Much later, in 1960, when Frost was in his eighties, he was asked to recall that issue of the *Atlantic Monthly*. Still overcome by its implication and importance, he said simply, "The splash made waves that still keep coming to me after forty-five years."[37]

GENERAL ROBERT LEE FROST ENTERS HEAVEN: WILLIAM DEAN HOWELLS, *HARPER'S MONTHLY*, AND FROST

Harper's in 1915, chock full of illustrations and far more committed to fiction and poetry than the *Atlantic*, had the feel of a quality commercial television network. In that magazine's September issue William Dean Howells, the "dean of American letters," publicly declared his enthusiasm for Robert Frost's poetry. Writing "The Editor's Easy Chair," as he had for years (just as Henry Mills Alden still wrote "The Editor's Study"), Howells made the New Poetry his topic. "If we could believe the publishers (and we are far from wishing to dispute them)," he wrote, "we are in the presence of such a poetic sunburst as has not flashed upon the world within something like a geological period." This light sarcasm coming from Howells had a particularly sharp ring. Back in the 1880s, he had been largely responsible for the turn to realism in the first place, but as a consequence he had also been blamed for turning the tide against poetry. As fiction veered toward realism, poetry after the 1880s became more and more idealist. It was with something of a wry smile that Howells now wrote about a resurgent realism in poetry. "The time was when their praise would not have been so lavish, so confident, so authoritative, from the trade; but now all is new."[38]

To illustrate the new turn to realism Howells then refers to a stack of recent poetry books on his desk that included Amy Lowell's *Sword Blades and Poppy Seeds*; Vachel Lindsay's *General William Booth Enters Heaven and Other Poems* (its title poem had won the first-ever *Poetry* magazine prize); Edgar Lee Masters's *Spoon River Anthology*, a poetic sensation from late 1914; as well as new collections from James Oppenheim, Conrad Aiken, John Gould Fletcher, Anna Hampstead Branch, Arthur Davison Ficke, and Robert Frost. Of them all, Howells devoted the most space to Frost's collections.

Thinking back on the postbellum decades, Howells asks the central question of the New Poetry: "*Is* all so new inside these books, which came to us, rustling in this tinsel of compliment, this machine-lace of professional glorification? We say no; there is a good deal of the eternal beautiful which cannot put on even a new form." If New Poetry means only free verse, then, Howells writes, even that is hardly new. "Walt Whitman broke loose sixty years ago," and since then "we have not forgotten the *Black Riders* of Stephen Crane [1896], very powerful things in the beat of their short lines, rhymeless, meterless." Nor does Howells find the new free verse appealing. Unlike those earlier poets, Howells says, the contemporary exponents of *vers libre* seem to lack rhythmic sensibility, writing only what Howells calls a freak form. Referring to Lowell's *Sword Blades and Poppy Seeds,* and Masters's *Spoon River Anthology,* Howells dismisses both as mere "shredded prose."[39]

In addition to "shredded prose," Howells finds in the New Poetry another freak form, which he calls "compressed verse." According to Howells, compressed verse does not tell a traditional story but instead depicts only the crisis of a dramatic moment and concentrates its artistic energy there. Comparing these two new styles, Howells writes, "Freak for freak, we prefer compressed verse to shredded prose." Hardly a compliment, this is Howell's rubric for appreciating and understanding Frost's two poetry collections.

One of the very instigators of the postbellum genteel tradition, Howells would have been as unlikely as Henry Holt to fall immediately under the spell of Frost's dramatic narratives. Still, Howells did appreciate its art and its deeper purpose. Predictably he preferred *A Boy's Will* to *North of Boston* but there, too, he recognized it for something new, not something old. "We should say the earlier book sings rather the most, but youth is apt to sing most, and there is strong, sweet music in them both. Here is no *vers libre,* no shredded prose, but very sweet rhyme and pleasant rhythm, though it does not always keep step (willfully breaks step at times, we should say), but always remains faithful to the lineage of poetry that danced before it walked."

Howells, the man who made realism the standard for serious fiction in America, accepts the new realist turn in poetry yet, one suspects, he could not help but prefer poetry to remain the high art of beauty and ideals he had long thought it to be. To Frost's credit the poetry in *North of Boston* had challenged that view. Howells could not help but recognize those poems' power, such that he had to define a new aesthetic category, "compressed verse," to explain it. Devoting most of his column to Frost's poetry, then, Howells particularly admired Frost's psychological depth of character. As he said, "His manly power is manliest in penetrating to the heart of womanhood in that womanliest phase of it, the New England phase." Howells had begun a realist tradition that had taken New England as its setting. After thirty years so many writers had followed in his wake that "one might have thought there was not much left to say of New England humanity, but here it is as freshly and keenly sensed as if it had not been felt before." Like Howells's own novels, Frost's poems find in New Englanders universal themes for the modern age. In Frost's poetry, Howells said, one finds at last "the unrecorded knowledge of humanity." Higher praise from the great realist to a new poet could hardly have been imagined. Altogether then, Howells could not but recognize in Frost's work genuine poetry, as the editor understood that term. "Amidst the often striving and straining of the new poetry, here is the old poetry as young as ever."[40]

• • •

Though he certainly had read the column already, Frost's new friend, the editor of the *Boston Herald,* Walter Prichard Eaton, also sent it to him. Writing to thank Eaton, Frost told him that "long ago my mother was a little schoolma'am in Columbus Ohio when he [Howells] was there and I have heard her speak of meeting him once or twice in society when Columbus society was gay in the sixties [1860s]. He has always stood for something to me away off and high up. So that I felt I had rounded some sort of a circle when he did what you say."[41]

FULL CIRCLE: THE *INDEPENDENT* "DISCOVERS" FROST

Frost's journey into the public sphere had begun in 1894 when the *Independent* had first welcomed his poetry into its pages. Since then the weekly had been increasingly reluctant to accept the New Poetry's reform of the genteel tradition. Always skeptical of realism both in fiction and in poetry, the editors Susan Hayes Ward and her brother, William, had long championed a high moral seriousness that excluded far more of Frost's submitted poems than it had accepted. By 1915, however, Frost's first mentors and advisers had retired and lived in Maine. In their place Hamilton Holt edited the magazine with Edwin E. Slosson as literary editor. Inheriting a magazine steeped in a crusty old-guard reputation of moral liberalism associated with the progressive wing of the Republican Party, the new editors recast the publication for a new era. It became far more political and less concerned with cultural and religious matters. While the Wards had long avoided too much illustration as low brow, the new editors loaded each week's issue with photographs and world news in short articles. To that end they had changed the religious declaration of moral fortitude on the masthead to a new nonreligious declaration of progressive Republican political ideas: "For sixty-six years the forward-looking weekly of America."

In literary matters the new editors no longer ensured that each week's issue would carry at least two poems and a short story. By 1915 many an issue would contain at best one short story and no poetry at all. They did, however, publish an abundance of criticism and had a lively literary review section. In the May 31, 1915, issue, that section included a review of the American editions of Frost's two books.

That week's front page carried the headline "Italy Enters the War." In the back a general roundup, "New Books," included three separate unsigned reviews (most likely written by Slosson) of three poets, including Robert Frost. It did not mention that many of his poems had first been published in the *Independent* itself. Apparently unaware of Frost's earlier connection to the magazine, the reviewer praises the otherwise unknown poet's bleak, cold, and harsh realism. Under the Wards such adjectives would have been meant as criticism. For Slosson, however, they were praise. In particular the reviewer applauds Frost's rare treatment of women as people rather than as ideals, either whores or angels. Complimenting his poetry for its artistic honesty as an accurate record of the times, a presentation of life "stripped to essentials," the reviewer declares the poetry's singular value. In fact, to accentuate Frost's work as part of the New Poetry, the reviewer mistakenly claims that *North of Boston*'s poems are written in free verse rather than meter. Overall the reviewer made of Frost the sort of poet that the editors meant to promote as part of the magazine's own new forward-thinking editorial direction.[42]

• • •

By September 1915 Robert Frost had become publicly recognized as an important poet. His work had been championed in the *New Republic, Poetry, New York Times, Boston Herald, Boston Evening Transcript, Chicago Evening Post, Atlantic, Harper's,* and the *Independent,* among other places. It would only be a matter of time before other reviewers and literary editors took notice and wrote their own assessments of this new poet and the New Poetry that he had made so visible.

Ironically the publicity attendant on Frost's newly published books, especially *North of Boston,* also had an unexpected financial consequence. From the time his family had first returned to the United States in February, they had been living at the farm of their friends the Lynches in Bethlehem, New Hampshire. That spring Frost and Elinor had at last found a suitable farm for the family in nearby Franconia. When he made an offer on the farm, though, the owner learned that Frost was a well-known poet (he had seen Braithwaite's lavish *Boston Evening Transcript* article, complete with the poet's picture) and so raised the asking price.

All would not be lost. By the end of 1915 the attention given to Frost's poetry, not to mention the more elusive word-of-mouth reviews that are never recorded, had made *North of Boston* a best-seller. In 1915 alone the book went through five separate printings totaling nearly twenty thousand copies, and, unlike Nutt, Holt did pay royalties to Frost.[43]

• • •

Nearly a hundred years later Robert Frost still makes the old poetry as new as ever. Beginning with these first two books, especially the poetry published in *North of Boston,* Frost brought the genteel idea of poetry into the modern age. Slowly and consistently in the public arena and not just in classrooms, his "kind of fooling" has persisted. "Nothing is quite honest that is not commercial," he once said. He never meant for his poetry to rely solely on the approval of coteries and small circles of like-minded readers and writers. In the anonymity of the public sphere, the anonymous market consisting of genteel and mass-circulation magazines, Frost tested both his artistic and his philosophical ideas. Remarkably that forum welcomed his poems.

That welcome continued into the electronic age. After World War II the new commercial television networks regularly courted him. It can also be said that, when the American governing class courted him, the politicians likely did so because, as intellectuals, they had grown up reading the popular genteel magazines that consistently published and discussed his work.[44] After all, of all the poets of his generation, only he became the first asked to recite a poem for the inauguration of the president of the United States. More to the point, John F. Kennedy, the youngest man ever elected president, had long admired Frost's work and read it for what it had to say as much as any other reason. In fact, when Frost told Kennedy over the phone that he would be reading "The Gift Outright," which he had published in his 1942 collection, *The Witness Tree*, Kennedy asked him to change the final line. This ambitious and ambiguous sixteen-line poem charts the full sweep of American history and was published in a time of war. Its final lines about westward expansion claim that the land was "still unstoried, artless, unenhanced, / Such as she was, such as she would become." Kennedy asked Frost to change that last line to "such as she will become." He wanted no ironic questions on that occasion.[45]

By 1963 Frost's poetry mattered as much to everyday readers as to those commanding the power of the American presidency. Frost had been asked to read not because the new Kennedy administration expected to hear a revival of the Gospel of Beauty, then long dead, nor because it expected a lush idealistic encomium but precisely because Frost had by then trained them to recognize in poetry a place for the hard truths and necessary wisdom that only literature can provide.

Even today Frost's poetry persists in the now commonplace metaphors of "roads not taken," "mending walls," and "silent, dark, and deep" woods. Among poets, meanwhile, he has had a global reach. In 1997 three Noble Prize winners—Joseph Brodsky, Seamus Heaney, and Derek Wolcott—paid homage to Robert Frost in a trade book of essays on the poet.[46] Russian Jewish, Irish Catholic, and Afro Caribbean, they are as far removed from genteel New England as one could get. Yet in Frost's poetry they found examples for their own life's work, and their own work has in turn ensured that Frost's legacy, real, honest, ambiguous, hard, sometimes bitter, often funny, will be made new and matter still.

Notes

INTRODUCTION

1. See Trachtenberg, *Incorporation of America* for a standard history of this period.

2. See Villanueva, *Theories of Literary Realism*. He offers an extensive and lucid treatment from Aristotle to the present of the problem of realism and mimesis for literature generally. For American literature some recent overviews of realism since the mid-1980s (none of which covers poetry) are A. Kaplan, *Social Construction of American Realism*; Glazener, *Reading for Realism*; and Lawson, *Downwardly Mobile*. I will have more to say about American literary realism in chapter 1.

3. Rubin, *Songs of Ourselves*, 389–90. Frost is especially beloved for one poem, "The Road Not Taken." Of the 970 entries, 343 readers chose "The Road Not Taken" as their favorite.

4. Kendall, *Art of Robert Frost*, 5. Richardson, *Ordeal of Robert Frost*, argues that Frost's ordeal concerned the ongoing tension in American culture between "village ideals" and intellectual life.

5. The genteels, as a sociological cohort, also established a particular "genteel tradition" that had its intellectual center in Boston. Of the many works that focus on Boston's intellectual, economic, and social elite, see Green, *Problem of Boston*; Story, *Forging of an Aristocracy*; and Dalzell, *Enterprising Elite*. Also relevant for a broader view are Persons, *Decline of American Gentility*, and Howe, "American Victorianism as a Culture."

6. Polanyi, *Great Transformation*.

7. These are the poets singled out as particularly important for the postbellum period by Edmund Clarence Stedman, who published the era's most significant anthology, *An American Anthology* (Boston: Houghton, Mifflin, 1900).

8. Kendell, *Art of Robert Frost*, 3. He is citing Frost's essay "The Constant Symbol" from *Collected Prose of Robert Frost*, 147.

CHAPTER ONE
THE WORLD THAT MADE ROBERT FROST:
THE GENTEELS, THEIR VALUES, AND THEIR PUBLICATIONS

1. The next year, 1893, "Seaward" was published as a book, complete with footnotes and an essay on its subject.

2. As told to an early biographer. See Sergeant, *Robert Frost: The Trial by Existence*, 28; also, the *Independent*, November 17, 1892.

3. See, for instance, Santayana's essay, "Genteel Tradition," first published in 1911 and collected in his *Genteel Tradition: Nine Essays*. Also see Howe's introduction to a special issue of *American Quarterly*, "American Victorianism as a Culture." There Howe makes the point that "Anglo-Saxon does not do justice to the importance of the Scottish, Welsh, and Scots-Irish contributions to American Victorian culture" (513). Also see Persons, *Decline of American Gentility*; Lears, *No Place of Grace*; and Jaher, *Urban Establishment*.

4. Jaher, *Urban Establishment*, 2.

5. In literary study three works have the most relevance to the genteels' tradition as I discuss it: Bercovitch, *Puritan Origins of the American Self*; Sollors, *Beyond Ethnicity*; and Buell, *New England Literary Culture*. Bercovitch explains how a particular group's ideology became a dominant feature of American literature, and Sollors extends Bercovitch's point to argue for the ability of a single culture's worldview to shape the views of immigrants from other communities in their literary expressions. Finally, Buell offers an extensive treatment of the contours of New England culture beyond what I am calling its genteel center.

6. Santayana, *Genteel Tradition*, 41.

7. Bushman, *Refinement of America*, xiii.

8. Santayana, *Genteel Tradition*, 40; Bushman, *Refinement of America*, 8, xii.

9. Bushman, *Refinement of America*, xvi–xvii.

10. Jones, *Age of Energy*, 59; Jaher, *Urban Establishment*, 9. More recently in *Downward Mobility* the literary historian Andrew Lawson adopts Jaher's findings and argues that it was precisely this distinctive "gentry-class rule" that literary realists protested.

11. Lears, *No Place of Grace*, 13; Lawson, *Downward Mobility*, 26.

12. Persons, *Decline of American Gentility*, 293; Mann, *Yankee Reformers in the Urban Age*, 3.

13. The standard history on that migration away from the farms is H. Barron's *Those Who Stayed Behind*. Also see Paton's study of Frost and Wyeth in relation to that depopulation, *Abandoned New England*.

14. Bushman, *Refinement of America*, xix.

15. Jones, *Age of Energy*, 223; Saum, *Popular Mood of America*, 76. According to Saum's research, however, the South proved an exception to a general trend of bleak pessimism and loss of large national purpose reflected in Northern publications (see 192).

16. Zboray, *A Fictive People*, 108.

17. Ibid., 108–31.

18. Leach, *Land of Desire*, 7.

19. The history of this transformation is extensive. See Blumin, *Emergence of the Middle Class*; Clark, *Roots of Rural Capitalism*; and Sellers, *Market Revolution*. Lawson argues that this transformation began in the 1830s and was marked by the panic of 1837 (*Downwardly Mobile*, 1–19). Regardless of the origins of the change, by the 1880s two distinctive cultural groups—the New England genteels and the nouveau riche—were vying for power.

20. Persons, *Decline of American Gentility*, 277; Jones, *Age of Energy*, 188.

21. See Green, *Problem of Boston*; Story, *Forging of an Aristocracy*; Dalzell, *Enterprising Elite*; Persons, *Decline of American Gentility*, 46. Persons adds that by the time of the Civil War this "inbred caste" could even be recognized "with a characteristic physiognomy readily apparent to the appreciative observer" (47).

22. Persons, *Decline of American Gentility*, 103, 55, 303.

23. See Ballou, *Building of the House*, for more on Houghton Mifflin.

24. Saum, *Popular Mood of America, 1860–1890*, 41–66. In one of the few histories to examine the views of "common people," Saum reports that his research turned up a view of bleak pessimism that helps explain why, to the genteels, cultural evangelism became all the more imperative after the Civil War. Saum's findings came from the diaries and letters of lower-middle-class Americans from the Civil War through 1890 that are scattered across archives throughout the nation.

25. See Jackson, *Word and Its Witness*, a groundbreaking study of the pervasive impact of particular Christian theological concepts from the first Pilgrims to the present day, particularly as they have shaped American realism.

26. Kete, *Sentimental Collaboration*.

27. The phrase comes from Jones, *Age of Energy*, 185. But historians as various as Lears, Jaher, and Bushman offer abundant examples, statistics, and history for it.

28. Howe, "American Victorianism," 516. After the Civil War the middle-class Anglo-Saxon Protestant core of the Republican Party had two geographic centers in the Northeast, the small villages and the newly industrializing cities. The Republican Party gained its strength postbellum precisely from its ability "to harmonize the rural and urban constituencies of American Victorian culture in its appeal to the values of modernization." Howe, "American Victorianism," 515. Also see Jaher, *Urban Establishment,* 87–125.

29. See Susman, "Personality and the Making of Twentieth-Century Culture," 271–85. Also see Hilkey, *Character Is Capital.* Her book explains an economic basis for this concept. Also see the more recent, *Word and Its Witness* by Jackson for the particularly Christian Protestant theological background for this idea of character (especially chaps. 1 and 2).

30. See Bercovitch, *Puritan Origins of the American Self,* in particular for a standard literary treatment of this point.

31. See A. Douglas, *Feminization of American Culture,* a standard history of this division. Also see Cott, *Bonds of Womanhood;* Kelley, *Private Woman, Public Stage;* Tompkins, *Sensational Designs;* and F. Kaplan, *Sacred Tears.*

32. See A. Douglas, *Feminization of American Culture,* for the approach of these institutions to gendered ideas of virtue.

33. Starr, *Creation of the Media,* 243. Summarizing the era from 1870 to 1900, Starr reports: "For the first time, Americans created private organizations specifically aimed at suppressing publications and other indecent items, undertook extensive prosecutions of people in the trade, and sent them to prison in significant numbers" (236).

34. See Tomsich, *A Genteel Endeavor,* 88. Although he overlooks the genteels' impact on Comstockery, Tomsich does argue that the genteels can be given credit ending nepotism and patronage in the federal civil service. He credits them with establishing the Pendleton Act and civil service reform generally (88).

35. Starr, *Creation of the Media,* 236.

36. His energies led to congressional action. The 1873 act itself would last until 1914 (Comstock himself died in 1915). See Starr, *Creation of the Media,* 241–43.

37. Ibid., 243, 244.

38. Jackson, *Word and Its Witness;* Susman, "Personality." In the 1890s there was a movement known as the Social Gospel. On the Social Gospel see the standard history, Hopkins, *Rise of the Social Gospel in American Protestantism.*

39. Glazener, *Reading for Realism.* She identifies only eleven institutions, all magazines and most of them monthlies. While I adopt her views in spirit, I disagree with many of the details, including her claim that monthly magazines

alone ought to define this group. The distinctions in format were not as relevant in the late nineteenth century as were the ideas and people responsible for creating those ideas.

40. The point and the phrase are Ellery Sedgwick's, in his important article, "American Genteel Tradition," 57.

41. Persons, *Decline of American Gentility*, 66.

42. An argument in support of this claim, though, is far beyond the scope of this book. For its application to literature see Jackson, *Word and Its Witness*.

43. I begin from the premise that the media constitute and define "the public," also called, more precisely, the public sphere. I have necessarily built on foundations laid out by Jürgen Habermas and Benedict Anderson. Both expanded the idea and meaning of *literature* and in so doing included journalism. Specifically I am discussing periodical journalism, defined as *periodically printed material concerning contemporary current affairs*. Until the development of printing, news of current events mostly arrived in the form of letters and proclamations. These were also eventually compiled into yearly (or longer) chronicles. Habermas's first major work, *The Structural Transformation of the Public Sphere*, published in German in 1962, made the case for the historical and cultural importance of journalism as writing, as a distinctive kind or genre of literature itself. There, for example, he writes: "A public sphere in the sense of a separate realm distinguished from the private sphere cannot be shown to have existed in the feudal society of the High Middle Ages" (6). The process itself began only in the Renaissance with the rise of states: "'Private' designated the exclusion from the sphere of the state apparatus; for 'public' referred to the state that in the meantime had developed under absolutism" (11). Then, with the rise of capitalism and high finance, these new distinctions between private and public took the shape that we understand as the norm today (14–26). His argument on behalf of journalism found its point of origin in the mercantilist era of the seventeenth century, when the state took charge of the economy and used journalism as its chief means of community building (Habermas, *Structural Transformation*, 23–26). Habermas's argument shocked the literary community insofar as it gave significant social and cultural power to a genre that had nothing to do with traditional categories of high literature—drama, fiction, poetry. For some, it seemed as if Habermas had, from a sociological perspective at any rate, granted more social and cultural authority to journalism than to any other kind of literature.

44. B. Anderson, *Imaginary Communities*, 135. The revised 2006 edition does not change the original but rather adds several chapters and a new preface. There Anderson argues that journalism did more than just create a public sphere with-

in an already existing national community. Anderson went so far as to claim that journalism also allowed elites to create "imagined communities," to create the very nations themselves. In short, journalism created nationalism as a consequence of its ability to produce a public sphere: "Print-language is what invents nationalism, not *a* particular language per se" (135). He is writing of Indonesia at this point but means his point to be applicable in general.

45. See Zboray, *A Fictive People*, on this point.

46. In 1865 the genteels' magazines—*Harper's Monthly* (established 1850), *Harper's Weekly* (1857), and the *Atlantic* (1857), *Godey's Lady's Book* (1830), and *Peterson's* (1842)—commanded large national readerships with circulations at or above 100,000 in a country of 35 million people. After the Civil War the genteel monthly with the highest circulation by far was the *Youth's Companion* (established 1824), which had become a family magazine.

47. In terms of the American publishing, by the end of the Civil War these periodicals were part of a booming industry of more than forty-five hundred newspapers and seven hundred magazines. Within that new industry the most growth had occurred among the newspapers. There were relatively few new magazines, in fact, only fifty more than had existed in 1850. For newspaper statistics see Mott, *American Journalism*, 404.

48. The *Sun* began the penny paper revolution in the 1830s but had ceased to be a penny paper in 1868, when Charles A. Dana, who had worked on the genteel *North American Review*, purchased it. Under his editorial control it forged a middle road between the genteels' *Atlantic* and the populist sensationalism of Bonner's *Ledger*. Bonner, it should be said, was himself an intellectual and ran a respected literary salon. He favored the more radical literary genres and ideas, publishing the renegade theology of Henry Ward Beecher and the stories of "Fanny Fern." In Philadelphia, meanwhile, the *Saturday Evening Post*, which sold for two cents an issue, also became a place where high literary ideals could speak to the cultural aspirations of a working- and lower-middle-class reader. It also became the leading magazine to espouse the views of the liberal mugwump wing of the new Republican Party. See Crouthamel, *Bennett's New York Herald*; Huntzicker, *Popular Press, 1833–1865*; Nord, *Comuunities of Journalism*; and Lehuu, *Carnival on the Page*.

49. Mott, *American Journalism*, 434; Starr, *Creation of the Media*, 256.

50. Mott, *American Journalism*, 441. The remark was made in regard to the *New York Evening Post*. An interviewer for *Pearson's Magazine* (March 1909, 246) had asked Pulitzer why he did not model his newspaper more along the lines of the high-toned liberalism of that daily.

Notes to Pages 23–27 • 257

51. Starr, *Creation of the Media,* 256. Also see Schudsen, *Discovering the News,* which explains how journalism adopted literary techniques; Fishkin, *From Fact to Fiction;* and Roggenkamp, *Narrating the News.*

52. Mott, *American Journalism,* 481.

53. For a brief overview of the national intrusion on the daily newspaper industry of the 1890s see Starr, *Creation of the Media,* 250–60.

54. "Mass advertising, riding on those communications, began to sell the mass-produced products to a mass audience." See Bagdikian, *Media Monopoly,* 144. He adds, "From 1880–1910 the American population grew from 50 to 92 million, thanks to immigration and public health laws that prevented disease and early death. Mass communications began to tie together the expanding country."

55. Starr, *Creation of the Media,* 261–62.

56. The popular publications I have defined were aimed at a nongenteel audience. The lower prices expanded the market and in just thirty years, increased the number of newspapers and magazines from 852 to 4,051, the overwhelming majority of which were two-cent newspapers. See Persons, *Decline of American Gentility,* 53.

57. "The number of periodicals with 100,000 circulation quadrupled from 21 to 85 between 1885 and 1900 and then nearly doubled again to 159 by 1905" (Starr, *Creation of the Media,* 262). In 1897 the circulation of *McClure's* was 260,000, *Cosmopolitan's* was 300,000, and *Munsey's* had 700,000 readers. Schneirov, *Dream of a New Social Order,* 11. More to the point, by 1893 the *Ladies' Home Journal* had already achieved a circulation of 700,000 (A. Douglas, *Feminization of American Culture,* 13); the *Journal,* established in 1883 as a genteel publication, became a mass-market phenomenon in the 1890s under its new editor, Edward Bok. By 1905 another mass-market leader, *McClure's,* was printing "an average of 165 pages of advertising a month at $400 a page" (17). Also see Castronovo, *Beautiful Democracy,* for a detailed look at the audiences of this period in terms of a theory of aesthetics.

58. Starr, *Creation of the Media,* 251, 254.

59. Mott, *A History of American Magazines,* 4:2; Mott, *American Journalism,* 512.

60. Most of Hovey's early books were self-published. Still, his poems had been published individually by many publications. His collections often won great acclaim in reviews, as did his verse drama, *Launcelot and Guinevere: A Poem in Dramas* (New York: U.S. Book, 1891).

61. *Independent,* November 17, 1892, 1617.

62. From that association Hovey had found his love of Provencal poetry. The poem itself was first written while Hovey was staying in Nova Scotia with Carman and learned of Parsons's death. As it happens Hovey wrote the poem at the home of Carman's cousin, the Canadian poet Charles G. D. Roberts. "The poem includes many references to the countryside around the Roberts house, Kingscroft, where it was written, and to Hovey's circle of literary contemporaries and forebears. Some of the best lines in the poem are found in his addresses to the nearby marshes as fellow mourners." Yearsley, "Richard Hovey."

63. *Independent,* November 17, 1892, 1.

CHAPTER TWO
REALISM AND GENTEEL PUBLISHING

1. Mott, *A History of American Magazines,* 4:2; Mott, *American Journalism* 411–514.

2. In addition weeklies like *Collier's,* established in 1888, became a mass-market muckraking weekly in 1895 under new editors. Mott, *A History of American Magazines,* 4:454. Another weekly, the *Saturday Evening Post,* though established in Philadelphia as early as 1821, became a mass-market publication in 1897 when the publisher of the wildly successful *Ladies' Home Journal,* Cyrus Curtis, bought it in a fire sale. The next year he appointed George Horace Lorimer as editor and inaugurated its reputation for muckraking. Mott, *A History of American Magazines,* 4:686–87.

3. Jackson, *Word and Its Witness,* 125–26, offers one of the best overviews of the importance and ongoing influence and impact of Bunyan on what I am calling genteel literature. As an example consider *McClure's.* Among the advertising and illustrations readers found "scientific articles, highlighting new discoveries," as well as articles on "locomotives and trains . . . wild animals and exploration . . . and a stress on personalities" (especially the series by Ida Tarbell on the life of Napoleon and Lincoln). Mott, *A History of American Magazines,* 4:590, 589–607.

4. For examples of this debate since the mid-1980s see A. Kaplan, *Social Construction of American Realism;* Glazener, *Reading for Realism;* Hochman, *Getting at the Author;* and Lawson, *Downwardly Mobile.*

5. A. Kaplan, *Social Construction of American Realism,* 161, 2. The summary is Kaplan's.

6. Auerbach, *Mimesis,* 491. Since the 1950s theorists have debated the issue across a number of fields from philosophy to linguistics. In his more recent overview of literary realism, the Spanish scholar Dario Villanueva (*Theories of Literary Realism*) identified a realism intrinsic to the literary work (which he calls

formal, or conscious) and one extrinsic (which he calls genetic, or correspondence). Referring to Benjamin Harshav and beginning from the premise that "the philosophical component determines the artistic component" (8), Villanueva defines literary realism as a weird synthesis of an "internal field of reference" and an "external field of reference" (8). Accounting for the phenomenology of reading on the one hand and of the writer's ideological impressions on the other, Villanueva's theory is appealing for its embrace of mimesis and its recognition that realist literature ultimately is just a set of words that invoke made-up possibilities.

7. In her introduction to *Social Construction of American Realism*, Amy Kaplan offers a guide to scholarly reaction to Chase's thesis through the late 1980s.

8. Lawson, *Downwardly Mobile*, 17. For details about why Howells found in realism the most pertinent literary method and style, see Lawson's chapter on Howells, "The Artist of the Floating World" (62–85).

9. Lawson, *Downwardly Mobile*, 17. Lawson's larger point is that such a need arose in the lower middle class. His case depends on the middle-class uncertainty of the leading American realists. However, regardless of the class from which that uncertainty emerged, the stylistic origins emerged when they did, Lawson says, because the American realists meant "to tether a world in danger of slipping away with some existential weight, to provide the fictional realm with referential grounding" (37). He calls this "realism's search for the tangible" (37).

10. In this Howells belongs to a much larger change in intellectual culture generally speaking. In *Objectivity* Lorraine Daston and Peter Galison explain that only in the mid-nineteenth century did the very idea of objectivity—that which is the opposite of subjectivity—"aspire to knowledge that bears no trace of the knower" (17), a concept that "first emerged in the mid-nineteenth century" and soon became the exclusive province of science (27). Meanwhile the literature on Howells's influence on American literary realism is extensive. For more recent assessments of his impact, see A. Kaplan's *Social Construction of American Realism*; Glazener's *Reading for Realism*; and Lawson's *Downwardly Mobile*.

11. Hochman, *Getting at the Author*, 11. See Daston and Galison's *Objectivity* for the implications of making things objective with regard to science in this same era.

12. Hochman, *Getting at the Author*, 91.

13. Jones, *Age of Energy*, 61. Jones cites the *Dictionary of American Biography*, 13:570.

14. Josiah Holland, "Goodness in Literary Material," *Scribner's*, September 1878, 743–44.

15. Information about Howells comes from Goodman, *William Dean Howells*, 248–74.

16. For example, the successor to *Scribner's Monthly*, the *Century*, edited by George Watson Gilder, was in the 1880s the most successful of the genteel monthlies with circulation of more than 100,000, and its editor received a $10,000 salary, too.

17. Sedgwick, "American Genteel Tradition," 158. Also see Joanna Levin, *Bohemia in America*, 1–69, esp. 67.

18. Tomsich, *Genteel Endeavor*, 145, 170, 141. In assessing Aldrich's own poetry and fiction, Tomsich says the editor was "devoted to the midrange of human experience; his interest was neither in the great and compelling events of the world nor in the private nuances of the self" (147). Aldrich was editor from 1881 to 1890.

19. Three of Howells's columns in particular make the larger moral point. In "Editor's Study," *Harper's*, April 1887, 825, he explains the moral failings of the romance tradition's fiction. In his next column in May he defended the realists' ability to promote equality. And in "Editor's Study," *Harper's*, September 1887, 638, he makes the case for the genteel idea of character according to his more liberal understanding of the concept.

20. William Dean Howells, "My Favorite Novelist and His Best Book," *Munsey's*, April 1897, 18–25.

21. In this the symbolists and decadents had classical rhetorical theory on their side, and they often invoked it. In theory *rhetoric* refers to the persuasive power of literature while belle lettres, and the new aestheticism, preferred the classical ideal of delight and teaching—anything but persuasion.

22. Weir, *Decadent Culture in the United States*, 53.

23. See Joanna Levin, *Bohemia in America*, for the class nuances the term evokes, particularly her chapter on San Francisco's elite Bohemian Club and the strange hybrid known as the bourgeois bohemian, 197–242.

24. Weir says the typical decadent, for instance, seeks a "counterculture of elites." Weir, *Decadent Culture in the United States*, 199.

25. Symons, *Symbolist Movement in Literature*, 9. This was the first significant book on symbolist literature and for decades a standard on the topic. It would have a powerful impact on such future poets as Wallace Stevens, T. S. Eliot, and Ezra Pound.

26. Symons wrote: "The latest movement in European literature has been called by many names, none of them quite exact or comprehensive—Decadence, Symbolism, Impressionism. . . . We shall find that Verlaine objects to being called a Decadent, Maeterlinck to being called a Symbolist, Huysmans to being called

an Impressionist. These terms, as it happens, have been adopted as the badge of little separate cliques, noisy, brainsick young people who haunt the brasseries of the Boulevard Saint-Michel, and exhaust their ingenuities in theorizing over the works they cannot write." Symons, "Decadent Movement in Literature," 858.

27. Ibid., 859–59. In a recent overview of this era Michael Levenson summarizes the symbolism of the 1890s as poetry that took particular delight in creating new symbols that were "not a return to romantic vision. . . . It was esoteric and partial rather than accessible and total. . . . On the one side, Symbolism faced the industrializing economy and a political impasse; on the other, it confronted the successes of realism and the prestige of *Parnassian* craft." Levinson, *Modernism*, 107. In *Modernism*'s first three chapters he offers one of the best recent overviews of the divide between realism and its alternatives in literature of the 1880s and 1890s.

28. The editors at *Harper's*, perhaps fearing that they had cast too many aspersions on the Jews, also decided to carry in this issue "The Mission of the Jews," an article about Jews in antiquity. Or perhaps not. For an overview of *Trilby*'s American success, see Hochman, *Getting at the Author*. Also see Levin, *Bohemia in America*, 190–95. To measure its continued impact in the twenty-first century, she tests readers by asking how many think Svengali was a real person.

29. Hochman, *Getting at the Author*, 61–69, offers a reading of *Trilby* in relation to American realism.

30. Iser, *Walter Pater*, 9, 31, 115.

31. Weir, *Decadent Culture in the United States*, 3. The tour would take Wilde to more than a hundred American cities and towns and would seal not only his reputation but also that of aestheticism in America.

32. As proof of wayward egotism gone berserk, and as proof of any larger social responsibility, *decadence* became a profound insult, most notably in *Degeneration* (1892 German; English 1895) by Max Nordau, a German literary intellectual and one of the leaders of the new Zionist movement. A literature detached from science and the social world was not for him. Many genteels, including Howells, agreed with Nordau and argued the new realism was the antidote to the disease of decadence. This is the tenor in many of Howells's columns in *Harper's* and of similar columns by George Watson Gilder and his associate editor Robert Underwood Johnson at the *Century*.

33. Parrish and Rollins, *Keats and the Bostonians*; Weir, *Decadent Culture in the United States*.

34. Today this group's claim to literary fame comes from Fanny Brawne's letters to John Keats, found by Day and Guiney in Europe. However, the letters remained unpublished until the 1930s.

35. For more details see Parrish and Rollins, *Keats and the Bostonians*, 1–21.

36. Melville Stone was one of the great newsmen of the 1880s and 1890s. He came up through the ranks of many Chicago newspapers and founded the *Chicago Daily News* in 1876. He adopted many of the reader-enticing methods of the *New York Herald* and other mass-market dailies and soon saw enormous profits. The *Chicago Daily News* became particularly beloved for its dialect poets and humorous columnists, particularly the poetic work of Eugene Field, whom Melville Stone put under contract in 1883. By 1888 Stone had sold the newspaper and devoted the rest of his career to the Associated Press. Field owed his almost overnight national fame to the syndication of his column, "Sharps and Flats."

37. Magazine historians often claim it to be the first ever little magazine (apparently ignoring Emerson's 1840 *Dial*). After a brief run in Boston the enterprise soon moved to Chicago, which was then undergoing a massive effort by the town's wealthy and genteel elite to make it a cultural capital. Building on the reputation of Chicago's genteel *Dial,* the local gentry in the 1890s also established the *Friday Literary Supplement.* In *Decadent Culture in the United States,* Weir finds that the first few months of the *Chap-Book's* Cambridge incarnation reflected the Tory politics typical of the crowd associated with Santayana, Charles Eliot Norton, and other Boston aesthetes. Once in Chicago, however, the magazine "settled into a largely Francophile but weirdly Americanized version of decadence," Weir says (106).

38. This led to a small turf war between Stone and Kimball and the rival decadent firm of Copeland and Day. When the American publication of the *Yellow Book* began, Stone and Kimball, who by then had moved the *Chap-Book* to Chicago, stopped including in their magazine the English writers who appeared in the *Yellow Book* and even ran an intensely hostile review of the *Yellow Book*. Ultimately, although both firms brought the new aestheticism to America, Stone and Kimball proved to be more prominent in the end. This was a result of their special book series, the Green Tree Library, and the Carnation Series, which was devoted to works from that movement. Before it went out of business in 1898, the firm of Stone and Kimball published 104 books. Also see Parrish and Rollins, *Keats and the Bostonians,* 17.

39. Herbert Stone was a dedicated Francophile, so most issues introduced American readers to the latest currents in French symbolism.

40. Weir, *Decadent Culture in the United States,* 103. It is probable that the young publishers closed both the *Chap-Book* and their publishing house after four years because they could no longer sustain the energy and sales of both.

41. Ziff, *American 1890s,* 134.

42. Before moving to England, Harland had made his reputation in America by pretending to be Jewish and by writing risqué stories about the Jewish Lower

East Side under the pseudonym Sidney Luska. Once in England, he used those experiences for his exploration of the underside of experience in stories and poems published in his new *Yellow Book*. That magazine came from a relatively new publisher, John Lane, who had just split from his partner, Elkin Mathews, at that eponymous firm. With the *Yellow Book* and decadence in general, Lane soon became the most modern of English publishers.

43. Brake, "Aestheticism and Decadence," 76–100. She adds that its cost "was cheaper than the single volumes of new fiction that began to prevail in 1894 and the old quarterlies . . . but more expensive than most of the monthly up-market reviews of the day . . . and far more expensive than the lavishly illustrated shilling monthlies such as the *Cornhill*" (78). Also see Mix, *A Study in Yellow*.

44. One of the best and only discussions of this forgotten magazine appears in Weir, *Decadent Culture in the United States*, 56–59.

45. Weir, *Decadent Culture in the United States*.

46. Tomsich, *A Genteel Endeavor*, 121.

47. Mott, *A History of American Magazines*, 4:37.

48. Harper, *House of Harper*, 530. Also see Ziff, *American 1890s*, 123. Ziff added this pithy phrase: "The difference between life and literature is such that the number of literary subjects is limited, while the range of human experience is not" (128).

49. Mott, *A History of American Magazines*, 4:122.

50. Dividing these twenty-four hundred books into three genres, or categories—genteelists, romanticists, and humorists—he uncovered a broad orthodoxy of subject matter and theme among all three: "Nature worship, sentimental love, primitivism, antiquarianism and exoticism, or supernaturalism." Kindilien, *American Poetry in the 1890s*, 55. He argues: "In their worship of the past, their fondness for historical myth and legend, their addiction to the exotic and the picturesque, and especially in their peculiar combination of the ideal, the spiritual, and the didactic, these poets of the Nineties manifested many of the qualities of genteelism" (30). Kindilien adds in summary: "American genteelism exploited a sentimental didacticism that had been inbred in verse during the preceding decades" (33).

51. In descending order of prominence the other publishers were to be found in the equally vibrant, though smaller, publishing centers of Chicago, San Francisco, and Philadelphia. Regardless, Kindilien emphasizes that these books from commercial publishers usually owed their existence to previous publication of individual poems in magazines and newspapers. Of the nineteen hundred poets who published books between 1870 and 1900, the majority were "critics, newspaper men, and writers of all kinds of prose." Kindilien, *American Poetry in the 1890s*, 6.

52. Ibid., 30, 10–11.

53. Weirick, *From Whitman to Sandburg in American Poetry*, 101.

54. "Impressions by the Way," 330.

55. Richard Hovey, *Seaward: An Elegy on the Death of Thomas William Parsons* (Boston: Lothrop, 1893). The book's first fifteen pages included the poem, followed by extensive notes to each stanza, as well as an essay on Parsons that Hovey had published in the *Atlantic*. Lothrop in these years made its profits from children's magazines, including *Pansy* (1874–96), and its constant profit generator, *Wide Awake* (1875–93), which had been the only children's magazine to feature regular articles about living writers by living writers. It included many contributions from Guiney's set, including Guiney herself. See Mott, *A History of American Magazines*, 3:177 and 508–9. In 1893 Lothrop also published a genteel large-size folio monthly, *Best Things: A Quarterly Illustrated Journal of Literature and Timely Topics for Family Reading*. It went out of business that same year, which also was the year Lothrop published Hovey's small book.

56. This book was simultaneously published in London by Elkin Mathews. By the end of that year Lane split with Mathews to start his own firm and to begin publishing the *Yellow Book*. Later Elkin Mathews became Ezra Pound's English publisher too.

57. After Oscar Wilde's 1895 trial, however, Boston's gentility got the better of Copeland and Day. They dropped their association with decadence. Weir, in his study of the firm's 108 publications, finds that only about 25 percent of its books could be properly classified as decadent (*Decadent Culture in the United States*, 74). These included works by both Lionel Johnson and W. B. Yeats, then part of the aestheticist Rhymer's Club that Yeats had formed at the Cheshire Cheese in London. Stephen Crane, though decidedly not an aesthete in the later nineteenth-century sense of lush beautiful poetry, did write strikingly original free verse, spare and precise poetry that the firm of Copeland and Day published in the same year (1895) that Crane published his first realist novel, *The Red Badge of Courage*.

CHAPTER THREE
AN INTELLECTUAL FINDS HIS WAY: ROBERT FROST GOES TO SCHOOL

1. For histories of San Francisco pertinent to Frost's family at this time, see Decker, *Fortunes and Failures*, and Etherington, *Public City*.

2. See Mott, *American Journalism*, 474. Mott also notes that the paper was actually owned by a conservative family that broadcast its views in another daily, the *Call*, thus hedging the market for opinionated dailies.

3. However, while the *San Francisco Bulletin* supported the Democratic Party, the *San Francisco Examiner* of the 1870s was the Democratic Party's house organ, and in the 1880s would become the leading newspaper in California for the Democratic Party (see Mott, *American Journalism*, 475). Eventually it was taken over by William Randolph Hearst and would become part of his national chain, helping to establish, as would Pulitzer, a mass market for journalism in America. During this period, too, Frost's father not only joined with the Christian Socialist aspirations of Henry George's single-tax idea but also became a close friend of his. For recent speculation about George's influence on Frost, see Sanders, *A Divided Poet*, 36–39.

4. I draw largely on Thompson, *Robert Frost: The Early Years*, 29–45, for the information in these paragraphs.

5. Thompson, *Robert Frost: Early Years*, 491–92; Frost, *Selected Letters of Robert Frost*, 498. The poem first appeared in the *San Francisco Evening Post* of March 29, 1884, 6.

6. Newdick, *Newdick's Season of Frost*, 21.

7. Ibid., 20–23. In fact, as Jay Parini makes clear, the grandparents did provide temporary shelter, and both parties were equally happy that it was temporary. Parini, *Robert Frost: A Life*, 21.

8. In a letter later in life he recalled with particular fondness his Greek and Latin teachers, "Miss Lear and Miss Newall who were really all the teachers I ever saw in my restriction to Greek and Latin." He had them each year he was in high school. Newdick, *Newdick's Season of Frost*, 30. Also see Thompson, *Robert Frost: Early Years*, 88–97. For the best biography of Frost, the one least tainted with overt hostility to its subject, see Jay Parini's *Robert Frost: A Life*.

9. Jackson, *Word and Its Witness*, 89; Jones, *Age of Energy*, 202.

10. She had homeschooled her son from third grade, and she continued to teach her son and daughter in her classroom after she was widowed and became a schoolteacher. Also, when Frost was twelve, he began work in a shoe factory followed by work on a local chicken farm and even as factotum in a New Hampshire resort one summer. The Salem school board met to fire his mother because she had always been unconventional by genteel standards. Happily she found another position in Methuen. Thompson, *Robert Frost: Early Years*, 56–77; Parini, *Robert Frost: A Life*, 23.

11. See Thompson, *Robert Frost: Early Years*, 98–107.

12. Ibid., 88–92. One of the more interesting views of this celebrated friendship can be found in Robert Hass, *Going by Contraries*, who says that Burrell's atheism had the most profound effect on Frost. Burrell had an extensive collection

of contemporary life-science books from Darwin and other biologists; through Burrell, Frost found encouragement to write poetry and learned to see the world through the irreglionist lens of the life sciences (45–48). When Burrell and Frost met, Burrell was living on his own, renting a room from Frost's great uncle (his grandmother's brother). Parini, *Robert Frost: A Life*, 25.

13. For a fine discussion of the influence of Proctor on Frost see Hass, *Going by Contraries*, 94–99.

14. Sorby, *Schoolroom Poets*, 167.

15. Thompson, *Robert Frost: Early Years*, 122–24.

16. Ibid., 511.

17. Having taken the conventional high school program in classics, Frost easily passed the six exams in Greek, Latin, Greek history, Roman history, algebra, and geometry. Thompson, *Robert Frost: Early Years*, 100–10.

18. Parini, *Robert Frost: A Life*, 32.

19. Mertins, *Robert Frost: Life and Talks Walking*, 46; Newdick, *Newdick's Season of Frost*, 33. Biographers differ as to just how dour the grandfather might have been. Parini, *Robert Frost: A Life*, describes him best: "Grandfather Frost, with his flowing white beard and small, wire-rimmed glasses—an important man in this working-class community, and a dominant figure in this small mill town—seemed austere" (20). They all agree that Frost's grandmother persuaded the grandfather to pay for Dartmouth rather than Harvard. At the time, unlike today, Dartmouth had a rigid, almost monastic, system of undergraduate regulations and the choice would have made sense. See Sergeant, *Robert Frost: Trial by Existence*, 26; Thompson, *Robert Frost: Early Years*, 134–46; Parini, *Robert Frost: A Life*, 32. Parini explains that Frost's grandfather made him account to the penny for his expenses, and this too led Frost to rebel (32).

20. A letter responding to a Dartmouth College librarian's inquiries about his college years details the hijinks among the students, such as barricading one another in their dorm rooms, massive "rushes," otherwise known as near-riots, in the chapel with first- and second-year students battling one another with foot stools and pew pillows, among other delights. See RF to Harold Rugg, April 20, 1915, in Frost, *Letters of Robert Frost*, 1:283.

21. Newdick, *Newdick's Season of Frost*, 35.

22. Given that it was 1892, he likely bought the most recent American edition, Francis Turner Palgrave, *The Golden Treasury of the Best Songs and Lyrical Poems in the English Language* (New York: Thomas Crowell, 1888). It is still unresolved where precisely this discovery occurred. According to Newdick, Palgrave's compendium was recommended to Frost by a professor at Dartmouth (Newdick,

Newdick's Season of Frost, 36), whereas Thompson says in *Robert Frost: Early Years* that the poet came upon the volume on his own (142). My own inclination is to believe them both: a professor mentioned it and he, being Frost, went to the bookstore, sought it out, and bought it.

23. Palgrave, preface to *Golden Treasury,* 7. Also see Pritchard, *Frost: A Literary Life Reconsidered,* 42–43. Pritchard reminds us that Frost later said he went to England "because it was the land of *The Golden Treasury*" (43). The conventional high school anthology of the era was J. W. Hale's *Longer English Poems* (1872), which Frost had encountered only recently in preparation for the Harvard exam on English literature.

24. Sergeant, *Robert Frost: Trial by Existence,* 30. However, he told his early biographer, Sergeant, "I was glad to seize the excuse" (29). See any number of biographies, including Sergeant, *Robert Frost: Trial by Existence,* 7–15.

25. Parini, *Robert Frost: A Life,* 41.

26. Newdick, *Newdick's Season of Frost,* 37, says that others are more skeptical.

27. Parini, *Robert Frost: A Life,* 38. To the great excitement of Methuen, Robert Frost's grade book from his 1893 year of teaching was found in 2011, put on exhibit, and attracted much publicity.

28. Newdick, *Newdick's Season of Frost,* 39.

29. As told to Burnshaw, *Robert Frost Himself,* 20. John Evangelist Walsh makes a compelling argument in *Into My Own* (24) for Thompson's massive, even overwhelming, sonic and intellectual effect on the young poet as revealed by his first published poem, "My Butterfly" (1896). In fact, even after Robert Frost's return from England in 1915, Sidney Cox recalls Frost's reading "The Hound of Heaven": "His voice ran with the emotion, wound through the labyrinths, darted, plunged, and yielded at last to the caressing hand and pursuing forgiveness." Cox, *A Swinger of Birches,* 21. Edward Rowland Sill also captured Frost's attention. He gave Sill's collected poems to Elinor (Thompson, *Robert Frost: Early Years,* 122). Lawrance Thompson, though he cites no source for it, claims Frost came across Francis Thompson only later, in the spring or summer of 1895, almost three years later and after Frost published his first poem in the *Independent* (198–200). Thomas Mosher also proved to be a huge fan of Francis Thompson's poem and in 1908 published his own edition of it as a separate book.

30. Many decades later Frost would define *belief* as having three central components, what he termed, "the self-belief, the love-belief, and the art-belief." All three, he said, "are all closely related to the God-belief." Frost, "Education by Poetry," first delivered as a 1930 talk to the Alumni Association of Amherst College, and later published in Frost, *Collected Poems, Prose, and Plays,* 726.

31. Thompson, *Robert Frost: Early Years,* 159; Newdick, *Newdick's Season of Frost,* 43. The Frost family's quarters at 96 Tremont Street in Lawrence survive.

32. Intellectually Frost wanted to "meet the challenge of Darwin with only a slight remodeling of his inherited religious beliefs." Hass, *Going by Contraries,* 46. Hass adds that Darwin and other scientists had proved the existence of a random world without purpose, where life was based solely on natural selection, which led to Frost's sense of "cosmic abandonment" (24).

33. See Parini, *Robert Frost: A Life,* and Thompson, *Robert Frost: Early Years.*

CHAPTER FOUR
ROBERT FROST, REALISM, POETRY, AND AMERICAN PUBLISHING OF THE 1890s
"MY BUTTERFLY: AN ELEGY," "THE BIRDS DO THUS"

1. Robert Frost, "My Butterfly: An Elegy," *Independent,* November 8, 1894, 1. "My Butterfly" appears on the cover.

2. Barthes, *Rustle of Language,* 142.

3. The version given here is the version published in the *Independent.* Readers familiar with the poem will detect numerous differences between this version and the version Frost eventually published in his first book, *A Boy's Will* (1913). The poem originally was published under Frost's full name, Robert Lee Frost.

4. Only Newdick believes this. Others, such as Thompson, Parini, and Jean Gould (*Robert Frost: The Aim Was Song*), take seriously Frost's later comments that he wrote it shortly before he mailed it, while he was living on Tremont Street in Lawrence. His memory of the poem was that, to gain some quiet reflective space, he had locked himself in the bathroom. As older sisters are wont to do, Jeanie soon pounded on the door demanding entrance. The memory seems particular enough to cast doubt on Newdick, but ultimately no one knows (see Thompson, *Robert Frost: Early Years,* 518–19, and Parini, *Robert Frost: A Life,* 42–43).

5. In 1898, when her brother became editor-in-chief, Susan Hayes Ward printed a short article on the importance of poetry to the early years of the *Independent* and spoke of its role in the magazine in "The Poetry of the Independent in Its First Decade," *Independent,* December 15, 1898, 1761–62.

6. Satelmajer, "When a Consumer Becomes an Editor," 86; the original appeared in the *Writer,* September 1895, 1359–63.

7. A. Kaplan, *Social Construction of American Realism.* Also see Habegger, *Gender, Fantasy, and Realism.* See Ziff, *American 1890s,* 104–5, for more on the distinction between romance and realism in fiction.

8. Satelmajer, "When a Consumer Becomes an Editor," 82. She explains in detail the weekly's connection to Dickinson. This interest in Emily Dickinson, by the way, was in marked contrast to the *Atlantic Monthly*, whose editor, Thomas Bailey Aldrich, wrote what is still a notorious review of Dickinson's 1892 collection, condemning it on genteel grounds.

9. Carman himself later wrote: "It was my business to give a first reading to all contributions, to recommend what I liked to my superior for final decision." Satelmajer, "When a Consumer Becomes an Editor," 87. Satelmajer is quoting from Bliss Carman's memoir of William Hayes Ward, which was published in the *Independent*, September 11, 1916, 374–87.

10. Maurice Thompson to William Hayes Ward, November 10, 1894, in Frost, *Selected Letters of Robert Frost*, 23. See also Sergeant, *Robert Frost: Trial by Existence*, 45. In 1900 Maurice Thompson would become well known for the novel *Alice of Old Vincennes*, his attempt to counteract what he felt to be the pernicious love of the ordinary and ugly in contemporary realism.

11. M. Thompson to Ward. See also Sergeant, *Robert Frost: Trial by Existence*, 45.

12. Robert Frost (hereafter RF in citations to his letters) to Susan Hayes Ward, January 30, 1895, in Frost, *Letters of Robert Frost*, 1:37.

13. Ibid.; RF to William Hayes Ward, March 28, 1894, in Frost, *Letters of Robert Frost*, 1:27. Also see Lawrance Thompson, *Robert Frost: Early Years*, 165, and Sergeant, *Robert Frost: Trial by Existence*, 39.

14. RF to W. H. Ward, 28. See also Sergeant, *Robert Frost: Trial by Existence*, 36–37; Thompson, *Robert Frost: Early Years*, 164–72.

15. See Francis, "Robert Frost and Susan Hayes Ward."

16. RF to Susan Hayes Ward April 22, 1894, in Frost, *Letters of Robert Frost*, 1:28. Also see Thompson, *Robert Frost: Early Years*, 165, and Sergeant, *Robert Frost: Trial by Existence*, 39.

17. RF to S. H. Ward, 30.

18. The new university's central purpose was its graduate research and education, an anomaly in the United States of that time. To convince the administration to hire him, Lanier in 1878 began a series of public lectures at the Peabody Conservatory of Music. Tragically Lanier did not live to see the impact his book would have. He died at thirty-nine in 1880 from tuberculosis contracted years earlier when, as a Confederate soldier for his native South Carolina, he had been a prisoner at Andersonville.

19. Mims, "The Achievement in Criticism and in Poetry," *Sidney Lanier*, 340–47. By studying rhythm, tune, and color, Lanier believed that one might receive

"a whole new world of possible delight" (340). He believed that "versification has a technical side quite as well capable of being reduced to rules as that of painting or any other fine art" (347). His book was intended to furnish students with such an array of facts and principles for pursuing further research.

20. As one recent scholar of Lanier puts it: "The link in Lanier's mind between music, feeling, and poetry was to lead him eventually to construe a 'science' of English verse, an attempt to discover similarities between the laws of musical rhythm and harmony." De Bellis, "Sidney Lanier," n.p.

21. De Bellis, "Sidney Lanier," n.p.; Lanier, *Science of English Verse*, 250. Although the book was published posthumously, Lanier's ideas had a powerful impact on the genteels. Also published posthumously was Lanier's *The English Novel* (1897). The radical surprise of this book was Lanier's insistence that novels be understood as if they, too, were poetry. He argued that novels are by definition subjective moral instruments in which form and theme relate intrinsically, creating in their harmony what we call meaning. Subtitled "A Study in the Development of Personality," Lanier's book, influenced by his reading of Charles Darwin, associated the art of fiction with the development of the human personality itself. Lanier insisted that serious fiction, like serious poetry, would be moral because it derived from moral beings, the authors. According to one scholar, Lanier's lectures were "founded on his insight that literature since the Greeks reflected increased concern with personality, or what 'the evolutionist' might call 'Spontaneous Variation peculiar to the human species.'" (De Bellis, "Sidney Lanier," n.p.) The more individualistic the work, the more obviously personal, and the more developed it must be, Lanier said. Bringing together his reading of Hegel and his reading of Darwin, Lanier argued that the human personality moved "toward nature" and was, as Jack De Bellis says, unified by "the conception of Love as the organic idea of moral order" (De Bellis, "Sidney Lanier," n.p.). Also see Rubin, *Songs of Ourselves*, 10–20; Golding, *From Outlaw to Classic*, especially chap. 1; and Mims, "Achievement in Criticism and in Poetry," 340–77.

22. Lanier, *Science of English Verse*, 252.

23. Sutton, *Newdick's Season of Frost*, 263.

24. RF to Susan Hayes Ward, June 10, 1894, in Frost, *Letters of Robert Frost*, 1:33.

25. Ibid., 1:35; Thompson, *Robert Frost: Early Years*, 519.

26. Sutton, *Newdick's Season of Frost*, 44–45; Mertins, *Robert Frost: Life and Talks Walking*, 197.

27. RF to Susan Hayes Ward, December 4, 1894, in Frost, *Selected Letters of Robert Frost*, 24.

28. Thompson, *Robert Frost: Early Years*, 194.

29. Field was a hugely influential figure of the day. His column, nationally syndicated from the *Chicago Morning News,* pushed the kind of personal journalism pioneered by Pulitzer. A poet as well as a columnist until his death in 1895, Field had done as much as anyone to establish something just short of a cult of innocent childhood in American genteel publications. See Sorby, *Schoolroom Poets,* 126–55.

30. RF to S. H. Ward, January 30, 1895; Frost, *Collected Prose of Robert Frost,* 247. Mark Richardson, editor of this collection, is quoting here from an interview with Frost published in 1954. Richardson's account of Frost's newspaper career, sadly confined to his endnotes in *Collected Prose,* is the best available.

31. Sutton, *Newdick's Season of Frost,* 122–23; RF to John Bartlett, March 18, 1913, in Frost, *Letters of Robert Frost,* 1:99.

32. RF to S. H. Ward, January 30, 1895; RF to Louis Untermeyer, February 21, 1950, in Frost, *Letters of Robert Frost to Louis Untermeyer,* 355.

33. Describing Frost's work on both newspapers, his early biographer, Robert Newdick, wrote that on the *Sentinel* Frost "served as reporter, editor, and general factotum," while on the *American* he worked as "an occasional paragrapher, . . . with sketches of local scenes, accounts of small but significant town happenings, and vignettes of community 'characters,' Frostian cartoons, as it were, for finished canvasses of *North of Boston* nearly two decades later." Newdick, "Robert Frost's Other Harmony," 410.

34. Jay Parini, *Robert Frost: A Life,* best details the difficult dynamics of this long marriage and is not afraid to chart Frost's failings as husband and father.

35. Parini, *Robert Frost: A Life,* 56. Also see Thompson, *Robert Frost: Early Years,* 217–23. Parini returns to Lawrance Thompson's insight to make explicit this profoundly important connection. And, amazingly, as of this writing, 2014, Dana's book is still in print with an edition from 1991.

36. RF to S. H. Ward, July 8, 1896, in Frost, *Letters of Robert Frost,* 1:38.

37. The other poems are "To Charista Musing," by Louise Guiney, and "The Bugle-Call," by Elizabeth Roberts MacDonald.

38. This is how the poem first appeared in the *Independent.*

39. The details appear in Thompson, *Robert Frost: Early Years,* 224–29; 533–36.

40. The phrase is Parini's, *Robert Frost: A Life,* 59. Parini's account is still the best (see 58–59).

41. As Parini, *Robert Frost: A Life,* puts it: "As before, his education was underwritten by his grandfather, who was so embarrassed by the incident with Herbert Parker [the mill owner's son] that he was glad to get his grandson out of town" (59).

42. A point stressed by Pritchard, *Frost: A Literary Life,* 46–47.

CHAPTER FIVE
DISCOVERING REALISM: FROST, 1897–99

1. "Caesar's Lost Transport Ships" was first published in the *Lawrence High Bulletin* while Frost was still in high school. It appeared relatively unchanged in the January 13, 1897, issue of the *Independent*. In a letter of July 8, 1896, Frost sent it to Ward for consideration.

2. "Greece" was first printed in the *Independent,* September 9, 1897, 1. Cramer, *Robert Frost Among His Poems,* believes it was written in 1895.

3. William Dean Howells in particular even went so far as to call the concept of literature itself a sacred space free from market considerations. "In the highest forms of literature, as in art, there still breathes the living spirit of all past excellence." *Harper's Monthly,* June 1902, 153.

4. And he should know, for he and Twain had given the era its singular epithet, the Gilded Age, in their 1876 novel of that name.

5. Robert Frost, "Warning," *Independent,* September 20, 1897, 1. All references and quotations are to this first published version of the poem. In this era a major push was made for reforming English spellings. Champions of that cause, the Wards also insisted that *though* be spelled "tho," among other simplifications of this movement.

6. Wilbur, *Things of This World.*

7. The poem expresses the very purpose and heritage of western civilization itself in a defense of Greece at a time when that country faced a new political crisis. He told Sergeant that in 1897 he had been reading Tacitus (in Latin) when he decided to face the question "How am I going to earn a living? All of a sudden it occurred to me; Why couldn't I go to college and become a teacher?" (Sergeant, *Robert Frost: Trial by Existence,* 52). Determined to go to Harvard, he discovered he had to take the entrance exams again. However, he feared only the examination in Greek, for which he felt particularly unprepared. Perhaps this explains why Greece was so much on his mind that summer of 1897.

8. At the time a writer not much younger than Frost, Stephen Crane, who was already making a reputation as one the country's foremost realist writers, was a war correspondent. His dispatches from Athens were almost universally attacked precisely because they carried too much of a "literary air," which is to say, they lacked the empirical focus on fact that reviewers expected from journalism. See Canada, *Literature and Journalism in Antebellum America,* 54–56. Canada relies on the trove of reviews in Crane's scrapbooks held in the research collections of the University of Virginia.

9. Sutton, *Newdick's Season of Frost,* 263.

10. The term was coined during the Dreyfus Affair in France. Initially an insulting pejorative coined by the forces of tradition, reaction, God, and country, it soon became a badge of honor. James did not make the case for this term until 1907, in a speech given to the Radcliffe Alumnae Association. Widely reprinted, "The Social Value of the College-Bred" argued that college graduates should be understood as intellectuals: "What prouder club-name could there be than this one, used ironically by the party . . . of every stupid prejudice and passion, during the anti-Dreyfus craze."

11. A. Taylor, *Thinking America,* 26.

12. They wished to make their views known in order to have an effect on "a public world—and a public language, the vernacular." A. Taylor, *Thinking America,* 89. Also see Menand, *Metaphysical Club,* 100; Hass, *Going by Contraries,* 50–52. About the term's coinage in France, Andrew Taylor adds: "By reaching beyond proscribed roles and socially acceptable divisions, the French intellectual, like the pragmatist, opposed rigidity and the urge to classify" (26).

13. As Persons puts it in *Decline of American Gentility*: "Eliot had irrevocably sundered the traditional bond between religion and learning" (190). Persons adds: "The failure to accommodate science to gentry culture had serious consequences. Ultimately, it was the scientist as investigator who displaced the gentleman as scholar" (185). Eliot came to Harvard in 1869 from MIT, where he saw firsthand the importance of practical education.

14. This in turn had not only opened the school up "to a wider demographic than the bourgeois Bostonian elite" of genteel culture, it had also made for a disparate and highly specialized student body. A. Taylor, *Thinking America,* 16.

15. Menand, *Metaphysical Club,* 100, xi. According to William James, Charles Sanders Peirce, another Harvard philosophy professor, had coined that term in his article "How to Make Our Ideas Clear" (*Popular Science Monthly,* January 1878). In a series of lectures to the Philosophical Union of the University of California, Berkeley, on August 28, 1898, James made pragmatism fundamental to philosophy. Later these lectures were published as a book, *Pragmatism: A New Name for Some Old Ways of Thinking, Popular Lectures on Philosophy* (New York: Longmans, Green, 1907). Philip Weiner, however, in *Evolution and the Founders of Pragmatism,* finds that the "undeniable fact is that no term like 'pragmatism' occurs" (25) in that or the other versions pointed to by James. On the other hand, the article does offer what Weiner calls a "practical test of clarity." The article declares an idea to be clear only "when we understand its *conceivable* effects or the logical consequences necessitated by adopting it as a premise or rule for the

resolution of a problem" (92). Ultimately from the 1870s through to the early twentieth century, both men so often discussed the idea that came to have that name that neither could recall who came to the term first. Weiner cites a 1900 letter from Peirce to James: "Who originated the term 'pragmatism,' I or you?" (23).

16. James, *Pragmatism*, 24, 26. James added that pragmatism had two aspects: "First, a method; and second, a genetic theory of what is meant by truth" (33).

17. Weiner, *Evolution*, 64, 84. He makes this point while discussing Lovejoy's critique of this method.

18. Daston and Galison, *Objectivity*, 223. For more detail about the meaning of this crisis of the self, see chap. 4, "The Scientific Self," 191–251.

19. According to Newdick, Frost was actually the principal of this school, having secured the job on the recommendation of the Salem School Board, which had come to admire him as a teacher. Sutton, *Newdick's Seasons of Frost*, 62. See Parini, *Robert Frost: A Life*, 60, for details.

20. L. Thompson, *Robert Frost: Early Years*, 234–37. In the spring semester his Greek professor, Frank Cole Babbitt, with whom Frost covered *The Odyssey*, sparked a lifelong interest in Greek epic poetry and the poetry of Theocritus.

21. Until confronted in 1946 by his biographer with incontrovertible proof that he had written it, Frost had disowned the poem. Robert Hass believes Frost must have written it as a youth, possibly in his early high school years. Perhaps he felt driven to print it just to get the better of his English composition teacher who, after learning that he had published poetry, sneered, "So we're a poet, are we?" For details on that confrontation see Lawrance Thompson's *Robert Frost: Early Years*, Sutton's *Newdick's Seasons of Frost*, and Jay Parini's *Robert Frost: A Life*. Also see Hass, *Going by Contraries*, 90.

22. Decades later, when Robert Newdick interviewed him in the 1930s, Frost could still repeat, almost verbatim, lectures he had first heard from Shaler in the 1890s. Sutton, *Newdick's Season of Frost*, 291.

23. Weiner, *Evolution and the Founders of Pragmatism*, 95.

24. Ibid.

25. Santayana had been an undergraduate at Harvard in the 1880s, when he had been instrumental in establishing the *Harvard Monthly*. On graduating he had gone on to obtain his Ph.D. at Harvard (only the third philosophy student to do so there) under Royce's direction. Royce championed his hiring. Duly appointed in 1889, Santayana spent the ten years of his professorship living in thrall to aesthetics and among students in a dorm on campus. Together they formed the Laodicean Club in 1891. It, along with the circle associated with Day and Guiney, established the *Mahogany Tree*. In 1898 Santayana moved off campus. See Padrón, "George Santayana."

26. In large part this is a result of the enormous impact Kant had, not just on philosophy but also on a wide array of intellectual inquiry, including science. Briefly, according to Daston and Galison in *Objectivity,* the Enlightenment conception of individuality had isolated specific faculties: will, reason, imagination, instinct, judgment, sensation. Each was subject to its own code and had its own characteristics. Following Kant, say Daston and Galison, the will was accepted as the single dominant faculty. They write of "the new Kantian views of a self unified around the will, [that] the shock of the impact sent heads spinning" (227). By the time Frost came to Harvard, then, scientists had accepted that "the will asserted (subjectivity) and the will restrained (objectivity)—the latter by a further assertion of will" (228). In short, the will was a paradox. In his attempt to explain it, in the 1890s William James wrote a book about "the will to believe," while Peirce continued to develop his conception of pragmatism as an aspect by which the human will actively submersed itself in a "cosmic community" to guarantee "the validity of logical inferences." For more on Peirce's views with regard to objectivity, see Daston and Galison, *Objectivity,* 257, and chap. 5.

27. To round out his courses Frost also took George Kittredge's class in Milton and further classes in Greek and Latin. There is some dispute concerning Shaler's class. Newdick has Frost taking the class, whereas Lawrance Thompson believes he simply audited it. Sutton, *Newdick's Season of Frost,* 64, 59–70; Thompson, *Robert Frost: Early Years,* 247.

28. Singer, *George Santayana, Literary Philosopher,* 21.

29. Santayana to Thomas Munro, 1928, in A. Taylor, *Thinking America,* 163; Singer, *George Santayana, Literary Philosopher,* 119.

30. Santayana, *Sense of Beauty,* chap. 1; Kindle version loc. 392.

31. To make his case for the necessity and importance of play, Santayana routinely taught three poets to his students: Lucretius, Dante, and Goethe. It is likely that Frost heard lectures based on the book that would eventually become *Interpretations of Poetry and Religion* (New York: Scribner's, 1900). There Santayana gave a literary and intellectual genealogy of his theory of *otium* and *eros.* Almost a decade later Santayana published *Three Philosophical Poets: Lucretius, Dante, and Goethe* (Cambridge, MA: Harvard University Press, 1910). This was a study of the three poets whose work he had taught in his philosophy classes and from whom, in addition to Aristotle and Spinoza, he derived the bulk of his ideas.

32. Santayana, *Sense of Beauty,* chap. 1; Kindle version loc. 391. Frost's lifelong admiration for Lucretius may well have had its source in Santayana's class. See Wilfred M. McClay (1982) for a fine summary of Santayana's cultural impact on modernist writers. An excellent recent study of Santayana's views of classicism and romanticism can be found in Singer, *George Santayana, Literary Philosopher.*

33. Daston and Galison, *Objectivity*, 201; James, *Will to Believe*, 208, 123, 135. According to Lawrance Thompson, "It may have seemed to Frost that James was speaking directly to him, at precisely the time when Frost was determining to give more scope to his own higher faculties. Hence his decision to go to Harvard not only as a student of the classics but also as one who sought direct inspiration from courses taught by Professor William James." Thompson, *Robert Frost: Early Years*, 232.

34. James, *Will to Believe*, xiv, 178. In his book *Pragmatism* he makes the case for that which is variously named truth, the Absolute, God, as a possibility that is as yet unproved. Yet as a possibility it has, and has had, profound consequences and practical effects on individuals and groups. See James's lecture "Pragmatism and Religion" in *Will to Believe*.

35. Daston and Galison, *Objectivity*, 201; James, *Will to Believe*, 178, 168, and 194.

36. James, *Will to Believe*, 17. No true empiricist or scientist could "thereby give up the quest or hope of the truth itself," James wrote (17).

37. James, *Will to Believe*, 30, 52, 62. Later, in his book *Pragmatism* James said that the will to believe is itself an example of pragmatism. Louis Menand in *The Metaphysical Club* adds, "James invented pragmatism . . . in order to defend religious belief in what he regarded as an excessively scientistic and materialistic age" (88). Menand also argues that William James "spoke of pragmatism, the philosophy he largely created, as the equivalent of the Protestant Reformation" against the deeply held anti-individualism and lèse majesté shared by the New England elite (353). Epigrammatically Menand declares: "William James invented pragmatism as a favor to Charles Peirce" (347).

38. James, "Pragmatism and Religion," *Pragmatism*, 134.

39. For scholarship on the impact James had on Frost, see Sears, "William James, Henri Bergson"; Poirier, *Robert Frost and the Work of Knowing*; Hass, *Going by Contraries*; Faggen, *Robert Frost and the Challenge of Darwin*; and L. Thompson, *Robert Frost: Early Years*.

40. For specifics on Frost's Harvard years of 1897–98 see Thompson, *Robert Frost: Early Years*, 230–49. Intriguingly Munsterberg in the 1890s worked closely with a favorite graduate student in his psychology lab, Gertrude Stein, then a student at Harvard's Extension School, soon to be Radcliffe.

41. Menand, *Metaphysical Club*, 268–84. Hall in fact had been appointed to the philosophy faculty of Johns Hopkins in the mid-1880s, only to leave in 1888 upon his appointment as president of the new Clark University in Worcester, Massachusetts. His reign was not a success, and when the University of Chicago

was founded in 1892 two-thirds of the Clark faculty and 70 percent of the students left, most heading directly for Chicago. See Menand, *Metaphysical Club*, 287. Hall is remembered today as the man who lured Sigmund Freud to America in 1903.

42. Heinze, *Jews and the American Soul*, 167. This book offers a fine discussion of the dispute between James and Munsterberg (165–91). More generally it charts the Jewish contribution to American psychological thinking.

43. If Frost was a regular reader of *McClure's* magazine, which he certainly did become, he would have read an 1893 profile of Munsterberg that made his empiricism clear.

44. Menand, *Metaphysical Club*, 146, 268–69.

45. Sergeant, *Robert Frost: Trial by Existence*, 54. On Frost's depression see Parini, *Robert Frost: A Life*, 65. His nearly two years at Harvard had made Frost "profoundly aware that the fin-de-siècle cosmos, newly expanded and mechanized by science, was now more than ever capable of reducing human aspirations and achievements to an almost total insignificance." Hass, *Going by Contraries*, 98. According to Hass, Frost began regularly reading *Scientific American* each month. Hass adds that Frost left Harvard with the "nagging suspicion that the Darwinian ideas he had absorbed from Harvard were not invented fictions"— they were empirically verifiable truth (92).

46. Poirier, *Work of Knowing*, 9; Francis, *Frost Family's Adventure in Poetry*, 4.

47. Parini, *Robert Frost: A Life*, 66.

48. In fact she even knew of the farm, thanks to her own mother. It turns out Elinor's mother had grown so worried about her daughter and family that she had already gone scouting for suitable farms and had been the one to show it to Frost and his wife, thereby planting the seed for Elinor to ask the grandfather for help in its purchase. On the other hand, Elinor's mother may have had her own psychological guilt to deal with since, as a Christian Scientist, she had dismissed the need for doctors during the early point of Elliot's illness. See Parini, *Robert Frost: A Life*, 70–71; L. Thompson, *Robert Frost: Early Years*, 260–62.

49. One of Frost's early biographers, Sergeant, recalls that in her conversations with Frost his grandfather "looms as a sort of fateful, archetypal image in the background of his adolescent and young life: an image of severity and power, gigantesque" (*Robert Frost: Trial by Existence*, 17).

50. Mertins, *Robert Frost: Life and Talks Walking*, 64. Lawrance Thompson's account in *Robert Frost: Early Years*, which consistently finds fault with a selfish Robert Frost, has been frequently challenged, and the proof now seems conclusive that Thompson interpreted his facts in a willfully misleading manner.

51. Mertins, *Robert Frost: Life and Talks Walking*, 65, 78. One way of looking at the Derry years is to summarize them as ones of "sickness, worry, and death." Burnshaw, *Robert Frost Himself*, 26. Viewed another way they become a kind of idyll when Frost could write and study his art, with a steady income to rely on. For another recent take on the Derry years and for more information about the town of Derry itself, see Sanders, *A Divided Poet*, esp. chap. 1, "Frost in Derry," 7–18.

52. L. Thompson, *Robert Frost: Early Years*, 530.

53. Dana, *How to Know the Wild Flowers*, 288; emphasis added. In a fascinating connection, the very next entry is "Self-Heal." This flower, also known as the "Heal-All," became the subject of one of Frost's most important and enduring poems, "Design." It is likely he composed its first version, "In White," during that same botanizing honeymoon in the summer of 1896.

54. Dana, *How to Know the Wild Flowers*, 320.

55. This is the view taken by Ron Thomas who looks at the 1942 version of this poem in "Thoreau, William James, and Frost's 'Quest of the Purple-Fringed': A Contextual Reading," *American Literature* 60, no. 3 (October 1988): 433–50, and writes: "So the complex epiphanic yet retrospective structure of this ironic, post-romantic, and highly modern flashback prompts us to ponder its maker's lifelong pursuit of poetic success. Frost's determined quest after himself in his otherness, then, as symbolized by an "orchis," in its present, past, and future dimensions represents respectively the poem, the image within the poem, and finally the poet himself" (435).

56. Faggen, *Robert Frost and the Challenge of Darwin*, 159. Faggen points out (158–59) that Darwin had written a book on the subject, *The Various Contrivances by Which Orchids Are Fertilized by Insects*.

57. "The Geology of the Soul" is followed by "The Manufacturers and the Tariff," hardly a soul-inspiring article. Yet the placement of the poem so close to the article "Geology of the Soul" could hardly be accidental, and its distance more likely a result of layout problems than randomness.

58. Later still, making a note about the poem on a copy of the *Independent* owned by his good friend Louis Untermeyer, Frost wrote: "I had almost forgotten this when I came on it a few years back and put it into one of my later books. This R.L. Frost sounds like a stranger to me. Doesn't he to you Louis?" Marginalia on copy in Mertins Collection of Robert Frost, Bancroft Library, University of California, Berkeley, http://archive.org/stream/inquestoforchis00frosrich#page/1494/mode/1up.

CHAPTER SIX
ROBERT FROST'S POETRY OF IDEAS, 1906–8
"TRIAL BY EXISTENCE," "THE LOST FAITH,"
"A LINE-STORM SONG," AND "ACROSS THE ATLANTIC"

1. Henry Holt, "The Commercialization of Literature: A Summing Up," *Putnam's Monthly*, February 1907, 565, 566.

2. May Sinclair, "Three American Poets of To-Day," *Atlantic Monthly*, September 1906, 325–35.

3. A selection of the poems scholars believe he wrote in these years includes "Loneliness" (1905, which becomes "The Hill Wife"); "Pea Brush"; "A Winter's Night"; "Love Being All One"; "The Mill City"; "What Thing a Bird Would Love"; "Wind and Window Flower"; "In Neglect"; "Going for Water"; "Midsummer Birds"; "Putting in the Seed"; "A Time to Talk"; "The Death of the Hired Man"; "I Will Sing You One-O" (perhaps earlier, 1896–1900); "In Hardwood Groves" (begun 1905, finished 1925).

4. Angyal, "Robert Frost's Poetry." Angyal finds at least three dates other than 1901 for the poem: Lawrance Thompson's from 1892; Frost's own report to the poet Genevieve Taggard, who recorded what he told her in her copy of a book of his collected poems, which dates it from 1898, and the report of his wife, Elinor, which says it came from 1895. The earliest surviving manuscript, at the Huntington Library, which came with the papers of the *Independent,* is dated 1905. Angyal, "Robert Frost's Poetry," 74.

5. See Frost, *Selected Letters of Robert Frost,* 35, for Ward's comment.

6. Specifically the poem is based on the myth of Er from the *Republic*. Most recently Tim Kendall has read this poem in light of that myth. He goes so far as to say, "The poem mimics its source in the Republic so closely as to seem like an act more of translation than of faith" (*Art of Robert Frost*, 33). I do not go quite that far in my reading.

7. See M. Taylor, *Men Versus the State,* esp. 1–80, for more on Spencer and these issues.

8. Faggen, *Robert Frost and the Challenge of Darwin,* 255–59, offers what is still the most complete and intriguing reading of the poem on precisely these terms. Faggen reads the poem as far less ambiguous and open than I do.

9. The lines quoted refer only to the first printing in the *Independent.*

10. In contrast Faggen argues that this poem proves that "for Frost, Christianity meant neither redemption nor salvation but [rather] acceptance of suffering

and mortification" (*Robert Frost and the Challenge of Darwin*, 258–59). Kendall has the same bleak assessment: "In Frost's poem the choosing of life itself causes the inevitable suffering" (*Art of Robert Frost*, 34).

11. RF to Susan Hayes Ward, October 29, 1906, in Frost, *Letters of Robert Frost*, 1:49.

12. Ibid., January 12, 1907, 1:51.

13. Mertins, *Robert Frost: Life and Talks Walking*, 88; also see Walsh, *Into My Own*, 94–95.

14. Parini, *Robert Frost: A Life*, 92.

15. Thompson, *Robert Frost: Early Years*, 316–34. It was a deeply genteel route involving William Wolcott, a Congregationalist minister whom Frost knew in Lawrence, Massachusetts, and Wolcott's Congregationalist minister friend, Charles Merriam, in Derry. In a memoir of Frost's close friend and former student, John Bartlett, Bartlett's daughter, drawing on her father's notes, quotes Frost himself as saying: "We were in debt, and somehow, coming to have a prejudice against debt. It occurred to us [he and Elinor] that I might take up teaching again." M. Anderson, *Robert Frost and John Bartlett*, 6.

16. Mertins, *Robert Frost: Life and Talks Walking*, 88–90; the quote is on page 90. The school board's behavior is from Sutton, *Newdick's Season of Frost*, 160.

17. Sutton, *Newdick's Season of Frost*, 260; Parini, *Robert Frost: A Life*, 97. Frost recounts this incident for Susan Hayes Ward in his letter to her of December 26, 1906, in Frost, *Letters of Robert Frost*, 1:50. For a different take on the effect of this poem on Pinkerton Academy, see L. Thompson, *Robert Frost: Early Years*, 328. Also see Sutton, *Newdick's Season of Frost*, 120–21, and Sanders, *A Divided Poet*, 13–15.

18. Thompson, *Robert Front: Early Years*, 327–28.

19. *Derry News*, March 1, 1907, 1, 4. Angyal's authoritative bibliography, "Robert Frost's Poetry," dates this poem to 1907 (91).

20. Frost had already dealt with these issues far more subtly in "The Black Cottage," the earliest drafts of which date to 1905. That poem's drama concerns a debate between a minister and a narrator about the metaphorical meaning of an abandoned cottage and its former occupant, a poem that ultimately connects American Protestantism to the Civil War through the issue of equality. See J. Barron, "A Tale of Two Cottages."

21. The most recent entry in the vast historiography on this issue is Oakes's *Freedom National*. He argues that the eradication of slavery was Lincoln's primary aim from first to last.

22. RF to S. H. Ward, August 6, 1907, in Frost, *Letters of Robert Frost*, 1:53; on the second poem see Mott, *American Magazines*, 4:79–80.

23. *New England Magazine*, October 1907, 204.

24. As with "The Lost Faith," Frost also chose never to republish "Across the Atlantic." Nor have subsequent scholars republished it. The poem does not appear even in the authoritative Library of America edition of Frost's work, a serious lapse in my opinion.

CHAPTER SEVEN
ROBERT FROST'S NEW POETIC REALISM, 1909–10
"INTO MINE OWN," "THE FLOWER BOAT"

1. When Frost published the poem in his first book, *A Boy's Will* (London: David Nutt, 1913), it had a new title, "Into Mine Own," the title by which it is still known today. Even then he thought so well of the poem that he published it as that book's first poem.

2. *New England Magazine*, May 1909, 281.

3. In addition to fiction the issue also had the following articles: "The Women's Congressional Club," and "Great Fights in Early New England."

4. A similar poem of love and longing was "Consummation" by Gertrude Brooke Hamilton, which appeared on page 297 of that issue.

5. Glazener, *Reading for Realism*; Poirier, *Robert Frost and the Work*, 80–81. Poirier's remains the most nuanced and considered account of the poem's inner grammatical workings. A more recent assessment can be found in Kendall, *Art of Robert Frost*, 16–18. He notes that "fear is one of Frost's great subjects" (17).

6. Although published in the issue of May 20, 1909, Frost evidently had written it as a twenty-year-old in 1894, at about the time he courted Elinor and convinced her to marry him. He signed a contract for the poem in March 1909 and received $10.

7. Jack Hagstrom, who knew Frost well in his later years, wrote: "Mark Antony DeWolfe Howe, then in his late eighties, had been the editor of the *Youth's Companion* when it published Frost's poems 'The Flower Boat,' 'October,' and 'Reluctance' in 1909 and 1912. . . . Mark Howe was graduated from Harvard in the Class of 1887." See Hagstrom, "Robert Frost and His Friends," *Dartmouth College Library Bulletin,* April 1996, www.dartmouth.edu/~library/Library_Bulletin/Apr1996/LB-A96-Hagstrom.html?mswitch-redir=classic#fn12.

CHAPTER EIGHT
COMING INTO HIS OWN: ROBERT FROST, 1910–12: "RELUCTANCE"

1. See Sutton, *Newdick's Season of Frost,* 261, 287–88, for Morrison's own account of observing Frost. Morrison himself eventually became a professor at the University of Chicago.

2. M. Anderson, *Robert Frost and John Bartlett,* 20.

3. See Cox, *A Swinger of Birches,* 51.

4. Biographers are quick to point out that the only openings available were for teaching the history of education and psychology.

5. In this passage Cox refers to a young professor whom he and Frost met in 1915; Cox's intention here is satire and to show how far removed from his and Frost's own views the professor's views were. Still, these *were* the views held by most of the modern writers Frost met in his English years. Cox, *Swinger of Birches,*19.

6. Mertins, *Robert Frost: Life and Talks Walking,* 106.

7. The *Forum* had long been a bastion of genteel opinion. It had recently been purchased by Mitchell Kennerley. He had made his name, as I mentioned earlier, publishing aestheticism, symbolism, and decadence, first in England with Alan Lane and then with his own firm in New York. Equally attracted to realism, Kennerley hoped his purchase of the *Forum* would give prestige to his eponymous publishing concern; he also used the magazine to highlight his forthcoming list of books.

8. The anthology ultimately included lush sensual aestheticist poetry and newer plainspoken realism, including Edna St. Vincent Millay's "Renascence" and realist poems by James Oppenheim ("Pittsburgh"), Edwin Markham, Sara Teasdale, and Louis Untermeyer ("Caliban in the Coalmines").

9. In 1891 at the age of forty Mosher, like Frost, had given up one career in order to embark on what seemed a wholly impractical and strange enterprise. Against all odds for nearly twenty years he had by 1911 made a decent living publishing the newer poets and their works from his office in Portland, Maine. He had made his mark through his books and the monthly *Bibelot,* and he had also become known for his catalogs, beautifully produced magazines in their own right. These lavishly printed catalogs, often accompanied by prose and poetry, contracted or stolen, had become his most effective promotional tool.

10. RF to Thomas Bird Mosher, February 19 and March 4, 1912, in Frost, *Letters of Robert Frost,* 1:61, 62.

11. "Reluctance," *Youth's Companion,* November 7, 1912, 612, first composed in 1899, according to Angyal, or even earlier, after the Dismal Swamp episode in 1894, according to Jeffrey S. Cramer. See John C. Kemp, *Robert Frost and New England* (Princeton, NJ: Princeton University Press, 1979), 146–47, for a view of the poem's regionalism and realism. For a more recent assessment see Kendall, *Art of Robert Frost,* 41–43. Originally begun in 1899, this poem seems to be another version of "A Late Walk," which Frost had published in the 1910 *Pinkerton Critic.* It tells the same story, and even uses the same flower, an aster. Unlike that poem, however, there is no love story here.

12. This is the version published in the *Youth's Companion.* There are notable differences in wording between it and subsequent versions, such as the change from *seemed* to *was* in line 20.

13. It almost never appears in Frost's poetry. In fact it occurs only in an unpublished poem, "Pan with Us," when Pan folds the leaves of an oak tree.

14. Frost "drifted along" with English rhyme. Many decades later, in a now-famous essay, "The Constant Symbol," first published in the *Atlantic Monthly* and then reprinted as an introduction to his *Collected Poetry,* Frost asserted that the English language had a horribly limited number of rhymes: "Does anyone believe I would have committed myself to the treason-reason-season rhyme-set…if I had been blasé enough to know that these three words about exhausted the possibilities? No rhyming dictionary for me to face the facts of rhyme." *Atlantic Monthly,* October, 1946, 52.

15. William James, *Pragmatism,* 115, 128; Ardoin, Gontarski, and Mattison, *Understanding Bergson, Understanding Modernism,* 3. For more on Le Roy with regard to problems of empiricism and objectivity, see Daston and Galison, *Objectivity,* 285–89

16. Daston and Galison, *Objectivity,* 284–85; Scott, "*Sub Specie Durantionis,*" 57.

17. Bergson, *Creative Evolution,* 369. All the quotations from Bergson are from his final paragraph, 369–70.

18. Scott, "*Sub Species Durationis,*" 60.

19. For more on the particulars of Bergson as he was understood by modernist writers see Ardoin, Gontarski, and Mattison, *Understanding Bergson, Understanding Modernism,* esp. Scott's essay, "*Sub Specie Durationis,*" 54–67.

20. Scholars who have studied the marginalia of Frost's copy of *Creative Evolution* at New York University note that he stops writing anything after the first chapter. Whether this means he also stopped reading the book is open for debate.

21. Frost, "The Figure a Poem Makes," *Collected Prose of Robert Frost*, 133, 132.

22. Much later, describing the sale of that farm, Frost said, "I have always looked on the sale of the Derry farm as my greatest financial achievement." Mertins, *Robert Frost: Life and Talks Walking*, 102. Thompson, *Robert Frost: Early Years*, goes on to make mincemeat of that claim by showing he barely broke even (367–68). Yet who is to say whether Frost meant by *financial* the profit measured in dollars that farm yielded? By the terms of the will he had to keep the property for ten years. The sale fundamentally freed him from financial obligations anywhere.

23. See Sergeant, *Robert Frost: Trial by Existence*, who quotes Frost's comments to her about the decision (88). Also Francis, *Frost Family's Adventure in Poetry*, who adds that Elinor wanted to be as near Shakespeare's Stratford as possible (33).

24. RF to Louis Untermeyer, May 16, 1915, in Untermeyer, *Letters of Robert Frost to Louis Untermeyer*, 7. For letter to Ward see Walsh, *Into My Own*, 32

25. So said his good friend John Haines, but in *Robert Frost: Life and Talks Walking*, Mertins says, "Frost denied this to me" (131).

26. Nutt actually had Frost sign a contract that obligated him for his next three books as well.

CHAPTER NINE
ROBERT FROST IN ENGLAND: *A BOY'S WILL*

1. M. L. Nutt, the widow of Peter Nutt who succeeded him as publisher, wrote to Frost on October 26, 1912, with an expression of interest. See Walsh, *Into My Own*, 78–79. Two weeks later she wrote and asked him to come in to discuss a contract, 80.

2. Walsh, *Into My Own*, 18.

3. RF to Susan Hayes Ward, September 15, 1912, in Frost, *Letters of Robert Frost*, 1:69–70. Also see Sergeant, *Robert Frost: Trial by Existence*, 94–95.

4. Brooker and Thacker, *Oxford Critical and Cultural History*, 145.

5. As it happened, Holbrook Jackson had his start in publishing by working with Alfred Orage on the leading Fabian socialist magazine in Britain, the *New Age*. In 1906 the two had established the Fabian Arts Group in an attempt to direct the taste of a newly expanded, newly literate public that had benefited from Britain's newly expanded public education system.

6. No biographer has ever identified this person, whom Frost always identified simply as "a former bobby." See Sutton, *Newdick's Season of Frost*, 76–77, and M. Anderson, *Robert Frost and John Bartlett*, 32.

7. Frost's friend, patron, and book collector Frederic Melcher claims Frost had already decided on Nutt because he admired his list of poets, most especially

William Henley, whose poem "Invictus" had long been one of Frost's favorites. Thornton, *Recognition of Robert Frost,* 133.

8. Parini, *Robert Frost: A Life,* 119. Kendall adds that the three sections can be read "as different phases of a spiritual and intellectual journey" (*Art of Robert Frost,* 13). According to Kendall, the poems are arranged in order to suggest "an arc of departure and return" (13). Concerning the glosses given to each poem that enforced the collection's unity as the supposed autobiography of a youth, Parini adds, "These headings provided, as it were, an inoculation against ruthless English reviewers who might cry sentimentality. 'But look,' the glosses seem to say, 'I am poking fun at the poor young man!'" (121).

9. See the first chapter of Glazener's *Reading for Realism.*

10. Mertins, *Robert Frost: Life and Talks Walking,* 108.

11. Walsh, *Into My Own,* 77–78, makes this speculation, which other biographers have since followed.

12. Economically speaking, the acceptance by Nutt was both good and bad news. Frost would receive the still generous royalty of 12 percent but only after the sale of 250 copies, and only a thousand would be printed. As it turned out, he never received a penny from M. L. Nutt. See Walsh, *Into My Own,* 80–81.

13. That series had just published *Lyrical Poems* by Lucy Lyttelton and a collection from William Sharp, the Irish Renaissance poet writing under the name of Fiona MacLeod. Both were reviewed widely, with Lyttelton receiving high praise from Alice Corbin Henderson in a recent issue of *Poetry* magazine. In short, Mosher's was no small offer.

14. RF to Thomas Mosher, November 19, 1912, in Frost, *Letters of Robert Frost,* 1:73–75. Also see Sergeant, *Robert Frost: Trial by Existence,* 98–99.

15. Francis, *Frost Family's Adventure in Poetry,* 75.

16. The poem had been first published in 1911 in the *English Review,* then edited by Austin Harrison. Ever since the novelist Ford Maddox Hueffer (Ford) had quit, the magazine's sales had declined and it was in dire shape. This one forty-four-page poem, according to Harrison, saved the magazine. Rogers, *Georgian Poetry,* 9.

17. Edward Marsh to Michael Sadleir, February 22, 1913, in Hassall, *A Biography of Edward Marsh,* 210; Ross, *Georgian Revolt,* 83.

18. Hassall, *A Biography of Edward Marsh,* 196.

19. Walsh, *Into My Own,* 153–54. The comments are actually margin notes in a copy of the December 1913 *Poetry and Drama* that included two of Frost's poems. He had sent the issue to Bartlett as a Christmas present.

20. See Hibberd, *Harold Monro: Poet of the New Age,* 3. Hibberd says of Monro that "all his achievements were based on socialist, futuristic ideals which he had

explored during years of enquiry and experiment before he settled in London." Before arriving in England, Munro and his college friend and cofounder, Maurice Browne, the soon-to-be impresario of the new drama in Chicago and a key figure in the burgeoning New Poetry scene now known as the Chicago Renaissance, had named the press after a utopian group in H. G. Wells's novel *A Modern Utopia* (1905). Browne and Monro had become devoted to the spartan virtues of the Japanese samurai and published literature that championed such ideals. Grant, *Harold Monro and the Poetry Bookshop*, 16–20. In addition to Browne, Monro was helped in the project by an American, Arthur Davidson Ficke, then in England. Ficke had been instrumental in gaining attention for *The Lyric Year* in 1912 and for jump-starting Edna St. Vincent Millay's career. Samurai Press published Drinkwater and Gibson with the goal of bringing poetry back to the people and to everyday life. Hibberd, "New Poetry, Georgians and Others," 176–98.

21. Ross, *Georgian Revolt*, 58; also see Grant, *Harold Monro and the Poetry Bookshop*, and Hibberd, "New Poetry, Georgians and Others."

22. Hibberd, *Harold Monro: Poet of the New Age*, 17.

23. Grant, *Harold Monro and the Poetry Bookshop*, 69. The first award went to Rupert Brooke for his realist poem "The Old Vicarage, Grantchester."

24. Harold Monro to Maurice Browne, November 10, 1911, in Grant, *Harold Monro and the Poetry Bookshop*, 39. Also see Hibberd, "New Poetry, Georgians and Others," 179. The subscriber list included six hundred to seven hundred of the most influential figures in the British literary establishment.

25. In fact the second issue of the American magazine, *Poetry*, carried a full-page advertisement for the *Poetry Review* that subsequently led to substantial sales in America.

26. Harold Monro, "The Future of Poetry," *Poetry Review* 1 (January 1912): 12.

27. Ibid., 11, 12.

28. The article about Gibson was written by Monro's former partner at Samurai, Maurice Browne. An American, he had led Chicago's Little Theater and was also a friend of Harriet Monroe's. She would soon do in Chicago with her magazine what Monro was doing in London. See Hibberd, "New Poetry, Georgians and Others," 180–81. Monroe, a poet, editor, and art and drama critic for Chicago newspapers, had become a devoted reader of Monro's magazine. She, too, felt Monro had made a mistake by putting too much prose about poetry in the magazine. She made sure to avoid that problem in her own *Poetry* magazine, founded that same year. See Grant, *Harold Monro and the Poetry Bookshop*, 43.

29. Hibberd, "New Poetry, Georgians, and Others," 115; Grant, *Harold Monro and the Poetry Bookshop*, 61. By October, having purchased a fourteen-year lease, Monro began to remake the building into a center for poetry that would house

his bookstore, publishing imprint, a space for lectures, and on its upper floors low-cost lodgings for poets and other artists. Hibberd, "New Poetry, Georgians, and Others," 115. Hibberd adds that the neighborhood was more lower-middle and working class than slum, though many of Monro's patrons would beg to differ.

30. Ross, *Georgian Revolt,* 69.

31. Ezra Pound, "Status Rerum," *Poetry,* January 1913, 127; Hassall, *A Biography of Edward Marsh,* 189–90. Hibberd, in *Harold Monro: Poet of the New Age,* however, thinks it likely that Marsh got the name from Monro and speculates that "perhaps he had actually picked it up in conversation with Harold" (86).

32. Hassall, *A Biography of Edward Marsh,* 274.

33. Ibid., 190. Marsh had admired Pound's realist portrayal of Jesus, "The Goodly Frere," which used the idiom of medieval troubadour lyrics to give a hard-hitting depiction of a rough-and-tumble Jesus and his friends. Marsh asked Pound for "The Goodly Frere" and for "Portrait d'Une Femme," his blank-verse portrayal of a woman entirely through a series of metaphors. Pound refused the first, saying "Frere" was not modern enough, and said he had already committed the other to his forthcoming *Ripostes,* from Elkin Mathews. Not wanting to be entirely left out, however, Pound asked Marsh to select a poem from his modern renderings of Calvalcanti in his *Canzoni.* Marsh did not find there the realist note he preferred, and Pound did not appear in the anthology.

34. Drinkwater would become famous in 1918 with his play *Abraham Lincoln,* which enjoyed as much fame in the United States as in Britain.

35. Many of the poets selected, however, wanted it dedicated to Yeats. Marsh objected that as an Irishman Yeats would make little sense as the progenitor of an anthology representing the British. Hassall, *A Biography of Edward Marsh,* 208.

36. Hassall, *A Biography of Edward Marsh,* 208. Specifically Marsh saw to it that prepublication copies went to influential reviewers, magazines, and the like. Ross, *Georgian Revolt,* 103.

37. In 1914 four of the poets—Abercrombie, Gibson, Drinkwater, and Brooke—started a literary magazine, *New Numbers.* It lasted only four issues, killed, like so much else, by the onset of World War I. In his overview of *Georgian Poets,* Ross finds that Brooke's poems depend on a dramatic situation, as do those of Walter de la Mare, Gibson, and Abercrombie (not to mention Masefield). See Ross, *Georgian Revolt,* 122–23.

38. Making precisely this point in Harold Monro's *Poetry Review,* Lascelles Abercrombie wrote an appreciation of the poet and playwright John Drinkwater, whose first collection, *Lyrical and Other Poems* (1908), had been published by Monro's Samurai Press.

39. Ross, *Georgian Revolt*, 17. When the book was published, Gibson had the best reputation. While he was on the staff of *Rhythm*, he also earned a respectable amount of royalties on his poetry books, especially his recent *Fires* (1912), which told in dramatic monologs the stories of the British working class, especially miners.

40. Marsh had become friendly with Monro. As Marsh and Brooke worked on the anthology, Marsh proposed that Monro be its publisher. For the most recent details of the history of the anthology, see Hibberd, "New Poetry, Georgians and Others," esp. 185–87.

41. Hibberd, "New Poetry, Georgians and Others," 107.

42. Nor should one think of the Georgian poets as somehow suspicious or disdainful of the new currents then emanating from France or even of the new imagism. In the same month their anthology was published, Brooke published in *Cambridge Magazine* a lavish appreciation of a show of the new postimpressionist—and then still very exotic—paintings by Henri Matisse.

43. Ross, *Georgian Revolt*, 33. Filippo Tommaso Marinetti read at the Poetry Bookshop in November 1913. He had first asserted the existence of futurism with "Futurist Manifesto," published in 1909 on the front page of *Le Figaro*, the conservative community organ of the French aristocracy. The piece touched off a firestorm of attention that Marinetti immediately capitalized on. After London he took his show to Berlin in 1912. By far the best account of the influence of Marinetti and futurism on Pound and imagism in 1912 is in Rainey, "Creation of the Avant-Garde." Such was the impact of Marinetti and futurism that Monro published a special issue of his magazine devoted to futurism in December 1913. It included a translation of the 1909 "Futurist Manifesto," as well as translations of the futurists' poetry. In his introduction Monro declared, "We claim ourselves, also, to be futurists." By that, however, he meant to align his ideals of poetry with the future rather than the genteel past and not with Marinetti's specific poetics.

44. Ross, *Georgian Revolt*, 107. Marsh took a hundred copies from the first run and gave them away to those among his vast network of influential friends who would either write about it or speak about it, both in England and abroad. The rest of that printing sold out within weeks, eventually leading to nine further printings averaging fifteen hundred copies each during the next year and a half. For the figures see Ross, *Georgian Revolt*, 99, 107.

45. Hibberd, "New Poetry, Georgians and Others," 119–20. Also see Hibberd, *Harold Monro: Poet of the New Age*, 105–38. As many as three hundred people filled the shop during its first two official opening days.

46. P. G. Wodehouse, *Piccadilly Jim* (1917; repr., New York: Overlook, 2004), 60.

47. Flint's publisher, Elkin Mathews, published Pound's most recent collection, *Ripostes*. Flint's article on French poetry had only just been published in the October issue of the Poetry Society's *Poetry Review* 1, no. 10 (1912): 355–414.

48. RF to F. S. Flint, January 21, 1913, Frost, *Letters of Robert Frost*, 1:89; Francis, *Frost Family's Adventures*, 76–77; and Walsh, *Into My Own*, 86.

49. RF to F. S. Flint, 1:90.

50. Parini, *Robert Frost: A Life*, 127.

CHAPTER TEN
ROBERT FROST: PUBLIC POET AT LAST "THE DEATH OF THE HIRED MAN"

1. RF to Ernest Silver, May 7, 1913, in Frost, *Letters of Robert Frost*, 1:104.

2. Ezra Pound, "The Approach to Paris, V," *New Age*, October 2, 1913, 662.

3. Ezra Pound to Harriet Monroe, March 1913, in Pound, *Selected Letters of Ezra Pound*, 51.

4. Pound to Alice Corbin Henderson, March 1913, in Pound, *Selected Letters of Ezra Pound*, 49; Thompson, *Robert Frost: Early Years*, 412.

5. Wagner-Martin, *Robert Frost: Critical Reception*, 1–2. Beginning in November 1913, Pound spent three periods over three years as Yeats's secretary at Stone Cottage. See Logenbach, *Stone Cottage*.

6. RF to John Bartlett, March 11, 1913, and RF to Thomas Mosher, June 15, 1913, both in Frost, *Letters of Robert Frost*, 1:97, 1:109–10.

7. Frost first mentions having tea with Sinclair in a letter to Bartlett, March 11, 1913, in Frost, *Letters of Robert Frost*, 1:97. By 1913 Sinclair had become deeply political, actively engaged in suffrage, feminism, and women's rights generally. In fact she had just published her first political tract, titled simply *Feminism* (1912).

8. Frost, *Letters of Robert Frost*, 1:97; Frost to Thomas Mosher, July 17, 1913, in Frost, *Letters of Robert Frost*, 1:132. Also see Sergeant, *Robert Frost: Trial by Existence*, 110.

9. Sergeant, *Robert Frost: Trial by Existence*, 103; also see Walsh, *Into My Own*, 109.

10. Frost to John Bartlett, March 11, 1913, in Frost, *Letters of Robert Frost*, 1:98.

11. As a result of their first major exhibition in the United States, the famed Armory Exhibition, the postimpressionists had made their radical break with visual expectations newsworthy.

12. F. S. Flint, *Poetry*, March 1913, 199; Pound, "A Few Don'ts by an *Imagiste*," 201. Also see Levenson, *A Geneaology of Modernism*, 43. The next month *Poetry* published no fewer than twelve of Pound's own poems to illustrate T. E. Hulme's

claim that poetry is also "the advance guard of language" (Levenson, *A Geneaology of Modernism*, 44).

13. See Rainey, "Creation of the Avant-Garde."

14. Gino Severini, "Get Inside the Picture: Futurism as the Artist Sees It," *Daily Express*, April 11, 1913, 4. One expected such things from intellectual publications such as the *New Age*, which had been one of the few English magazines to prepare the ground for such avant-garde antics.

15. Walsh, *Into My Own*, 116.

16. Hassall, *A Biography of Edward Marsh*, 229.

17. Frost was not the only poet Pound bullied. According to legend, Pound challenged Abercrombie to a duel over his claim that poets should write like Wordsworth. Wilhelm, *Ezra Pound in London and Paris*, 117. The story goes that after demanding the duel Abercrombie avoided Pound. One day Abercrombie went to Yeats for advice, only to find Pound at Yeats's door, at which point Abercrombie ran away. In the end, when given the choice of weapons, Abercrombie said they must use one another's own books, and so the episode ended.

18. Frost, *Letters of Robert Frost*, 1:132; Sergeant, *Robert Frost: Trial by Existence*, 106. It seems probable to me that the poem in question was "The Death of the Hired Man," which Pound so admired he tried to have it published in both *Smart Set* and *Poetry*.

19. William Pritchard puts it like this: "Frost's attempt, generally, was to make the nature of 'reaching out' so inclusive as not to exclude any possible reader anywhere from membership in his audience." Pritchard, *Frost: A Literary Life Reconsidered*, 70.

20. It is impossible to know the precise details of Frost's revisions. The internal evidence suggests to me a profound influence from the poets he had met after arriving in England. Still, he did say to Edward Lathem in an interview many decades later that he had written the whole poem in one two-hour burst. Frost, *Interviews with Robert Frost*, 25.

21. RF to Flint, July 6, 1913. Also see Walsh, *Into My Own*, 111.

22. Wilhelm, *Ezra Pound in London and Paris*, 112.

23. From 1913 until 1923, when Nathan and Mencken quit, *Smart Set* published a roll call of modernist writers. From Britain and Ireland: "D.H. Lawrence, George Moore, May Sinclair, Robert Bridges, Joseph Conrad, William Butler Yeats." From the rest of Europe: Arthur Schnitzler, Franz Wedekind, August Strindberg, D'Annunzio. From the United States: "Theodore Dreiser, Floyd Dell, . . . Robinson Jeffers, Sara Teasdale, Harriet Monroe, Louis Untermeyer, Ezra Pound, Elinor Wylie, Edna St. Vincent Millay, Maxwell Bodenheim." G. Doug-

las, *Smart Magazines*, 80. After Nathan, Mencken, and Alfred A. Knopf failed to buy the magazine outright in 1923, and after Nathan and Mencken quit *Smart Set*, they simply founded their own magazine, *American Mercury*.

24. Ezra Pound to Homer Pound, June 3, 1913, in Pound, *Selected Letters of Ezra Pound*, 57. Also see Cook, *Robert Frost: A Living Voice*.

25. In 1950 Frost told editors who wished to use the poem for an anthology, *The World's Best*, "By the way, it's in blank verse, not free verse." Cramer, *Robert Frost Among His Poems*, 32.

26. In keeping with my practice, all quotations come from the first published magazine version of this poem. Although Frost had sent it to *Smart Set* and *Poetry*, it ultimately was published by the *New Republic*, February 6, 1915, 19–20. These lines are found there on page 20.

27. Or almost. Late in his life Frost admitted during a reading that the first line unintentionally had six feet. Cramer, *Robert Frost Among His Poems*, 32. Cramer cites a reading Frost gave in 1960 and that was reproduced in Cook, *Robert Frost: A Living Voice*, 139. Also see Barry, *Robert Frost on Writing*.

28. Cramer, *Robert Frost Among His Poems*, 29; Frost, *Interviews with Robert Frost*, 219. Also see Cramer, *Robert Frost Among His Poems*, 32.

29. There is a rich and extensive critical library concerning this poem. Relevant to my discussion is Richard Poirier's reading, which sees the poem as an analog for Frost's views of poetry in general. Poirier, *Robert Frost and the Work of Knowing*, 135. Also the ethical dimension of the poem is uncovered with great subtlety by Timmerman, *Robert Frost: Ethics of Ambiguity*, 120–22. He reads the poem in light of the parable of the prodigal son from Luke 15:11–32. For other more recent views of the poem, see Sanders, *A Divided Poet*, 39–40, as well as Kendall, *Art of Robert Frost*, 60–63. Kendall attends particularly to the concept of value, as well as to the issue of home, in this poem.

30. Kilcup, *Robert Frost and the Feminine Literary Tradition*, 83; also see Evans, *Robert Frost and Sidney Cox*, 84–101, for the most thorough treatment of this poem. In *Robert Frost and the Challenge of Darwin*, 115–16, Faggen reads this poem in terms of what it has to say about a vanishing type: the farmhand. As far as Frost was concerned, Silas was in many ways the last of his kind. Faggen reads the poem, then, in terms of survival itself and reads its formal method as an elegy to that social role and to that kind of work.

31. All quotations are from *New Republic*, February 6, 1915, 20. Later Frost told Sidney Cox that some of his imagery concerning the moon could seem like "the older poetry." Even there, though, Frost calls attention to the drama made entirely through speech and the implications of Mary's and Warren's tones. Ev-

ans, *Robert Frost and Sidney Cox,* 98, 89. One of the best readings of this poem in terms of a more aesthetic romantic inclination can be found in Walsh, *Into My Own,* 112–14.

32. In contrast to my view of the poem, Richardson, *Ordeal of Robert Frost,* 49–50, finds its gender politics far too conventional to warrant much attention. This, as I have hoped to show, mistakes one theme for another. Hoffman, *Robert Frost and the Politics of Poetry,* 103–5, offers a corrective to Richardson's reading, though he attends more to Frost's experimentation with tones of speech than do I.

33. Evans, *Robert Frost and Sidney Cox,* 89.

34. Walsh, *Into My Own,* 112–13. See also Thompson, *Robert Frost: Early Years,* 43.

35. RF to F. S. Flint, June 26, 1913, in Frost, *Letters of Robert Frost,* 1:120. Also see Francis, *Frost Family's Adventure in Poetry,* 77, and Thompson, *Robert Frost: Early Years,* 437. Walsh adds, "Then came a day when Pound blandly announced that unless Frost espoused Imagist principles he would no longer enjoy Pound's sponsorship—the threat also implied the severing of all the important contacts already made, starting with Yeats, and others in prospect" (*Into My Own,* 109).

36. RF to Sidney Cox, January 2, 1915, in Frost, *Letters of Robert Frost,* 1:244.

37. "The July Smart Set," *Smart Set,* June 1913, 174.

38. Kemp, *Robert Frost and New England,* 81, 82.

CHAPTER ELEVEN
INVENTING A NEW POETRY: "A HUNDRED COLLARS," "THE FEAR"

1. The *Athenaeum* review was penned anonymously by Edward Thomas, whom Frost later called "the best friend I ever had" (they had not yet met when the review appeared). Wagner-Martin, *Robert Frost: Critical Reception,* 1.

2. Ibid. See also Walsh, *Into My Own,* 124.

3. Wagner-Martin, *Robert Frost: Critical Reception.*

4. Ibid., 1.

5. Ibid., 3.

6. Frost lists most of these poems in RF to John Bartlett, August 1913, in Frost, *Letters of Robert Frost,* 1:134. There he refers to "Birches" as "Swinging Birches."

7. RF to F. S. Flint, July 10, 1913, in Frost, *Letters of Robert Frost,* 1:130. Also see Walsh, *Into My Own,* 125.

8. The seriousness of their ideas did not preclude the antics associated with a bohemian avant-garde. "Hulme once emphasized a point in an aesthetic dispute

[by] holding Wyndham Lewis upside down over the railings in Fitzroy Square." Hassall, *Edward Marsh*, 187.

9. In 1913 Hulme established a new salon that met on Frith Street. The salon itself, unlike the bohemian excess of his earlier café salons, had a decidedly high tone. It took place weekly on Tuesdays "in a magnificent house at 67 Frith Street in the very heart of London." It is described as a "house, which had once been the Venetian embassy and was in 1911 the residence of his close friend Ethel Kibblewhite. . . . His salon was the scene of legendary arguments and has been described by many who attended from week to week." J. Brooker, "T(homas) E(rnest) Hulme."

10. A central figure in the Action Française, Ferdinand Lasserre made anti-Bergsonism central in his essay "La Philosophie de Bergson," which he had published in *Action Française* in 1911. Lasserre was the principal philosopher of this French movement. Charles Maurras was the group's literary critic. Levenson adds that the attack on Bergson hit Hulme like a physical blow to the stomach. In fact he traveled to Paris to meet Lasserre to see why Bergson and Bergsonism should be anathema. Whatever he may have discovered there, Hulme continued his own Bergsonian ways, even finishing and publishing his translation of Bergson's *Introduction to Metaphysics*. By 1913, however, Hulme was thoroughly convinced that Bergson did not offer a means to social order and health but only justified further chaos. Although Hulme ignores the group's anti-Semitism, Levenson offers a fine overview, *A Geneology of Modernism*, 80–102. Hulme's first public declaration of his new views appeared in the *Cambridge Magazine* of May 1912 under the appropriate headline "A Tory Philosophy." See also Hewitt, *Fascist Modernism*.

11. Levenson, *A Genealogy of Modernism*, 86. Levenson adds, "After his return from Berlin [July 1913]—and primarily under the influence of Worringer and Husserl—he moved to a new attitude which found classicism as unsatisfactory as romanticism; the goal became not a classical, but an anti-humanist and geometric art," 98. Levenson further adds, "Husserl and [G. E.] Moore had persuaded him [Hulme] that truth, meaning and value were independent of the individual" and that genuine art would express truth, meaning and value rather than something called "vital human form" (99). See also 96–102.

12. RF to Flint, June 25, 1913, in Frost, *Letters of Robert Frost*, 1:119.

13. RF to Flint, July 6, 1913, in Frost, *Letters of Robert Frost*, 1:125; also see Walsh, *Into My Own*, 118.

14. RF to John Bartlett, July 4, 1913, in Frost, *Letters of Robert Frost*, 1:121–23. From the letters it seems likely he met Hulme the day before, July 3, 1913. Flint

said he was seeing Hulme on June 28 and would ask if he could meet Frost then. Frost, *Letters of Robert Frost*, 1:119. On Sunday, July 6, Frost told Flint that his "ideas had gotten the rub they needed." The remaining days between June 28 and July 6, or "last week," would have been when the meeting occurred. That Frost wrote to Bartlett the first serious assertion of his poetic theory on July 4 suggests he had just come to its formulation, that he had just had his discussion with Hulme and Flint.

15. RF to Bartlett, July 4, 1913. Also see M. Anderson, *Robert Frost and John Bartlett*, 52–54.

16. Vander Ven, "Robert Frost's Dramatic Principle of 'Oversound,'" 250. He adds, "Given a context of signals which indicate fear or doubt [or any other emotional nuance], the reader will experience the sound of fear or doubt [or other emotional nuance] in the poem only if he has heard those sounds carried in the human voice" (250).

17. See Francis, *Frost Family's Adventure in Poetry*, 77.

18. RF to Sidney Cox, July 10, 1913, and RF to William Stanley Braithwaite, March 22, 1915, both in Frost, *Letters of Robert Frost*, 1:126, 1:266. To this letter Pritchard adds that Frost is "at all times careful to keep his hands off the characters, as if their speech were issuing forth of its own accord, untouched by the creator's thumb of moral judgment and assessment" (*Frost: A Literary Life Reconsidered*, 104).

19. RF to Thomas B. Mosher, July 17, 1913, in Frost, *Letters of Robert Frost*, 1:131–33.

20. Robert Frost, "The Fear" and "A Hundred Collars," *Poetry and Drama*, December 1913, 406–15. All quotations from these poems are taken from this edition of *Poetry and Drama*.

21. Readers familiar with the poem from later published versions will notice a variety of differences in Lafe's name, spelled Layfayette in later versions, as well as in punctuation and even various phrases, such as "naked above the waist" instead of "unclad above the waist," as given here.

22. At some point Frost must have decided that even a size 15 collar spoke too generously of Magoon's physical size. In subsequent versions of the poem he changed it to size 14.

23. Bushman, *Refinement of America*, 411.

24. In subsequent versions Frost changed this to read, "There's nothing I'm afraid of like scared people."

25. The extensive criticism of this poem focuses on its ethical issues. Noting that the plot revolves around Lafe's attempt to give away his collars, one critic,

John Kemp, *Robert Frost and New England*, 116–17, found there a metaphor for intellectual, social, and artistic freedom from constraint: Lafe's collars, he says, manifest "his increasing independence, for the poem indicates that he makes little of both physical and mental constraints." Kemp does not make anything of the class issues, however, and reads the convulsive clutching of his throat as Magoon's sudden recognition of his own social restrictions. In contrast Timmerman, *Robert Frost: Ethics of Ambiguity*, is one of very few critics to focus precisely on Magoon's fear and to read it as anything *but* comic (160). Faggen meanwhile says that rather than celebrating a Jeffersonian equality, the poem "undermines Jeffersonian ideals of the virtue of agrarian democracy and natural aristocracy." Faggen, *Robert Frost and the Challenge of Darwin*, 143. Rather than establish the two as friends, this poem, according to Faggen, says that people face one another as antagonists and remain such. According to Faggen, Darwinian biology informs this poem (143–48). Kilcup, *Robert Frost and Feminine Literary Tradition*, is one of the only critics to concentrate on the importance of gender. She reads this poem as "the comic triumph of a (homoerotic) hypermasculine" man "over a feminized man" (177). Even though Lafe clearly does triumph, Kilcup does not believe the poem necessarily sides with him. Nor do I. More likely Frost knew both sides of the gender divide. He, like his male friends, as poets, had to confront cultures, Anglo and American, that increasingly belittled their choice of profession, declaring them feminine and unworthy as real men. Most recently Nancy Nahra reveals a striking connection to one of Horace's satires in this poem. Nahra, "'My Kind of Fooling.'" Also see Sanders, *A Divided Poet*, 49–55, and Kendall, *Art of Robert Frost*, 79–81.

26. This poem also was most likely written that August; he wrote to Bartlett claiming to have finished a poem he thought about calling "The Lantern." RF to John Bartlett, August 1913, in Frost, *Letters of Robert Frost*, 1:133.

27. In the scholarship concerning this poem only Faggen, *Cambridge Introduction to Robert Frost*, 104–5, has raised the issue that the woman may well be correct to fear the stranger in the woods. See Kendall, *Art of Robert Frost*, 153–55, for a treatment of the poem as a psychological study of fear without relief or solace.

28. Robert Frost, "The Fear," *Poetry and Drama*, December 1913, 409.

29. RF to John Bartlett, August 6, 1913, in Frost, *Letters of Robert Frost*, 1:136. Also see M. Anderson, *Robert Frost and John Bartlett*, 58–59.

30. See Francis, *Frost Family's Adventure in Poetry*, 94–95.

31. Walsh, *Into My Own*, 144–45.

32. Frost's recollection is in Walsh, *Into My Own*, 152.

33. An admirer of Gibson's poetry, Frost had appealed to Monro to arrange a meeting. After they met, the two became fast friends.

34. Gibson, however, did not last long upstairs in his artist apartment. He soon fell in love with the store's secretary, married her, left London, and settled in the Dymock area in Gloucestershire, near the town of Ryton. Absconding with his most important employee may have angered Monro; worse, Gibson, along with another Georgian resident of the Dymock area, Lascelles Abercrombie, began *New Numbers,* a rival magazine to *Poetry and Drama.*

35. Their first meeting can be precisely dated to October 6, 1913. When they met, Thomas had already published no fewer than twenty-four books, which barely kept his family afloat. The meeting came about when the Georgian poet Ralph Hodgson gave Thomas the manuscript of "The Death of the Hired Man." Thomas read it and asked to meet the poet. Hodgson then arranged the meeting.

36. Francis, *Frost Family's Adventure in Poetry,* 81. In fact Frost began to frequent a number of distinct poetic circles that fall. Burnshaw, *Robert Frost Himself,* 16, describes some of them: "The old Guard at the Poetry Society [Noyes and Bridges] versus Harold Monro, . . . another group, friends of Monro, who called themselves "Georgians" to impugn Victorians and Edwardians. . . . A fourth group welcomed T. E. Hulme for his emphasizing the image." To that list one can also add Hulme's regular Thursday salon and for a while Yeats's regular Monday evening salon.

37. Walsh, *Into My Own,* 148.

38. RF to John Bartlett, November 5, 1913, in Frost, *Letters of Robert Frost,* 1:154. Also see M. Anderson, *Robert Frost and John Bartlett,* 63–66.

39. RF to John Bartlett, December 8, 1913, in Frost, *Letters of Robert Frost,* 1:162. Also see Francis, *Frost Family's Adventure in Poetry,* 58.

40. RF to Gertrude McQuestern [ca. October 1913], in Frost, *Letters of Robert Frost,* 1:148–51. Also see Walsh, *Into My Own,* 157.

41. RF to Gertrude McQuestern [ca. October 1913], in Frost, *Letters of Robert Frost,* 1:151.

CHAPTER TWELVE
ROBERT FROST, A REALIST IN THE MAGAZINES OF MODERNISM: "THE HOUSEKEEPER" AND "THE CODE"

1. Rogers, *Georgian Poetry, 1911–1922,* 9.

2. Campbell, "Contemporary Poetry."

3. It also published in the essay section an extended appreciation by J. C. Squire of Francis Thompson, the poet who had meant so much to Frost when he first read "The Hound of Heaven" as a teenager.

4. His bookshop also regularly sponsored readings by poets, still a relatively unusual thing to do in 1913. "We make a regular practice of reading poetry aloud, and anyone who wishes to stroll in and listen may do so." Harold Monro, "Varia: The Bookshop," *Poetry and Drama*, December 1913, 387.

5. Untermeyer, *From Another World*, 206–7.

6. Robert Frost to Ernest Silver, February 23, 1914, in Frost, *Letters of Robert Frost*, 1:178–82. The phrase is on page 181. Alford, recently graduated from King's College, Cambridge had become, in many respects, central to the operations of the Poetry Bookshop. From a wealthy family, he had even lent it £200, in part to publish his own book of poems under the Poetry Bookshop imprint. His youth and inexperience explain why, in his letter to Bartlett, Frost refers to Alford as a cub. See Hibberd, *Harold Monro*, 140.

7. Frost, *Selected Letters of Robert Frost*, 105–6.

8. In a letter accompanying Untermeyer's response, Charles Ryder summarized Alford's review: "American poetry, with the exception of a few poems by men now dead, is insignificant." Ryder, letter to editor, *Poetry and Drama*, March 1914, 110.

9. Louis Untermeyer, letter to editor, *Poetry and Drama*, March 1914, 107, 109–10.

10. Alford, "American Poetry: A Response to Louis Untermeyer," 241; Edward J. Wheeler, "Voices of the Living Poets," *Current Opinion*, August 1914, 136–38; Alford, "American Poetry: An Explanatory Note," 306.

11. Alford, "American Chronicle," 410.

12. Robert Frost, "Home Burial," in "Extracts from Recent Books," *Poetry and Drama*, September 1914, 310–13.

13. It also took up a full two pages of the double-columned quarto magazine. *Egoist*, January 15, 1914, 31–32.

14. In fact, as biographers have long made it a point to emphasize, the main character of John was modeled on John Hall, Frost's neighbor and friend from his Derry years whose life parallels in many ways that depicted in the poem. Hall died in 1906, and biographers believe Frost wrote the first drafts of the poem then. See L. Thompson, *Robert Frost: Early Years*, and Walsh, *Into My Own*, 57–61. Scholars, too, have long made this connection, most recently David Sanders, "John Hall and 'The Housekeeper,'" in his *A Divided Poet*, 82–88.

15. Lespi, "'Is It the Neighbor?,'" makes a striking case for the neighbor's profound implication in the story of Estelle and John. That speculation and attention to other intriguing ambiguities in the poem can be found in Lespi's fine article.

16. Scholarship on the poem has never associated it with the comic as it has "A Hundred Collars." Instead the poem's more sinister themes have been addressed.

Kemp, *Robert Frost and New England,* describes it as a "macabre study," and that has been the general reading ever since (128). Later Faggen, *Robert Frost and the Challenge of Darwin,* read the poem in terms of its critique of eugenics and playing God with nature—John, the jilted lover, raises prized hens for show and lets the work of his actual farm fall to ruin (232–37). In contrast Rotella, "'Synonymous with Kept,'" reads the poem as a critique of economic issues (256). Also see Kendall's reading, *Art of Robert Frost,* 146–48.

17. Kilcup, *Robert Frost and Feminine Literary Tradition,* details four distinct aspects of gossip that Frost emphasizes to poetic effect: "its creation of intimacy"; its fundamental purpose to prove one's power with secret knowledge; its "alliance with the erotic"; and "its affiliation with women" (110).

18. O'Brien, *Names, Proverbs, Riddles, and Material Text,* 92–93.

19. Robert Frost, "The Code—Heroics," *Poetry,* February 1914, 167–71. From its publication in *North of Boston* Frost revised the title to the shorter "The Code."

20. In his treatment of the issue Poirier, *Work of Knowing,* says that both "The Code" and "A Hundred Collars" "are about cultural confrontations about the way things ought to be said" (109). Also see Kemp, *Robert Frost and New England,* which emphasizes the cultural rather than class bias dramatized through these characters' speech (128–29). Richardson, in *Ordeal of Robert Frost,* was the first scholar to explore in any serious depth the implicit gendered implications of the talk in this poem (63–64). Faggen, *Robert Frost and the Challenge of Darwin,* in contrast, makes an excellent case for the class dynamics of this poem (134–35).

21. In his recent look at the poem O'Brien writes in *Names, Proverbs, Riddles, and Material Text* that it is also about the "problem of ever being able to say just the right thing . . . the issue of how to find a way, some conventional and at the same time acceptable way, of talking about the unknowable" (87). Kendall, in *Art of Robert Frost,* highlights not only the linguistic implications but also the humor of this poem (120–23).

CHAPTER THIRTEEN
POET OF THE NEW AMERICAN POETRY
NORTH OF BOSTON, "PUTTING IN THE SEED"

1. It was promoted under that title in the Nutt company catalog announcing forthcoming books for 1914. The original table of contents for the English edition lists only fifteen poems. Neither "The Pasture" nor "Good Hours" is listed among them. Instead "The Pasture" constitutes the introduction to the book and "Good Hours" its conclusion. When the American edition was published in 1915, it followed the same format, except a blank page was added before "Good Hours." For more information about these variations see Sanders, "Correcting the Record."

In 1923, when Frost issued his first *Selected Poems,* he removed "The Pasture" from this collection altogether and let it serve, still in italics, as the introduction to all his work, as it has done in successive issues of his collected poems ever since.

2. William Stanley Braithwaite, ed., *Anthology of Magazine Verse for 1914* (Cambridge, MA: [n.p.] 1914), ix.

3. *Times Literary Supplement,* May 28, 1914, 263 (brief mention). An anonymous review followed in *TLS,* July 2, 1914, 316. Other reviews included Lascelles Abercrombie, "A New Voice," *Nation,* June 13, 1914; Ford Maddox Hueffer, "Mr. Robert Frost and *North of Boston,*" *Outlook,* June 27, 1914, 879–80; Wilfrid Gibson, *Bookman,* July 1914, 46; and Edward Thomas, "A New Poet," *London Daily News,* July 22, 1914 (reprinted in Thomas, *Elected Friends,* 16–17).

4. Thomas, "A New Poet"; Thomas, *Elected Friends,* 20, 24.

5. Elinor Frost to Leona White Harvey, June 20, 1914, in Frost, *Selected Letters of Robert Frost,* 126. In a letter to John Haines, meanwhile, Frost explains not only how much he liked Abercrombie's review but also how much it derived from his conversations with Abercrombie. RF to John Haines [ca. July 20, 1914], in Frost, *Letters of Robert Frost,* 1:209.

6. Wagner-Martin, *Robert Frost: Critical Tradition,* 11–14.

7. Ibid., 297. "Home Burial" appears on pages 310–13.

8. Harold Monro, "New Books," *Poetry and Drama,* September 1914, 297.

9. Alford, "American Chronicle," 410.

10. See John Haines's memoir of the area in Thornton, *Recognition of Robert Frost,* 89–97.

11. Francis, *Frost Family's Adventure in Poetry,* 108.

12. RF to John Cournos, July 8, 1914, in Frost, *Letters of Robert Frost,* 1:208.

13. All quotations are from the version published in *Poetry and Drama,* December 1914, 349.

14. Kendall, *Art of Robert Frost,* finds it both misplaced and mistaken for Robert Pinsky to have included this poem in his anthology *Great Poems About Sex,* because "what is successful in Frost's poem is precisely the subtlety, the uncertainty and the understatement which such an anthology must, by the promise of its title, opt to ignore" (217).

15. This poem would be incorporated as part of a narrative sequence of five lyrics, "The Hill Wife," which he published in his third book, *Mountain Interval* (New York: Holt 1916). The five lyrics form a longer narrative.

16. RF to Thomas Mosher, October 1914, in Frost, *Letters of Robert Frost,* 1:226. I believe he was relying on Mosher's inherent generosity and knew that Mosher would always give him royalties.

17. RF to Mosher, December 27, 1914, in Frost, *Letters of Robert Frost*, 1:238.

18. Florence Holt's letter to Frost is printed in Frost, *Selected Letters of Robert Frost*, 130–31.

19. Henry Holt to David Nutt and Co., September 2, 1914, in Frost, *Selected Letters of Robert Frost*, 133.

20. The letters are in Frost, *Selected Letters of Robert Frost*, 130–34.

21. Ross, *Georgian Revolt*, 110–11. As a result of the war the second Georgian anthology did not get published until late in 1915. It would go on to outsell even the first edition with nineteen thousand copies sold. See Ross, *Georgian Revolt*, 114.

22. The war also delayed the publication of the fourth, and what would also be the final, number of *New Numbers*. It also led to the demise of Monro's *Poetry and Drama* and would delay his publication of Marsh's second *Georgian Anthology*. See Francis, *Frost Family's Adventure in Poetry*, 158.

CHAPTER FOURTEEN
THE AMERICAN MAGAZINES OF 1915 AND THE MAKING OF ROBERT FROST

1. Arthur Davidson Ficke, "In Defense of Vers Libre," *Little Review*, December 1914, 19.

2. Damon, *Amy Lowell*, 289; Lathem, *Robert Frost:"His American Send-off,"* 3.

3. Wagner-Martin, *Robert Frost: Critical Reception*, 17–21.

4. Ibid.

5. Ibid.

6. RF to Sidney Cox, March 2, 1915, and RF to William Stanley Braithwaite, March 22, 1915, both in Frost, *Letters of Robert Frost*, 1:260–61, 264–67.

7. The full correspondence between Holt and Nutt detailing the negotiations for this event can be read in Lathem's *Robert Frost: "His American Send Off,"* no page numbers but see 2–3 and notes 3 and 4. Note 4 contains the complete correspondence between Nutt and Holt.

8. The anecdote is in note 5 (n.p.) of Lathem's *Robert Frost: "His American Send-off."*

9. See J. Barron, "Louis Untermeyer." This is still the most recent biographical treatment of the poet.

10. Untermeyer, *New Era in American Poetry*, 10–11; Louis Untermeyer, "North of Boston," *Chicago Evening Post*, April 23, 1915, 25, in Wagner-Martin, *Robert Frost: Critical Reception*, 24–27.

11. Untermeyer, "*North of Boston*," 26.

12. Ibid. Untermeyer added, though, that Frost was "less rhapsodic" and "more local" than Whitman ever was.

13. RF to Louis Untermeyer, April 3, 1915, in Untermeyer, *Letters of Robert Frost to Louis Untermeyer*, 4.

14. The information that follows comes largely from L. Thompson, *Robert Frost: Years of Triumph*, 1–46. Typically Thompson interprets Frost as a mere careerist. His interpretation of these events is at odds with my own.

15. Sylvester Baxter, "Talk of the Town," *Boston Herald*, March 9, 1915, 12. Baxter also wrote an extensive essay introducing Frost to an American audience, "New England's New Poet," *American Review of Reviews*, April 1915, 432–34, in Wagner-Martin, *Robert Frost: Critical Reception*, 21–24.

16. Ellery Sedgwick to Edward Garnett, May 26, 1915, in Lathem, *Robert Frost, "His American Send-Off,"* n.p. [7].

17. Braithwaite, "A Poet of New England." In a delightful, not to say almost uncanny, coincidence the review that appeared immediately following Braithwaite's introduction to Robert Frost was of a book on Henri Bergson by a Danish philosopher, Harald Hoffding, *Modern Philosophers and Lectures on Bergson*.

18. *Boston Evening Transcript*, May 6, 1915, 16; William Stanley Braithwaite, "Robert Frost, New American Poet," *Boston Evening Transcript*, May 8, 1915, sec. 3, 4. The second article also carried a subheading that implied that Frost was an example of the very idea of modern poetry itself: "His Opinions and Practice—An Important Analysis of the Art of the Modern Bard."

19. Braithwaite, "Robert Frost: New American Poet," 10. In 1959 Frost would make his view of Emerson's poem public in a talk about Emerson, published that year as "On Emerson," *Daedalus* (fall 1959): 712–18. For more on what Frost intended by his reference to "Monadnock" see Grenier, *Robert Frost: Poet and His Critics*, 156.

20. Braithwaite, "Robert Frost: New American Poet," 10.

21. Ibid., 4.

22. Ibid.

23. Thompson, *Robert Frost: Years of Triumph*, 54; Grenier, *Robert Frost: Poet and His Critics*, 82. Thompson cites D. D. Paige, *The Letters of Ezra Pound 1907–1941* (New York: Harcourt Brace, 1950), 62–63.

24. Paige, *Letters of Ezra Pound*, 62–63.

25. Jessie Rittenhouse, review of *North of Boston, New York Times Book Review*, May 16, 1915, 189; RF to Sidney Cox, May 16, 1915, in Frost, *Letters of Robert Frost*, 1:295–96; Grenier, *Robert Frost: Poet and His Critics*, 86.

26. This story and quotations come from Lathem, *Robert Frost: "His American Send-Off,"* n.p. [3–4].

27. Garnett had heard a great deal about Frost from their mutual friend Edward Thomas. Unsolicited, in May 1915 Garnett wrote to the editor of the *Atlantic* suggesting this article. The letters between Sedgwick and Garnett are available in Frost, *Selected Letters of Robert Frost,* 169–70; 175–76, and in Lathem, *Robert Frost: "His American Send-Off."* Also see RF to Edward Garnett, June 12, 1915..

28. Sedgwick to Garnett, May 26, 1915.

29. RF to Garnett, June 12, 1915. Nearly fifty years later, when Edward Connery Lathem compiled a small collection about these events, Frost wrote to Lathem, saying, "Ellery Sedgwick had been teasing me about publishing the poems he had already accepted. . . . He had been teasing me about publishing them and had gone on to tease me about the article. He said he wasn't sure he would publish them, but he probably meant to publish both, and he now did at the best time of the year for all concerned." RF to Lathem [1960?], in Lathem, *Robert Frost: "His American Send-Off,"* n.p. [12].

30. Edward Thomas to Edward Garnett, March 17, 1915, in Lathem, *Robert Frost: "His American Send-Off,"* note 8.

31. Edward Garnett to Ellery Sedgwick, April 17, 1915, in Lathem, *Robert Frost: "His American Send-Off"* n.p. [4]. Initially Sedgwick was taken aback. He told Garnett that he already had assigned *North of Boston* to an omnibus review of recent books for April 1915. He did not see the need for more discussion of book or poet. In response Garnett made the case that Frost needed an essay, not a review.

32. Thomas to Garnett, May 1915, in Lathem, *Robert Frost: "His American Send-Off,"* note 8.

33. Edward Garnett to Ellery Sedgwick, April 24, 1915, in Lathem, *Robert Frost: "His American Send-Off,"* n.p. [5]; Sedgwick to Garnett, May 26, 1915.

34. Edward Garnett, "A New American Poet," *Atlantic Monthly,* September 1915, 214, 215, 217–19.

35. Ibid., 220, 219, 216–17.

36. RF to Edward Garnett, June 12, 1915.

37. Robert Frost to Edward Connery Lathem [1960?].

38. William Dean Howells, "The Editor's Easy Chair," *Harper's Monthly,* September 1915, 634. Well before he published this column, Howells wrote to Frost about his keen admiration for his poetry. He hoped, even, to meet Frost. Accordingly, on one of his frequent trips to New York City, Frost did in fact meet Howells

in the late summer of 1915, and that meeting likely led Howells to publish this column on Frost.

39. Howells, "Editor's Easy Chair," 634. He compliments Lowell as a poet only when she returns to meter and/or rhyme, and he acknowledges the power of Masters's stories but cannot help but lament their "shredded prose without even a slow, inscriptional pulse in it" (635).

40. Ibid., 635.

41. RF to Walter Prichard Eaton, September 18, 1915, in Frost, *Letters of Robert Frost*, 1:354–55.

42. Another collection, Gertrude Huntington McGiffert's *A Florentine Cycle and Other Poems* (New York: Putnam, 1915), also received praise in the same issue. She manifestly rejected the new realism in verse consisting exclusively of conventional meters, rhyme, and lush religious themes.

43. Thornton, *Recognition of Robert Frost*, 136.

44. Parini, *Robert Frost: A Life*, 412–14, offers the best overview of the people behind choosing Frost as the first-ever poet for a presidential inauguration in American history.

45. Frost actually wrote a special poem for John F. Kennedy's 1963 inauguration, "Dedication." On the day itself, January 20, 1963, the weather, among other things, conspired against Frost and he could not see his new poem. He recited only "The Gift Outright" from memory, adding Kennedy's correction. Parini, *Robert Frost: A Life*, 412–14.

46. Brodsky, Heaney, and Walcott, *Homage to Robert Frost*.

Bibliography

Abbott, Craig. "Publishing the New Poetry: Harriet Monroe's Anthology." *Journal of Modern Literature* 11 (1984): 89–108.

Alford, John. "American Chronicle." *Poetry and Drama*, December 1914, 407–12.

———. "American Poetry: An Explanatory Note." *Poetry and Drama*, September 1914, 305–6.

———. "American Poetry: A Response to Louis Untermeyer." *Poetry and Drama*, June 1914, 229–41.

Anderson, Benedict. *Imaginary Communities*. Rev. ed. London: Verso, 2006.

Anderson, Margaret B. *Robert Frost and John Bartlett: The Record of a Friendship*. New York: Holt, Rinehart, Winston, 1963.

Angyal, Andrew J. "Robert Frost's Poetry Before 1913: A Checklist." *Proof*, no. 5 (1977): 67–125.

Ardis, Ann L. "Democracy and Modernism: The New Age Under A. R. Orage (1907–22)." In Brooker and Thacker, *Oxford Critical and Cultural History*, 1:205–25.

Ardoin, Paul, S. E. Gontarski, and Laci Mattison, eds. *Understanding Bergson, Understanding Modernism*. New York: Bloomsbury Academic, 2013. Kindle Edition.

Auerbach, Erich. *Mimesis*. Princeton, NJ: Princeton University Press, 1953.

Bagdikian, Ben. *Media Monopoly*. Boston: Beacon, 1983.

Ballou, Ellen B. *The Building of the House: Houghton Mifflin Company—The Formative Years*. Boston: Houghton Mifflin, 1970.

Barron, Hal S. *Those Who Stayed Behind: Rural Society in Nineteenth Century New England.* 2d ed. New York: Cambridge University Press, 1988.

Barron, Jonathan N. "A Tale of Two Cottages: Frost and Wordsworth." In *Roads Not Taken: Rereading Robert Frost.* Edited by Earl J. Wilcox and Jonathan N. Barron. Columbia: University of Missouri Press, 2000.

———. "Louis Untermeyer." In *American Writers,* suppl. 14, 293–318. Edited by Jay Parini. New York: Scribner, 2006.

Barry, Elaine. *Robert Frost on Writing.* New Brunswick, NJ: Rutgers University Press, 1973.

Barthes, Roland. *The Rustle of Language.* Translated by Richard Howard. Oxford: Blackwell, 1986.

Bercovitch, Sacvan. *The Puritan Origins of the American Self.* New Haven, CT: Yale University Press, 2011.

Bergson, Henri. *Creative Evolution.* Translated by Arthur Mitchell. New York: Henry Holt, 1911.

Blumin, Stuart M. *The Emergence of the Middle Class: Social Experience in the American City.* Cambridge: Cambridge University Press, 1989.

Brake, Laurel. "Aestheticism and Decadence: *The Yellow Book* (1894–7), *The Chameleon* (1894), and *The Savoy* (1896)." In Booker and Thacker, *Oxford Critical and Cultural History of Modernist Magazines,* 1:76–100.

Brodsky, Joseph, Seamus Heaney, and Derek Walcott. *Homage to Robert Frost.* New York: Farrar, Straus and Giroux, 1997.

Brooker, Jewel Spears. "T(homas) E(rnest) Hulme." In *British Poets, 1880–1914.* Edited by Donald E. Stanford. Detroit: Gale Research, 1983.

Brooker, Peter. "Harmony, Discord, and Difference; Rhythm, Blue Review, and the Signature." In Brooker and Thacker, *Oxford Critical and Cultural History,* 1:314–36.

Brooker, Peter, and Andrew Thacker, eds. *The Oxford Critical and Cultural History of Modernist Magazines.* New York: Oxford University Press, 2009.

Browne, Francis F. "American Publishing and Publishers." *Dial* 28 (May 1900): 340–43.

Buell, Lawrence. *New England Literary Culture*. New York: Cambridge University Press, 1986.

Burnshaw, Stanley. *Robert Frost Himself*. New York: George Braziller, 1986.

Bushman, Richard L. *The Refinement of America: Persons, Houses, Cities*. New York: Alfred A. Knopf, 1992.

Campbell, Roy. "Contemporary Poetry." In *Scrutinies by Various Writers*. Edited by Edgell Rickwood, 168–72. London: Wishhart, 1928.

Canada, Mark. *Literature and Journalism in Antebellum America: Thoreau, Stowe, and Their Contemporaries Respond to the Rise of the Commercial Press*. New York: Palgrave Macmillan, 2011.

Castronovo, Russ. *Beautiful Democracy*. Chicago: University of Chicago Press, 2007.

Chase, Richard. *The American Novel and Its Tradition*. New York: Doubleday, 1957.

Churchill, Suzanne W. *The Little Magazine Others and the Renovation of Modern American Poetry*. Aldershot, UK: Ashgate, 2006.

Clark, Christopher. *The Roots of Rural Capitalism: Western Massachusetts, 1780–1860*. Ithaca, NY: Cornell University Press, 1990.

Cook, Reginald. *Robert Frost: A Living Voice*. Amherst: University of Massachusetts Press, 1974.

Cott, Nancy. *The Bonds of Womanhood: Women's Sphere in New England*. New Haven, CT: Yale University Press, 1977.

Cox, Sidney. *A Swinger of Birches: A Portrait of Robert Frost*. 1957. Reprint, New York: New York University Press, 1961.

Cramer, Jeffrey S. *Robert Frost Among His Poems*. Jefferson, NC: McFarland, 1996.

Crouthamel, James. *Bennett's* New York Herald *and the Rise of the Popular Press*. Syracuse, NY: Syracuse University Press, 1989.

Dalzell, Robert Jr. *Enterprising Elite: The Boston Associates and the World They Made*. Cambridge, MA: Harvard University Press, 1987.

Damon, S. Foster. *Amy Lowell: A Chronicle*. Boston: Houghton Mifflin, 1935.

Dana, Mrs. William Starr (Theodora Parsons). *How to Know the Wild Flowers*. New York: Chas. Scribner's Sons, 1893.

Daston, Lorraine, and Peter Galison. *Objectivity*. 2007. New York: Zone Books, 2010.

De Bellis, Jack. "Sidney Lanier." In *American Literary Critics and Scholars, 1850–1880.* Edited by John Wilbert Rathbun and Monica M. Grecu. Detroit: Gale Research, 1988.

Decker, Peter R. *Fortunes and Failures: White-Collar Mobility in Nineteenth-Century San Fransisco.* Cambridge, MA: Harvard University Press, 1978.

Douglas, Ann. *The Feminization of American Culture.* New York: Farrar, Straus and Giroux, 1998.

Douglas, George H. *The Smart Magazines: Fifty Years of Literary Revelry and High Jinks at* Vanity Fair, New Yorker, Life, Esquire *and the* Smart Set. Hamden, CT: Archon Books, 1991.

Emerson, Ralph Waldo. "Nature." In *Emerson's Prose and Poetry,* 27–55. Edited by Joel Porte and Saundra Morris. New York: W. W. Norton, 2001.

Etherington, Philip J. *The Public City: The Political Construction of Urban Life in San Francisco, 1850–1900.* Cambridge: Cambridge University Press, 1994.

Evans, William R. *Robert Frost and Sidney Cox: Forty Years of Friendshp.* Hanover, NH: University Press of New England, 1981.

Exman, Eugene. *The House of Harper: One Hundred and Fifty Years of Publishing.* New York: Harper & Row, 1967.

Faggen, Robert, ed. *The Cambridge Companion to Robert Frost.* Cambridge: Cambridge University Press, 2001.

———. *The Cambridge Introduction to Robert Frost.* Cambridge: Cambridge University Press, 2008.

———. *Robert Frost and the Challenge of Darwin.* Ann Arbor: University of Michigan Press, 1997.

Fishkin, Shelley Fisher. *From Fact to Fiction: Journalism and Imaginative Writing in America.* Baltimore: Johns Hopkins University Press, 1985.

Flint, F. S. "Imagisme." *Poetry,* March 1913, 198–99.

Francis, Lesley Lee. *The Frost Family's Adventure in Poetry: Sheer Morning Gladness at the Brim.* Columbia: University of Missouri Press, 1994.

———. "Robert Frost and Susan Hayes Ward." *Massachusetts Review* 26, no. 2/3 (1985): 341–50.

Fredeman, William E. "Thomas Bird Mosher and the Literature of Rapture." *Papers of the Bibliographic Society of Canada* 26 (1988): 27–65.

Frost, Robert. *Collected Poems, Prose, and Plays.* Edited by Mark Richardson and Richard Poirier. New York: Library of America, 1997.

———. *The Collected Prose of Robert Frost.* Edited by Mark Richardson. Cambridge, MA: Harvard University Press, 2012.

———. *Interviews with Robert Frost.* Edited by Edward Connery Lathem. New York: Holt, Rinehart and Winston, 1966.

———. *The Letters of Robert Frost to Louis Untermeyer.* New York: Holt, Rinehart and Winston, 1963.

———. *The Letters of Robert Frost: Volume 1, 1886–1920.* Edited by Mark Richardson, Robert Faggen, Donald Sheehy. Cambridge, MA: Harvard University Press, 2014.

———. *The Notebooks of Robert Frost.* Edited by Robert Faggen. Cambridge, MA: Harvard University Press, 2006.

———. *Selected Letters of Robert Frost.* Edited by Lawrance Thompson. New York: Holt, Rinehart and Winston, 1964.

Gioia, Dana. *Can Poetry Matter?* St. Paul, MN: Milkweed Editions, 1991.

Glazener, Nancy. *Reading for Realism: The History of a U.S. Institution, 1850–1910.* Durham, NC: Duke University Press, 1997.

Golding, Alan. *From Outlaw to Classic: Canons in American Poetry.* Madison: University of Wisconsin Press, 1995.

Goodman, Susan J. *William Dean Howells: A Writer's Life.* Berkeley: University of California Press, 2005.

Gould, Jean. *Robert Frost: The Aim Was Song.* New York: Dodd, Mead, 1964.

Grant, Joy. *Harold Monro and the Poetry Bookshop.* London: Routledge and Kegan Paul, 1967.

Green, Martin. *The Problem of Boston: Some Readings in Cultural History.* New York: W. W. Norton, 1966.

Gregory, Horace. *Amy Lowell: Portrait of the Poet in Her Time.* New York: Thomas Nelson and Sons, 1958.

Grenier, Donald J. *Robert Frost: The Poet and His Critics.* Chicago: American Library Association, 1974.

Gura, Philip. *The Wisdom of Words: Language, Theology, and Literature in the New England Renaissance*. Middletown, CT: Wesleyan University Press, 1981.

Habegger, Alfred. *Gender, Fantasy, and Realism in American Literature*. New York: Columbia University Press, 1982.

Habermas, Jürgen. *The Structural Transformation of the Public Sphere*. Translated by Peter Burger. Boston: MIT Press, 1991.

Harper, J. Henry. *The House of Harper*. New York: Harper and Brothers, 1912,

Hass, Robert. *Going by Contraries: Robert Frost's Conflict with Science*. Charlottesville: University of Virginia Press, 2002.

Hassall, Christopher. *A Biography of Edward Marsh*. New York: Harcourt Brace, 1959.

Heinze, Andrew R. *Jews and the American Soul: Human Nature in the Twentieth Century*. Princeton, NJ: Princeton University Press, 2004.

Hewitt, Andrew. *Fascist Modernism: Aesthetics, Politics, and the Avant-Garde*. Stanford, CA: Stanford University Press, 1993.

Hibberd, Dominic. *Harold Monro: Poet of the New Age*. New York: Palgrave Macmillan, 2001.

———. "The New Poetry, Georgians and Others." In Brooker and Thacker, *Oxford Critical and Cultural History*, 1:176–98.

Hilkey, Judy. *Character Is Capital: Success Manuals and Manhood in Gilded Age America*. Chapel Hill: University North Carolina Press, 1997.

Hochman, Barbara. *Getting at the Author: Reimagining Books and Reading in the Age of American Realism*. Amherst: University of Massachusetts Press, 2001.

Hoffman, Tyler. *Robert Frost and the Politics of Poetry*. Hanover, NH: University Press of New England, 2001.

Holt, Henry. *Garrulities of an Octogenarian Editor*. Boston: Houghton Mifflin, 1923.

Hopkins, Charles Howard. *The Rise of the Social Gospel in American Protestantism*. New Haven, CT: Yale University Press, 1940.

Howe, Daniel Walker. "American Victorianism as a Culture." *American Quarterly* 27, no. 5 (1975): 507–32.

Howells, William Dean. "The Man of Literature as a Man of Business." *Literature and Life*, 1–35. New York: Harper and Brothers, 1902.

———. *The Rise of Silas Lapham.* Edited by Don L. Cook. 1885. New York: W. W. Norton, 1982.

Huntzicker, William E. *The Popular Press, 1833–1865.* Westport, CT: Greenwood, 1999.

"Impressions by the Way," *Munsey's Magazine,* December 1894, 330.

Iser, Wolfgang. *Walter Pater.* Translated by David Henry Wilson. 1987. Reprint, Cambridge: Cambridge University Press, 2010.

Jackson, Gregory S. *The Word and Its Witness: The Spiritualization of American Realism.* Chicago: University of Chicago Press, 2009.

Jaher, Frederic Cople. *The Urban Establishment: Upper Strata in Boston, New York, Charleston, Chicago, and Los Angeles.* Urbana: University of Illinois Press, 1982.

James, William. *Will to Believe.* New York: Longmans, Green, 1897.

John, Arthur. *The Best Years of the Century: Richard Watson Gilder,* Scribner's Monthly, *and the* Century Magazine, *1870–1909.* Urbana: University of Illinois Press, 1981.

Johnson, Ben, III. *Fierce Solitude: A Life of John Gould Fletcher.* Fayettville: University of Arkansas Press, 1994.

Jones, Howard Mumford. *The Age of Energy: Varieties of American Experience, 1865–1915.* New York: Viking, 1971.

Kaplan, Amy. *The Social Construction of American Realism.* Chicago: University of Chicago Press, 1987.

Kaplan, Fred. *Sacred Tears: Sentimentality in Victorian Literature.* Princeton, NJ: Princeton University Press, 1987.

Kelley, Mary. *Private Woman, Public Stage: Literary Domesticity in Nineteenth-Century America.* New York: Oxford University Press, 1984.

Kemp, John C. *Robert Frost and New England: The Poet as Regionalist.* Princeton, NJ: Princeton University Press, 1979.

Kendall, Tim. *The Art of Robert Frost.* New Haven, CT: Yale University Press, 2012.

Kenner, Hugh. "Imagism." In *The Pound Era,* 173–222. Berkeley: University of California Press, 1971.

Kete, Mary Louise. *Sentimental Collaboration: Mourning and Middle-Class Identity in Nineteenth-Century America.* Durham, NC: Duke University Press, 1999.

Kilcup, Karen. *Robert Frost and the Feminine Literary Tradition*. Ann Arbor: University of Michigan Press, 1998.

Kindilien, Carlin. *American Poetry in the 1890s*. Providence, RI: Brown University Press, 1956.

Lanier, Sidney. *The Science of English Verse*. New York: Chas. Scribner's Sons, 1880.

Lathem, Edward Connery. *Robert Frost: 'His American Send-off,'* 1915. Lunenburg, VT: Stinehour Press, 1963.

Lawson, Andrew. *Downwardly Mobile: The Changing Fortunes of American Realism*. Oxford: Oxford University Press, 2012.

Leach, William. *Land of Desire: Merchants, Power, and the Rise of a New American Culture*. New York: Pantheon, 1993.

Lears, T. J. Jackson. *No Place of Grace*. New York: Pantheon, 1981.

Lehuu, Isabelle. *Carnival on the Page: Popular Print Media in Antebellum America*. Chapel Hill: University of North Carolina Press, 2000.

Lespi, Jeremy. "'Is It the Neighbor?': A Close Reading of Robert Frost's 'The Housekeeper.'" *Robert Frost Review* 15 (2005): 51–67.

Levenson, Michael. *A Genealogy of Modernism: A Study of English Literary Doctrine, 1908–1922*. Cambridge: Cambridge University Press, 1984.

———. *Modernism*. New Haven, CT: Yale University Press, 2011.

Levin, Joanna. *Bohemia in America: 1858–1920*. Stanford, CA: Stanford University Press, 2010.

Lidderdale, Jane, and Mary Nicholson. *Dear Miss Weaver: Harriet Shaw Weaver, 1876–1961*. New York: Viking, 1970.

Logenbach, James. *Stone Cottage*. New York: Oxford University Press, 1988.

Mann, Arthur. *Yankee Reformers in the Urban Age*. Cambridge, MA: Harvard University Press, 1954.

Marek, Jayne E. *Women Editing Modernism*. Lexington: University Press of Kentucky, 1995.

McClay, Wilfred M. "Two Versions of the Genteel Tradition: Santayana and Brooks." *New England Quarterly* 55, no. 3 (1982): 368–91.

Menand, Louis. *The Marketplace of Ideas: Reform and Resistance in the American University*. New York: W. W. Norton, 2010.

———. *The Metaphysical Club: A Story of Ideas in America*. New York: Farrar, Strauss and Giroux, 2001.

Mertins, Louis. *Robert Frost: Life and Talks Walking.* Norman: University of Oklahoma Press, 1965.

Milford, Nancy. *Savage Beauty: The Life of Edna St. Vincent Millay.* New York: Random House, 2001.

Mims, Edwin. *Sidney Lanier.* Boston: Houghton Mifflin, 1905.

Mix, Katherine Lyon. *A Study in Yellow.* Lawrence: University Press of Kansas, 1960.

Moody, A. David. *The Young Genius, 1885–1920.* Vol. 1 of *Ezra Pound: Poet.* Oxford: Oxford University Press, 2007.

Mott, Frank Luther. *A History of American Magazines, 1850–1865.* Vol. 2. Cambridge, MA: Harvard University Press, 1938.

———. *A History of American Magazines, 1865–1885.* Vol. 3. Cambridge, MA: Harvard University Press, 1938.

———. *A History of American Magazines, 1885–1905.* Vol. 4. Cambridge, MA: Harvard University Press, 1957.

———. *American Journalism.* New York: Macmillan, 1941.

Nahra, Nancy. "'My Kind of Fooling': Robert Frost's 'A Hundred Collars' and *North of Boston's* Variations on Horace." *Robert Frost Review,* nos. 23/24 (2013–2014): 86–105.

Newdick, Robert S. *Newdick's Season of Frost: An Interrupted Biography of Robert Frost.* Edited by William Sutton. Albany: State University of New York Press, 1976.

———. "Robert Frost's Other Harmony." *Sewanee Review* 48, no. 3 (1940): 410–18.

Nord, David Paul. *Communities of Journalism: A History of American Newspapers and Their Readers.* Urbana: University of Illinois Press, 2001.

Nussbaum, Martha. *Not for Profit: Why Democracy Needs the Humanities.* Princeton, NJ: Princeton University Press, 2010.

Oakes, James. *Freedom National: The Destruction of Slavery in the United States, 1861–1865.* New York: W. W. Norton, 2014.

O'Brien, Timothy. *Names, Proverbs, Riddles, and Material Text in Robert Frost.* New York: Palgrave Macmillan, 2010.

Orr, David. *Beautiful and Pointless: A Guide to Modern Poetry.* New York: Harper Perennial, 2012.

Padrón, Charles. "George Santayana." In *American Philosophers Before 1950*. Edited by Philip Breed Dematteis and Leemon B. McHenry. Detroit: Gale Research, 2003.

Palgrave, Francis Turner. *The Golden Treasury of the Best Songs and Lyrical Poems in the English Language*. New York: Thomas Crowell, 1888.

Parini, Jay. *Robert Frost: A Life*. Boston: Henry Holt, 1999.

Parrish, S. Maxfield, and Hyder Edward Rollins. *Keats and the Bostonians*. Cambridge, MA: Harvard University Press, 1951.

Paton, Priscilla. *Abandoned New England: Landscape in the Works of Homer, Frost, Wyeth and Bishop*. Hanover, NH: University Press of New England, 2003.

Persons, Stow. *The Decline of American Gentility*. New York: Columbia University Press, 1973.

Poirier, Richard. *Robert Frost and the Work of Knowing*. 2d ed. Palo Alto, CA: Stanford University Press, 1990.

Polanyi, Karl. *The Great Transformation: The Political and Economic Origins of Our Time*. 1944. Boston: Beacon, 2001.

Pondrom, Cyrena. "H. D. and the Origins of Imagism." In *Signets: Reading H.D.*, 85–109. Edited by Susan Stanford Friedman and Rachel Blau Duplessis. Madison: University of Wisconsin Press, 1990.

Pound, Ezra. "A Few Don'ts by an *Imagiste*." *Poetry*, March 1913, 200–6.

———. *The Selected Letters of Ezra Pound 1907–1941*. Edited by D. D. Paige. London: Faber and Faber, 1942.

Pritchard, William. *Frost: A Literary Life Reconsidered*. New York: Oxford University Press, 1984.

Rabate, Jean-Michel. "Gender and Modernism: *The Freewoman, The New Freewoman, The Egotist.*" In Brooker and Thacker, *Oxford Critical and Cultural History*, 1:269–89.

Rainey, Lawrence. "The Creation of the Avant-Garde: F. T. Marinetti and Ezra Pound." In *Institutions of Modernism: Literary Elites and Public Culture*, 10–41. New Haven, CT: Yale University Press, 1998.

Richardson, Mark. *The Ordeal of Robert Frost*. Urbana: University of Illinois Press, 1997.

Rogers, Timothy. *Georgian Poetry, 1911–1922: The Critical Heritage*. London: Routledge and Kegan Paul, 1977.

Roggenkamp, Karen. *Narrating the News: New Journalism and Literary Genre in Late Nineteenth-Century Newspapers and Fiction.* Kent, OH: Kent State University Press, 2005.

Ross, Robert H. *The Georgian Revolt, 1910–1922.* Carbondale: University of Southern Illinois Press, 1965.

Rotella, Guy. "'Synonymous with Kept': Frost and Economics." In Faggen, *Cambridge Companion to Robert Frost,* 241–60.

Rubin, Joan Shelley. *Songs of Ourselves: The Uses of Poetry in America.* Cambridge, MA: Harvard University Press, 2007.

Sandel, Michael J. *What Money Can't Buy: The Moral Limits of Markets.* New York: Farrar Straus and Giroux, 2012.

Sanders, David. *A Divided Poet: Robert Frost,* North of Boston, *and the Drama of Disappearance.* Rochester, NY: Camden House, 2011.

———. "Correcting the Record: Good Hours and *North of Boston.*" *Robert Frost Review,* nos. 23/24 (December 3, 2014): 70–85.

Santayana, George. *The Genteel Tradition: Nine Essays.* Edited by Douglas L. Wilson. Cambridge, MA: Harvard University Press, 1967.

———. *The Sense of Beauty.* New York: Chas. Scribner's Sons, 1896.

Satelmajer, Ingrid. "When a Consumer Becomes an Editor: Susan Hayes Ward and the Poetry of *The Independent.*" *Textual Cultures* 2, no. 1 (2007): 78–100.

Saum, Lewis O. *The Popular Mood of America, 1860–1890.* Lincoln: University of Nebraska Press, 1990.

Schneirov, Matthew. *The Dream of a New Social Order: Popular Magazines, 1893–1914.* New York: Columbia University Press, 1994.

Schudsen, Michael. *Discovering the News: A Social History of American Newspapers.* New York: Basic Books, 1978.

Scott, David. "*Sub Specie Durantionis,* or the Free Necessity of Life's Creativeness in Bergson's Creative Evolution." In Ardoin, Gontarski, and Mattison, *Understanding Bergson, Understanding Modernism,* chap. 4.

Sears, John F. "William James, Henri Bergson, and the Poetics of Robert Frost." *New England Quarterly* 48, no. 3 (September 1975): 341–61.

Sedgwick, Ellery, III. "The American Genteel Tradition in the Early Twentieth Century." *American Studies* 25, no. 1 (1984): 49–67.

Sellers, Charles. *Market Revolution: Jacksonian America.* Oxford: Oxford University Press, 1994.

Sergeant, Elizabeth Shepley. *Robert Frost: The Trial by Existence.* New York: Holt, Rinehart, Winston, 1960.

Singer, Irving. *George Santayana, Literary Philosopher.* New Haven, CT: Yale University Press, 2000.

Sokol, B. J. "What Went Wrong Between Robert Frost and Ezra Pound." *New England Quarterly* 49, no. 4 (December 1976): 521–41.

Sollors, Werner. *Beyond Ethnicity: Consent and Descent in American Culture.* New York: Oxford University Press, 1987.

Sorby, Angela. *Schoolroom Poets: Childhood and the Place of American Poetry.* Hanover, NH: University Press of New England, 2005.

Stansell, Christine. *American Moderns: Bohemian New York and the Creation of a New Century.* New York: Henry Holt, 2000.

Starr, Paul. *The Creation of the Media: Political Origins of Modern Communications.* New York: Basic Books, 2004.

Stedman, Edmund Clarence. *An American Anthology.* Boston: Houghton, Mifflin, 1900.

Stedman, Laura, and George M. Gould. *Life and Letters of Edmund Clarence Stedman.* New York: Moffat, Yard, 1910.

Story, Ronald. *The Forging of an Aristocracy: Harvard and the Boston Upper Class.* Middleton, CT: Wesleyan University Press, 1980.

Susman, Warren. "Personality and the Making of Twentieth-Century Culture." In *Culture as History: The Transformation of American Society in the Twentieth Century,* 271–85. New York: Pantheon, 1984.

Swinnerton, Frank. *The Georgian Literary Scene: 1910–1955, A Panorama.* New York: Farrar, Strauss, 1950.

Symons, Arthur. "The Decadent Movement in Literature." *Harper's,* November 1893, 858–67.

———. *The Symbolist Movement in Literature.* London: Heinemann, 1899.

Taylor, Andrew. *Thinking America: New England Intellectuals and the Varieties of American Identity.* Durham, NH: University Press of New England, 2010.

Taylor, M. W. *Men Versus the State: Herbert Spencer and Late Victorian Individualism.* Oxford: Clarendon, 1992.

Thomas, Edward. *Elected Friends: Robert Frost and Edward Thomas to One Another.* Edited by Matthew Spencer. Boston: Handsel Books, 2004.

Thompson, Lawrance. *Robert Frost: The Early Years, 1874–1915.* New York: Holt, Rinehart and Winston, 1966.

———. *Robert Frost: The Years of Triumph, 1915–1938.* Boston: Henry Holt, 1970.

Thornton, Richard, ed. *Recognition of Robert Frost.* New York: Henry Holt, 1937.

Timmerman, John. *Robert Frost: The Ethics of Ambiguity.* Lewisburg, PA: Bucknell University Press, 2002.

Tompkins, Jane. *Sensational Designs: The Cultural Work of American Fiction.* New York: Oxford University Press, 1985.

Tomsich, John. *A Genteel Endeavor: American Culture and Politics in the Genteel Age.* Palo Alto, CA: Stanford University Press, 1971.

Trachtenberg, Alan. *The Incorporation of America.* New York: Hill and Wang, 1982.

Untermeyer, Louis. *From Another World: The Autobiography of Louis Untermeyer.* New York: Harcourt, Brace, 1939.

———. *The Letters of Robert Frost to Louis Untermeyer.* New York: Holt, Rinehart and Winston, 1963.

———. *The New Era in American Poetry.* New York: Henry Holt, 1919.

Vander Ven, Tom. "Robert Frost's Dramatic Principle of 'Oversound.'" *American Literature,* May 1973: 238–51.

Villanueva, Daraio. *Theories of Literary Realism.* Translated by Mihai Spariosu ad Santiago Garcia-Castanon. Albany: State University of New York Press, 1997.

Wagner-Martin, Linda. *Robert Frost: The Critical Reception.* New York: Burt Franklin, 1977.

Walsh, John Evangelist. *Into My Own: The English Years of Robert Frost.* New York: Grove, 1988.

Weiner, Philip. *Evolution and the Founders of Pragmatism.* Cambridge, MA: Harvard University Press, 1949.

Weir, David. *Decadent Culture in the United States: Art and Literature Against the American Grain, 1890–1926.* Albany: State University of New York Press, 2008.

Weirick, Bruce. *From Whitman to Sandburg in American Poetry.* New York: Macmillan, 1924.

Wilbur, Richard. *Things of This World.* New York: Harcourt, Brace, 1956.

Wilhelm, J. J. *Ezra Pound in London and Paris: 1908–1925.* University Park: Penn State University Press, 1990.

Williams, Ellen. *Harriet Monroe and the Poetry Renaissance.* Urbana: University of Illinois Press, 1977.

Woolley, Lisa. *American Voices of the Chicago Renaissance.* DeKalb: Northern Illinois University Press, 2000.

Wulfman, Cliff. "Ford Maddox Ford and the English Review." In Brooker and Thacker, *Oxford Critical and Cultural History,* 1:226–39.

Yearsley, Meredith. "Richard Hovey." In *American Poets, 1880–1945, Third Series.* Edited by Peter Quartermain, 54:182. Detroit: Gale Research, 1987.

Zboray, Ronald. *A Fictive People: Antebellum Economic Development and the American Reading Public.* Oxford: Oxford University Press, 1993.

Ziff, Lazer. *The American 1890s: Life and Times of a Lost Generation.* New York: Viking, 1966.

Index

Page numbers in italics refer to illustrations

Republican Party, 30, 118, 254n28
Rhyme, 68, 119, 128, 134–35, 283n14
Rhythm, 71–72, 167, 169, 174
Rhythm, 155
Richardson, Mark, 2, 298n20
Riley, James Whitcomb, 1–2, 4
Ripostes (Pound), 289n47
Rittenhouse, Jessie, 212, 230, 237
"Road Not Taken, The," 238–40
Roberts, Charles G. D., 40, 68, 258n2
Roberts, George G. D., 84
Robinson, Edwin Arlington, 2, 108, 163–64, 201, 236
Rogue, 226
Romance tradition, 37; challenges to, 33, 35, 260n19; criteria for poetry in, 44, 69; realism *vs.,* 31–32
Roosevelt, Theodore, 30–31
Ross, Ronald, 157
Rossetti, Dante Gabriel, 36, 40, 124–25
Royce, Josiah, 89
Rural people, 291n30; speech in Frost's poems, 205, 208; stereotypes of New England's, 170, 228–29, 231
Russell, Bertrand, 137

"Sachem of the Clouds," 53
Salem, New Hampshire, 78–79
Salem Depot, New Hampshire, 53
Samurai Press, 149, 152, 154, 285n20
San Francisco, Frost's early years in, 49
Santayana, George, 274n25, 275n31; Frost resisting teachings of, 91–92; on genteel tradition, 7–9, 252n3; in Guiney's decadent circle, 39–40; teaching at Harvard, 89–91
Saturday Evening Post, 258n2
Saum, Lewis O., 253n24
Schoolroom Poets, 15

Schoolteacher, Frost as, 58, 61, 63, 74–75, 77–78, 118, 272n7; "The Birds Do Thus" alluding to, 80–81; at Pinkerton Academy, 113–15, 118, 129–30, 280n15; at Plymouth Normal School, 130–31; redesigning English curriculum, 129–30
Schudson, Michael, 23
Science, 139, 277n45; faith and, 61, 67–68, 89, 104; faith *vs.,* in Frost's poetry, 108–9, 134; Frost's interests in, 54, 78; Harvard's focus on, 86–89; Lanier presenting poetics as, 71–72
Science of English Verse, The (Lanier), 71
Science of Poetic Meter (Lanier), 71–72
Scott, David, 139
Scudder, Horace, 15
Secularism, in education, 14
Sedgwick, Ellery, 131, 232; commissioning Garnett's essay, 238, 241, 302n27, 302n31; publishing Frost's poems, 238, 302n29
Self, James on, 92–93
Severini, Gino, 165
Sexuality, 17, 42, 216, 217, 220; in "Putting in the Seed," 217–20, 299n14; in "The Quest of the Orchis," 102, 104–5; in realism, 42–43
Shakespeare, William, 123, 127
Shaler, Thomas, 89, 274n22, 275n27
Short stories, Frost's, 113
Sill, Edward Rowland, 54, 267n29
Silver, Ernest, 129–30
Sinclair, May, 108, 163–64, 289n7
Singer, Irving, 90
Slosson, Edwin E., 248
Small presses, 29, 42, 151–52
Smart Set, 168–69, 174–75, 290n23
"Smile, The," 217, 220
Smith, J. C., 192–93